CHRONICLE OF AMERICAN PHYSICAL EDUCATION

Editors' note:

To preserve the language of the period the selections have not been edited. The occasional grammatical error, misspelling, and quaint use of a word have been unaltered throughout.

CHRONICLE OF AMERICAN PHYSICAL EDUCATION

SELECTED READINGS 1855 - 1930

Aileene S. Lockhart
University of Southern California

Betty Spears
Wellesley College

WM. C. BROWN COMPANY PUBLISHERS
Dubuque, Iowa

Library of Congress Catalog Card Number: 76—187834

ISBN 0–697–07158–8

Printed in the United States of America

Contents

Preface

There are many ways to present history, and we have chosen to tell it in the words of those who made it. *Chronicle of American Physical Education* provides a selection of primary sources so that the reader may examine directly the writer's approach to his subject and the development of his ideas. The student usually begins the study of history with a textbook, seeing history through the eyes of its author-historian on whom he must rely for a synthesis and interpretation of selected facts and ideas. The student's exposure to primary sources is limited to quotations selected by the historian, and the student must depend on him for accuracy, context, and interpretation. While it may be hoped that the textbook of history enables the student to gain an overall view of a period and a condensation of facts and ideas as seen by the author, it does not introduce him to the historical process nor to the ways in which history itself is studied.

The study of history is based on the available evidence of the thoughts and actions of men and women. While the historian has the benefit of knowing the consequences of the events he is investigating, it is the analysis of those events and the evidence on which the analysis is based that hold the key to the study of history. Evidence takes many forms, including eyewitness accounts, diaries, memories, and the writings of men and women. The student of history should learn to question the evidence and to develop valid criteria on which to select or reject it. The authors of *Chronicle of American Physical Education* believe that the evidence for the study of history should be made available in the original language and concepts of the period being investigated.

Thousands of articles, books, pamphlets, and other primary sources were examined during the process of selecting the material included in this anthology. The only interpretations which the authors permitted themselves were the selection and arrangement of the material. While it was recognized that many events outside the United States influenced the development of American physical education, it was decided to limit the present collection to works by American authors. Not only are there included herein the well-known physical educators, but also scientists such as Scripture and Lincoln and educators such as G. Stanley Hall, for persons such as these also influenced physical education. Though the readers will find many familiar names, *ideas rather than names* motivated the authors in their selection of material; as a result, readers may find articles of historical consequence written by authors quite unknown to them. Physical educators who have come to associate certain individuals with specific achievements will find that these people also have made other notable contributions. For example, the work we have chosen to include by Jessie Bancroft is not on the theories and uses of games but on the place of automatism in gymnastic exercise.

Most of these articles have not been reproduced elsewhere and therefore are difficult to locate. They have been selected because it was felt that the ideas they contain made a significant contribution to the history of physical education in the United States. To preserve the language of the period the selections have not been edited and, in almost all cases, have been printed in their entirety. The practices of the different original publications relating to the title and how or whether authors were identified have been observed; this accounts for differences in style which the alert reader will recognize in this volume. Thus, for example, President C. W. Eliot is identified with Harvard University, but E. M. Hartwell's affiliation is not noted in one article, and the *Atlantic Monthly* of 1861 did not identify authors at all. The occasional grammatical error, misspelling, and quaint use of a word have been unaltered throughout. If a bibliography was a part of the original selection, it has been included to give the student the sources used by the writer.

After careful consideration it was decided to present the material in chronological order rather than by topics. This arrangement permits the student to see the chronicle as a whole and in sequence rather than divided into unnatural sections. In the history of physical education in the United States there are certain identifiable events which helped us group the selections into three periods. The authors recognize that there are no clear-cut distinctions from one period to the next and that the germs of the next period are evident in the preceding one. The first period from 1855 to 1888 represents the beginnings of physical education in the United States. The Conference in the Interest of Physical Education in 1889 begins the second period, which continues the chronicle of development to the twenty-fifth year of the American Physical Education Association. In the third period, 1912-1930, the trends toward modern physical education evolve. It should be noted, however, that changes in philosophy, the use of scientific knowledge, evolving programs, the existence of professional associations and organizations and their activities are apparent from the first article by Beecher to the last selection by McCloy.

In part one, "The Beginnings," Catharine Beecher's and Dio Lewis's vision of a healthy population with symmetrical bodies, Higginson's description of a gymnasium of the 1860s, and Ellis's boyish recollection of student days at Round Hill School present some of the significant origins of physical education in the United States. While a number of articles dating from 1885 deal with the growing importance of discovering the "correct" system of gymnastics, the wholesome effects of exercise on women, and the development of physical training or physical education in the colleges, during this period more diverse programs were also proposed and new sports such as basketball and volleyball were introduced.

The first article in part two is the opening address presented by the United States Commissioner of Education at the 1889 Conference in the Interest of Physical Training. Throughout this period well-known scientists and educators emphasized the value of the motor and physical aspects of education. Lincoln's writings on the motor elements in education, Bancroft's studies on automation, and Stiles's article on the now familiar all-or-none principle helped shape the concepts of physical education. One is aware of the rapid and widespread growth of this "new profession" as physical educators of the 1890s wrote about training teachers, the formation of professional associations, and the effect of increasing scientific knowledge on physical education. Leonard's bibliography of the history of physical training illustrates the interest in history and makes the reader aware of the then available sources on this subject. The four broad objectives—organic, motor, mental, and social—on which programs were based for many years were identified in 1909 by Hetherington.

To emphasize their place in the history of physical education, readings on sports and dance were selected for inclusion. Reports of creating and inventing new sports such as basketball and volleyball, conducting longitudinal research on Harvard oarsmen, and encouraging the participation of women in sports all affected the development of physical education in the United States. Trends in programs for women appear and reappear as physical educators demonstrated that physical activity did not harm women, introduced new sports for women, and argued the extent to which they should engage in athletics. Men's athletics and intercollegiate programs with their attendant problems and attempts to control them reflect a growing concern as the Intercollegiate Athletic Association of the United States proposed changing its name to the National Collegiate Athletic Association. By this time the concept of play was accepted as a basic part of the philosophy and programs, and physical education moved away from gymnastics as its central concern as "natural" programs evolved. At the end of this period, Meylan's presidential address to the American Association of Physical Education in 1911 emphasized the changes which had occurred during the twenty-five years of the association and reported that the playground and hygiene associations were investigating possible affiliation with the physical education association.

In part three readers will find that traditional concepts were reexamined, new directions proposed, and research and its contribution to the growth of the profession accepted. The lack of physical fitness of the draftees of World War I gave impetus to legislation requiring physical education in most states. The reports of the National Amateur Athletic Federation of America provide evidence of the concern about competition for girls and women. The chapter from H'Doubler's book demonstrates the aesthetic attitude toward dance and the developing recognition of dance as a part of modern education. By the end of the last period, just prior to the 1930s, Brace's article on the measurement of achievement in physical education, Williams's views of physical education as a means to a fuller life, Nash's support of health and character as appropriate objectives, and McCloy's article setting standards for research bring readers directly to modern physical education.

Chronicle of American Physical Education may be used as a text for a course in the history of physical education in the United States or as a supplementary source in courses in the general history of physical education. It will be a valuable addition to every physical educator's library. Also, it will provide primary sources for students interested in a particular subject in history.

It is hoped that this volume will stimulate students to undertake additional study and research in the history of physical education in the United States. The authors were privileged to have available to them many historical libraries in New England, some of them of particular interest to the student of physical education. This was essential for a work of this sort, since New England witnessed the birth of physical education. Among these libraries were the Edith Hemenway

Eustis Library of Wellesley College which houses one of the oldest collections on physical education in the United States, the Physical Education Library at Smith College, the Frost Library at Amherst College, the Goodell Library at the University of Massachusetts, and the Marsh Library at Springfield College. For permission to reprint, we are indebted to the various publishers and publications.

There is no reason, of course, to plead the value of the study of history. Physical education students, however, remain much more aware of current literature than that of the past, on which the present rests. In an era of reevaluation and of questioning, and in an era in which concepts are especially important, it is instructive and perhaps surprising for the initiate to history to find relevant and contemporary ideas in the early writing of those who were so instrumental in shaping today's thoughts. The scholar is never satisfied with only the literature of the hour. He finds value, pride, friendships at a distance, and vitality in his heritage and in the judgments of those who preceded him. He possesses the basis for making comparative judgment. The unique purpose of this collection is to provide the opportunity for students to begin the exciting exploration of the development of physical education in the United States through *primary sources.*

AILEENE S. LOCKHART
BETTY SPEARS

Part I

THE BEGINNINGS

1855 - 1888

EXERCISE AND AMUSEMENT

Catharine Beecher

Next to pure air, *healthful exercise and amusements* are the most important remedies for the evils set forth.

The modes for securing these are not so easily indicated. A great part of the American people exercise certain portions of their muscular system too much, while their intellect has little activity, and their spirits are rarely cheered and animated by amusements. Another portion keep their brain in constant labor, without the balancing influence of muscular activity, or the relief of recreation. And still another portion give up their whole being to pleasure-seeking and amusement, without any useful activity either of body or mind.

There are various measures which might be adopted, that each in its place would tend to a better adjustment of this difficult matter. To illustrate what *might* be done, let it be imagined that, for the sake of an experiment, funds were provided, and the inhabitants of a community should all agree to give the method here suggested a fair trial.

In the first place, a course of lectures should be given, for the purpose of making the people fully understand the evils to be remedied, and the benefits to be secured.

Next, a central site should be provided, on which should be erected a large and beautiful building—a *Temple of Health.* Around it should be every variety of pleasant walks, and shades, and flowers, to attract and please in the summer months, and other arrangements provided for outdoor sports and exercises in winter. Within the building should be arranged a great variety of apparatus and accommodations for in-door amusements that *exercise the muscles,* and those which in most cases could be performed *in measures and to the sound of music.* These

Catharine Beecher, "Exercise and Amusement," *Letters to the People on Health and Happiness* (New York: Harper & Brothers, Publishers, 1855), pp. 168-171.

exercises should be under the direction of scientific and medical men, and no one should be admitted to these premises except on condition that they would strictly obey the direction of these managers.

All persons attending should then be examined in regard to their daily avocations, their diet, the ventilation of their sleeping and business rooms, the defects of their physical system, and any disease they may suffer, and advice appropriate be given. Then a course of exercise, fitted to each case, should be marked out, and superintendents appointed to see that all these directions are obeyed. The aim should be, not only to secure exercise, but that kind which is appropriate to each case, and also that which would prove *exhilarating* and *amusing*. For exercise that is sought as a pleasure is more than doubled in value.

In short, every arrangement should be made in strict conformity to the laws of health, and all excess should be excluded. Here, too, parents should be instructed in family plays and games, and thus induced to join with their children in home amusements. For nothing so binds the young to those who control them, as aid and sympathy in amusing sports.

It is believed that if any community would once fairly test such a plan as this for six months, nine-tenths of the diseases, infirmities, low spirts, and ill-temper of that place would vanish away, while every social, domestic, and religious virtue would take a new start.

The preceding method is suggested mainly with reference to adults. In regard to the rising generation, the grand remedy must be in connection with schools and other institutions for education.

As these are now conducted, all the money, time, and efforts are spent in training and exercising the intellect. In our higher institutions, one department is *endowed* that a teacher may give all his time and efforts to cultivating the mathematical faculties. Another endowment supports a teacher to train the linguistic powers. Another endowment secures a teacher for chemistry—another provides for some other of the natural sciences. Thus, there is a constantly accumulating outlay for divisions and subdivisions of labor, and all for the intellectual department of education. Stringent rules also are made, and laws enforced to secure obedience to arrangements that often involve most flagrant violations of the laws of health.

But where in the wide circuit of our nation is an institution where even *one* teacher is sustained, whose official duty it is to secure the health and perfect development of that wonderful and curious organism on which the mind is so dependent? Why should not the students in our colleges and other institutions of learning be required to breathe pure air; to exercise their muscles appropriately and sufficiently; to retire as well as to rise at proper hours; to take care of the skin, and to avoid the use of stimulating herbs and drinks? And why should not endowments be provided to sustain a well qualified and able man, whose official duty it shall be to give instructions, and exercise the supervision that would secure so important a result?

In regard to all our common and other schools for young children to the proper ventilation of their school-rooms should be added a complete and scientific training of their bodies to perfect health and the full development of every part. This is entirely practicable, and would be immediately adopted by every teacher did the public demand it. One half hour of every school session ought to be spent by every teacher and pupil in a regular course of calisthenic and gymnastic exercises, that should be as imperative as any other school duty.

A universal course of training of this kind, scientifically arranged and applied, in connection with obedience to other laws of health, might, in one generation, transform the inhabitants of this land from the low development now so extensive to the beautiful model of the highest form of humanity.

Children, too, can be made to understand all that is contained in this book as to the construction of their own bodies and the laws of health. And such knowledge is as important for them, in order to secure their obedience to these laws, as it is for grown persons. Nothing can be made more interesting to children than information in regard to the curious construction of their own bodies; while this alone will secure an intelligent and cheerful submission to rules that regulate their appetites and propensities.

Food and Drink

Next in importance to air and exercise comes the selection of diet and drink. And in this matter the practical adoption of one common-sense maxim would do almost all that needs to be done. The maxim is this: *In cases where one of two courses involves danger and risk and another is perfectly safe, always choose the path of safety.*

We have seen that the great mass of this nation is fast hastening to disease and deterioration, and that individual misery and domestic unhappiness are widely increasing as the result. We have seen that owing to needless varieties, to stimulating food and drinks, and to the use of condiments, *excess* in loading the digestive organs is one great cause of this extensive suffering.

Now there is a rich variety and abundance of simple, healthful food and drinks that are fitted for the perfect development and nutrition of the body, and involve little liability to perversion and excess. And when all stimulating food, drinks, and condiments are relinquished and a simple diet maintained, a *healthful appetite* returns, which is a safe guide to the proper amount to be taken, provided always that enough pure air and exercise are secured.

Moreover, I have found by my own experience, and have learned from others, that after living for several months on simple food, there is an increased susceptibility of taste and a keener relish for the delicate flavors that simple food offers. Does any one remember the delicious relish of childhood for a bit of good bread? This same relish will again return when solicited aright. Let a person for several weeks try the experiment of drinking only water, eating nothing but bread and butter, potatoes, baked fruit, and milk, and at the same time exercise abundantly in the fresh air, and if their experience corresponds with that of most I have known who have tried the experiment, they will say, "Never did food of the richest variety and composition furnish such an exquisite relish!"

The more a person will limit a meal to *a few articles,* and these of the *simplest kind,* the more will they regain the appetite and relish of early life.

Now the course here suggested is perfectly safe, is equally productive of enjoyment, and is in obedience to the laws of health, which are the laws of God. The common course pursued in this land of abundance and gormandizing is certainly one of risk and danger to the delicate and deteriorated constitutions of the adult and rising generations. Is not here the place to practice the Christian "daily" duty of "self-denial?" And if the strong and healthy feel no need of it for themselves, is there not a duty set forth for them in this inspired command, "We that are strong ought to bear the infirmities of the weak, and not to please ourselves."

In reference to stimulating drinks, how often have I seen the need of this divine injunction. The parents of a family drink strong tea and coffee. They teach their children perhaps, that it is a dangerous and unhealthy practice, and train them to entire abstinence. But after a few years these children draw to manhood and womanhood, and begin to claim the privileges of acting by their own judgments. Then, after a period of deprecation and remonstrance, the luxury is conceded. Some one of the flock is weak, the strong can bear it but the weak one falters. No eye but that of the Heavenly Parent marks how this one single cause is daily draining the already stinted nervous fountain. And when the flower is cut down, the weeping parents mourn over the sacrifice offered by themselves to their own self-indulgence—to their neglect of that beneficent law, "We that are strong ought to bear the infirmities of the weak, and not to please ourselves."

Oh, tender parents, who provide these dangerous beverages, look around your beloved circle and see which one you can select as the hapless victim!

And so in reference to that disgusting and baleful use of tobacco, which all over the nation is draining the nervous fountain of thousands of pale and delicate young men. The clergyman, the church elder, the father of the family, indulge in a useless and dangerous practice, merely to gratify a morbid appetite. While they teach others to "deny fleshly lusts," and upbraid the young if they fall, in their own cherished fleshly appetite they see no sin, because they say it does not hurt *themselves.*

But every young victim to this appetite who has been led on by their example, or has not been withheld when their arguments and example might have saved them, is set down to their account by Him who seeth not as man seeth. He whose example of self-denying benevolence they profess to follow, whose last teachings on earth were, "If ye love me feed my sheep; feed my lambs"—He has left to them, above all others, the sacred monition, "We that are strong ought to bear the infirmities of the weak, and not to please ourselves."

In regard to the use of tobacco, it seems to me the American people, for want of little consideration, are invading their high character for respectful kindness and deference to woman. In this matter, there are few that have so much occasion as myself to render a grateful acknowledgment of this most chivalrous virtue in my countrymen; for during the last period of my life I have crossed from West to East, or from East to West, not less than thirty times, and have traveled in all the Free States and five of the Southern; and in all this varied experience, when, in a large portion of the cases also, I was without a protector, I have never *once* known of a coarse or disrespectful word or act toward myself, or witnessed one toward any other woman. At the same time, all that father or brother could render has been accorded by strangers.

But in my recent travels, especially at the West, I have constantly been made to feel what a *selfish* as well as disgusting and ungallant habit is induced by the use of tobacco! The majority of ladies are offended by the effluvium of that weed, and disgusted by its marks on the mouth and face, while the puddles of tobacco juice that infest our public conveyances, the breath of smokers, and the wads and squirting of chewers, not only defile the dress but keep a sensitive stomach in constant excitement and agitation. There have been times in my experience when it seemed to me I must give up a journey from this cause alone. Certainly, if those who practice this vice will insist on perfuming public conveyances with dead tobacco smoke from their dress and lungs, and rendering all their premises filthy and disgusting with their expectorations, the managers of these conveyances should provide rooms and cars for ladies and all other persons who are annoyed by this vice, from which all who either smoke or chew shall be excluded.

GYMNASTICS

So your zeal for physical training begins to wane a little, my friend? I thought it would, in your particular case, because it began too ardently and was concentrated too exclusively on your one hobby of pedestrianism. Just now you are literally under the weather. It is the equinoctial storm. No matter, you say; did not Olmsted foot it over England under an umbrella? did not Wordsworth regularly walk every guest round Windermere, the day after arrival, rain or shine? So, the day before yesterday, you did your four miles out, on the Northern turnpike, and returned splashed to the waist; and yesterday you walked three miles out, on the Southern turnpike, and came back soaked to the knees. To-day the storm is slightly increasing, but you are dry thus far, and wish to remain so; exercise is a humbug; you will give it all up, and go to the Chess-Club. Don't go to the Chess-Club; come with me to the Gymnasium.

Chess may be all very well to tax with tough problems a brain otherwise inert, to vary a monotonous day with small events, to keep one awake during a sleepy evening, and to arouse a whole family next morning for the adjustment over the breakfast-table of that momentous state-question, whether the red king should have castled at the fiftieth move or not till the fifty-first. But for an average American man, who leaves his place of business at nightfall with his head a mere furnace of red-hot brains and his body a pile of burnt-out cinders, utterly exhausted in the daily effort to put ten dollars more of distance between his posterity and the poor-house,—for such a one to kindle up afresh after office-hours for a complicated chess-problem

Thomas Wentworth Higginson, "Gymnastics," *Atlantic Monthly,* vol. VII, no. XLI, March 1861, pp. 283-302.

seems much as if a wood-sawyer, worn out with his week's work, should decide to order in his saw-horse on Saturday evening, and saw for fun. Surely we have little enough recreation at any rate, and, pray, let us make that little un-intellectual. True, something can be said in favor of chess,—for instance, that no money can be made out of it, and that it is so far profitable to us overworked Americans: but even this is not enough. For this once, lock your brains into your safe, at nightfall, with your other valuables; don't go to the Chess-Club; come with me to the Gymnasium.

Ten leaps up a steep, worn-out stairway, through a blind entry to another stairway, and yet another, and we emerge suddenly upon the floor of a large lighted room, a mere human machine-shop of busy motion, where Indian clubs are whirling, dumb-bells pounding, swings vibrating, and arms and legs flying in all manner of unexpected directions. Henderson sits with his big proportions quietly rested against the weight-boxes, pulling with monotonous vigor at the fifty-pound weights,—"the Stationary Engine" the boys call him. For a contrast, Draper is floating up and down between the parallel bars with such an airy lightness, that you think he must have hung up his body in the dressing-room, and is exercising only in his arms and clothes. Parsons is swinging in the rings, rising to the ceiling before and behind; up and down he goes, whirling over and over, converting himself into a mere tumbler-pigeon, yet still bound by the long, steady vibration of the human pendulum. Another is running a race with him, if sitting in the swing be running; and still another is accompanying their motion, clinging to the *trapèze.* Hayes, meanwhile, is spinning on the horizontal bar, now backward, now forward, twenty times without stopping, pinioned through his bent arms, like a Fakir on his iron. See how many different ways of ascending a vertical pole these boys are devising!—one climbs with hands and legs, another with hands only, another is crawling up on all-fours in Feegee fashion, while another is pegging his way up by inserting pegs in holes a foot apart,—you will see him sway and tremble a bit, before he reaches the ceiling. Others are at work with a spring-board and leaping-cord; higher and higher the cord is moved, one by one the competitors step aside defeated, till the field is left to a single champion, who, like an India-rubber ball, goes on rebounding till he seems likely to disappear through the chimney, like a Ravel. Some sturdy young visitors, farmers by their looks, are trying their strength, with various success, at the sixty-pound dumb-bell, when some quiet fellow, a clerk or a tailor, walks modestly to the hundred-pound weight, and up it goes as steadily as if the laws of gravitation had suddenly shifted their course, and worked upward instead of down. Lest, however, they should suddenly resume their original bias, let us cross to the dressing-room and, while you are assuming flannel shirt or complete gymnastic suit, as you may prefer, let us consider the merits of the Gymnasium.

Do not say that the public is growing tired of hearing about physical training. You might as well speak of being surfeited with the sight of apple-blossoms, or bored with roses,—for these athletic exercises are, to a healthy person, just as good and refreshing. Of course, any one becomes insupportable who talks all the time of this subject, or of any other; but it is the man who fatigues you, not the theme. Any person becomes morbid and tedious whose whole existence is absorbed in any one thing, be it playing or praying. Queen Elizabeth, after admiring a gentleman's dancing, refused to look at the dancing-master, who did it better. "Nay," quoth her bluff Majesty,—" 'tis his business,—I'll none of him." Professionals grow tiresome. Books are good, —so is a boat; but a librarian and a ferryman, though useful to take you where you wish to go, are not necessarily enlivening as companions. The annals of "Boxiana" and "Pedestriana" and "The Cricket-Field" are as pathetic records of monomania as the bibliographical works of Mr. Thomas Dibdin. Margaret Fuller said truly, that we all delight in gossip, and differ only in the department of gossip we individually prefer; but a monotony of gossip soon grows tedious, be the theme horses or octavos.

Not one-tenth part of the requisite amount has yet been said of athletic exercises as a prescription for this community. There was a time when they were not even practised generally among American boys, if we may trust the foreign travellers of a half-century ago, and they are but just being raised into respectability among American men. Motley says of one of his Flemish heroes, that "he would as soon have foregone his daily tennis as his religious exercises"—as if ball-playing were then the necessary pivot of a great man's day. Some such pivot of physical enjoyment we must have, for no other race in the world needs it so much. Through the immense inventive capacity of our people, mechanical avocations are becoming almost as sedentary and intellectual as the professions. Among Americans, all hand-work is constantly being transmuted into brain-work; the intellect gains, but the body suffers, and needs some other form of physical activity to restore the equilibrium. As machinery becomes perfected, all the coarser tasks are constantly being handed over to the German or Irish immigrant,—not because the American cannot do the particular thing required, but because he is promoted to something more intellectual. Thus transformed to a mental laborer, he must somehow supply the bodily deficiency. If this is true of this class, it is of course true of the student, the statesman, and the professional man. The general statement recently made by Lewes, in England, certainly holds not less in America:—"It is rare to meet with good digestion among the artisans of the brain, no matter how careful they may be in food and general habits." The great majority of our literary and professional men could echo the testimony of Washington Irving, if they would only indorse his wise conclusion:—"My own case is a proof how one really loses by over-writing one's self and keeping too intent upon a sedentary occupation. I attribute all my present indisposition, which is losing the time, spirits, everything, to two fits of close application and neglect of all exercise while I was at Paris. I am convinced that he who devotes two hours each day to vigorous exercise will eventually gain those two and a couple more into the bargain."

Indeed, there is something involved in the matter far beyond any merely physical necessity. All our natures need something more than mere bodily exertion; they need bodily enjoyment. There is, or ought to be, in all of us a touch of untamed gypsy nature, which should be trained, not crushed. We need, in the very midst of civilization, something which gives a little of the zest of savage life; and athletic exercises furnish the means. The young man who is caught down the bay in a sudden storm, alone in his boat, with wind and tide against him, has all the sensations of a Norway sea-king,—sensations thoroughly uncomfortable, if you please, but for the thrill and glow they bring. Swim out after a storm at Dove Harbor, topping the low crests, diving through the high ones, and you feel yourself as veritable a South-Sea Islander as if you were to dine that day on missionary instead of mutton. Tramp, for a whole day, across hill, marsh, and pasture, with gun, rod, or whatever the excuse may be, and camp where you find yourself at evening, and you are as essentially an Indian on the Blue Hills as among the Rocky Mountains. Less depends upon circumstances than we fancy, and more upon our personal temperament and will. All the enjoyments of Browning's "Saul," those "wild joys of living" which make us happy with their freshness as we read of them, are within the reach of all, and make us happier still when enacted. Every one, in proportion as he develops his own physical resources, puts himself in harmony with the universe, and contributes something to it; even as Mr. Pecksniff, exulting in his digestive machinery, felt a pious delight after dinner in the thought that this wonderful apparatus was wound up and going.

A young person can no more have too much love of adventure than a mill can have too much water-power; only it needs to be worked, not wasted. Physical exercises give to energy and daring a legitimate channel, supply the place of war, gambling, licentiousness, highway-robbery, and office-seeking. De Quincey, in like manner, says that Wordsworth made pedestrianism a substitute for wine and spirits; and Emerson thinks the force of rude periods "can rarely be compensated in tranquil times, except by some analogous vigor drawn from occupations as hardy as war." The animal energy cannot and ought not to be suppressed; if debarred from its natural channel, it will force for itself unnatural ones. A vigorous life of the senses not only does not tend to sensuality in the objectionable sense, but it helps to avert it. Health finds joy in mere existence; daily breath and daily bread suffice. This innocent enjoyment lost, the normal desires seek abnormal satisfactions. The most brutal prize-fighter is compelled to recognize the connection between purity and vigor, and becomes virtuous when he goes into training, as the heroes of old observed chastity, in hopes of conquering at the Olympic Games. The very word *ascetic* comes from a Greek word signifying the preparatory exercises of an athlete. There are spiritual diseases which coil poisonously among distorted instincts and disordered nerves, and one would be generally safer in standing sponsor for the soul of the gymnast than of the dyspeptic.

Of course, the demand of our nature is not always for continuous exertion. One does not always seek that "rough exercise" which Sir John Sinclair asserts to be "the darling idol of the English." There are delicious languors, Neapolitan reposes, Creole siestas, "long days and solid banks of flowers." But it is the birthright of the man of the temperate zones to alternate these voluptuous delights with more heroic ones, and sweeten the reverie by the toil. So far as they go, the enjoyments of the healthy body are as innocent and as ardent as those of the soul. As there is no ground of comparison, so there is no ground of antagonism. How compare a sonata and a sea-bath, or measure the Sistine Madonna against a gallop across country? The best thanksgiving for each is to enjoy the other also, and educate the mind to ampler nobleness. After all, the best verdict on athletic exercises was that of the great Sully, when he said, "I was always of the same opinion with Henry IV. Concerning them: he often asserted that they were the most solid foundation, not only of discipline and other military virtues but also of those noble sentiments and that elevation of mind which give one nature superiority over another."

We are now ready, perhaps, to come to the question, How are these athletic enjoyments to be obtained? The first and easiest answer is, By taking a long walk every day. If people would actually do this, instead of forever talking about doing it, the object might be gained. To be sure, there are various defects in this form of exercise. It is not a play to begin with, and therefore does not withdraw the mind from its daily cares, the anxious man recurs to his problems on the way; and each mile, in that case brings fresh weariness to brain as well as body. Moreover, there are, according to Dr. Grau, "three distinct groups of muscles which are almost totally neglected where walking alone is resorted to, and which consequently exist only in a crippled state, although they are of the utmost importance, and each stands in close *rapport* with a number of other functions of the greatest necessity to health and life." These he afterwards classifies as the muscles of the shoulders and chest, having a bearing on the lungs,—the abdominal muscles, bearing on the corresponding organs,—and the spinal muscles, which are closely connected with the whole nervous system.

But the greatest practical difficulty is that walking, being the least concentrated form of exercise, requires a larger appropriation of time than most persons are willing to give. Taken liberally, and in connection with exercises which are more concentrated and have more play about them, it is of great value, and, indeed, indispensable. But so far as I have seen, instead of these other pursuits taking the place of pedestrianism, they commonly create a taste for it; so that, when the sweet spring-days come round, you will see our afternoon gymnastic class begin to scatter literally to the four winds; or they look in for a moment, on their way home from the woods, their hands filled and scented with long wreaths of the trailing arbutus.

But the gymnasium is the normal type of all muscular exercise,—the only form of it which is impartial and comprehensive, which has something for everybody, which is available at all seasons through all weathers, in all latitudes. All other provisions are limited: you cannot row in winter nor skate in summer, spite of parlor-skates and ice-boats; ball-playing requires comrades; riding takes money; everything needs daylight: but the gymnasium is always accessible. Then it is the only thing which trains the whole body. Military drill makes one prompt, patient, erect, accurate, still, strong. Rowing takes one set of muscles and stretches them through and through, till you feel yourself turning into one long spiral spring from finger-tips to toes. In cricket or baseball, a player runs, strikes, watches, catches, throws, must learn quickness of hand and eye, must learn endurance also. Yet, no matter which of these may be your special hobby, you must, if you wish to use all the days and all the muscles, seek the gymnasium at last,—the only thorough panacea.

The history of modern gymnastic exercises is easily written: it is proper to say modern,—for, so far as apparatus goes, the ancient gymnasiums seem to have had scarcely anything in common with our own. The first institution on the modern plan was founded at Schnepfenthal, near Gotha, in Germany, in 1785, by Salzmann, a clergyman and the principal of a boys' school. After eight years of experience, his assistant, Gutsmuths, wrote a book upon the subject, which was translated into English, and published at London in 1799 and at Philadelphia in 1800, under the name of "Salzmann's Gymnastics." No similar institution seems to have existed in either country, however, till those established by Voelckers, in London, in 1824, and by Dr. Follen, at Cambridge, Mass., in 1826. Both were largely patronized at first, and died out at last. The best account of Voelcker's establishment will be found in Hone's "Every-Day Book"; its plan seems to have been unexceptionable. But Dr. James Johnson, writing his "Economy of Health" ten years after, declared that these German exercises had proved "better adapted to the Spartan youth than to the pallid sons of pampered cits, the dandies of the desk, and the squalid tenants of attics and factories," and also adds the epitaph, "This ultra-gymnastic enthusiast did much injury to an important branch of hygiene by carrying it to excess, and consequently by causing its desuetude." And Dr. Jarvis, in his "Practical Physiology," declares the unquestionable result of the American experiment to have been "general failure."

Accordingly, the English, who are reputed kings in all physical exercises, have undoubtedly been far surpassed by the Germans, and even by the French, in gymnastics. The writer of the excellent little "Handbook for Gymnastics," George Forrest, M. A., testifies strongly to this deficiency. "It is curious that we English, who possess perhaps the finest and strongest figures of all European nations, should leave ourselves so undeveloped bodily. There is not one man in a hundred who can even raise his toes to a level with his hands, when suspended by the latter members; and yet to do so is at the very beginning of gymnastic exercises. We, as a rule, are strong in the arms and legs, but weak across the loins and back, and are apparently devoid of that beautiful set of muscles that run round the entire waist, and show to such advantage in the ancient statues. Indeed, at a bathing-place, I can pick out every gymnast merely by the development of those muscles."

It is the Germans and the military portion of the French nation, chiefly, who have developed gymnastic exercises to their present elaboration, while the working out of their curative applications was chiefly due to Ling, a Swede. In the German manuals, such, for instance, as

Eiselen's "Turnübungen," are to be found nearly all the stock exercises of our institutions. Until within a few years, American skill has added nothing to these, except through the medium of the circus; but the present revival of athletic exercises is rapidly placing American gymnasts in advance of the *Turners,* both in the feats performed and in the style of doing them. Never yet have I succeeded in seeing a thoroughly light and graceful German gymnast, while again and again I have seen Americans who carried into their severest exercise such an airy, floating elegance of motion, that all the beauty of Greek sculpture appeared to return again, and it seemed as if plastic art might once more make its studio in the gymnasium.

The apparatus is not costly. Any handful of young men in the smallest country-village, with a very few dollars and a little mechanical skill, can put up in any old shed or shoe-shop a few simple articles of machinery, which will, through many a winter evening, vary the monotony of the cigar and the grocery-bench by an endless variety of manly competitions. Fifteen cents will bring by mail from the publishers of the "Atlantic" Forrest's little sixpenny "Handbook," which gives a sufficient number of exercises to form an introduction to all others; and a gymnasium is thus easily established. This is just the method of the simple and sensible Germans, who never wait for elegant upholstery. A pair of plain parallel bars, a movable vaulting-bar, a wooden horse, a springboard, an old mattress to break the fall, a few settees where sweethearts and wives may sit with their knitting as spectators, and there is a *Turnhalle* complete,—to be henceforward filled, two or three nights in every week, with cheery German faces, jokes, laughs, gutturals, and gambols.

But this suggests that you are being kept too long in the anteroom. Let me act as cicerone through this modest gymnastic hall of ours. You will better appreciate all this oddly shaped apparatus, if I tell you in advance, as a connoisseur does in his picture-gallery, precisely what you are expected to think of each particular article.

You will notice, however, that a part of the gymnastic class are exercising without apparatus, in a series of rather grotesque movements which supple and prepare the body for more muscular feats: these are calisthenic exercises. Such are being at last introduced, thanks to Dr. Lewis and others, into our common schools. At the word of command, as swiftly as a conjuror twists his puzzle-paper, these living forms are shifted from one odd resemblance to another, at which it is quite lawful to laugh, especially if those laugh who win. A series of windmills,—a group of inflated balloons,—a flock of geese all asleep on one leg,—a circle of ballet dancers, just poised to begin,—a band of patriots just kneeling to take an oath upon their country's altar,—a senate of tailors,—a file of soldiers,—a whole parish of Shaker worshippers,—a Japanese embassy performing *Ko-tow:* these all in turn come like shadows,—so depart. This complicated attitudinizing forms the preliminary to the gymnastic hour. But now come and look at some of the apparatus.

Here is a row of Indian clubs, or sceptres, as they are sometimes called,—tapering down from giants of fifteen pounds to dwarfs of four. Help yourself to a pair of dwarfs, at first; grasp one in each hand, by the handle; swing one of them round your head quietly; dropping the point behind as far as possible,—then the other,—and so swing them alternately some twenty times. Now do the same back-handed, bending the wrist outward, and carrying the club behind the head first. Now swing them both together, crossing them in front, and then the same back-handed; then the same without crossing, and this again backward, which you will find much harder. Place them on the ground gently after each set of processes. Now, can you hold them out horizontally at arm's length, forward and then sideways? Your arms quiver and quiver, and down come the clubs thumping at last. Take them presently in a different and more difficult manner, holding each club with the point erect instead of hanging down; it tries your wrists, you will find, to manipulate them so, yet all the most graceful exercises have this for a basis. Soon you will gain the mastery of heavier implements than you begin with, and will understand how yonder slight youth has learned to handle his two heavy clubs in complex curves that seem to you inexplicable, tracing in the air a device as swift and tangled as that woven by a swarm of gossamer flies above a brook, in the sultry stillness of the summer noon.

This row of masses of iron, laid regularly in order of size, so as to resemble something between a musical instrument and a gridiron, consists of dumb-bells weighing from four pounds to a hundred. These playthings, suited to a variety of capacities, have experienced a revival of favor within a few years, and the range of exercises with them has been greatly increased. The use of very heavy ones is, so far as I can find, a peculiarly American hobby, though not originating with Dr. Windship. Even he, at the beginning of his exhibitions, used those weighing only ninety-eight pounds; and it was considered an astonishing feat, when, a little earlier, Mr. Richard Montgomery used to "put up" a dumb-bell weighing one hundred and one pounds. A good many persons, in different parts of the country, now handle one hundred and twenty-five, and Dr. Windship has got much farther on. There is, of course, a knack in using these little articles, as in every other feat, yet it takes good extensor muscles to get beyond the fifties. The easiest way of elevating the weight is to swing it up from between the knees; or it may be thrown up from the shoulder, with a simultaneous jerk of the whole body; but the only way of doing it handsomely is to put it up from the shoulder with the arm alone, without bending the knee, though you may bend the body as much as you please. Dr. Windship now puts up one hundred and forty-one pounds in this manner, and by the aid of a jerk can elevate one hundred and eighty with one arm. This particular movement with dumb-bells is most practised, as affording a test of strength; but there are many other ways of using them, all exceedingly invigorating, and all safe enough, unless the weight employed be too great, which it is very apt to be. Indeed, there is so much danger of this, that at Cambridge it has been deemed best to exclude all beyond seventy pounds. Nevertheless, the dumb-bell remains the one available form of home or office exercise: it is a whole athletic apparatus packed up in the smallest space; it is gymnastic pemmican. With one fifty-pound dumb-bell, or a pair of half that size,—or more or less, according to his strength and habits,—a man may exercise nearly every muscle in his body in half an hour, if he has sufficient ingenuity in positions. If it were one's fortune to be sent to prison,—and the access to such retirement is growing more and more facile in many regions of our common country,—one would certainly wish to carry a dumb-bell with him, precisely as Dr. Johnson carried an arithmetic in his pocket on his tour to the Hebrides, as containing the greatest amount of nutriment in the compactest form.

Apparatus for lifting is not yet introduced into most gymnasiums, in spite of the recommendations of the Roxbury Hercules: beside the fear of straining, there is the cumbrous weight and cost of iron apparatus, while, for some reason or other, no cheap and accurate dynamometer has yet come into the market. Running and jumping, also, have as yet been too much neglected in our institutions, or practised spasmodically rather than systematically. It is singular how little pains have been taken to ascertain definitely what a man can do with his body,—far less, as Quetelet has observed, than in regard to any animal which man has tamed, or any machine which he has invented. It is stated, for instance, in Walker's "Manly Exercises," that six feet is the maximum of a high leap, with a run,—and certainly one never finds in the newspapers a record of anything higher; yet it is the English tradition, that Ireland, of Yorkshire, could clear a string raised fourteen feet, and that he once kicked a ladder at sixteen. No springboard would explain a difference so astounding. In the same way,

Walker fixes the limit of a long leap without a run at fourteen feet, and with a run at twenty-two,—both being large estimates; and Thackeray makes his young Virginian jump twenty-one feet and three inches, crediting George Washington with a foot more. Yet the ancient epitaph of Phayllus the Crotonian claimed for him nothing less than fifty-five feet, on an inclined plane. Certainly the story must have taken a leap also.

These ladders, aspiring indefinitely into the air, like Piranesi's stairways, are called technically peak-ladders; and dear banished T. S. K., who always was puzzled to know why Mount Washington kept up such a pique against the sky, would have found his joke fit these ladders with great precision, so frequent the disappointment they create. But try them, and see what trivial appendages one's legs may become,—since the feet are not intended to touch these polished rounds. Walk up backward on the under side, hand over hand, then forward; then go up again, omitting every other round; then aspire to the third round, if you will. Next grasp a round with both hands, give a slight swing of the body, let go, and grasp the round above, and so on upward; then the same, omitting one round, or more, if you can, and come down in the same way. Can you walk up on *one* hand? It is not an easy thing, but a first-class gymnast will do it,—and Dr. Windship does it, taking only every third round. Fancy a one-armed and legless hodman ascending the under side of a ladder to the roof, and reflect on the conveniences of gymnastic habits.

Here is a wooden horse; on this noble animal the Germans say that not less than three hundred distinct feats can be performed. Bring yonder spring-board and we will try a few. Grasp these low pommels and vault over the horse, first to the right, then again to the left; then with one hand each way. Now spring to the top and stand; now spring between the hands forward, now backward; now take a good impetus, spread your feet far apart, and leap over it, letting go the hands. Grasp the pommels again and throw a somerset over it,—coming down on your feet, if the Fates permit. Now vault up and sit upon the horse, at one end, knees the same side; now grasp the pommels and whirl yourself round till you sit at the other end, facing the other way. Now spring up and bestride it, whirl round till you bestride it the other way, at the other end; do it once again, and, letting go your hand, seat yourself in the saddle. Now push away the spring-board and repeat every feat without its aid. Next, take a run and spring upon the end of the horse astride; then walk over, supporting yourself on your hands alone, the legs not touching; then backward, the same. It will be hard to balance yourself at first, and you will careen uneasily one way or the other; no matter, you will get over it somehow. Lastly, mount once more, kneel in the saddle, and leap to the ground. It appears at first ridiculously impracticable, the knees seem glued to their position, and it looks as if one would fall inevitably on his face; but falling is hardly possible. Any novice can do it, if he will only have faith. You shall learn to do it from the horizontal bar presently, where it looks much more formidable.

But first you must learn some simpler exercises on this horizontal bar: you observe that it is made movable, and may be placed as low as your knee, or higher than your hand can reach. This bar is only five inches in circumference; but it is remarkably strong and springy, and therefore we hope secure, though for some exercises our boys prefer to substitute a larger one. Try and vault it, first to the right, then to the left, as you did with the horse; try first with one hand, then see how high you can vault with both. Now vault it between your hands, forward and backward: the latter will baffle you, unless you have brought an unusual stock of India-rubber in your frame, to begin with. Raise it higher and higher, till you can vault it no longer. Now spring up on the bar, resting on your palms, and vault over from that position with a swing of your body, without touching the ground; when you have once managed this, you can vault as high as you can reach: double-vaulting this is called. Now put the bar higher than your head; grasp it with your hands, and draw yourself up till you look over it; repeat this a good many times: capital practice this, as is usually said of things particularly tiresome. Take hold of the bar again, and with a good spring from the ground try to curl your body over it, feet foremost. At first, in all probabiilty, your legs will go angling in the air convulsively, and come down with nothing caught; but ere long we shall see you dispense with the spring from the ground and go whirling over and over, as if the bar were the axle of a wheel and your legs the spokes. Now spring upon the bar, supporting yourself on your palms, as before; put your hands a little farther apart, with the thumbs forward, then suddenly bring up your knees on the bar and let your whole body go over forward: you will not fall, if your hands have a good grasp. Try it again with your feet outside your hands, instead of between them; then once again flinging your body off from the bar and describing a long curve with it, arms stiff: this is called the Giant's Swing. Now hang to the bar by the knees,—by both knees; do not try it yet with one; then seize the bar with your hands and thrust the legs still farther and farther forward, pulling with your arms at the same time, till you find yourself sitting unaccountably on the bar itself. This our boys cheerfully denominate "skinning the cat," because the sensations it suggests, on a first experiment, are supposed to resemble those of pussy with her skin drawn over her head; but, after a few experiments, it seems like stroking the fur in the right direction, and grows rather pleasant.

Try now the parallel bars, the most invigorating apparatus of the gymnasium, and in its beginnings "accessible to the meanest capacity," since there are scarcely any who cannot support themselves by the hands on the bars, and not very many who cannot walk a few steps upon the palms, at the first trial. Soon you will learn to swing along these bars in long surges of motion, forward and backward; to go through them, in a series of springs from the hand only, without a jerk of the knees; to turn round and round between them, going forward or backward all the while; to vault over them and under them in complicated ways; to turn somersets in them and across them; to roll over and over on them as a porpoise seems to roll in the sea. Then come the "low-standing" exercises, the grasshopper style of business; supporting yourself now with arms not straight, but bent at the elbow, you shall learn to raise and lower your body and to hold or swing yourself as lightly in that position as if you had not felt pinioned and paralyzed hopelessly at the first trial; and whole new systems of muscles shall seem to shoot out from your shoulder-blades to enable you to do what you could not have dreamed of doing before. These bars are magical,—they are conduits of power; you cannot touch them, you cannot rest your weight on them in the slightest degree, without causing strength to flow into your body as naturally and irresistibly as water into the aqueduct-pipe when you turn it on. Do you but give the opportunity, and every pulsation of blood from your heart is pledged for the rest.

These exercises, and such as these, are among the elementary lessons of gymnastic training. Practise these thoroughly and patiently, and you will in time attain evolutions more complicated, and, if you wish, more perilous. Neglect these, to grasp at random after everything which you see others doing, and you will fail like a bookkeeper who is weak in the multiplication-table. The older you begin, the more gradual the preparation must be. A respectable middle-aged citizen, bent on improving his *physique,* goes into a gymnasium, and sees slight, smooth-faced boys going gayly through a series of exercises which show their bodies to be a triumph, not a drag, and he is assured that the same might be the case with him. Off goes the coat of our enthusiast and in he plunges; he gripes a heavy dumb-bell and strains one shoulder, hauls at a weight-box and strains the other, vaults the bar and bruises his knee, swings in the rings once or twice till his hand slips and he falls to the floor. No matter, he thinks the cause demands sacrifices; but he subsides, for the next fifteen minutes, into more moderate exercises, which he still makes immoderate by his awkward way of doing them. Nevertheless, he goes home, cheerful under difficulties, and will try again to-morrow. To-morrow finds him stiff, lame, and wretched; he cannot lift his arm to his face to shave, nor lower it sufficiently to pull his boots on; his little daughter must help him with his shoes, and the indignant wife of his bosom must put on his hat, with that ineffectual one-sidedness to which alone the best-regulated female mind can attain, in this difficult part of costuming. His sorrows increase as the day passes; the gymnasium alone can relieve them, but his soul shudders at the remedy; and he can conceive of nothing so absurd as a first gymnastic lesson, except a second one. But had he been wise enough to place himself under an experienced adviser at the very beginning, he would have been put through a few simple movements which would have sent him home glowing and refreshed and fancying himself half-way back to boyhood again; the slight ache and weariness of next day would have been cured by next day's exercise; and after six months' patience, by a progress almost imperceptible, he would have found himself, in respect to strength and activity, a transformed man.

Most of these discomforts, of course, are spared to boys; their frames are more elastic and less liable to ache and strain. They learn gymnastics, as they learn everything else, more readily than their elders. Begin with a boy early enough, and if he be of a suitable temperament, he can learn in the gymnasium all the feats usually seen in the circus-ring, and could even acquire more difficult ones if it were worth his while to try them. This is true even of the air-somersets and hand-springs which are not so commonly cultivated by gymnasts; but it is especially true of all exercises with apparatus. It is astonishing how readily our classes pick up any novelty brought into town by a strolling company,—holding the body out horizontally from an upright pole, or hanging by the back of the head, or touching the head to the heels, though this last is oftener tried than accomplished. They may be seen practising these antics, at all spare moments, for weeks until some later hobby drives them away. From Blondin downwards, the public feats derive a large part of their wonder from the imposing height in the air at which they are done. Many a young man who can swing himself more than his own length on the horizontal ladder at the gymnasium has yet shuddered at *l'échelle périlleuse* of the Hanlons; and I noticed that even the simplest of their performances, such as holding by one hand, or hanging by the knees, seemed perfectly terrific when done at a height of twenty or thirty feet in the air, even to those who had done them a hundred times at a lower level. It was the nerve that was astounding, not the strength or skill; but the eye found it hard to draw the distinction. So when a gymnastic friend of mine, crossing the ocean lately, amused himself with hanging by one leg to the mizzen-topmast-stay, the boldest sailors shuddered, though the feat itself was nothing, save to the imagination.

Indeed, it is almost impossible for an inexperienced spectator to form the slightest opinion as to the comparative difficulty or danger of different exercises, since it is the test of merit to make the hardest things look easy. Moreover, there may be a distinction between two feats almost imperceptible to the eye,—a change, for instance, in the position of the hands on a bar,—which may at once transform the thing from a trifle to a wonder. An unpractised eye can no more appreciate the difficulty of a gymnastic exercise by seeing it executed, than an inexperienced ear, of the perplexities of a piece of music by hearing it played.

The first effect of gymnastic exercise is almost always to increase the size of the arms and the chest; and new-comers may commonly be known by their frequent recourse to the tape-measure. The average increase among the students of Harvard University during the first three months of the gymnasium was nearly two inches in the chest, more than one inch in the upper arm, and more than half an inch in the fore-arm. This was far beyond what the unassisted growth of their age would account for; and the increase is always very marked for a time, especially with thin persons. In those of fuller habit the loss of flesh may counter-balance the gain in muscle, so that size and weight remain the same; and in all cases the increase stops after a time, and the subsequent change is rather in texture than in volume. Mere size is no index of strength: Dr. Windship is scarcely larger or heavier now than when he had not half his present powers.

In the vigor gained by exercise there is nothing false or morbid; it is as reliable as hereditary strength, except that it is more easily relaxed by indolent habits. No doubt it is aggravating to see some robust, lazy giant come into the gymnasium for the first time, and by hereditary muscle shoulder a dumb-bell which all your training has not taught you to handle. No matter; it is by comparing yourself with yourself that the estimate is to be made. As the writing-master exhibits with triumph to each departing pupil the uncouth copy which he wrote on entering, so it will be enough to you, if you can appreciate your present powers with your original inabilities. When you first joined the gymnastic class, you could not climb yonder smooth mast, even with all your limbs brought into service; now you can do it with your hands alone. When you came, you could not possibly, when hanging by your hands to the horizontal bar, raise your feet as high as your head,—nor could you, with any amount of spring from the ground, curl your body over the bar itself; now you can hang at arm's length and fling yourself over it a dozen times in succession. At first, if you lowered yourself with bent elbows between the parallel bars, you could not by any manœuvre get up again, but sank to the ground a hopeless wreck; now you can raise and lower yourself an indefinite number of times. As for the weights and clubs and dumb-bells, you feel as if there must be some jugglery about them,—they have grown so much lighter than they used to be. It is you who have gained a double set of muscles to every limb; that is all. Strike out from the shoulder with your clenched hand; once your arm was loose-jointed and shaky; now it is firm and tense, and begins to feel like a natural arm. Moreover, strength and suppleness have grown together; you have not stiffened by becoming stronger, but find yourself more flexible. When you first came here, you could not touch your fingers to the ground without bending the knees, and now you can place your knuckles on the floor; then you could scarcely bend yourself backward, and now you can lay the back of your head in a chair, or walk, without crouching forward, under a bar less than three feet from the ground. You have found, indeed, that almost every feat is done originally by sheer strength, and then by agility, requiring very little expenditure of force after the precise motion is hit upon; at first labor, puffing, and a red face,—afterwards ease and the graces.

To a person who begins after the age of thirty or thereabouts, the increase of strength and suppleness, of course, comes more slowly; yet it comes as surely, and perhaps it is a more permanent acquisition, less easily lost again, than in the softer frame of early youth. There is no doubt that men of sixty have experienced a decided gain in strength and health by beginning gymnastic exercises even at that age, as Socrates learned to dance at seventy; and if they have practised similar exercises all their lives, so much is added to their chance of preserving physical youthfulness to the last. Jerome and Gabriel Ravel are reported to have spent near three-score years on the planet which their winged feet have so lightly trod; and who will dare to say how many winters have passed over the head of the still young and graceful Papanti?

Dr. Windship's most important experience is, that strength is to a certain extent identical with health, so that every increase in muscular development is an actual protection against disease. Americans, who are ashamed to confess to doing the most innocent thing for the sake of mere enjoyment, must be cajoled into every form of exercise under the plea of health. Joining, the other day, in a children's dance, I was amused by a solemn parent who turned to me, in the midst of a Virginia reel, still conscientious, though breathless, and asked if I did not consider dancing to be, on the whole, a *healthy* exercise? Well, the gymnasium is healthy; but the less you dwell on the fact, the better, after you have once entered it. If it does you good, you will enjoy it; and if you enjoy it, it will do you good. With body, as with soul, the highest experience merges duty in pleasure. The better one's condition is, the less one has to think about growing better, and the more unconsciously one's natural instincts guide the right way. When ill, we eat to support life; when well, we eat because the food tastes good. It is a merit of the gymnasium, that, when properly taken, it makes one forget to think about health or anything else that is troublesome; "a man remembereth neither sorrow nor debt"; cares must be left outside, be they physical or metaphysical, like canes at the door of a museum.

No doubt, to some it grows tedious. It shares this objection with all means of exercise. To be an American is to hunger for novelty; and all instruments and appliances, especially, require constant modification: we are dissatisfied with last winter's skates, with the old boat, and with the family pony. So the zealot finds the gymnasium insufficient long before he has learned half the moves. To some temperaments it becomes a treadmill, and that, strangely enough, to diametrically opposite temperaments. A lethargic youth, requiring great effort to keep himself awake between the exercises, thinks the gymnasium slow, because he is; while an eager, impetuous young fellow, exasperated because he cannot in a fortnight draw himself up by one hand, finds the same trouble there as elsewhere, that the laws of Nature are not fast enough for his inclinations. No one without energy, no one without patience, can find permanent interest in a gymnasium; but with these qualities, and a modest willingness to live and learn, I do not see why one should ever grow tired of the moderate use of its apparatus. For one, I really never enter it without exhilaration, or leave it without a momentary regret: there are always certain special new things on the docket for trial; and when those are settled, there will be something more. It is amazing what a variety of interest can be extracted from those few bits of wood and rope and iron. There is always somebody in advance, some "man on horseback" on a wooden horse, some India-rubber hero, some slight and powerful fellow who does with ease what you fail to do with toil, some terrible Dr. Windship with an ever-waxing dumb-bell. The interest becomes semi-professional. A good gymnast enjoys going into a new and well-appointed establishment, precisely as a sailor enjoys a well-rigged ship; every rope and spar is scanned with intelligent interest; "we know the forest round us as seamen know the sea." The pupils talk gymnasium as some men talk horse. A particularly smooth and flexible horizontal pole, a desirable pair of parallel bars, a remarkably elastic spring-board,—these are matters of personal pride, and described from city to city with loving enthusiasm. The gymnastic apostle rises to eloquence in proportion to the height of the hand-swings, and points his climax to match the peak-ladders.

An objection frequently made to the gymnasium, and especially by anxious parents, is the supposed danger of accident. But this peril is obviously inseparable from all physical activity. If a man never leaves his house, the chances undoubtedly are, that he will never break his leg, unless upon the stairway; but if he is always to stay in the house, he might as well have no legs at all. Certainly we incur danger every time we go outside the front door; but to remain always on the inside would prove the greatest danger of the whole. When a man slips in the street and dislocates his arm, we do not warn him against walking, but against carelessness. When a man is thrown from his horse and gratifies the surgeons by a beautiful case of compound fracture, we do not advise him to avoid a riding-school, but to go to one. Trivial accidents are not uncommon in the gymnasium, severe ones are rare, fatal ones almost unheard of,—which is far more than can be said of riding, driving, hunting, boating, skating, or even "coasting" on a sled. Learning gymnastics is like learning to swim,—you incur a small temporary risk for the sake of acquiring powers that will lessen your risks in the end. Your increased strength and agility will carry you past many unseen perils hereafter, and the invigorated tone of your system will make accidents less important, if they happen. Some trifling sprain causes lameness for life, some slight blow brings on wasting disease, to a person whose health is merely negative, not positive,—while a well-trained frame throws it off in twenty-four hours. It is almost proverbial of the gymnasium, that it cures its own wounds.

A minor objection is, that these exercises are not performed in the open air. In summer, however, they may be, and in winter and in stormy weather it is better that they should not be. Extreme cold is not favorable to them; it braces, but stiffens; and the bars and ropes become slippery and even dangerous. In Germany it is common to have a double set of apparatus, out-doors and in-doors; and this would always be desirable, but for the increased expense. Moreover, the gymnasium should be taken in addition to out-door exercise, giving, for instance, an hour a day to each, one for training, the other for oxygen. I know promising gymnasts whose pallid complexions show that their blood is not worthy of their muscle, and they will break down. But these cases are rare, for the reason already hinted,—that nothing gives so good an appetite for out-door life as this indoor activity. It alternates admirably with skating, and seduces irresistibly into walking or rowing when spring arrives.

My young friend Silverspoon, indeed, thinks that a good trot on a fast horse is worth all the gymnastics in the world. But I learn, on inquiry, that my young friend's mother is constantly imploring him to ride in order to air her horses. It is a beautiful parental trait; but for those born horseless, what an economical substitute is the wooden quadruped of the gymnasium! Our Autocrat has well said, that the livery-stable horse is "a profligate animal"; and I do not wonder that the Centaurs of old should be suspected of having originated spurious coin. Undoubtedly it was to pay for the hire of their own hoofs.

For young men in cities, too, the facilities for exercise are limited not only by money, but by time. They must commonly take it after dark. It is every way a blessing, when the gymnasium divides their evenings with the concert, the book, or the public meeting. Then there is no time left, and small temptation, for pleasures less pure. It gives an innocent answer to that first demand for evening excitement which perils the soul of the homeless boy in the seductive city. The companions whom he meets at the gymnasium are not the ones whose pursuits of later nocturnal hours entice him to sin. The honest fatigue of his exercises calls for honest rest. It is the nervous exhaustion of a sedentary, frivolous, or joyless life which madly tries to restore itself by the other nervous exhaustion of debauchery. It is an old prescription,—

"Multa tulit fecitque puer, sudavit et alsit, *Abstinuit venere et vino.*"

There is another class of critics whose cant is simply can't, and who, being unable or unwilling to surrender themselves to these simple sources of enjoyment, are grandiloquent upon the dignity of manhood, and the absurdity of full-grown men in playing monkey-tricks with their bodies. Full-grown men? There is not a person in the world who can afford to be a "full-grown man" through all the twenty-four hours. There is not one who does not need, more than he needs his dinner, to have habitually one hour in the day when he throws himself with boyish eagerness into interests as simple as those of boys.

No church or state, no science or art, can feed us all the time; some morsels there must be of simpler diet, some moments of unadulterated play. But dignity? Alas for that poor soul whose dignity must be "preserved,"—preserved in the right culinary sense, as fruits which are growing dubious in their natural state are sealed up in jars to make their acidity presentable! "There's beggary in the love that can be reckoned," and degradation in the dignity that has to be preserved. Simplicity is the only dignity. If one has not the genuine article, no affluence of starch, no snow-drift of white-linen decency, will furnish any substitute. If one has it, he will retain it, whether he stand on his head or his heels. Nothing is really undignified but affectation or conceit; and for the total extinction and annihilation of every vestige of these, there are few things so effectual as athletic exercises.

Still another objection is that of the medical men, that the gymnasium, as commonly used, is not a specific prescription for the special disease of the patient. But setting aside the claims of the system of applied gymnastics, which Ling and his followers have so elaborated, it is enough to answer, that the one great fundamental disorder of all Americans is simply nervous exhaustion, and that for this the gymnasium can never be misdirected, though it may be used to excess. Of course one can no more cure over-work of brain by over-work of body than one can restore a wasted candle by lighting it at the other end. But by subtracting an hour a day from the present amount of purely intellectual fatigue, and inserting that quantum of bodily fatigue in its place, you begin an immediate change in your conditions of life. Moreover, the great object is not merely to get well, but to keep well. The exhaustion of over-work can almost always be cured by a water-cure, or by a voyage, which is a salt-water cure; but the problem is, how to make the whole voyage of life perpetually self-curative. Without this, there is perpetual dissatisfaction and chronic failure. Emerson well says, "Each class fixes its eye on the advantages it has not,—the refined on rude strength, the democrat on birth and breeding." This is the aim of the gymnasium, to give to the refined this rude strength, or its better substitute, refined strength. It is something to secure to the student or the clerk the strong muscles, hearty appetite, and sound sleep of the sailor and the ploughman,—to enable him, if need be, to out-row the fisherman, and out-run the mountaineer, and lift more than his porter, and to remember head-ache and dyspepsia only as he recalls the primeval whooping-cough of his childhood. I am one of those who think that the Autocrat rides his hobby of the pavements a little too far; but it is useless to deny, that, within the last few years of gymnasiums and boatclubs, the city has been gaining on the country, in physical development. Here in our town we had all the city- and college-boys assembled in July to see the regattas, and all the country-boys in September to see the thousand-dollar base-ball match; and it was impossible to deny, whatever one's theories, that the physical superiority lay for the time being with the former.

The secret is, that, though the country offers to farmers more oxygen than to anybody in the city, yet not all dwellers in the country are farmers, and even those who are such are suffering from other causes, being usually the very last to receive those lessons of food and clothing and bathing and ventilation which have their origin in cities. Physical training is not a mechanical, but a vital process; no bricks without straw; no good *physique* without good materials and conditions. The farmer knows, that, to rear a premium colt or calf, he must oversee every morsel that it eats, every motion it makes, every breath it draws,—must guard against over-work and under-work, cold and heat, wet and dry. He remembers it for the quadrupeds, but he forgets it for his children, his wife, and himself: so his cattle deserve a premium, and his family does not.

Neglect is the danger of the country; the peril of the city is in living too fast. All mental excitement acts as a stimulant, and, like all stimulants, debilitates when taken in excess. This explains the unnatural strength and agility of the insane, always followed by prostration; and even moderate cerebral excitement produces similar results, so far as it goes. Quetelet discovered that sometimes after lecturing or other special intellectual action, he could perform gymnastic feats impossible to him at other times. The fact is unquestionable; and it is also certain that an extreme in this direction has precisely the contrary effect, and is fatal to the physical condition. One may spring up from a task of moderate mental labor with a sense of freedom like a bow let loose; but after an immoderate task one feels like the same bow too long bent, flaccid, nerveless, all the elasticity gone. Such fatigue is far more overwhelming than any mere physical exhaustion. I have lounged into the gymnasium, after an afternoon's skating, supposing myself quite tired, and have found myself in excellent condition; and I have gone in after an hour or two of some specially concentrated anxiety or thought, without being aware that the body was at all fatigued, and found it good for nothing. Such experiences are invaluable; all the libraries cannot so illustrate the supremacy of immaterial forces. Thought, passion, purpose, expectation, absorbed attention even, all feed upon the body's powers; let them act one atom too intensely or one moment too long, and this wondrous physical organization finds itself drained of its forces to support them. It does not seem strange that strong men should have died by a single ecstasy of emotion too convulsive, when we bear within us this tremendous engine whose slightest pulsation so throbs in every fibre of our frame.

The relation between mental culture and physical powers is a subject of the greatest interest, as yet but little touched, because so few of our physiologists have been practical gymnasts. Nothing is more striking than the tendency of all athletic exercises, when brought to perfection, to eliminate mere brute bulk from the competition, and give the palm to more subtile qualities, agility, quickness, a good eye, a ready hand,—in short, superior fineness of organization. Any clown can learn the military manual exercise; but it needs brain-power to drill with the Zouaves. Even a prize-fight tests strength less than activity and "science." The game of base-ball, as played in our boyhood, was a simple, robust, straightforward contest, where the hardest hitter was the best man; but it is every year becoming perfected into a sleight-of-hand, like cricket; mere strength is now almost valueless in playing it, and it calls rather for the qualities of the billiard-player. In the last champion-match at Worcester, nearly the whole time was consumed in skilful feints and parryings, and it took five days to make fifty runs. And these same characteristics mark gymnastic exercises above all; men of great natural strength are very apt to be too slow and clumsy for them, and the most difficult feats are usually done by persons of comparatively delicate *physique* and a certain artistic organization. It is this predominance of the nervous temperament which is yet destined to make American gymnasts the foremost in the world.

Indeed, the gymnasium is as good a place for the study of human nature as any. The perpetual analogy of mind and body can be appreciated only where both are trained with equal system. In both departments the great prizes are not won by the most astounding special powers, but by a certain harmonious adaptation. There is a physical tact, as there is a mental tact. Every process is accomplished by using just the right stress at just the right moment; but no two persons are alike in the length of time required for these little discoveries. Gymnastic genius lies in gaining at the first trial what will cost weeks of perseverance to those less happily gifted. And as the close elastic costume which is worn by the gymnast, or should be worn, allows no merit or defect of figure to be concealed, so the close contact of emulation exhibits all the varieties of temperament. One is made indolent by success, and another is made ardent; one is discouraged by failure, and another aroused by it; one does everything best the first time and slackens ever after, while another always begins at the bottom and always climbs to the top.

One of the most enjoyable things in these mimic emulations is this absolute genuineness in their gradations of success. In the great world outside, there is no immediate and absolute test for merit. There are cliques and puffings and jealousies, quarrels of authors, tricks of trade, caucusing in politics, hypocrisy among deacons. We distrust the value of others' successes, they distrust ours, and we all sometimes distrust our own. There are those who believe in Shakespeare, and those who believe in Tupper. All merit is measured by sliding scales, and each has his own theory of the sliding. In a dozen centuries it will all come right, no doubt. In the mean time there is vanity in one half the world and vexation of spirit in the other half, and each man joins each half in turn. But once enter the charmed gate of the gymnasium, and you leave shams behind. Though you be saint or sage, no matter, the inexorable laws of gravitation are around you. If you flinch, you fail; if you slip, you fall. That bar, that rope, that weight shall test you absolutely. Can you handle it, it is well; but if not, stand aside for him who can. You may have every other gift and grace, it counts for nothing; he, not you, is the man for the hour. The code of Spanish aristocracy is slight and flexible compared with this rigid precedence. It is Emerson's Astræa. Each registers himself, and there is no appeal. No use to kick and struggle, no use to apologize. Do not say that to-night you are tired, last night you felt ill. These excuses may serve for a day, but no longer. A slight margin is allowed for moods and variations, but it is not great after all. One revels in this Palace of Truth. Defeat itself is a satisfaction, before a tribunal of such absolute justice.

This contributes to that healthful ardor with which, in these exercises, a man forgets the things which are behind and presses forward to fresh achievements. This perpetually saves from vanity; for everything seems a trifle, when you have once attained it. The aim which yesterday filled your whole gymnastic horizon you overtake and pass as a boat passes a buoy: until passed, it was a goal; when passed, a mere speck in the horizon. Yesterday you could swing yourself three rounds upon the horizontal ladder; to-day, after weeks of effort, you have suddenly attained to the fourth, and instantly all that long laborious effort vanishes, to be formed again between you and the fifth round: five, five is the only goal for heroic labor to-day; and when five is attained, there will be six, and so on while the Arabic numerals hold out. A childish aim, no doubt; but is not this what we all recognize as the privilege of childhood, to obtain exaggerated enjoyment from little things? When you have come to the really difficult feats of the gymnasium,—when you have conquered the "barber's curl" and the "peg-pole,"—when you can draw yourself up by one arm, and perform the "giant's swing" over and over, without changing hands, and vault the horizontal bar as high as you can reach it,—when you can vault across the high parallel bars between your hands backward, or walk through them on your palms with your feet in the vicinity of the ceiling,—then you will reap the reward of your past labors, and may begin to call yourself a gymnast.

It is pleasant to think, that, so great is the variety of exercises in the gymnasium, even physical deficiencies and deformities do not wholly exclude from its benefits. I have seen an invalid girl, so lame from childhood that she could not stand without support, whose general health had been restored, and her bust and arms made a study for a sculptor, by means of gymnastics. Nay, there are odd compensations of Nature by which even exceptional formations may turn to account in athletic exercises. A squinting eye is a treasure to a boxer, a left-handed batter is a prize in a cricketing eleven, and one of the best gymnasts in Chicago is an individual with a wooden leg, which he takes off at the commencement of affairs, thus economizing weight and stowage, and performing achievements impossible except to unipeds.

In the enthusiasm created by this emulation, there is necessarily some danger of excess. Dr. Windship approves of exercising only every other day in the gymnasium; but as most persons take their work in a more diluted form than his, they can afford to repeat it daily, unless warned by headache or languor that they are exceeding their allowance. There is no good in excess; our constitutions cannot be hurried. The law is universal, that exercise strengthens as long as nutrition balances it, but afterwards wastes the very forces it should increase. We cannot make bricks faster than Nature supplies us with straw.

It is one good evidence of the increasing interest in these exercises, that the American gymnasiums built during the past year or two have far surpassed all their predecessors in size and completeness, and have probably no superiors in the world. The Seventh Regiment Gymnasium in New York, just opened by Mr. Abner S. Brady, is one hundred and eighty feet by fifty-two, in its main hall, and thirty-five feet in height, with nearly a thousand pupils. The beautiful hall of the Metropolitan Gymnasium, in Chicago, measures one hundred and eight feet by eighty, and is twenty feet high at the sides, with a dome in the centre, forty feet high, and the same in diameter. Next to these probably rank the new gymnasium at Cincinnati, the Tremont Gymnasium at Boston, and the Bunker-Hill Gymnasium at Charlestown, all recently opened. Of college institutions the most complete are probably those at Cambridge and New Haven,—the former being eighty-five feet by fifty, and the latter one hundred feet by fifty, in external dimensions. The arrangements for instruction are rather more systematic at Harvard, but Yale has several valuable articles of apparatus—as the rack-bars and the series of rings—which have hardly made their appearance, as yet, in Massachusetts, though considered indispensable in New York.

Gymnastic exercises are as yet but very sparingly introduced into our seminaries, primary or professional, though a great change is already beginning. Frederick the Great complained of the whole Prussian school-system of his day, because it assumed that men were originally created for students and clerks, whereas his Majesty argued that the very shape of the human body rather proved them to be meant by Nature for postilions. Until lately all our educational plans have assumed man to be a merely sedentary being; we have employed teachers of music and drawing to go from school to school to teach those elegant arts, but have had none to teach the art of health. Accordingly, the pupils have exhibited more complex curves in their spines than they could possibly portray on the blackboard, and acquired such discords in their nervous systems as would have utterly disgraced their singing. It is something to have got beyond the period when active sports were actually prohibited. I remember when there was but one boat owned by a Cambridge student,—the owner was the first of his class, by the way, to get his name into capitals in the "Triennial Catalogue" afterwards,—and that boat was soon reported to have been suppressed by the Faculty, on the plea that there was a college law against a student's keeping domestic animals, and a boat was a domestic animal within the meaning of the statute. Manual labor was thought less reprehensible; but schools on this basis have never yet proved satisfactory, because either the hands or the brains have always come off second-best from the effort to combine: it is a law of Nature, that after a hard day's work one does not need more work, but play. But in many of the German common-schools one or two hours are given daily to gymnastic exercises with apparatus, with sometimes the addition of Wednesday or Saturday afternoon; and this was the result, as appears from Gutsmuth's book, of precisely the same popular reaction against a purely intellectual system which is visible in our community now. In the French military school at Joinville, the degree of Bachelor of Agility is formally conferred; but Horace Mann's remark still holds good, that it is seldom thought necessary to train men's bodies for any purpose except to destroy those of other men.

However, in view of the present wise policy of our leading colleges, we shall have to stop croaking before long, especially as enthusiastic alumni already begin to fancy a visible improvement in the *physique* of graduating classes on Commencement Day.

It would be unpardonable, in this connection, not to speak a good word for the hobby of the day,—Dr. Lewis, and his system of gymnastics, or, more properly, of calisthenics. Aside from a few amusing games, there is nothing very novel in the "system," except the man himself. Dr. Windship had done all that was needed in apostleship of severe exercises, and there was wanting some man with a milder hobby, perfectly safe for a lady to drive. The Fates provided that man, also, in Dr. Lewis,—so hale and hearty, so profoundly confident in the omnipotence of his own methods and the uselessness of all others, with such a ready invention, and such an inundation of animal spirits that he could flood any company, no matter how starched or listless, with an unbounded appetite for ball-games and bean-games. How long it will last in the hands of others than the projector remains to be seen, especially as some of his feats are more exhausting than average gymnastics; but, in the mean time, it is just what is wanted for multitudes of persons who find or fancy the real gymnasium to be unsuited to them. It will especially render service to female pupils, so far as they practise it; for the accustomed gymnastic exercises seem never yet to have been rendered attractive to them, on any large scale, and with any permanency. Girls, no doubt, learn as readily as boys to row, to skate, and to swim,—any muscular inferiority being perhaps counterbalanced in swimming by their greater physical buoyancy, in skating by their dancing-school experience, and in rowing by their music-lessons enabling them more promptly to fall into regular time,—though these suggestions may all be fancies rather than facts. The same points help them, perhaps, in the lighter calisthenic exercises; but when they come to the apparatus, one seldom sees a girl who takes hold like a boy: it, perhaps, requires a certain ready capital of muscle, at the outset, which they have not at command, and which it is tedious to acquire afterwards. Yet there seem to be some cases, as with the classes of Mrs. Molineaux at Cambridge, where a good deal of gymnastic enthusiasm is created among female pupils, and it may be, after all, that the deficiency lies thus far in the teachers.

Experience is already showing that the advantages of school-gymnasiums go deeper than was at first supposed. It is not to be the whole object of American education to create scholars or idealists, but to produce persons of a solid strength,—persons who, to use the most expressive Western phrase that ever was coined into five monosyllables, "will do to tie to"; whereas to most of us it would be absurd to tie anything but the Scriptural millstone. In the military school of Brienne, the only report appended to the name of the little Napoleon Bonaparte was "Very healthy"; and it is precisely this class of boys for whom there is least place in a purely intellectual institution. A child of immense animal activity and unlimited observing faculties, personally acquainted with every man, child, horse, dog, in the township,—intimate in the families of oriole and grasshopper, pickerel and turtle,—quick of hand and eye,—in short, born for practical leadership and victory,—such a boy finds no provision for him in most of our seminaries, and must, by his constitution, be either truant or torment. The theory of the institution ignores such aptitudes as his, and recognizes no merits save those of some small sedentary linguist or mathematician,—a blessing to his teacher, but an object of watchful anxiety to the family physician, and whose career was endangering not only his health, but his humility. Introduce now some athletic exercises as a regular part of the school-drill, instantly the rogue finds his legitimate sphere, and leads the class; he is no longer an outcast, no longer has to look beyond the school for companions and appreciation; while, on the other hand, the youthful pedant, no longer monopolizing superiority, is brought down to a proper level. Presently comes along some finer fellow than either, who cultivates all his faculties, and is equally good at spring-board and black-board; and straightway, since every child wishes to be a Crichton, the whole school tries for the combination of merits, and the grade of the juvenile community is perceptibly raised.

What is true of childhood is true of manhood also. What a shame it is that even Kingsley should fall into the cant of deploring maturity as a misfortune, and declaring that our freshest pleasures come "before the age of fourteen"! Health is perpetual youth,—that is, a state of positive health. Merely negative health, the mere keeping out of the hospital for a series of years, is not health. Health is to feel the body a luxury, as every vigorous child does,—as the bird does when it shoots and quivers through the air, not flying for the sake of the goal, but for the sake of the flight,—as the dog does when he scours madly across the meadow, or plunges into the muddy blissfulness of the stream. But neither dog nor bird nor child enjoys his cup of physical happiness—let the dull or the worldly say what they will—with a felicity so cordial as the educated palate of conscious manhood. To "feel one's life in every limb," this is the secret bliss of which all forms of athletic exercise are merely varying disguises; and it is absurd to say that we cannot possess this when character is mature, but only when it is half-developed. As the flower is better than the bud, so should the fruit be better than the flower.

We need more examples of a mode of living which shall not alone be a success in view of some ulterior object, but which shall be, in its nobleness and healthfulness, successful every moment as it passes on. Navigating a wholly new temperament through history, this American race must of course form its own methods and take nothing at second-hand; but the same triumphant combination of bodily and mental training which made human life beautiful in Greece, strong in Rome, simple and joyous in Germany, truthful and brave in England, must yet be moulded to a higher quality amid this varying climate and on these low shores. The regions of the world most garlanded with glory and romance, Attica, Provence, Scotland, were originally more barren than Massachusetts; and there is yet possible for us such an harmonious mingling of refinement and vigor, that we may more than fulfill the world's expectation and may become classic to ourselves.

PHYSICAL EDUCATION

Dio Lewis

I have nothing to say of the importance of Physical Education.

He who has not seen in the imperfect growth, pale faces, distorted forms and painful nervousness of the American People, enough to justify any and all efforts to elevate our physical tone, would not be awakened by words, written or spoken. Presuming that all who read this work are fully cognizant of the imperative need which calls it forth, I shall enter at once upon my task.

My object is to present a new system of Gymnastics. Novel in philosophy, and practical details, its distinguishing peculiarity is a complete adaptation, alike, to the strongest man, the feeblest woman, and the frailest child. The athlete finds abundant opportunities for the greatest exertions, while the delicate child is never injured.

Dispensing with the cumbrous apparatus of the ordinary gymnasium, its implements are all calculated not only to impart strength of muscle, but to give flexibleness, agility and grace of movement.

None of the apparatus, (with one or two slight exceptions,) is fixed. Each and every piece is held in the hand, so that any hall or other room may be used for the exercises.

Public Interest in Physical Education

The true educator sees in the present public interest in physical education, a hope and a promise.

And now he is only solicitous that the great movement so auspiciously inaugurated, may not degenerate into some unprofitable speciality.

Dio Lewis, *The New Gymnastics for Men, Women and Children* (Boston: Ticknor and Fields, 1864), pp. 5-6, 9-18.

One man strikes a blow equal to five hundred pounds; another lifts eleven hundred pounds; another bends his back so that his head rests against his heels; another walks a rope over the great cataract; another runs eleven miles in an hour; another turns sixty somersets without resting.

We are greatly delighted with all these—pay our money to see them perform; but as neither one of these could do what either of the others does, so we all know that such feats, even if they were at all desirable, are not possible with one in a thousand. The question is not what shall be done for these few extraordinary persons. Each has instinctively sought and found his natural speciality.

But the question is, what shall be done for the millions of women, children and men, who are dying for physical training? My attempt to answer this momentous question will be found in this work.

Do Children Require Special Gymnastic Training?

An eminent writer has recently declared his conviction, that boys need no studied muscle culture. "Give them," he says, "the unrestrained use of the grove, the field, the yard, the street, with the various sorts of apparatus for boys' games and sports, and they can well dispense with the scientific gymnasium."

This is a misapprehension, as is easy to convince all, who are disposed to think!

With all our lectures, conversations, newspapers, and other similar means of mental culture, we are not willing to trust the intellect without scientific training. The poorest man in the State demands for his children the culture of the organized school; and he is right. An education left to chance and the street, would be but a disjointed product. To insure strength, patience and consistency, there must be methodical cultivation and symmetrical growth. But there is no need of argument on this point. In regard to mental training, there is, fortunately, among Americans, no difference of opinion. Discriminating, systematic, scientific culture, is our demand.

No man doubts that chess and the newspaper furnish exercise and growth; but we hold, and very justly too, that exercise and growth without qualification, are not our purpose. We require that the growth shall be of a peculiar kind—what we call scientific and symmetrical. This is vital. The education of chance would prove unbalanced, morbid, profitless.

Is not this equally true of the body? Is the body one single organ, which, if exercised, is sure to grow in the right way? On the contrary, is it not an exceedingly complicated machine, the symmetrical development of which requires discriminating, studied management? With the thoughtful mind, argument and illustration are scarcely necessary; but I may perhaps be excused by the intelligent reader for one simple illustration. A boy has round or stooping shoulders: hereby the organs of the chest and abdomen are all displaced. Give him the freedom of the yard and street—give him marbles, a ball, the skates! Does any body suppose he will become straight? Must he not, for this, and a hundred other defects have special, scientific training? There can be no doubt of it!

Before our system of education can claim an approach to perfection, we must have attached to each school a Professor, who thoroughly comprehends the wants of the body, and knows practically the means by which it may be made symmetrical, flexible, vigorous and enduring.

Military Drills

Since we have, unhappily, become a military people, the soldier's special training has been much considered as a means of general physical culture. Numberless schools, public and private, have already introduced the drill and make it a part of each day's exercises.

But this mode of exercise can never furnish the muscle culture which we Americans so much need. Nearly all our exercise is of the lower half of the body—we walk, we run up and down stairs, and thus cultivate hips and legs, which, as compared with the upper half of the body, are muscular. But our arms, shoulders and chests are ill-formed and weak. Whatever artificial muscular training is employed, should be specially adapted to the development of the upper half of the body.

Need I say that the military drill fails to bring into varied and vigorous play the chest and shoulders? Indeed in almost the entire drill, are not these parts held immovably in one constrained position? In all but the cultivation of uprightness, the military drill is singularly deficient in the requisites of a system of muscle training, adapted to a weak-chested people.

The exercises employed to invigorate the body, should be such as are calculated to make the form erect, and the shoulders and chest, large and vigorous.

Dancing, to say nothing of its almost inevitably mischievous concomitants, brings into play chiefly that part of the body which is already in comparative vigor, and which, besides, has less to do directly, with the size, position and vigor of the vital organs.

Horse-back exercise is admirable, and has many peculiar advantages which can be claimed for no other training, but may it not be much indulged, while the chest and shoulders are left drooping and weak?

Skating is graceful and exhilarating, but to say nothing of the injury which not unfrequently attends the sudden change from the stagnant heat of our furnaced dwellings to the bleak winds of the icy lake, is it not true that the chest muscles are so little moved, that the finest skating may be done with the arms folded?

I suggest these thoughts for the intelligent reader, and then take the liberty to request his careful examination of the "Ring" and other exercises which appear in this work. Are they not completely adapted to the obvious necessities of our bodies?

Music With Gymnastics

A party may dance without music. I have seen it done. But the exercise is a little dull.

Exercises with the upper extremities are as much improved by music as those with the lower extremities. Indeed with the former there is much more need of music, as the arms make no noise, such as might secure concert in exercises with the lower extremities.

A small drum, costing perhaps $5, which may be used as a bass drum, with one beating stick, with which any one may keep time, is, I suppose, the sort of music most classes in gymnastics will use at first. And it has advantages. While it is less pleasing than some other instruments, it secures more perfect concert than any other.

The violin and piano are excellent, but on some accounts the hand-organ is the best of all.

Feeble and apathetic people, who have little courage to undertake gymnastic training, accomplish wonders under the inspiration of music. I believe five times as much muscle can be coaxed out, under this delightful stimulus, as without it.

The Gymnasium

The gymnasium must not be cold, but should be well ventilated. The best plan is to raise it to 65 or 68, and when the class begins, drop the upper sash of the windows, raising them again when the teacher announces a period of rest.

It is a common mistake to suppose that the gymnast should exercise in a cold room until he is warm. It is not difficult to accomplish this, but cold air is unfavorable to the development of muscle.

My own rule is to make the hall as warm as for a lecture, and then open the windows freely during the exercise.

The floor of the gymnasium should be marked as shown in the cut. The lines must be about fifty-five inches apart, both lengthwise and crosswise of the room. The feet must have exactly the relations ex-

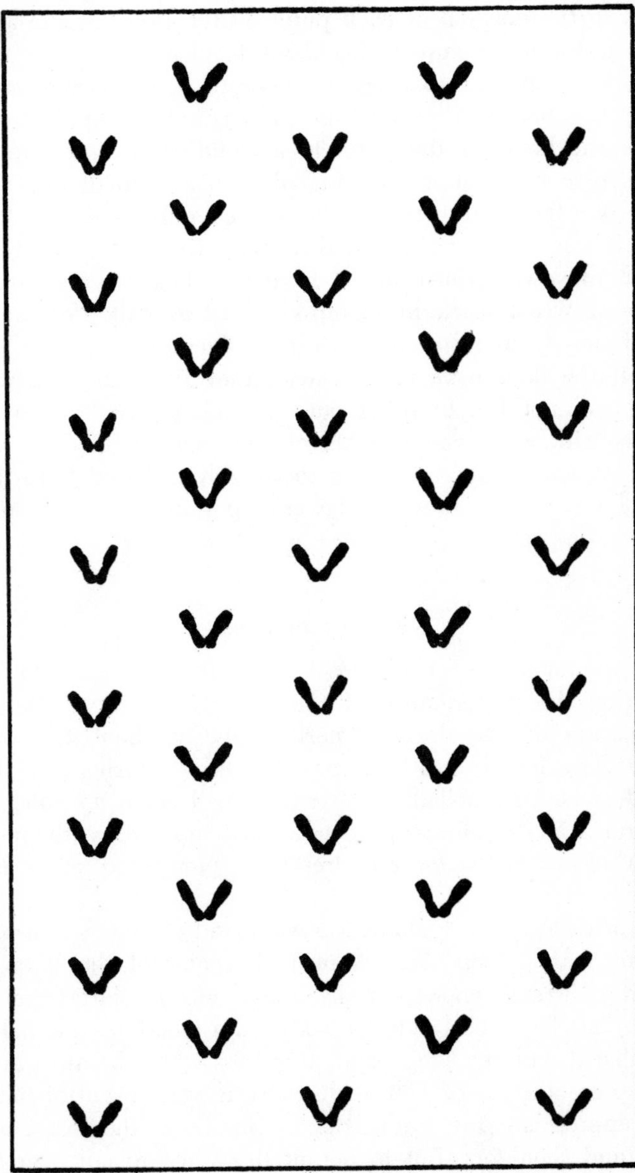

hibited in the cut. A large piece of tin, cut out in the shape of a pair of feet, and laid on the floor at the right points, may be used with a stencil brush, to make the marks. The painters will furnish a black paint which contains no oil. It is very little trouble to mark a floor in this way.

With a floor thus marked, you have to make no explanations, either in regard to the position of each pupil on the floor, or the attitude of the feet, and you are sure to avoid all accidents.

It is very difficult to keep the floor of a gymnasium sufficiently clean, but it is better to refrain from gymnastic training altogether, than to expose the lungs of the pupil to a cloud of dust. Complete gymnastics involve much foot stamping, designed to invigorate the circulation in our feet and legs, which are generally cold. No feature of the exercises is more important. How shall freedom from dust be secured? In my own gymnasium, I have the floor cleansed with water three times a week. Scattering damp saw dust over the floor and sweeping it off, has been resorted to with satisfaction.

But if the floor have many cracks, they fill with dust, which the stamping will not fail to bring out. In such a case it is well to fill the cracks with wax, which, being melted, can be filled in with little difficulty. When the wax has been thoroughly cleansed from the upper surface of the boards, it will not work up from the cracks and make the boards slippery.

Gymnasium Dress

The accompanying cuts present good illustrations of the costume worn during the performance of the New Gymnastics. The most essential feature of the dress is perfect liberty about the waist and shoulders. The female costume may be never so short, if the waist or shoulders be trammelled, the exertions will serve no good purpose. If the arms can be thrust perpendicularly upward without drawing a quarter of an ounce on the dress, the most vital point has been secured.

It is made very loose about the waist and shoulders, worn without hoops, but with a thin skirt as near the color of the dress as possible, and only stiff enough to keep the outside skirt from hanging closely to the legs. This skirt should be fastened to the belt of the dress so that it will not hang below the dress when the arms are raised.

The present style of Garibaldi waist is very beautiful. It is particularly appropriate for gymnastics, as it allows the freest action of the arms and shoulders. But to permit this waist to fall over the belt,

which is its peculiar feature, the belt is usually made tight enough to keep it in its position. This is wrong. Buttons should be placed on the inside of the belt, the same as on gentlemen's pants for suspenders, and the same kind of suspenders should be worn. In this way the belt may be very loose, and yet being supported over the shoulders, it will remain in its proper position.

It will be observed the gentlemen's dress has no belt. The jacket is buttoned to the pants, as is the fashion with small boys. The tailor will easily manage to conceal the buttons. The dress about the shoulders should be *very loose*. The pants must be loose, and may be fastened at the knee, as in the Zouave dress, or worn down to the ankle.

At all seasons of the year the material should be flannel.

The shoe I am in the habit of wearing is low quartered, fastened with a strong buckle, and the bottom is covered with a layer of rubber. In many of the difficult feats the foot is apt to slip, unless the rubber is added.

A majority of my pupils simply remove their coats and exercise in the street dress, but the garb I have described, has signal advantages.

RECOLLECTIONS OF ROUND HILL SCHOOL

I can give only boyish recollections of Round Hill School, for I was not twelve years of age when I went there, as a pupil of Messrs. Cogswell and George Bancroft, and their assistants. Indeed, the original scheme of the institution planned for boys even younger than twelve at their entrance, though there were really but few as young as myself, and most of them were much my elders. The scheme or plan was, I think, brought home by Mr. Bancroft from Germany, and was modeled after preparatory educational institutions which he had known abroad. A sketch of it and of the aims and methods of the founders of the school is to be found in the privately printed memoir of Mr. Cogswell. The number of the scholars also far exceeded the limits originally intended, and there came to be a long list of applicants waiting for vacancies. The school soon attained popularity and a wide repute, but faded away after a brief period of seeming prosperity. This was before the rising of alienations of feeling between the sections of the country. Though there were many excellent schools, academies, and seminaries in Massachusetts at the time, those in New York were not of a high character, and farther south they were still more deficient. The aim of those in the South was to procure teachers from the North and East. It was not strange, therefore, that the noising abroad of the method, the corps of teachers, and the promise of success of the institution of Northampton, should have rapidly drawn together, as it did, pupils from prominent and prosperous families in all parts of the Union. The highest names in the country were borne by boys in the school. Mr. Cogswell, especially, was very proud of his constituency. His own charming manners, his geniality of spirit, and

George E. Ellis, "Recollections of Round Hill School," *Educational Review*, vol. I, April 1891, pp. 337-344.

his kindly relations with the young made him a favorite with parents as with their children.

The staff of instructors, tutors, and helpers engaged in various departments was so large that I think the expense to the parents of a pupil must have exceeded that of a student in Harvard College at that time. I have not had opportunity to revert to the catalogue of the college in those years, and to compare the numbers on the list of the faculty, but I recall from memory the names of the teachers—all of them supposed to have been of marked ability—who were associated with the principals at Round Hill, viz.: Dr. Beck, a German, who taught Latin; Dr. Bode, a German, Greek; Mr. Gardara, a Frenchman, French; Mr. Gherardi, an Italian,—who afterward married Mr. Bancroft's sister,—Italian; San Martin, a Spaniard, Spanish; Mr. T. Walker, afterward judge in Ohio, who, with another Mr. Bancroft, taught mathematics; Drs. Follen and Grater, Germans, German and drawing; Mr. Lucas and Mr. Robinson, singing and writing; Messrs. John and Eugene Watson, and Mr. George S. Hilliard, English branches; a dancing and gymnasium master, a Mr. Cantwell, an English gentleman, who acted as *custos morum*, attending the boys at play—and, it may be, other subordinates that I have forgotten. There were two schoolrooms—one of them was used mainly for classes at recitations.

There was a row of sightly and spacious buildings, two of them, I believe, detached, the others united, with columns and piazzas, that stretched across the brow of a high and extended hill, commanding a superb view of river, valley, and wooded mountains. The streets in the town were lined with stately elms. On the hill were many chestnuts. The back slopes of the hill, running far down into levels, were disposed for three different uses. The first of these gave spacious playgrounds, with a gymnasium, and a large space on a declivity, called "Crony Village," where the boys might make huts, shanties, and burrows, in which, singly or in partnership, they could roast potatoes, apples, corn and chestnuts, frogslegs, and various other good things for out-door appetites. The second division was laid off for garden-lots, where each boy who wished might raise flowers or vegetables, with seeds and tools furnished to him. The third took in Mr. Cogswell's extensive farm-grounds for fruits, hay, and vegetables. There were spacious barns for cattle, horses, hay, and many wagons, one or more of huge size. The boys in turn might ride these horses; the wagons were used for journeys far and wide, often a mountain or other excursion by large or small companies. Dr. Beck, a splendidly formed and muscular man, would in the summer accompany groups of boys to Mill River to teach them swimming. In the winter he would go there with them for skating, but not on the Connecticut. The boys were forbidden to go down into the village without especial leave, even to visit parents or friends. The long hill up which ran the only road to the school, afforded a splendid and safe "coast" for the boys in winter.

No corporal punishment was practiced in the school. Deprivation of meals and retention in the school-room were the lighter penalties. A graver one was the being shut into a dark apartment in the cellar, called the "Dungeon," of which the stalwart Newton, a general factotum, was the keeper. Great efforts, with kindness, amusements, and a degree of indulgence, were used to promote the happiness of the boys. Cleanliness and neatness were exacted. Several public rooms were provided, kept warm in bad weather, where they might gather to play, read, or enjoy themselves at their pleasure. Tools for carpentry, for making bows and arrows, squirrel-traps and kites were at hand. On Sunday morning the lines would be formed in procession, by two and two, instructors taking their places at the head of sections, as each was to attend either the Unitarian, the Orthodox, or the Episcopal Church. The return to the Hill was in the same order, no scattering or loitering being allowed.

The large school-room, square, and with comfortable desks and seats, was in the entrance story of one of the buildings, with four doors opening on the grass. In cases like that soon to be mentioned, when there was not a sharp pair of eyes on the platform, boys found these doors convenient for occasionally slipping out; and as Messrs. Cogswell and Bancroft took turns, in general, in occupying the platform, the former always intent on his duty, the latter apt to be engrossed in some book of his own, boys would creep out on all fours. The school work was opened daily with Scripture reading and prayer. The other school-room—or rather two of them in separate stories—were used, if I rightly remember, for separate classes in turn, for recitations to the different teachers in their special branches. Being used thus alternately for several hours, the large common school-room was left for quiet study or writing.

Practically, though the two associate principals were understood to have equal authority and responsibility, their relations with the scholars proved to be quite different in intimacy and sociability. Mr. Cogswell had no wife, but an unmarried sister, greatly loved by him and the boys. Much depended upon a housekeeper and her assistants,—some excellent matrons, above the grade of menials, who looked after the boys' clothing, and allowed a comfortable seat by their firesides for special favorites, for whom they would do some friendly mending, or furnish molasses to be made into candies, or dispense goodies from their private stores. For our common meals there was a large dining-room, with horseshoe table, Mr. Cogswell always sitting at the head of the outer curve. I never heard any complaint either of the quality or the amount of the food. The boys sat alphabetically, divided into messes of five—with equal portions of the various kinds of food; instructors were dispersed among them, all faring alike, and allowed to call for "more." The breakfast scene daily brought a somewhat exciting pleasure. The aforesaid Newton went down to the town daily to carry and bring a very large mail, to obtain supplies, and to do miscellaneous errands. A box was provided in the dining-room into which the boys might put slips of paper, signed by their names, stating their wants and wishes. These covered a very extensive range of necessities, whims, and fancies. Large indulgence was shown to them in this respect, and anything which a parent would not think unreasonable when charged upon his son's bill was generally allowed. But there was an element of fun in connection with this usage. As the breakfast was closing, Mr. Cogswell would take the box and examine its contents. If he found anything ludicrous, or any fault of grammar or spelling, he would read it aloud with the signature. Thus, a boy had written, "I want a *fir* cap." Mr. Cogswell gravely announced, "Our trees do not bear caps."

Mr. Bancroft dwelt at a little distance from the school, and so could see but little of the boys except in school hours and at recitations. He was absent-minded, dreamy, and often in abstracted moods as well as very near-sighted. I have seen him come into the recitation room at an exercise held before breakfast, with a slipper or shoe on one foot and a boot on the other. More than once he sent me across the road to his library for his spectacles. These were generally to be found shut into a book, which he had been reading before going to bed. The boys, who called him familiarly "the Crittur," were fond of playing tricks upon him, which they could do with impunity, owing to his shortness of vision. The wall back of the platform where he sat, poring over a book, was thickly bespattered with "spit balls," thrown at him. I recall a sultry autumn afternoon, when, in the large school-room, a boy deliberately tossed at him an over-ripe muskmelon, got from his own grounds. His features and garb were well sprinkled with it. As the offending boy crawled out of one of the doors, Mr. Bancroft rose sternly, shook himself, and said, "I want the boy who threw that melon at me to come right up here." There was no response. Then, ordering the doors closed, he came down among the desks, putting the question to each boy. Of course they could all answer "No." The pursuit was not followed up, as many were at various recitations and the culprit was covered by others. As to the rich fruit in his garden, much of it, even before fully ripe, strangely disappeared after dark and before daylight. I think Mr. Bancroft and his family could have had only the smaller portion of it. I recall that one afternoon, as his fine peaches were ripening, he sought to make a compact with the boys, that if they would be patient he would give them a treat. So, as the occasion came, naming three boys with whom he was a little more familiar—I thought simply because their Christian names were the same as his own,—he said, "I wish George Riggs, George Rivers, and George Ellis to come to my garden after school to gather peaches; the other boys will collect outside the fence to partake in the distribution." On presenting ourselves for duty, Mr. Bancroft directed us, with baskets, to pick up the windfalls and to pluck from some trees—not the most luscious—and then to pass the fruit to the waiting boys through the pickets of the fence. They were received with ominous looks of disappointment. After holding a brief consultation, a group of the boys proceeded to return the gift to the donor by a vigorous "peppering" of Mr. Bancroft with his own peaches, till he found refuge from the missiles.

I suppose that Mr. Bancroft, though meaning in all things to be kind and faithful, was, by temperament and lack of sympathy with the feelings and ways of young boys, disqualified from winning their regard and from being helpful and stimulating to them. He seemed to be more earnestly bent on learning for himself than on helping them to learn. His single year as a tutor in Harvard College, before going to Round Hill, resulted in experiences wholly unsatisfactory to himself as well as to the beloved President Kirkland, his associates in the faculty, and the students. There was a continual restiveness and embroilment excited by what were viewed as his crotchets. It should be said, however, that these infelicities showed themselves only in Mr. Bancroft's relations with boyish pupils. For scholars of maturer years and high ambitions, he was a most warm-hearted, kindly, and helpful friend, doing them various and highly valued service. I have heard from many American young men pursuing their studies in Germany and in the universities while Mr. Bancroft was our minister to Prussia and Germany, that he was ever most ready to perform all manner of kindnesses for them, to advance their plans and win them privileges.

The boys at Round Hill, with all the rules and provisions for their health, bathing, play, and exercise, were generally of the robuster sort, and full of animal spirits, which sought lively outbursts. These were manifested in their own way on the loaded stages when going to and returning from vacations. It required three, four, perhaps more, of the old-fashioned stage-coaches to transport them to and from Boston, Salem, and the neighborhood. The road was hilly, rough, and hard to travel. At first, the journey of a hundred miles was broken by a night passed at Worcester. But the inn-keeper, Mr. Thomas, a resolute man, soon refused to receive us as guests. He complained that the boys, after eating out everything he had in his house, and pretending to go to their beds, several in a room, would at midnight rush out into the halls and entries, with unearthly noises, for a pillow-fight. His other guests protested, and Mr. Thomas said that thenceforward he would only furnish us a mid-day dinner; and he did not much desire our company even for that. So after that we had to adapt ourselves to the usual mail stages, which left Boston daily soon after midnight, taking, in bad traveling, near twenty-four hours for the route. A forerunner, with a lantern, would ring at our respective homes, announcing the coming stage, and one by one we would mount it for the dark enterprise. But not a boy took the inside, which was given up for trunks, boxes, and traps. The boys clustered over the top and the outside, most of them having fish horns and whips, which were used diligently along the country roads. Simple travelers, women, and boys on these roads would often be frightened,—till they understood who the alarmists were—by being told that a linch-pin was out, or that a wheel was coming off. No tutors or guardians accompanied the boys, and they had the course to themselves.

Round Hill School was opened for pupils and for work in the autumn of 1823. Its auspices were most propitious. A high enthusiasm was excited in its favor, and a long future of success and prosperity seemed to be insured for it. It came to disaster and grief about 1830. Being then in college, if I had, as I doubt, any full and intelligent information and knowledge of the causes of its misfortunes, they are not now distinctly in my memory. I have a vague idea that these causes were extravagant outlays,—which resulted in a burdensome debt and mortgage,—lack of internal discipline, and a loss of harmony, with discordant variances, between principals Cogswell and Bancroft, as to the conduct of affairs. No doubt all these unfortunate conditions contributed to the catastrophe. Probably the last mentioned was the most effective for harm. It must have been very difficult for men of such widely different temperaments, sentiments, and views as to methods of teaching and discipline, to have accorded in complicated arrangements involving much business. The rupture was a serious one, and the partners separated. There had been up to that time 290 scholars, 99 of whom were from Massachusetts, 46 from New York, 32 from Maryland, 28 from South Carolina, 18 from Georgia, with others from

Virginia, North Carolina, Mississippi, Louisiana, Tennessee, Ohio, Michigan, the Canadas, the West Indies, Mexico, and Brazil. Only one had died at the school.

In 1831 a pamphlet was published in Boston, connected with an attempt to revive and reinstate the institution; but the hope was a failure. The list of instructors, as published, is sadly shorn of the names of scholars from Europe which had given the school so eminent a repute. Some of these, the most able, had found places in other institutions. Mr. Cogswell appears alone as principal. Nine other young men, of whom Benjamin Pierce attained distinction, were associated with him. Bankruptcy soon followed, and those fine buildings, once so bright with happy young life, were left to desolation and decay. Some fifteen years after I had been a pupil there, I visited the melancholy scene. A public establishment for summer boarders, connected with a water cure, occupied a small portion of the edifices. The remainder, with piles of bedsteads, broken furniture, and like rubbish, were sad relics of the then recent past.

George E. Ellis

Boston, Mass.

A BRIEF HISTORY OF THE NORTH AMERICAN GYMNASTIC UNION

Henry Metzner

German-American gymnastics, as embodied in the North American Gymnastic Union, date back to the middle of the last century, the history of the Union embracing over sixty years of tireless activity. Since the days of its beginning, when the ambitious and inspired young men, imbued with the spirit of progress and freedom, transplanted the ideals of Jahn to American soil, this organization has cleared its own path and, in spite of numerous internal and external conflicts, has never lost sight of the ultimate goal.

The impetuosity of the early days has made way for the thoughtful deliberation of later years, to which the *Turnerbund* owes its flourishing Normal College, its many successful turning schools, its influence upon the public school system throughout the land, as well as the spirit of unity and brotherhood, which inspires the individual members.

The Establishment of the Turnerbund

The first gymnastic societies in the United States were organized toward the close of the year 1848. Until the middle of the fifties all of these societies owed their organization and their flourishing state to the many German immigrants, who came to this country when the revolutionary movement in Germany in 1848-1849 was suppressed. For all those who had been friendly to the cause of the people were forced to flee from their native land in order to escape persecution and the pressure of the reaction. Among the thousands of political refugees that fled to American soil, there were many who had been members of a *Turnverein,* who prized the cause of turning, and who were eager to establish it in their new home.

Henry Metzner, *A Brief History of the North American Gymnastic Union* (Indianapolis, Indiana: The National Executive Committee of the N.A.G.U., 1911), pp. 22-27, 54-62.

Although there was no legislative barrier to the founding of these organizations, the influence of the Know-Nothing party, narrow minded, puritanical and opposed to everything foreign, was used against these societies. These men who had sacrificed all for their ideals, and had come to this country as political refugees, were not received with open arms, but were regarded by many with mistrust and suspicion. It was not easy for them to overcome these barriers and to establish gymnastic societies.

The oldest *Turnverein* in the United States which flourishes to the present day, is the *Cincinnati Turngemeinde,* founded November 21, 1848, at the instigation of Friedrich Hecker. The *New York Turngemeinde* was also organized in 1848. The *Philadelphia Turngemeinde,* which today is considered one of the strongest societies in the Bund, was founded May 15, 1849. Internal dissensions arose, and the dissatisfied members established the *Sociale Turngemeinde* in November of that year. A third society, the *Socialer Turnverein,* was organized at almost the same time. Several months after the gymnastic festival of the Bund, in 1854, these three societies combined to organize the *Socialdemokratische Turngemeinde.* A society with a similar name was founded in Baltimore in 1849. Very little is known of the *Socialistischer Turnverein* of Brooklyn, established in 1850 and dissolved during the civil war. On June 6, 1850, the *Socialistischer Turnverein* of New York was founded.

These six societies had barely gained a foothold when they established a *Turnerbund.* The *Socialistischer Turnverein* of New York gave the first impetus to this end in its resolution of July 15, 1850, urging a closer union of all the societies in order to insure their own existence, to protect the common interests and to give a basis for mutual cooperation. A plan of organization presented by the representatives of the New York and Brooklyn societies was accepted, and it was further resolved to invite representatives of all the societies to a convention (*Tagsatzung*), which was finally held in the home of the *Philadelphia Turngemeinde* on the 4th and 5th of October, 1850. Many differences of opinion came to light at this first meeting, particularly on political questions, for one party wished to make the promotion of Socialism one of the main functions of the organization. The other faction advocated that the *Turnverein* should confine itself solely to physical training. On one point, however, all were agreed, that the *Turnerbund* should manifest a tendency toward freethought in the broadest sense.

The first year of the gymnastic union did not pass as smoothly as had been hoped. The societies had not come to realize their duties toward the central organization and barely heeded the proclamation of the provisional central executive committee. The *Philadelphia Turngemeinde* invited all the societies to take part in a general gymnastic festival to be held in that city September 29 and 30, 1851, and the executive committee took advantage of this opportunity to call together a second convention.

The *Turnfest* and the convention proved to be complete successes, according to the first number of the *Turnzeitung,* the official organ of the Bund. At the convention the following societies were represented: New York, Boston, Cincinnati, Brooklyn, Utica, Philadelphia and Newark. The *Indianapolis Turngemeinde,* as well as the *Rochester Turnverein,* had signified their intention of joining the *Turnerbund.* After a heated debate it was finally decided to name the organization *Socialistischer Turnerbund.* The most important resolution was undoubtedly that which called for the establishment of a newspaper which was to be the official organ of the union, and was to be kept free of all personal polemics and of any tendency toward partisanship. The societies were reminded of their duty to maintain the practice of military drill.

When the *Turnerbund* had finally been assured of a permanent organization, the practice of the German system of physical training was gradually taken up by all the large cities in the land. Even in the South, although the Germans were not so numerous as they were farther north in the East and in the West, and although the *Turnerbund* was not in accord with the South on the question of slavery, many gymnastic societies were organized. These societies had become the gathering places for the Germans. Vehement opposition toward these so-called "aliens" was gradually evinced by the fanatic party press, and from the pulpit they were scored for their un-Christian conduct and attitude. As a result of this many-sided opposition, the *Turnvereine* gathered strength and gradually gained influence and the respect of fair-minded citizens.

It is characteristic of those days that the revolutionary tendency which had driven these men from their fatherland was still maintained. Political refugees received their support; an agitation was on foot to encourage their erstwhile brothers to renewed revolutionary demonstrations; the resolution by which the societies were urged to continue the practice of arms was prompted by a desire to return to Germany at the first sign of an outbreak, and to take an active part in the uprising of the people.

The *Turnzeitung* of November 15, 1851, showed that 22 societies had been organized in the United States, of which 11 had joined the

Turnerbund, and that the total membership of these *Turnvereine* amounted to 1,672. Much space in this paper was devoted to the practice of physical training and to illustrated articles on this subject. The larger societies established turning schools, and the first attempts were made to initiate boys and girls in this new practice.

Physical training bore the stamp of Jahn's time. There were no professional teachers of physical training, and classes were conducted by those best qualified. The gymnastic apparatus was of primitive and awkward construction in comparison with that of to-day.

In the year 1852 two gymnastic festivals were held, one in Baltimore and one in Cincinnati. Thirty societies were represented at the convention held in conjunction with the *Turnfest* in Cincinnati. A resolution was passed at this meeting by which each gymnastic society was forced to subscribe for as many copies of the *Turnzeitung* as it had members. This resolution later became the bone of bitter contention.

The book on gymnastics which was published in 1853 under the title "Das Turnen," did not meet with the popular success which had been expected for it. It had been written by Eduard Mueller with the hope that it would help the smaller gymnastic societies in the practice of physical training, but it contained so many technicalities of language that it proved of no value to those who were not acquainted with the terms applied to the many physical exercises.

Gymnastic festivals were held in Louisville and in New York in the year 1853, and in September of the same year a convention was called at Cleveland. At this time the *Turnerbund* was divided into five districts, according to locality. An executive committee was placed at the head of each district, and these in turn made their reports to the central organization.

At the convention in Cleveland it had been resolved to urge the establishment of non-sectarian German schools. Many societies sought to realize this ambition and either organized *Schulvereine* (school societies) or lent their financial support to those which were already in existence. Many a German-American school of that time owed its success to the energy and efforts of the *Turnvereine,* which thus honored German traditions. . . .

The Influence of the North American Turnerbund on Gymnastics in the Public Schools

Dr. Edward Mussey Hartwell, in his admirable report to the United States Commissioner of Education, 1897-98, in the chapter on Physical

Education, speaking of gymnastics in the city schools in the United States says: "Neither the colleges nor the athletic organizations of the country have earned the right to speak with authority on the question of what constitutes a well-ordered and practicable system of physical training for elementary and secondary schools. Therefore, the more or less successful introduction of school gymnastics, since 1884, by the cities of Chicago, Kansas City, Cleveland, Denver, Indianapolis, St. Louis, Milwaukee, Cincinnati, St. Paul, San Francisco, and Boston, through the action of their respective school boards, has been chiefly due to the zeal and insistence of the advocates of the German and Swedish systems of gymnastics, who were prepared to speak with knowledge and to act with intelligence. In every city named above, excepting Boston, German free and light gymnastics have been adopted, and the directors of physical education are graduates of the Seminary or Normal School of the North American *Turnerbund.* In Boston, Worcester, Cambridge, and a considerable number of other cities in Massachusetts and New England, Swedish gymnastics have been introduced more or less completely into the public schools. Mixed systems of an eclectic character are in vogue in the schools of Brooklyn, Washington, New York, and Providence. The promotion of gymnastic teaching in the public schools has ever been one of the cherished aims of the *Turnerbund.*"

While the Turner societies were primarily organized for physical and mental education of adults, the maintenance of schools of gymnastics for boys and girls was made obligatory for all societies of the Bund, until such time when the public schools should give adequate physical training to their pupils. Whenever, therefore, a favorable opportunity presented itself, boards of education were petitioned to introduce gymnastics. The Turner societies were always ready to co-operate with school boards, and in many cities the teachers and leaders of these societies taught gratuitously (often for years) in order to let results convince skeptical school boards of the value of school gymnastics.

Although introduced into the school systems of some of the cities of the middle western states in the sixties and seventies (in Cincinnati as early as 1860) gymnastics never became an integral part of the school work for any great length of time. In fact, Dr. Hartwell states in his report "that even now (1898) no important city or town of the United States has succeeded in maintaining for fifteen successive years a genuine and adequate system of school gymnastics."

It is, therefore, with some measure of pride, that we are able to report that practically all the cities Dr. Hartwell refers to are at present, thirteen years later, not only successfully conducting free exercises in their schools, but have adopted the policy of installing in all school buildings, gymnasiums, or playrooms, and of equipping the schoolyards as open-air gymnasiums or playgrounds.

The successful introduction of physical training into the public schools naturally had its influence upon private and parochial schools, and even upon some colleges and universities with the result that these also made gymnastics part of their regular work.

But there is another part of physical education which owes much of its success to the early efforts of the Turners. We refer to the play movement. Play ever was an integral part of *Turnen,* of gymnastics. Guts Muths', as well as Jahn's gymnastics, were conducted in the open. The activities upon these grounds were mainly games and what is now grouped under the name of track and field work. Exercises upon apparatus were added later, as being essential for winter and for indoor work. As early as the late sixties boys and girls in Cincinnati enjoyed the giant stride and swings in the large playground or garden, as it was then called, back of the old Turner Hall, and did stunts upon the horizontal bars, jumped and vaulted into jumping pits filled with tan-bark, threw the javelin and played ball. And, as in Cincinnati, so it was in other cities. It was, therefore, perfectly natural when the modern playground movement swept over Europe and over the United States that the *Turnerbund* was again to be found in the foreground as one of its most ardent and intelligent advocates, and that the Bund's teachers and leaders were again willing to co-operate in organizing and supervising playgrounds.

A recent questionnaire sent to cities where there are Turner societies shows that gymnastics were introduced into the schools of fifty-two cities either by the direct efforts of the Turner societies of these cities or through the efforts of the district organizations. These cities in the year 1910 had a population of 16,083,400, and a school population of 2,085,763.* The physical training work in these cities is supervised by 352 teachers.

The time devoted daily to gymnastics averages fifteen minutes in primary and grammar grades, and two weekly periods of forty-five minutes each in the high schools. While the work is obligatory for practically all elementary grades, only about one third of the cities have gymnastics obligatory for all four high school years; two years seem to be the rule.

The questionnaire showed that recent years have brought about several marked developments in the physical training work of the public

*These figures, as well as all others, apply only to cities in which it was reasonably certain that gymnastics were introduced through the efforts of the *Turnerbund.*

schools. The first is the installation of gymnasiums in the buildings devoted to elementary education (the high schools in most cities have long since had gymnasiums). Forty-one cities report that they are beginning to equip their schools with gymnasiums; the total number of gymnasiums is 323. Chicago reports that it has 70 gymnasiums in its schools, while St. Louis reports 37 and Cincinnati 28. Quite a number state that all new buildings are being equipped with gymnasiums or playrooms.

The second development is the building of shower baths and even of swimming pools in the elementary schools. The third is the equipping of playrooms for indoor play. The greatest forward step, however, is the recognition that the yard of every school is the natural playground for most of the children attending the school. This brought with it the enlargement of school yards and the equipment of the same with gymnastic and play apparatus. Thirty-three cities report that their school grounds are being equipped. The total number of equipped schoolyards is 537. Indianapolis reports that all of her 61 schools have equipped yards. Philadelphia reports 58 and Kansas City 40; and quite a number of smaller cities report that practically all of their schoolyards (numbering from 10 to 25) are equipped. It is interesting and encouraging to note that although this wider use of the schoolyards is of more recent origin, and has been introduced in fewer cities as yet, the number of equipped school yards or playgrounds is already greater than the number of equipped gymnasiums and playrooms, i.e., 41 cities with 323 gymnasiums as against 33 cities with 537 playgrounds.

Summarizing, the results of this investigation show that the *Turnerbund* has been and still is an active and efficient agent promoting rational physical training in the schools of the United States.

History of the Normal College of the North American Gymnastic Union

The Normal College of the North American Gymnastic Union is the oldest American institution for the education of teachers of physical training.

The Normal School of the North American Gymnastic Union was reorganized in 1866. Prior to 1875, the school was a traveling institute of gymnastics, whose earliest courses were completed in the city of New York. The institute was then transfered to Chicago. In October, 1871, the great fire in Chicago ended the existence of the institute in that city, and in 1872 the school was reopened in the city of New York.

From 1875 to 1888, Milwaukee was the seat of the Normal School. From 1889 to 1891, the school temporarily made its home in the city of Indianapolis. At the end of this transitional period, the North American Gymnastic Union had completed a gymnasium building adjoining the new home of the National German-American Teachers' Seminary and the German and English Academy at Milwaukee. The three schools were united in a way that enabled each to preserve its individuality, and at the same time to utilize the teaching facilities of the other two schools.

In 1902, the scope of the work of the Normal School was materially extended. From 1902 to 1907, the following courses were given: *Course A.* A special course for the students of the National German-American Teachers' Seminary.—*Course B.* A one-year course for male students of the Normal School who had attained the knowledge of German required for admission to the first-year class of the Teachers' Seminary, but did not meet the entrance requirements for course C.—*Course C.* 1902-1904: A one-year course for students of the Normal School who had attained the knowledge of English required for admission to the second-year class of the Teachers' Seminary. 1904-1907: A one-year course for students of the Normal School who held an American high school diploma or had passed equivalent entrance examinations.—*Course D.* A one-year course for students of the Normal School who, in addition to the qualifications prescribed for course C, had a thorough knowledge of the German language.

At a joint meeting of the governing boards of the three schools, held September 29, 1906, it was agreed that after August 31, 1907, the National German-American Teacher's Seminary and the Normal School of Gymnastics should be conducted as separate and independent institutions. At the same meeting, the gymnasium building was sold to the German and English Academy.

In January, 1907, the National Executive Committee of the North American Gymnastic Union adopted resolutions to the effect that after August 31, 1907, the Normal School of Gymnastics be conducted in the city of Indianapolis under the name of "The Normal College of the North American Gymnastic Union"; that one-year, two-year, and four-year college courses be offered prospective teachers of physical training who, prior to matriculation, completed the four-year course of an approved American high school, or who pass equivalent entrance examinations in high school subjects, including at least three years of high school English; and that in addition to physical training and practice in teaching, the work of each college year includes courses in letters and science equivalent to one year's work as counted by universities toward the baccalaureate degree.

In March, 1907, the Normal College was incorporated under the laws of the State of Indiana as an institution of learning empowered to confer academic titles and degrees. In June, 1910, the College was accredited in Class A by the Indiana State Board of Education, which exempts applicants for positions in the Public and High Schools of Indiana from examination.

The Normal College was opened in the German House at Indianapolis on September 23, 1907.

Conclusion

It is not presumptuous to remark that in the sixty-one years of its existence the *Turnerbund* has been an important factor in the cultural development of this republic. From the very inception of their organization, in whatever principles they have advocated, it has always been the serious aim of the Turners to contribute their share toward the fruitful development of the country. To be sure, these men may not always have been on the right track. In their eager desire for reform they may have overshot the mark at times, but every unprejudiced historian will agree that as citizens of this country they have been honest and unselfish in their activities. They were never diverted from their goal by harsh criticism or by the superior smiles of those who claimed to know better, for they have kept in mind the spirit of Goethe's words:

> "*Wer fertig ist, dem ist nichts recht zu machen;*
> *Ein Werdender wird immer dankbar sein!*"

> "A mind, once formed, is never suited after.
> One, yet in growth, will ever grateful be."

ATHLETICS IN AMERICAN COLLEGES

By Prof. Edward Hitchcock

Amherst College

The desire to prolong his life and enjoy it to the fullest extent, is a regnant idea in almost every man. And to this end nearly every one labors to the best of his abilities. This the individual does.

But national and state governments, some corporations, local communities, and educational institutions also, have duties to perform in this direction. For in every community there are sure to be some selfish and negligent persons, who are not only willing to injure themselves, but greatly endanger others. Hence National, State and local laws are enacted to protect the public health, and officials are appointed to execute sanitary and hygienic measures.

The attention given to the health of body and mind among educational institutions, is one of the marked features of modern progress. Its beginnings have been shown in attempts to secure physical exercise for students, by manual labor, work-shops, agriculture, horticulture, military discipline, calisthenics, and gymnastics.

About the close of the last century, Pestalozzi and Salzmann seem to have given us our earliest ideas of physical exercise, as gained by the fixed apparatus of modern gymnasiums. In 1811, Jahn opened in Berlin the Turnplatz, or gymnasium which was the alma-mater of all the gymnasiums in Germany. In Switzerland, in 1815, gymnastics were introduced into the schools and colleges of the country. At the Royal Military Academy at Woolwich, England, German gymnastics were introduced in the year 1823. At the Round Hill School, in Northampton, Mass., a gymnasium was established in 1825; also one in the Salem Latin School at about this period, and one on Charles Street, in Baltimore. And between 1830 and 1840, so-called gymnasiums were established in several

Edward Hitchcock, "Athletics in American Colleges," *Journal of Social Science,* no. XX, July 1885, Saratoga Papers of 1884, part II, pp. 27-44.

colleges and academies in New England, where with limited apparatus, usually in a cold, cheerless building, or a grove, students were allowed to exercise their bodies when and how they pleased, with no guidance, system or protection. Like music, and some other branches of education, physical culture has been appended to and recommended by many educational institutions, but in only a very few, up to the present time, has it been made a vital part of the regular course of culture.

The modern idea is to recognize, control and direct physical culture, recreation and amusements as a part of our educational systems, in order to make use of all the energy of the student while in college or school. Probably 1859 is the period when first a rational and systematic idea of physical culture came to the minds especially of the leading educational institutions in this country. And right here comes up the practical question to every educator, how much must the institution do for the individual in the matter of private and public health? To how much must the college give direction and demand attention, and how much must be left the individual to provide for himself?

At the age when students go to college, it is to be presumed that they have had the early training of mother and nurse, and generally that they will remember and act up to it. But with the growth and development of their powers, additional instruction must be given them which home does not afford, in regard to their growth and more mature abilities. At this period, if healthy, they need special guidance and control, not because they are ignorant, but because much more self-reliant, they have more confidence in their ability to direct themselves and others, are more impulsive, and if injured or under the power of a slight malady, recover more readily than later in life. They need at this period some definite laws laid down to them, more or less explained in connection with their anatomy and physiology. It is time they understood the reason of many of these things. Hence by recitations and lectures, students should be early taught the common laws of hygiene, specially as pertaining to college life, and exactly for the same reason, and in essentially the same manner, as they are taught how properly and advantageously to use their mental powers. After they have been directed how to take good care of the body, the college is bound to give facilities, apparatus, appliances and inducements to obey these rules of health, in certainly as accessible and profitable ways as it gives apparatus, charts, blackboards and libraries to develop and guide the intellectual powers. A college is at fault if it furnishes incorrect or imperfect apparatus, or those means which are obsolete, or are shown to be injurious to the student.

The student comes to college with presumably a good physical and mental health. The college should furnish him with such healthful surroundings as will promote his growth, and not tend to impair his health. Locations and buildings must be approved by the laws of hygiene and the Commonwealth. The laws of the proper heating, ventilation and drainage of buildings must be obeyed most rigidly by the college authorities. More strict attention must be given to these laws in a college, than in other more sparsely settled portions of the community, because of the close crowding and the greater danger of the contagious diseases.

As the idea of a college is to so train men that they may most profitably use all their powers in the advancement of knowledge and culture among men, it is its duty so to arrange its whole course as to promote this culture in as profitable a manner as is possible. It should give the best instructors, the most approved apparatus, and other means of developing the mental powers, and so condense, arrange and methodize all work, as in the best way to economize the time and the strength of the student. The courses of study should be so arranged that one subject prepares the way for another, which should supplement the first. Time and energy must not be lost by a change from one department to another. And facilities should be furnished so that the best work may be grafted directly upon previous good work.

And the necessary care and culture of the body must be so provided for that it may come in at proper times and places, when the man needs muscular activity and rest from study, or demands recreation, or at least a change in the way of using his nerve force. This is where a Department of Physical Education serves its purpose. It is not enough for the faculty of a college to enlarge upon the value of long walks, inspiring pure air, an occasional bath, as the condition of the weather, the inducements of the natural surroundings, or the inclination or daily duties of the student may allow. With the present material surroundings of nearly all our homes, in these days of steam and electricity, and the many conveniences, comforts and luxuries of every-day life, it is demanded of the college that good facilities be offered to its students for pleasant, profitable and well-directed muscular exercise, and in an attractive form: exercise which is not excessive, but regular and healthful, which is pleasurable, which may be carried on amidst such surroundings as are equal to those in other departments of the college; and the matter of personal bodily cleanliness should be provided for, since the student cannot enjoy the comforts of a home. Hence it should be the duty of the college to direct its public health, by the provision of proper baths and the necessary attachments.

In fine, then, the advanced idea of a college should recognize as a part of its work a supervisory care over the conditions of the health of the student, and an education how to use the physical powers in harmony with the intellectual, by instruction and enforced attendance, healthful and recreative duties, so far as to be able to maintain the highest powers of the whole man to keep them thoroughly active in the summer time of existence.

If one were asked to state the important point to be secured in the education of the body, he would probably say endurance, strength, activity, and grace of motion; and in systems of physical culture these have been striven for with earnestness and zeal. We admire the crew who can hold out well to the end of the course; the runner or the boxer who has the best wind, and the gymnast who sustains himself in a trying position for the longest period. And we are pleased with the strong and agile feats of the gymnast, vaulting, dipping, turning or leaping, with an ease and strength so graceful and accomplished, with apparently so little exertion. And yet we never find the man who is master of all these accomplishments at once. The boating man has a gait most peculiar to himself, and one not marked with ease and grace; the ball-players and athletic men do not exhibit grace in the dance, though they may well measure the step, and be in accord with the cadence of the music.

Yet, in many of our systems of physical education, there is a radical error, because the desire is to produce a powerful effect by proclaiming strength alone, or endurance alone, or grace alone, as the end to be secured. The mistake has been to create a high market value in a limited part of the body, to unduly develop muscle or lung power, which while essential, are not the only or perhaps the main ends to be attained.

A modern writer and philosopher has said, "To be well is the first duty of man." Thence the attainments sought after in a system of physical culture should be to sustain *all the powers of man,* symmetrically, equably, and harmoniously, *up to the normal standard.* No steamboat or railroad will arrange its time-table squarely up to the utmost speed of its engines. No bank will divide all its earnings. And the possibilities of hygiene in college should be to be *well,* to be *happily* and *comfortably well;* not to be an athlete or gymnast at the expense of mental and moral powers, but to secure for this end whatever things may tend to keep up, in the growing period, the normal and natural strength of mind and body. Gymnastics and athletic sports are a part, and an essential part, of college education, but when these dominate the man, then he is in a great peril, as great as he incurs who makes himself only a philologist, mathematician, metaphysician, or anything else, in disregard of any or all his possibilities as a physical, intellectual, and accountable being.

About the year 1856, the late President Stearns, of Amherst College, developed the idea that physical culture, or a proper care and knowledge of the body, should be as necessary a part of a college system as the mental or moral discipline, and that the maintenance of all the normal powers of the body in a college student, is as important to his present and future work, as is the intellectual and moral training which the college imparts. As the student must know what are the leading faculties of mind and heart, and how to keep them in their highest efficiency, so should he be familiar with his bodily powers and their mutual action and reaction upon mind and soul; and it is as much the duty of college to ensure facilities for the one as for the other. This, of course, implies that activity must be enjoined upon all faculties, mental and bodily, especially in the growing and developing stage of young men. Hence the correct and dominant idea that physical, muscular activity, in its proper amount and direction, is a great regulator of health, and an important aid in the bodily development of all people,—especially the young. This is based on the fact that about half of the human body is muscle—lean meat—and the only way to keep it healthy, active, and vigorous, up to the normal standard, is by actively and properly using this muscular tissue, or by "taking exercise," as it is commonly termed. This use is necessary in order to furnish the muscles with a healthy growth, to promote sufficient circulation of blood through them, to induce a sufficient absorption of the waste, to so excite and control the nerve force, that it will readily, promptly, and efficiently arouse the muscular fibre to activity, when either automatically, or by demand of the will, the action is required. And it is a fact of great importance that if the muscles are normally strong and in good order, the other organs of the body are much more likely to be in good condition. One of the tests, oftentimes, in ascertaining occult disease is to try the muscular strength of the forearm, and if it is up to a fair standard to give encouragement to the patient.

Good bodily muscles almost always imply good lungs; "capacious lungs" are important points to life insurance companies—a large heart with an abundance of blood; and a stomach and bowels competent to nourish every part of the body. A strong man is apt to have a will of his own, and a power to direct his intellectual forces intelligently, whether the mental capacity be great or small. A strong man usually has a voice able to make himself felt by others. In fine, properly regulated physical prowess, the world over, does give the advantage to a man over all his own powers, and those of his fellow-men also.

But muscular strength and agility are not the sole attainments of physical culture in educational institutions. Nor is it to growth and development entirely that attention should be given. As the health of a city in ordinary times depends as much on the cleanliness of its inhabitants, its streets, and back yards, and the efficiency of its sewers, as it does on its food markets, so does the body need to maintain in full vigor its excreting or waste organs. Of these the principal ones for the student to give attention to are the skin and the lungs. Of the six pounds of food and water taken by the average man daily, at least one half is taken from the body by these two waste organs, and through an almost infinite number of minute glands and tubes. If now these organs do not maintain the average activity and carry off deleterious substances, these must either remain in the body, or the work be performed vicariously by other organs, thus overtasking them and disturbing the healthy balance of work in the different parts of the body. These organs are ordinarily stimulated to healthy action by muscular activity which regulates the amount of blood sent to them, and at the same time excites normal nervous impulses, and thus secures a proper secretion of the matter to be rejected from the body. But in addition to the impulse of activity of the body other stimuli are necessary, such as the solvent power of water and the excitement of heat. These are accomplished by the application of, or the immersion in, water or steam of varying temperatures, as well as dry heat. Pure air also, with the proper amount of moisture in it, is an essential for the health of both skin and lungs. Both the skin and lungs are furnished with an almost infinite number of sensitive nerve fibres, which if maintained in proper health and sensitivity not only keep these excreting organs in health and vigor, but by their reaction and reflex influence greatly control other and more important organs of the body, and not only the emotions and feelings, but the intellectual states also. Or, as Dr. Sargent, of Harvard College, says: "The object of muscular exercise is not to develop muscle only, but to increase the functional capacity of the organs of respiration, circulation, and nutrition: not to gain in physical endurance merely, but to augment the working power of the brain: not to attain bodily health and beauty alone, but to break up morbid mental tendencies, to dispel the gloomy shadows of despondency, and to insure serenity of spirit."

Based upon these general ideas, Amherst College has, for twenty-four years, sustained a Department of Physical Education and Hygiene, by which is meant the instruction of all students in the laws of the structure and use of the body, and some specific instructions to the individual for his health, and a required system of physical exercise, combined, so far as possible, with recreation and enjoyment. This instruction has not been of such a nature as to make anatomists or physiologists, nor a study in the direction of disease, or how to treat disordered bodies, nor to create or maintain athletes; but only such knowledge as will help the better to understand how to keep healthy and vigorous minds and bodies working harmoniously together; how to keep the growing powers active while in the developing period of college life, so that the training may tell in the world's work. It has been accomplished by plain, simple and familiar lectures and recitations, amply illustrated by the well-known classic models of Auzoux of Paris, and a series of lectures to the freshman directly on entering college.

The idea has been carried out at Amherst, that a college can be furnished with such means for some physical exercise by which *all the students* may be benefited, and this when they are in a class together, as in other departments; thus securing the stimulus and animation of fellowship in the duty, as well as a personal benefit at the same time. As Mr. C. F. Adams says, "The contact with his equals in the class and on the playground, is the best education a boy ever gets." This community or associated exercise must be of such a kind as not to have military rigidity on the one hand, or the looseness of rowdyism on the other; and this feature is an essential part of the whole plan which is the most difficult to manage and arrange, and the benefit of which must be judged of more by the opinion of the graduates who have gone through it, than by the passing judgment of outside parties. The nucleus of the work has been an exercise with wooden dumb-bells by each class at a stated hour each day, guided by the music of a piano, under the leadership of a captain. And this exercise does not over-develop the muscles, nor tend to make mere muscular men. The muscle is not put to a severe trial, but is only actively and moderately called into action, so as to keep up its normal or healthy growth. It is only swinging light dumb-bells for a short time; and yet, only those who have gone through the actual work of swinging wooden bells to lively music, for even twenty consecutive minutes, know the healthy exercise and stimulus that is furnished to the muscles, skin and lungs. The exercise may be called gymnastics or calisthenics, or by whatever name is acceptable—a rose would smell as sweet if called by any other name,—but the exercise, as carried out in this way, gives fuller breathing, a more vigorous circulation, an increased action of the sweat glands and the supple and active muscles, to which no young man of an average body can offer objection. Professor Wilder, of Cornell University, says: "For students, agility is more desirable than great strength.

It may be attained by movements of the body and limbs, with or without light weights, or dumb-bells, or Indian clubs." It is not asserted that this exercise with light bells and piano music is sufficient exercise for every student in college. It only claims to be a minimum. The demand for food, for fresh air, for sleep, for study, vary exceedingly, and the personal equation in these hygienic demands must vary as well as in the necessary amount of muscle use. Probably, every other man who has come to Amherst College to get the most out of the college, in any way he can, by using every aid the department furnishes—required and voluntary—will obtain recreation and exercise enough to keep himself in good working order by living up to the *requirements* of this department. But others do not get a full amount of physical care and culture to keep them up to the highest standard of physical health by these required facilities of college. A goodly number of the class—perhaps a half,—will never do more than is required of them in any branch of study. And if this is not a characteristic of nearly everybody outside of college, as well as in it, to do as little of anything which they are required to do, without an immediate and personal and selfish gain, then some of us have observed human nature in vain. Will any teacher in college tell us what proportion of his *whole class* make the most of work under him when it is required, and not optional work? Does he find one in ten or five? While a majority will do as well as they can with ordinary work under his direction, does he find the enthusiasm, the zeal, the eagerness to embrace every point, as perhaps the five per cent. of any college enthuse when a regatta or base-ball season is at hand?

Is it right, then, to expect that young men, averaging from twenty to twenty-two, generally of good physical inheritance, with vacations of one-fifth of the year,—more than one day in a week,—when the elasticity and buoyancy of hope, good cheer and present comfort are at their maximum, when sickness is at its minimum, when experience of pain and dark days are unknown to them—when all these are matters of their every-day lives—can we expect many of them to give special attention to the health which they seem to possess, and especially if it interferes with their present comfort and pleasure, *if it be left to their own choice to provide for it,* or without some special attractions towards it? And again, I ask, do even a majority of older, wiser and more experienced men, on the average,—more than ten per cent. even,—take any better care of themselves than the same percentage of college students!

If, however, this be the just statement of things, in regard to the care of the health, which people will take when in ordinary circumstances, it does not mean that we should let things alone, or allow them to drift. It is in an adverse direction which Amherst College has been tending for nearly twenty-five years. She has endeavored to adopt those means and employ those agencies, by which the students shall secure for themselves such physical exercise as can be provided without making it tedious, burdensome or objectionable, but wholly necessary and pleasant. She has directed the students to follow such guidance, and do so much for their recreation and exercise, as can be secured without interference with study, at the same time enforcing so much attention to the rules and practice of health as will the better enable them to find out what are their intellectual, moral and physical powers, and how to handle them to the best advantage. For the college does not strive to make specialists, monstrosities, or athletes, but only so to train the powers that the graduates may become successful in that special direction which they may choose, when they settle down to the work of life, after college discipline, training, and direction have done their full work. And without doubt, to nine-tenths of college graduates, for the solid work of life, physical endurance will be far more important to success than simply the highest intellectual attainments.

The required exercises of this department, as at present conducted, furnish *all of* the students a modicum. The college *requires all of them* to get a regular, constant and uniform physical exercise with recreation: gathers them together at a stated time and place, and tries to induce by the surroundings to help them to secure a change of occupation, a good time, and forgetfulness of study for the short hour. The object aimed at is, *to secure and keep in good health and activity all the powers,* making them to act in perfect harmony, and not seeking to secure only handsome and well shapen bodily forms, or the greatest amount of power in lungs, heart, nutritive organs, and muscles. To secure that health and general power and endurance of the body, which shall the most completely supplement and associate with mental and moral culture, is the object of the methods adopted by the Amherst gymnasium.

Thus far Amherst College has been considered in the Department of Physical Education only, as it has been, and is at present. It started on a new experiment twenty-five years ago, with somewhat crude ideas, and without the immense strides of material progress which the nation has taken since the civil war. It began with the wants of two hundred students; now it has three hundred and fifty; and with the paternal idea of college full in view. Now it deals with students of the average age of twenty-one years and one month. Twenty-five years ago, bare—

very bare—necessities were furnished to the student in his surroundings. Now, by the facilities of steam, electricity, and material developments everywhere, in public and private, bodily comforts, care and attention, and legal governmental supervision, the college must keep pace, and perhaps a little ahead, in order to make itself the most efficient in its work. So that the plain, simple, and cold gymnasium, with but very little apparatus for individual development and attention, with no means for bathing, must be supplemented by something abreast of the times.

And for this very appreciation and aid, the college is most fortunate in one of its alumni; not a mere "*pro auctoritate mihi commissa*" graduate, but one who, as the captain of the class of '79 for three years, most thoroughly appreciates the wants of the college in its physical culture, and who has handsomely come to the front, and proposes to put this department in such a position that it may accomplish for the future what it has steadily tried to do for the past; or, in his own words, "to increase the usefulness of the Alma Mater in that department in which he ever felt an interest." Charles M. Pratt, of Brooklyn, has given to the college such a superior building as the department recognizes the necessity of, for today and the future. And the Pratt Gymnasium stands as a munificent gift of an alumnus to his alma mater, and a gift expressing an appreciation of the needs in the direction of physical education in our schools and colleges.

This new gymnasium does not only mean more and better appliances which the student may use for his health, but will require more knowledge of, and better guidance of the student. He is not only to have more and better means to do with, but is to be better instructed how to use the methods and opportunities for his individual good. At the same time, it is not best to require and oversee all the physical exercise of a student, any more than a literary professor can watch all the time over the men in his department. Be it in physical health or mental study, each student must have not a little freedom to work in his own way, somewhat according to his own taste and choice, and not by an inflexible method with no allowance for the personal equation. Students are urged, allowed and induced to secure recreation, exercise, and a daily outing, and some fun aside from the requirements of the class exercises. And a majority of the students will avail themselves of this unrequired exercise and recreation. And yet, the new gymnasium, well apportioned in all its parts, is so furnished with appropriate appliances as to give every man a chance for some physical exercise, in spite of the, at times, uninviting climate, and other contingencies, which keep us within walls and under roofs.

While it is proposed to maintain the daily class drill as the rallying point for all the physical exercises of college, the great number of pieces of special apparatus and machines now introduced, will not only give greater advantage of voluntarily varied exercise to the well-developed and entirely normal student, but advantages will be offered and prescribed to the few who are unsymmetrically developed or only well developed in a portion of their bodies.

The earliest study of the human form and its proportion, so far as can be ascertained, dates back to the early centuries of the Christian Era. And the first record of such study we find in a Sanscrit manuscript of the remote civilization of India, called the "Silpi Sastri," or, "A Treatise on the Fine Arts." The leading idea of this monograph is that of the vertical measure of the body, and its division into certain parts, which, when existing in the proper proportion, constitute the perfect human body. These parts number 480, and are divided as follows:

The hair,	15
" face,	55
" neck,	25
" chest,	55
From the chest to the umbilicus,	55
Thence " " pubes,	53
Thence " " knee,	90
The knee itself,	30
The leg and foot,	102
	480

The idea suggested by these "parts" of the Silpi Sastri, is, that the body is planned and constructed according to certain "canons," "modules," or "standards," which are determined by arithmetic or geometrical proportions, and up to almost the present day the artistic idea has been to discover what this occult, mysterious, and wonderful quality of triangles, squares, circles, and numbers, is, that will furnish the key to unlock the absolute perfection of the human form.

In the Egyptian monuments we find a wonderful and vigorous adherence to a definite scale of proportions, and the persistent unwillingness of these artists to represent their figures in any manner except that of sitting or standing upright, gives an inaccurate idea of the human form as it then existed. And still the characteristic features of the negro are so well preserved here, that we can but wonder at the physical change which has come over this race during 4000 years.

Almost 400 B.C., Polykleitus, a Grecian sculptor, wrote a treatise on human proportion entitled the "canon." This was illustrated by a statue called Doryphoros or Spear Bearer, which history confirms as a work of almost perfect proportions, and which Vitruvius, a Roman of later date, dwelling upon at great length, gives an intelligent account of, and describes in many of its details.

Phidias—it is said—to arrive at elegance, employed 20 models: he borrowed from each of them the most beautiful parts, his knowledge of the human form permitting him to arrange them with all the necessary strength and dignity.

During the "Renaissance" the artists of Italy, Germany, France, Belgium, and Holland, as well as mathematicians and anatomists, made the study of the proportions of the human body the subject of theory, practice or treatise, to a very considerable extent.

In 1770, Sir Joshua Reynolds, in England, seemed to appreciate a most clear conception of the true theory of human proportion (and like a true artist sought to carry out the theory on canvass), though he took no pains to establish his views by measurements and weights of the body. His language is this: "From reiterated experience and a close comparison of the objects of nature, the artist becomes possessed of a central form from which every deviation is deformity. To the principle I have laid down, that the idea of beauty in each species of being is an invariable one, it may be objected that in every particular species there are various central forms, which are separate and distinct from each other, and yet are undoubtedly beautiful; that in the human figure, for instance, the beauty of Hercules is one, of the Gladiator another, of Apollo another, which makes so many ideas of beauty. It is true, indeed, that these figures are each perfect in their kind: but still none of them is the representation of an individual, but of a class. And as there is one general form which belongs to the human kind at large, so in each of these classes there is one common idea and central form, which is the abstract of the various individual forms belonging to that class. But I must add, further, that though the most perfect forms of each of the general divisions of the human figure are ideal, and superior to any individual form of that class, yet the highest perfection of the human figure is not to be found in any one of them. It is not in Hercules, nor in the Gladiator, nor in the Apollo: but in that form which is taken from them all, and which partakes equally of the activity of the Gladiator, of the delicacy of the Apollo, and the muscular strength of the Hercules."

Up to the early years of the present century, the study of this subject was exclusively given to find out the mysterious key or idea of the plan of the human form. The desire was to find the artificial idea of the body, as Linnæus classified plants and animals by a simple numerical quality. But between 1820 and 1830 the natural system of investigation and discovery was introduced, and was, by Sir John Herschel of England, and Baron Quetelet of Belgium, applied to the human form. This depended upon a certain use of numbers, it is true—that of measuring and weighing—but it was a simple collation of data, and so comparing and arranging them that the much-coveted "idea," or "canon," or "module," could be obtained by finding the variations in the body, and thus deducing the true form, casting aside the irregularities, the greater first and then the lesser ones, till an approximation to the ideal was exhibited. The examination, the weighing and the measuring of the body and its parts, was quite extensively carried out by these two men, who, by establishing a "*mean individual,*" *not* an "*average,*" are bringing us nearer to the determination of the typical man or woman, than ever before.

And here must be considered the difference between the typical "average man" and the typical "mean man." By an *average individual* is meant the young man who is like the greater part of his fellows in certain matters—say height or weight: that is, if all are arranged together for comparison, the average man will be most like the largest number. And the mean student, too, will be somewhat near to the average student; but in arranging all the students to show the mean student, we shall find the mean at the top of a curve descending both ways, called the "binomial curve." The mean student represents a central magnitude, all deviations from which are to be regarded as deviations from a standard. An average gives us the medial sum or quantity between two or more sums or quantities, while the mean gives the intermediate point between two extremes. The mean gives us a regular march of groups, from the least up to the standard, and then a march down to the smallest, while the average shows the irregular groups here and there. "An average gives us no assurance that the future will be like the past; a mean may be reckoned on with the most implicit confidence."

The method at present employed to ascertain the average, or mean man, and thus the typical man, is by comparing as many as possible of certain outline measurements of the living man, and from these to construct the type. With this object in view, very many men—especially medical ones—have been compiling them by the tens of thousands. These have been mainly of persons congregated in prisons, hospitals, and armies, and latterly schools and colleges. When work was first begun in this department at Amherst College, twenty-four years ago, "vital statistics," as they were termed, were taken of every man entering, and yearly afterwards during his course. These were "anthropometric"—man-measuring—items such as weight, height, several girths, lung capacity, and a simple test of strength, secured mainly for anatomical and physiological science, and to allow the student by annual comparisons to see what his development might be. These have been carefully maintained, and enlarged extensively up to the present time, and valuable tables secured therefrom.

But a more extensive series of measurements, and a more accurate examination of the student, and some knowledge of his antecedents is now demanded. For all people, young and old, are not equally developed. And in every college class a few are sure to be defective in certain points, and at their age may be furnished some development of their weaker parts, by judicious inspection, advice, and proper gymnastic apparatus. Or, as an old English poet says:—

> "Few bodies are there of that happy mould,
> But some one part is weaker than the rest;
> The leg or arm perhaps refuse their load,
> Or the chest labors. These assiduously
> But gently in their proper arts employed,
> Acquire a vigor and elastic spring,
> To which they were not born."

Thus, with the means at hand of the Pratt gymnasium, the old system of statistics is greatly increased in number and minuteness, there being sixty-two items now secured of each man, as he enters college, and twice afterwards during the course. This examination not only considers his present and hereditary condition, but his arms, legs, body and bones are tested, and the more important vital organs such as heart and lungs are specially looked into by stethoscope and percussion, as well as the eyes considered in regard to near sight, astigmatism and color blindness. An accurate record of this examination is kept on file at the gymnasium, which may be consulted by the student at any time; that is, each man may know and study his own record. This record is also the basis for advice, prescription and suggestion by the department; and on his entrance to college, every student is furnished with the average condition and measures of a student of his own height, which he may use, and the professor also, as a basis for advice and gymnastic training. And, while a student is to enjoy the advantage of the class exercise, as heretofore, he may now be able to attend to the growth and development of any parts of the body which are not up to the normal standard. And by the large additions of new apparatus, not only is the defective man guided and helped, but the average man will find more apparatus, appliances and baths to supplement the service of his dumb-bells, and will be invited to give his muscles, skin and lungs a quota of increased relaxation from study and physical exercise, such as he may desire.

The matter of athletic sports and games, indoors and out, seems to need a recognition and reasonable support from the authorities of college. In spite of the excess of competition, not only in games, but in business and intellectual and religious life at the present day, there is a feature of much good and recreation in the games of today, which demand a proper recognition, support and control. Were our climate without its rigors of cold and its pungency of heat, no doubt it would be best to have no covered gymnasiums, but use only the field and grove for recreation and exercise. But when military men tell us that through the average year, only about half the days are suitable for the ordinary drill of the soldier out of doors, we must provide walls, roofs and artificial heat. And yet during the delightful out-door months of the year, all people should be incited to be out of doors for work, exercise and recreation to the fullest extent possible. And while it is very true that for the most harmonious development, the games of base-ball, foot-ball and tennis are not equal to the symmetrical work of dumb-bells, gymnastic apparatus, or even boxing gloves, yet the exhilaration, freedom and fresh air of these games are excellent means of promoting and maintaining the health of very many, and especially young people. It, therefore, seems safe and wise to say that clubs for these games are to be encouraged in a college. And the formation of the club is a very essential part, that the games may be controlled and guided by what are the rules and methods obtained by experience and practice. That while many may enjoy and profit by a regular half or whole hour daily, there should be a centre to rally around, and a method to be followed to gain a good result from the exercise. For the good effect of most of these games is not only muscular work, sweat of the skin and inspirations of the lungs; but the playing by rule, the spirit of submission to decisions, of obedience, of quick determination and coöperation are of great value, specially to the young man in process of mental and moral training.

Results of course are expected. And accurate statistical data have been secured at the college during the existence of the department, but not before that time. Hence comparisons are very difficult to secure, because anything reliable and carefully recorded, as to the condition of body or health, previous to about 1860, is merely a matter of present opinion or tradition. No earlier records of health are preserved, not even the deaths noted in official returns, nor the physical condition of the students made of any account, in any college so far known to the writer, save where the faculty accounts of the intellectual or moral standing of the student incidentally bring up the matter.

Perhaps the earliest note of warning and need of the subject was made by President Stearns, of Amherst, in his yearly report to the Trustees in 1859, when he says: "By the time junior year is reached many students have broken down their health, and every year some lives are sacrificed"; and "during the year two of the most promising students in the senior class have just deceased." Dyspepsia used to be heard of and endured. But during the last twenty-four years only two cases are recorded as causes of disease. Nervousness and exhaustion formerly were sources of much trouble to students. There has not, however, been a single case in each of these years. Boarding-house keepers say that they are compelled to furnish more and better food, such as oatmeal, bread and meats. And the opinion of the faculty is most positive that a much better condition of health prevails than before the establishment of a Department of Health in the college.

It is not possible to state the amount of sickness in any community with exactness, it is such a peculiar quantity, and is so varied a factor with different individuals. But careful observations have shown that in England, for every death there are two persons constantly sick, and there are seven hundred and twenty days of disability for every death. And in Europe every individual loses from nineteen to twenty days by sickness, each year. In Massachusetts, during 1872, there were 13.9 days lost to each person from labor by sickness. The average loss of time of the entire men—not officers—of the United States navy, on account of sickness and accident, for the year 1881, was 11.9 days. These were men known as "under treatment."

The manner of estimating the amount of sickness among the students of Amherst College, has been to enter a man on the sick list if he has lost more than two consecutive days from all college work by sickness or accident. As a result, during twenty years—1860 to 1880—we find the amount of time which has been lost by sickness, when averaged upon the whole number of students, to be 2.65 days to each man.

Another fact which seems to reflect credit upon the value of this department, is the decrease of illness during college life. As it stands in a tabulated form, we find the following per cent. of the class who lost by illness:—

Freshmen,	29	Juniors,	23
Sophomores,	28	Seniors,	19

Or a decrease of disability of about ten per cent. And this has not been a sudden increase at either part of the course, but a steady growth, year by year. The number of Amherst students from whom the data were obtained is 2,106, and their average age 21.1 years; the period of their observation was four years, and their average per cent. of good health was seventy-five per cent. of the whole number.

Part II

THE DEVELOPMENT

1889 - 1911

PHYSICAL TRAINING

William T. Harris

A Conference in the Interest of Physical Training was held at Huntington Hall, Massachusetts Institute of Technology, Boston, on Friday and Saturday, Nov. 29 and 30, 1889. William T. Harris, United States Commissioner of Education, presided. In opening the Conference, Dr. Harris said:

We open this morning a Conference devoted to the consideration of physical exercises for the development of the body. Physical training, I take it, is a part of the subject of hygiene in its largest compass, which includes dietary and digestive functions, and matters of rest and repose as well as matters of muscular training. We wish to discuss physical training in view of hygiene, and to avoid, if we can, all narrow interpretation of our subject. The advantage of such a Conference as this is that extremes come together; and, by comparison of views, each one learns to supplement his own deficiencies. We shall all be delighted to find new phases of the subject. Hygiene wishes to make the most of the body for human purposes,—not for animal purposes, but for *human* purposes. Hygiene includes several departments, of which physical training is one.

I shall define physical training as the conscious or voluntary training of the muscular side of our system, which is the special side under the control of the will. Of course we understand that the vital processes go on without the will, and that this is an advantage,—it is better that they should remain involuntary. Of course the voluntary system has relations to the involuntary system, and this is one of the first questions which have been considered by persons who have thoroughly studied physical training. What can we do with our wills? What can

Isabel C. Barrows, ed., *Physical Training Conference 1889* (Boston: George H. Ellis, 1890), pp. 1-4.

we do with our muscles that shall help on the vital processes and develop them? That is a deep subject. It should be the first which attracts the attention of persons interested in physical education, and it should be also the last one. We ask what we can do by the action of our wills in the matter of developing the muscles of the chest, of the legs, and of the arms, and inquire what are the relations of muscle-action to digestion and sleep and such matters. We have not yet probed these subjects to the bottom, nor have we ascertained the fundamental relations of the voluntary to the involuntary functions in diseased conditions. We are continuously finding some new phases, and I suppose the medical profession discover more new facts in relation to this than persons specially interested in physical training alone. Physicians discover cases in which some oversight in regard to will-training has resulted in interfering more or less with the involuntary processes, so that the latter have been retarded, thus injuring some of their functions. We all acknowledge the importance of discovering and settling the limits between these two processes and defining all the relations between the involuntary vital processes and the conscious voluntary movements, and the transition of these voluntary movements into involuntary ones again through the principle of habit. The exercise of the muscles by voluntary effort calls into action the higher nervous motor-centres of the body and brain. That is to say, physical training such as is advocated by us relates especially to the will, and therefore to the very highest nerve-centres of the physical system. This reveals its relation to rest and recreation. Now, when one, for instance, is studying science or art or literature or any school studies, he is exercising these same high nerve-centres. Let him pass from study to one of these systematic physical exercises, and he does not get the required rest. It is not rest and repose from the exercise of these higher nerve-centres, at least. Of course all of our specialists in physical training know that it is not a relief from will-tension, and the question remains: In how far is such exercise as that valuable? In what way is it a relief? Those who put forward theories of physical exercise and training have their views with regard to this, and the opinions of different individuals vary. I take it that one of the most important results of this Conference will be the adjusting of differences of opinion with regard to this point,—in how far the use of the muscles by the will can afford rest and recreation from studies and from sedentary occupations, and in how far they will serve so well as free play. We all know the difference between play and work. In our play, caprice governs, and there is real repose for the will. But in work the will takes the body and the mind and puts them under forms prescribed by others or under such forms as it has adopted for itself in its rational hours. Its action in work is as much inhibitory and holding back as it is spontaneous and free exercise. But play is not inhibitory. Play has its use in education. We are discovering more and more how play is an exceedingly important function; that it is the source of the development of individuality through spontaneity. The individual through play learns to know, to command, to respect himself, and to distinguish between his own impulses and inclinations and those of others. Great strength of individuality grows from play. Nations that postpone play until maturity fail in this respect. In China it is said that old men of sixty enjoy flying kites. In this country boys of twelve or fifteen fly kites; but there aged men love to do it; and children do not feel the same interest in play in China as they do here.

These considerations, with regard to the relation of the voluntary culture of the body to the involuntary, the relation of the muscles to the vital organs, have been receiving much attention in *the new physical education:* the old physical education thought that muscular education was all that was necessary to the training of the body, and this view prevailed here up to about the year 1860. The new physical education began with the work of Dr. Hitchcock at Amherst, and was followed up by Dr. Sargent in the Hemenway Gymnasium at Cambridge, Dr. Hartwell at the Johns Hopkins, and their co-workers in the various colleges and universities. The student now studies this problem broadly, and focuses his attention on the relation of the voluntary to the involuntary, and tries to discover whereby the vital organs,—the lungs, the heart, the stomach, all the digestive organs, the kidneys,—in short, how all the functions that are involuntary in their action may be assisted and influenced by voluntary action and motion. The old gymnastic did not pay attention enough to this relation of exercise to the vital organs to discover its negative effects. It did not determine the limits of muscular training. In the case of calisthenics, for example, the will-power is called into play, and it is no relief from the strain on the brain to go from the study of arithmetic or from the concentration of attention on the work in recitation to the performance of physical manœuvres that demand close attention to the teacher who gives the signal for the calisthenic exercises. A very powerful exercise of the will is demanded in calisthenics, whereas free play (not systematic games) is rest for the will. The recess spent in play in the school-yard is a great rest and refreshment. I mention this because there has been a movement throughout the country, commencing long ago in Evansville, Ind., to do away with the recess. A superintendent who had given much time to studying the moral development of children came to believe that the recess is the cause or the means of a great deal of immorality, and that by abolishing it he would bring the pupil more under the control of the teacher, thereby increasing the moral hold on the pupil. That movement spread to various places in this country. Rochester for a long time has had no recess. At Albany, also, the schools have no recess. This abolishing of the recess has led our conservative educators who hold their faith in the old regulation to look with suspicion on this experiment, and to try to discover in what forms there is apparent a physical reaction, and in what forms there are counter-movements on the part of physicians and others, tending to mould public opinion.

I hope that the papers and discussions will discuss elaborately and settle these questions which naturally arise in our minds. I have the pleasure of introducing as the first speaker Dr. Edward M. Hartwell of Johns Hopkins University, who will speak on the Nature of Physical Training and the Best Means of securing its Ends.

THE NEW ATHLETICS

John S. White, LL.D.

Until recently we could not be said in America to have any national system of gymnastics. The movement for the better physical education of the masses has been sporadic and inefficient. The system of heavy gymnastics introduced by Dr. Winship, of Boston, 20 years ago, produced a limited number of over-developed athletes, who could raise to arm's length a dumb bell weighing 225 pounds, who could toss a barrel of flour into a cart, and who could lift a ton and a quarter with a machine attached to their shoulders. The other extreme of Winship's methods was the system of calisthenics, or light gymnastics, devised by Dr. Dio Lewis, whose name will surely hold a very high place in the annals of physical training and in the educational system of America, for to no one individual more than to him is due the credit of stimulating a keen and abiding interest in physical exercise. Following Dr. Lewis, with methods that are much more thorough, systematic and far-reaching, came Dr. Edward Hitchcock, of Amherst College; Dr. D. A. Sargent, director of the Hemenway gymnasium at Harvard University; Dr. Watson L. Savage, director of the Berkeley Lyceum; Professor Hartwell, of Johns Hopkins University; Mr. William Blaikie, and a few others, whose expert judgment in the training of youth at all ages, as well as of maturer individuals is beyond value, and whose success in the correction of physical deficiencies by gymnastic training has been marked and progressive. The result attained by these experts will shortly give to us a national system superior to any ever before devised. The essential principles of the new gymnastics, as stated in Dr. Savage's words, are these: "All exercise, to be truly beneficial, must be adapted to the individual by competent judgment, and apparatus

John S. White, "The New Athletics," *Proceedings of the American Association for the Advancement of Physical Education,* no. 3, 1889, pp. 46-52.

must be provided which shall afford ready means for the correct development of every muscle of the body."

Sterne says: "The body and the mind are like the jerkin and its lining; if you rumple the one you rumple the other." In this bit of wisdom lies the gist of the whole matter. The scholar, the preacher, and the business man, in this driving metropolitan life, will speedily break down unless he recognizes the fact that the constant drain upon his nerves and the trituration of the tissues of the brain must be balanced by regular and judicious exercise. Charles Kingsley said of the Greeks: "Their notion of education was to produce the highest type of health—that is, harmony and sympathy and grace in every faculty of mind and body;" and so closely upon a par did they place the action of mind and body that their commonplace definition of an "ignoramus" was "a man who could neither read nor swim;" and the Persians swung the balance far off to the side of bodily care, for, says Herodotus, "from their fifth year to their twentieth the boys were carefully taught three things only—to ride, to draw the bow, and to speak the truth."

For the new era of athletics I should set this primary and crucial test: All physical exercise to be beneficial, must have in it the element of fun. Schiller even declares that the "play-impulse" in human nature is the foundation of all art. If you recommend dumb-bells to a man seeking development for the chest and arms, you will merely impose upon him a few unhappy hours of unfruitful occupation (for he will drop the exercise in disgust in a week), and you will prejudice him forever against your methods. Advise walking or horseback riding, and give him no companion, and you will fail just as soon of improving his physical condition as in the other case. But let him engage in any real sport presenting the elements of enjoyment and a desire to win, and the exercise will immediately become its own advocate. Two thousand books have been written upon the use or misuse of the digestive organs, and nobody reads them. Possibly ten books have been written upon physical education and they are eagerly devoured. No system of class instruction in the gymnasium can be successful, either with adults or with children, unless the exercises are done to music and with a military or dance step. In other words, the exercises must seem to be play and not work.

It is peculiarly appropriate in this connection for me to call your attention in a practical way to such of our national sports as may deserve special commendation or criticism. Baseball—the most truly American of sports and the finest game in the world for boys—a grand inheritance from our copper-skinned predecessors; cricket—that splendid exotic which steadily refuses to be transplanted into the hotbed of our versatile American life; running, jumping, throwing the hammer and pole vaulting—these need no champion; but so much criticism has been brought to bear, in one way and another, against tennis, rowing and football, that they merit at least an impartial judgment. One of the New York periodicals recently opened its pages for the discussion of the various kinds of physical exercise, and two contributors, a physician and a professional pedestrian, took up the cudgel for their respective hobbies. One claimed that horseback riding, of which he was personally very fond, was the best exercise in the world for men, if not for women. The other naturally favored walking. But they united in the statement that lawn tennis was an unmanly and injurious sport. One claimed that it was babyish; the other that it produced the disease known to physicians as the "tennis arm."

It is a pity that such a comment should ever be made upon that sport which combines more of the qualities essential for permanent health and the training of all muscles of the body than any other game which has ever been invented. The only criticism of any weight that can be brought against it is that it develops the muscles of the right arm more than those of the left; but every exercise has the same tendency—cricket, billiards, baseball, or lacrosse, to fully as great an extent as tennis. Let a player secure his left arm to his side so that he cannot move it freely, and he will find it impossible to play the game. Only one exercise in the world can be said to be perfect in this respect—of securing the development of the muscles of both sides of the body to the same degree—and that is rowing straight forward with two oars in a boat having no rudder, where there is no current and no wind. It is self evident that in order to propel the boat in a straight line under these circumstances, the same effort must be made by each arm and that the muscles of both sides of the back will be strengthened with absolute equality.

In the game of lawn tennis the strain is so short in the effort to reach and return the ball, that persons of all ages can play it without injury or excessive weariness. The back, the loins and the lower limbs are exercised practically to the same extent. Being a game of skill, there is no limit to the proficiency which can be acquired, so the game can never lose its popularity. Both the essential elements of pleasure and honorable contention are always present, whether in a game of two persons or four; and as there is in common parlance, "no money in it," lawn tennis will never be encroached upon by the professional element, but will always remain peculiarly a game by amateurs. The game can also be enjoyed by beginners, and is therefore suitable as a means of exercise for the greatest possible number. But the best of all arguments in its favor is that women can participate in the sport to the same extent as men; and, I need not add that for the last reason it is the most conducive of outdoor sports to courtesy and good manners. Let the carper at lawn tennis spend an hour or two on some pleasant autumn afternoon watching the players upon the beautiful turf courts of our various grounds, and let him note the keen enjoyment manifested by all the players, their courtesy toward each other and the flush of health on every face, with never a suggestion of discontent or exhaustion, and his prejudice will speedily vanish—nay, I believe he will at once experience a change of heart.

Rowing, or still better, canoeing, must be ranked among the very best forms of outdoor exercise. But the rowing of races and the excessive training necessary to success in a close and prolonged contest can by no means be recommended to the same extent, nor are they open as a means of exercise to any very great proportion of a college or athletic club. But short boat races, like short running races, are above criticism. The practice of rowing races over a four-mile course is greatly to be deplored. The fashion appears to have originated in imitation of the contests in England between the Varsity crews of Oxford and Cambridge. But these races are rowed on the Thames, with a strong downward current, so that the time and physical strain are thus greatly reduced.

In a circular letter issued by an intercollegiate athletic conference held in New York city in 1884, are these words: "Nearly every college boat race has been won at the end of the third mile. The result has been a 'procession' for the fourth mile, or a desperate attempt on the part of the defeated crew to retrieve themselves. The consequent tendency has been to lessen the interest in college boating, or to injure the health of the participants by over-exercise and heart-strain. The style of rowing for a four-mile race is essentially different from that of a two-mile race, and requires different qualifications.

"*Resolved, therefore,* That no intercollegiate boat race should be for a longer distance than three miles."

In reply to a question which I addressed upon this point to several prominent college boating men I received an almost unanimous response that a boat race ought never to exceed this limit. One stated that in a four-mile race, before entering upon the last quarter, the rowers are, as a rule, absolutely exhausted. They almost lose consciousness of time and place, and their motions become purely mechanical. It seems impossible to them to row a dozen more strokes. Incessant encouragement is necessary from the coxswain or from the shouts of the spectators to enable them even to keep their senses long enough to finish the race. Of course these statements do not apply as closely to the crew which is in the lead, since for that very reason their powers of endurance have not been so severely tested. One believer in long distance rowing objected that he, personally, never reachéd the point of exhaustion. "But," said I, "I believe you were a member of the Harvard freshmen crew of 1875, and can you tell me why you lost the race to Columbia?" "Oh, we had the best of them all the way," was the reply, "but, unfortunately, our strongest man fainted just at the end of the third mile."

It is a matter of much regret that the recommendation of the athletic conference failed of the concurrent adoption of five colleges, and no subsequent attempt has been made to secure an intercollegiate athletic code, either in reference to rowing or other contests.

The same objection may be forcibly brought against long-distance bicycle racing. One mile should never be exceeded by contestants under 20 years of age.

When I said that all games of permanent value must possess the two elements of "fun" and "honorable contention," I might have added that a game, to be permanently attractive to the athlete, must have in it also the element of danger. The modern reader will never lose his fascination for the Field of the Cloth of Gold, the Knights of the Round Table, and their deeds of derring-do, so long as he is human and manly and courageous. It was not that men and women held life less dear than now; but honor, bought at the price of life, filled a higher niche in their hearts than a cowardly existence without it. It is difficult to understand how a mother could so bravely bid good-by to her boy, not yet of age, as he set off upon the perilous expedition to recover the Holy City from the Saracens; or how a girl would permit her lover to enter the lists to ride in the tournament to certain danger, if not death. But personal bravery and physical prowess have always won the respect and admiration of women and men, and we cannot tell how much those splendid chivalric days, false, perhaps, in fashion and reason, but shining with brave deeds, have contributed to that basis of character in the Anglo-Saxon race which makes their descendants famous for pluck and endurance to this day.

Of all our athletic contests, only one replaces in any sense the mediæval tournament in its salient features—the hardening of the muscles, the training of the powers of endurance, the sense of danger to limb if not to life, and the stimulus to deeds of courage amounting almost to exaltation—and that is football. The penalty of greatness is criticism, and football, whose ardent admirers claim it to be the greatest of all games, does not lack this qualification, for its enemies are legion. Sorry will be the days for the boys of America if ever football should be ousted from its high place of honor among the best of their sports. It is the grandest of all tests of activity and muscular endurance, fineness of spirit and self control. It demands the shrewdest tactics and the ablest generalship; the noblest humility in victory, the best philosophy under defeat, of all contests, short of actual warfare, which are open to the boy or the man. "Of all athletic sports," says Sargent, "football is the best game to test a man physically." In the pushing and hauling, the jostling, trampling struggle for supremacy, few muscles of the body are inactive. The legs are almost constantly in motion, and the arms, chest, abdomen and back get their share of activity; the lameness and soreness in these regions of the body after a fierce contest is due as often to great muscular effort as to collision with opposing rushers. In spite of the accidents attending this game, as at present played, no sport affords better opportunity for vigorous training. "If I am ever called to lead a force of men in defence of my country," says the staid Professor Luther, of Trinity College, "I want to ride against the enemy behind a regiment of men who have met and fought, earned victory and suffered defeat on the football ground, and I shall know that when I face the foe on fairly equal terms, nothing short of superhuman power can conquer me!" What really matters an occasional bruise, or even a broken limb, when you cultivate in the football player, a toughness of muscle, a presence of mind in sudden danger, a quickness of thought in emergencies, a discretion in the face of overwhelming odds, and a dexterity of limb and motion, which, without any doubt, will prevent in the after-life of a player a thousandfold more accidents than he can possibly meet with on the football field. The trained athlete is not apt to sprain his ankle by a false step from a street car, or wrench his back by the lifting of an unusually heavy burden.

It is high time that a more generous attitude be shown by the community toward the athletic sports of the college and the school. Let us put upon the shelf, once for all, the time worn jest that the boy goes to college to learn to row and play ball. Some excess there is in this direction, something of overtraining and neglect of studies on the part of individuals, but where one man receives injury or devotes overmuch time to sport and physical exercise a hundred average men receive inestimable benefit from the added stimulus to a more intelligent comprehension of the laws of health, and a wiser care of their own muscular development which the single overt example has awakened.

Statistics show that the average length of life of college graduates is greater than that of other men in nearly similar conditions, and that dissipation among the unprincipled men in college is greatly diminished by athletic training. Somebody has defined all crime as disease, and certainly morbid dispositions do not exist in perfectly healthy bodies.

But do not stop with your encouragement of sports for boys. Do yet more for the girls. There is a reason why the girls of 16 in America are taller and more robust than their mothers. We can trace it directly to more intelligent ideas of dress and open-air exercise, to horseback riding and to lawn tennis. Increase these opportunities and let the girls play hockey and cricket—as, indeed, they are already doing in the English schools—let them fence and shoot and swim, but above all give them gymnasiums in every city and town in the land.

I hail with enthusiasm the athletic spirit of the present time, and I prophecy that before many years our American young men and women will show a robustness and vigor of constitution, and a familiarity with the best forms of physical exercise, both for the training of the muscles and the maintenance of health, unparalleled since the days of Plato, the mighty wrestler; Socrates, the invincible soldier, and the magnificently trained boys and girls of the Dorians, in ancient Greece.

The man of the future is to be a man of action, and he must have big lungs, brawny muscles and a constitution of iron. Already the pessimist is asking: "Where today are the counterparts of the great statesmen, orators, poets and painters who have in past days studded the sky of history with the jewels of their intellect?" My reply is: "They are here, but this busy age of evolution has claimed them for other work; they are factors of a new and higher civilization, and art, for the nonce, must yield to utility."

Your Chathams, your Harry Vanes and your Websters are managing colossal railroad systems stretching their lines of steel thousands of miles into the wilderness, and demanding the best energies of 50,000 men.

The Galileos, the Newtons and the Franklins have chained the lightning, and are illuminating the world with its majestic energy. The Shakespeares and the Miltons, the Raphaels and the Rembrandts are standing today at the bar of nations, pleading causes whose decisions make the world to tremble, or wielding a pen through the pages of marvellous newspapers and magazines mightier than the sword of Alexander or Joshua; or wearing a mitre and a robe whose potent sway reaches to the uttermost parts of a great land—not as through the enforced and narrow tenets of former days, but by the subtle, golden influence of a broad Christianity.

The fundamental principle, then, of the new physical education is this; aim not to produce great athletes, who can lift vast weights or hurl a ponderous hammer, while the multitude go untaught; but endeavor to train every individual to the highest symmetrical development, and the maximum of health and physical beauty of which nature has made him capable. Let Hercules stand aside for Apollo!

PHYSICAL EDUCATION
A New Profession

Luther Gulick, M.D.

There seems to be a very general misapprehension, even among intelligent men, as to the nature of the work in which we are engaged. By many it is regarded simply as a specialty in medicine; others think it merely a department in athletics; others still, with more gross ideas, regard us as men who devote our time and energy to the building up of muscular tissue.

Perhaps I can best define the profession by stating its objects. It is difficult to formulate any classification that is at once logical and complete. The following, therefore, is presented, not without feelings of diffidence, as in some respects at least, it differs from any that have been hitherto presented.

I will make three grand divisions of exercises, according to their purpose: namely, Educative, Curative and Recreative gymnastics. Hard and fast lines cannot be drawn, assigning each exercise to a particular one of these classes, as frequently it will be found that one exercise belongs to two or more classes at once, as in medicine, opium is a hypnotic, cardiac stimulant, antispasmodic, cerebral stimulant, anodyne, etc., etc. This is a division of the objects of exercise, and not of exercises themselves. I will now take up the divisions somewhat in detail.

1. *Educative Exercises,* or Physical Education. We adopt the following definition for the object of educative exercises: "To lead out and train the physical powers; to prepare and fit the body for any calling or business, or for activity and usefulness in life." This may be divided as follows:

Luther Gulick, "Physical Education: A New Profession," *Proceedings of the American Association of Physical Education,* 5th Annual Meeting, no. 4, 1890, pp. 59-67.

(*a*) *Muscular Strength.* This includes strength of the heart and respiratory muscles, as well as the arms, legs and body.

(*b*) *Endurance,* a matter of the heart, lungs and nervous system as well as of the extrinsic muscles.

(*c*) *Agility* or quickness of action, being largely an affair of the central nervous system.

(*d*) *Muscular Control.* Excellence in almost any art or trade involves accurate control or discipline of certain parts of the body. In playing the violin, a great deal is demanded in this direction; first as to the coordination of the fingers of the left hand, being able to place them rapidly, independently, and with absolute precision, both as to time and locality, upon the finger board of the violin, in a position that is naturally awkward; second, to be able to use the right and left arms with entire independence, the muscles of the wrist being used principally in one case, and of the fingers in the other. In piano playing there is similar training. The hands have to learn to work independently, and even the fingers independently of each other. They have to learn to act with extreme rapidity, with absolute certainty, with automatic regularity. And so on with all the musical instruments, there is a large amount of work to be done which is primarily, fundamentally, and essentially, Physical Training.

In the trades there is a similar state of affairs. Perfect control is fundamental and is usually secured only by years of practice on the thing to be done. Thus filling a flat surface is an extremely difficult thing, not because it is difficult of comprehension, but because it is difficult of execution. The movement is perfectly simple, placing the file on the surface to be filed, observing that the surface of the file exactly coincides with the surface to be filed, with one hand on each end of the file, a certain desired pressure is brought to bear, traction being made at the same time with both hands. As the file moves over the surface there is a constant variation of the position of the fulcrum, the two arms of the lever are thus constantly altering in length; the forces required at each end to produce a uniform pressure on the surface to be filed is one which is thus constantly changing, and which must be met by the varying strength of the muscles which do the work. Here again we see Physical Training.

There are numerous departments in the trades, the arts, and daily life, where the excellence of work depends largely upon physical training in some branch. To-day these are manned by specialists,—specialists, not in Physical Training, but in the end for which the training exists. To make my meaning plainer, let me refer to the violin player again. The music teacher teaches the violin, and gives finger exercises, and a large portion of the time of the music teacher is spent, not in teaching music, but in physical training. Now, the music teacher, unless exceptionally qualified, as music teachers are not ordinarily in this direction, is not as competent in physical training as a man of equal abilities would be who gave his whole time to the subject. Thus the physical training part of learning to play the violin or piano could be better done by a man who made a specialty of physical training than by a man who was primarily a very fine musician, and who took up this physical training as an incidental matter. Flexibility of the wrist, perfect control and coordination of the muscles, independent action of the hands, action and quickness of the fingers, can all be gained better by other means than by mere finger exercises on the violin or piano; but in general it is not the teacher of music who is best qualified to take up this work, for the questions are primarily those of physiology rather than of music. Let each do what he can do best, physical trainer, physical training, music teacher, music and not physical training.

(*e*) *Physical Judgment.* This may be called a correlative of muscular control, this the intelligence telling when and where. "It is a sort of psychic trigonometry by which the trained mind calculates the distance, position and motion of objects." None of the important points already considered can take the place of this, nor can we get along without it. A man wishes to jump a ditch; he has no time to measure it and calculate how much muscular effort will be required to clear it, but physical judgment enables him to do all this at once. There seems to be confusion as to the difference between muscular control and physical judgment. Take a catcher behind a base ball bat; physical judgment tells him where to put his hands, and the exact instant that the ball will reach them; muscular control enables him to put his hand where he chooses. One might be able to put his hands where he chose, but not know where; or he might know where without being able to place his hands there.

(*f*) *Self Control.* This may be described as the power of the mind over itself. It is the power which gives self-possession, allowing a man to act naturally in times of excitement and danger.

(*g*) *Physical Courage,* that which renders a person willing to undertake, that quality which comes to one naturally, from a knowledge of his ability, gained through experience. "There is sometimes a constitutional timidity, or lack of what we may call physical faith, that has to be overcome." A presumptuous daring is not physical courage, being born usually of ignorance of the real dangers rather than a calm meeting of them.

(*h*) *Symmetry,* harmonious, or all round development of the body. The strength of a chain is represented by the weakest link, and this is not untrue of the body.

(*i*) *Grace,* which is fundamentally economy of action. It differs from muscular strength and from muscular control. A man may have both these and not be graceful. Comparing grace and symmetry, grace is beauty of action, while symmetry is beauty of form.

(*j*) *Expression.* In this country we do not know very much about these special exercises. The Delsarte gymnastics, perhaps, are the best example of this type, their aim being primarily to enable the body to express the thoughts, ideas, emotions of the mind in the most intelligible way to other minds through their eyes and ears, thus including much of gesture, elocution, etc.

2. We now come to the second division, *Curative Exercises.* It is not designed to trench upon the field of the medical profession; but it is well known that some disturbances of the system can be cured, and many prevented, by the correct use of exercise. The same is true in relation to some bodily deformities. Certain cardiac, spinal and nervous diseases and disorders of the nutritive system are peculiarly susceptible to gymnastic treatment. I will not speak further of this branch, as its importance is already coming to be understood.

3. *Recreative Exercises.* There is a real and fundamental difference between recreative or play exercises and educative gymnastics. It consists primarily in the attitude of the will, and it matters little so far as this is concerned whether it has to exercise itself in confining the mind to a difficult task in arithmetic, or to keeping a fixed and sustained attention on the leader of a calisthenic drill. To illustrate,—you will all recognize the picture in some form or other,—a class of young ladies, students, are to take exercise, they are already taxed mentally to their utmost. This is the argument for their exercise. Calisthenics are prescribed. Then one of two things will follow, either they memorize a series of exercises, so many movements, so many counts to each movement, and subsequently do these exercises together, or they follow a leader by word of command. In each of these there is more required of the nervous system than of the muscular system. From twelve to twenty-four different movements are done, from fourteen to sixteen counts on each movement, each one being required to remember the movement that comes next, etc. The amount of muscular work demanded is trifling, the degree of attention required is large. In the other case where a leader is followed, but no set of movements has to be committed, at the word "attention" every eye is fixed on the leader, and at the word of command each one does

the exercise with all the precision possible, both as to time and movement.

In both these classes of exercises the will, the attention, must be controlled. They may be educative, but they are not recreative. If brain centers need recreation, it is a radical and fundamental mistake to give gymnastics that shall call upon those same centers. If school children need gymnastics that shall further tax their wills, and thus the nervous system, then by all means let us give them these exercises, but if not let us prescribe exercises which shall take and secure more muscular strength and have less nervous drain. I am not criticising all calisthenic drills for school children, only those which demand attention and will, when recreation is needed. Automatic movements are not included in this class. The mere fact that a lesson is interesting is no proof that it is not exhausting; the same is true of exercise.

I wish next to speak of the opportunities that are offered for scientific work in this profession. It is hardly possible at the present day for a man to look forward to adding materially to the sum total of knowledge in any of the older professions. A man who goes into physical education with fair abilities and preparation expects in the course of a few years to have acquired all that has been known up to his time (the scientific side of the subject is as yet young) and to add materially to the sum total of knowledge on this subject. In this respect, then, does this profession differ from others, in that it is new, and every man may expect to do that scientific work which will be not merely original with him, but original to the world. In fact, each man will have to depend to a considerable extent on the results of his own investigations, for he has not as in medicine, reliable and elaborate treatises on which to rely. The science is as yet too young to have developed them. He must expect to assist in the development of such works for the use of those who come afterward. An oak tree during the first year of its existence is susceptible to slight influences which would be entirely unfelt a few years later, even if multiplied a thousandfold. This profession has still to be defined, it has not yet crystallized, and thus it is possible to stamp it with one's own character as it will never be possible again. What physician in the world could now alter the practice of medicine? And yet the time was when medicine was in the same plastic state that physical education is in to-day. Men of foresight will see in this fact the possibility of a permanent influence not offered in the professions that are already formed.

It would be out of place here to attempt to discuss the nature of the various scientific problems which are presented in this field. They vary from the study of the exact effects on the heart of long and short distance running, the consideration of the relative effects of complicated movements on the brain and nerve centers, the relation between different kinds of muscular work and the intellectual activities, to the study of the laws of heredity, the relation which the rapidity of blood-flow bears to the psychical activities, and so on and so forth. The problems are without number, and are multiplying every day. Every problem which is solved in this field seems to bring to view ten, which are of more vital importance, of more difficulty and more interest than the one before them. There are few scientific fields to-day which offer opportunities for the study of problems of greater value to the human race, or more fundamental in regard to its ultimate success, than does that of physical education. It is a factor in modern life, that is as yet unappreciated. It deals with life on a broad side, is in line with the most thorough modern physiological psychology in its appreciation of the intimate relations of body and mind, is in line with our modern conception of evolution, as it works to develop a superior race. This profession offers to its students a large and broad field for intellectual activity, involving for its fullest appreciation a profound knowledge of man through psychology, anatomy, physiology, history and philosophy. To sum up this part of the argument, I would say that physical education offers a greater field for original work than almost any other. Second, on account of its youth and plasticity it offers the possibility of a permanent influence that is never offered except in the youth of such professions. Third, this work is intrinsically of great value. Fourth, it offers a great field for intellectual activity.

This profession, then, differs from any that now exists. It is readily seen that it is not merely a department of medicine, which relates primarily to the prevention and cure of disease. The mere fact that a man is an excellent medical practitioner will not qualify him to take hold of educative gymnastics, although it would qualify him to understand curative gymnastics. On the other hand, the study of psychology and pedagogy will not qualify a man to take hold of curative gymnastics, although it might qualify him to understand educative exercises.

I take it that there is no other factor which is as prominent in the development of any profession as the kind of men who take upon themselves the functions of that profession. The advance of physical education will depend more upon the kind of men who take up this work as their profession, than upon any other one factor. If it is largely taken up by men of little education and small abilities, the work will never become of the greatest value, nor will it be favorably known to the general public. If however, on the contrary, men of collegiate training, philosophic minds, of broad purposes and earnest hearts, are induced to enter this field, the profession will show that it is intrinsically a broad, scientific, philosophic field, and it will be recognized by thinking men as one of the departments in education, fundamental in the upbuilding of the nation.

I have endeavored in this paper to show: *First,* that this is a profession, and in the rough to define its aims. *Second,* to show that opportunities for valuable work are abundant. *Third,* that great importance is to be attached to the kind of men who enter this profession.

TEACHING TEACHERS

Those who dig the earth or handle other raw material seldom make much money. Intelligent persons, seeing this, turn to work that pays better. They make the money, but not mainly with their muscles. The brain and nerves do the chief work. In some lines the muscles help a good deal. In others not much. In many not at all. But muscles not used, or little used, get weak. And a worse thing comes. The vital organs get weak, too. The man or woman loses vigor, loses looks, runs down, gets ill more easily, shortens life. They lose also much of the power to enjoy life, and seriously cripple their usefulness as well. To the bilious man, for example, no food tastes good. But the hunter enjoys every bite with keen relish. So does the boy or girl just in from a ten-mile skate.

But if millions who live in the city and towns, and very many in the country as well, find that their occupation not only adds nothing to their vigor of body, but instead actually reduces it, they must either get that vigor in some other way or do without it. And most of them do without it, so narrowing their effectiveness throughout their lives, no matter what field of labor they may enter. Spirited young men see this. They admire strength, and will gladly do whatever they think will bring it. "The glory of young men is their strength," is just as true now as when Solomon wrote it three thousand years ago.

And how shall they best get the coveted strength and its twin sister, vigor? Shall it be by outdoor pastimes? By farm work? By some trade?

No, not for thorough development, for each of these is but partial in its development. No known outdoor sport, for instance, will develop

William Blaikie, "Teaching Teachers," *Physical Education*, vol. I, no. 4, June 1892, pp. 63-69.

the arm or the chest. Farm work brings size and strength to the muscles used and to no others, as does every known trade. And so does every pastime. Emerson's rule, "In all human action those faculties will be strong which are used," applies to the muscles and the vital organs, if possible, even more directly than to the mental powers. And the body, moreover, can be trained in a fifth of the time required for the mind. To develop all parts, then, there must obviously be work for all. But if neither pastime nor occupation brings the thorough development, just what will bring it? Simply varied exercise, some for certain muscles, some for others, until all are called into play, and into sensible, vigorous, systematic play, for that is about all the sort that pays. It had best be had under favorable surroundings, in good air, with pleasant companions, suitable apparatus, a skillful and wise director, an intelligent idea of the end sought and of the best means to attain it.

And where can this be had? At any well appointed and rightly managed gymnasium. A good gymnasium is in itself no guaranty that it will be rightly used, or even used at all. Good boots do not make a good walker. A wealthy club or university may have a superbly appointed gymnasium, built at vast expense; may even take accurate measurements of a man in half a hundred different parts; may go further, and tell him where he needs building up, and how to build there; but, if it does no more than that, a skillful teacher, with a hundred dollars' worth of apparatus, in a moderate sized room, by *daily personal effort and guidance with each pupil,* will, in a few years, often in a few months, make his every pupil a sound, strong, evenly developed man or woman, well equipped physically for any place in life which he may be called to fill.

The successful gymnasium, then, must not only be well appointed, but rightly managed. There must be intelligent use of it. And that comes, as in everything else, either by long trial for one's self, or, better yet, from good leading by one who has had the experience, and who hence knows how to use it to the most advantage.

But where can you get such leading? Where are such teachers made? For ours is a large country and it will take quite a number to go around. Normal schools in every state equip teachers for the *mental* training of the youth, but there are few "normal schools for bodily training."

During the past six years normal classes for physical education have been successfully conducted in a few cities. The Young Men's Christian Associations, with the marvelous enterprise which has marked their work during the last ten years, were very early in the field. Already they were far in the lead in trying to supply the country with gymnasiums, for, where a live college, private club, or university had occasionally built one, they had put up a dozen. Not that they cared only to build a race of vigorous and enduring men. They had another and broader aim. They saw that nothing among all the varied attractions they hold out of cheerful quarters, fresh and pleasant papers and periodicals, pictures and selected libraries, games and practical talks, music and entertainments, began to draw the youth like the gymnasium and the swimming pool. Many a young fellow who cared little for his moral welfare, and even less for mental improvement, had learned something of the value and charm of a good body, and was eager to get his into shape. He naturally sought the most attractive place where that could be done. He did not find it in any public gymnasium, which any respectable man could join, on paying a moderate fee, and the few wealthy athletic clubs imposed a tariff far too high for his slender purse. But the Young Men's Christian Associations found it for him, and in nearly 300 cities they have live, active gymnasiums, most of them fairly, and some, notably those at Brooklyn, Harlem, Worcester, Boston, Syracuse, Burlington, Vt., Albany, Utica, Detroit, Milwaukee, Kansas City, Omaha, Atlanta, and Baltimore, well equipped, and with a moderate percentage of really competent teachers.

But this is, at best, only partial work, and does not begin to meet the situation. The great lack, and the hardest one to fill, is of teachers. As there was no normal school, no place where such teachers were trained, the Associations had to make one. And fortunately they were able to make it aid other excellent work. For other needs had arisen. The General Secretary of each Association has so much power in his hands, and such opportunity, that he needs careful and skillful preparation for his work. For they long ago gave up putting in dull men as General Secretaries. It did not pay. The Rev. David Allen Reed, of Springfield, Mass., recognizing this fact, conceived the idea of affording to this class of men an opportunity to greatly increase their usefulness by special training for this work. Accordingly he organized in January, 1885, the School for Christian Workers, which had as one department the Young Men's Christian Association Training School, to train General Secretaries. Inter-denominational in its character, its Board of Trustees, and its Board of Instructors, it is more than national in its aim and scope, for already students go there, not only from every section of our country and the British Provinces, but also from Great Britain, France, Germany, Sweden, and the Orient as well, and the demand for its trained men far outruns the supply. For here they found a range of work so broad yet thorough, so well fitted to the demands of to-day, and of the troops of youth who are quick to avail themselves of this skill and knowledge, that, were the gymnasium instructor of even ten years ago to attempt to lead a class now, he would be left hopelessly behind. The pupil is here taught the history of gymnastics, ancient, mediæval, and modern, that which Sweden, Germany, and France can teach, and their influence on national life, as shown by the Greeks, Romans, and Germans; the use of the sphygmograph, and the various dynamometers and other instruments found so necessary in gauging a man's powers to-day; and in anthropometry, which already, thanks to Galton, Sargent, Hitchcock, and others, is doing such valuable work. But he studies physiology, anatomy, etc., from quite a different standpoint from the physician. For while the latter learns anatomy mainly with reference to surgery and pathology, and physiology chiefly that it may aid him in the arrest and cure of disease, and hygiene only incidentally, the physical director's first work is body-building, and then such care of the body as shall keep it in its best order for anything it may be called on to do.

Many a man now broken, or prematurely old, might have kept himself strong and effective clear through seventy or eighty years of active useful life, had his bodily education been under such intelligent guidance as this. The wonder is that medical men of to-day have not been swifter than they have to see how vastly such a knowledge of body-building and body-training would aid them in their own high calling. Masters of the healing art in the past were quick to make judicious gymnastic work aid in curing disease. Not only among the Greeks "were their gymnastics, aleiptes, tetraleiptes, and pædotribæ at the same time physicians, and the aleiptes in particular were called physicians," but Ikkus of Tarentum and Herodicus are mentioned by Plato as "the inventors of gymnastic medicine" who, notwithstanding the imperfect pharmacy and ætiology of their time, and their inferiority in the whole art of physic, yet "treated diseases with great success." Galen "divides the whole of gymnastics into the warlike, injuriously athletic, and truly medicinal," and speaks very strongly of the advantages of friction of the skin either in thinning the fleshy or fattening the lean. Hippocrates, the most celebrated physician of antiquity, made exercise a prominent factor in healing disease, and was intimately acquainted with gymnastic work, and the treatment of injuries received in the arena. In later days Francis Fuller, an eminent English physician, in his "Medicina Gymnastica," says: "Exercise is to physic what bandage is to surgery, an assistance or medium, without which any other administrations, though ever so noble, will not succeed. It is a kind of reserve, but yet of the efficacy that the thing you most depend on, though in itself very powerful, may yet receive its *dernier puissance* from this reserve, and to this it is that we must attribute the wonderful success which the ancients had in their curing with such indifferent material as their pharmacy afforded them."

Now is there anything strange in such results from vigorous, though never violent, systematic exercise? In many forms of disease there is more or less congestion, and often the chief thing to do is to allay that congestion. But a strong, regular, and normal circulation is one of the rewards one gets for keeping himself in good physical condition by judicious bodily exercise. And with such a circulation there is no congestion. Take a familiar case, the congestion of blood in the head in an ordinary headache. Yet Professor Goldie, the director of the famous New York Athletic Club, a vigorous, hearty man, accustomed for almost fifty years to gymnastic exercise, says that he never had a headache in his life, and his looks indorse his words. Constipation, the fruitful mother of so much neuralgia, headache, rheumatism, hemorrhoids, hypochondria, and of so many other ailments all too common in this sedentary land, has no enemies like vigorous, systematic exercise and coarse food. The man with a first-class brain and a third-class stomach and a fourth-class liver is beginning to find out that he is not really a strong man; and that, while with ample vital and muscular power, kept by sensible exercise in good condition, he might have staid like Webster or Bismarck till seventy, or, like Gladstone or Bancroft, past eighty, his obituary is very likely to be written by or soon after the time he is fifty. If, as eminent physicians say, six hours' mental work is enough a day, and he averages ten, he must not be surprised if something wears out early. The late ex-Justice Benjamin R. Curtis, of the United States Supreme Bench,—probably the greatest lawyer this country has yet produced,—said that a lawyer can do a year's work in ten months, but he cannot do it in eleven; and his words fit all other men who uniformly overwork their brain and nerves, quite as aptly as they do the hard-pressed lawyer.

Is it not then a matter of congratulation that we have at last such a training school? All kinds of gymnastics, acrobatic and athletic, exercises that are mere feats, have been tried in this country almost as they never were anywhere else before. And they have clearly failed to bring to our millions of boys and girls, men and women, true and lasting vigor. But while the feats are good things to omit, the vigorous yet never violent work in each line is, under judicious guiding, a most valuable aid. And one of the very encouraging features is the deep interest already being taken in this work by a goodly number of physicians, interest of a practical sort, where they put themselves under the leadership of the men in charge of the physical department of this training school. Leaders of men, skilled in a thousand different exercises, they rush you, whether you like it or not, through a mazy round of work, with such magnetic dash and pace that you can hardly stop if you want to; and they never rest, nor do you, till they have stretched every muscle in you, voluntary and involuntary, till a bed tastes uncommonly good when they get through with you. Finely developed themselves, somehow in following them, you cannot get rid of the idea that you yourself are one day going to be as opulent as they in muscular and vital power. No wonder that such men soon turn out fine classes.

Indeed, so searching is the director's scrutiny into a man's character, and all his past life, before he may enter this training school, that an actual majority of applicants are rejected. For there is a purpose in this scrutiny. A reprobate will often drag down other men almost as fast as a rotten apple will kill all the apples about it. But a clean, pure, strong, all-round man will lift other men, and better them as John Hardy bettered Tom Brown. And just such men they want to let loose to lead in the gymnasiums of our country, and they are letting loose to-day. Devoting their lives to the work with a depth and earnestness of purpose, and a persistent determination, it will not be many years till, with the rapidly widening knowledge and increasing interest in bodily vigor, and hence in making men and women fitter for every possible position in life, they will be recognized as very potent factors in our American education, and in adding to our effectiveness as a nation. Where now we have one strong, efficient man, we will have them then by the score, simply because we will have used the means to get them. Recently a general secretary in a large northwestern city said that he could find ten good physical directors places at once. But what a pity it is that not merely the scores of thousands of young men in the Christian associations, but that all our young men and all our young women, and the boys and girls as well, should not have the advantage of such most valuable instruction! Over and over has such training saved human life. Indeed, the very director of this training school now so helpful to others, himself expected to be an invalid for life, if not to die some years ago, from spinal and brain trouble, and says that exercise which he was induced to take by reading, in Japan, a little book called *How to Get Strong*, saved his life and built him up. Henry Ward Beecher well says: One whole half of the force of human life is squandered by reason of weakness and sickness. It is a matter for educators, for naturalists, and for economists to study as fundamental to posterity." Where now they have found how to substitute for this weakness and sickness, strength and vigor, and how to do it so easily, effectively, and cheaply, would it not indeed be well, as the great preacher suggests, for our educators to provide this boon of systematic and judicious bodily training for every child in the land? Largely to just such training Germany has twice owed her freedom, and her great power and prestige as a nation. If we are far behind her to-day in this regard, there is one comfort,—when America undertakes to do a thing, it is very likely to be done, and done without delay.

William Blaikie.

FORM IN GYMNASTICS

W. G. Anderson, M.D.
Yale University,
New Haven, Conn.

This article on form is intended not alone for those who teach gymnastics, but for any one who may be interested in good work. Skill in the execution of any exercise is always desirable. It denotes more than we perhaps are willing to admit at first thought that it does.

Any one who has visited the German and Swedish gymnasia in this country, or who has taken time to make a comparison of the work found there and in our American institutions will have noticed the difference between the work of the American and the foreigner. A man of experience can tell a German gymnast as soon as he has seen him execute a simple movement in the gymnasium, whether on the apparatus or in light gymnastics. One of the distinctions lies in what we may be pleased to term form. We Americans are lacking much in this respect. It is to be deplored that this is true. Possibly the American way of rushing through a thing is the cause. Nevertheless, when the time comes to judge the merits of the work of the different representatives, it will be found that the one who is careful about his form, whether in light or heavy work is more successful.

What Is Form?

It is the finish that should be given to an exercise, whether heavy or light. It is a proof that the person executing a motion with his body has mastered the component parts of the exercise and placed them together to make a perfect whole. It will be seen when a teacher executes a most difficult feat with the utmost ease and grace. Form is grace. Grace is controlled strength. Form is a visible result of the

W. G. Anderson, "Form in Gymnastics," *Physical Education,* vol. 8, no. 6, August 1892, pp. 106-109.

easiest and best controlled expenditure of great force in gymnastic work. It is conservation of physical energy. Form is the same to physical training that the "touch" is in handling musical instruments. Form is the result of close application to work, which indicates will power, and being the result of will power is in turn an educator of the will.

Form is one of the results of gymnastic training in free work with bells, clubs, wands, etc. The teacher of gymnastics excels his pupils not only on account of his familiarity with the various kinds of apparatus found in the gymnasia, but because of the finish to his work which places him above his pupils. Of two persons who perform the same trick the one who possesses form is superior to the other. It is a thorn in the flesh to many teachers of gymnastics that some of their pupils are so much better than they are. It is also a source of worry to instructors who are not proficient in executing exercises that some one may join their classes who will excel them in their own specialty. Pupils in our gymnasia respect those who are superior to them, not those they can defeat. The acquisition of form will give the teacher the power he should possess over his pupils. The acquiring of skill in the execution of gymnastic exercises requires time, but it will more than repay the teacher, because of the supremacy it gives him.

When to Begin to Teach

When you believe in teaching gymnastics, and believe that the subject should be well taught and well done. As soon as you have made up your mind that form is desirable. When you have the right idea of form, and when you have the will and patience to work for it. When you make up your mind what is right. When you are a good exponent of the work. When you have had drill in light gymnastics, which will do away with the stiffness of the heavy work, and will make your muscles much more pliable. Then is the time to begin. Remember that the stiffness of the first movements will gradually give way to the grace of the perfected exercises, as the straight lines of the beginner in drawing lead to the curves, so the awkward movements of the beginner in gymnastics will later become the easy movements that denote controlled strength.

Begin at the beginning in any form of exercises. This is not an easy thing to do, because a number of teachers have not the correct idea of what the beginning is. Teach the proper standing position, which is that of a soldier (according to the new regulations). This, or modified forms of it, are used in all standing starting positions for work on any of the hanging apparatus, to which a person leaps. To illustrate:

We wish to teach the hanging position on the horizontal bar. The pupil under the bar, holding the position of a soldier, with this exception, the head being slightly thrown back, the eyes raised, the backs of the hands front, thumbs and first finger touching the side of the thigh. Now, after bending the knees, raise the heels, swing the arms hip high, back, look at the bar, fill the lungs. Next leap up and catch the bar. So much for the start. Let us observe the hanging position: Taken as a whole the body presents a long, beautiful curve; the hips slightly back, the chest arched forward, the knees, heels and toes touching, the toes pointing down.

I have found from personal experience that for all long swings, including the giant swing, the thumb should rest along the first finger, thus permitting the hand to slide further on the bar; but in this as many other things one cannot make arbitrary rules. It is to a great extent a matter of training. Habit will govern. In any exercise in heavy gymnastics, there are generally three parts: The fundamental starting position; the execution of the exercise; and the finish. The last part of any exercise, or finish, is one that should be, but seldom is practiced. The competent teacher believes in thorough work, at the start, during the work and at the end. We Americans are apt to spend too much time on the performance itself, and to slight the beginning and the end. The fundamental starting and hanging position in the exercise mentioned above are not difficult, but the finish, or drop, is. To drop and stand in place requires that the center of gravity of the body should be over the balls of the feet. If it is forward or back, the body will naturally fall in one of these directions. It is not easy for a person to hang perfectly still, but this should be acquired. As soon as it is, drop to the feet, leaving the arm raised, until the landing is safe, and then again resume the position of attention.

It has been mentioned that it is somewhat difficult for a pupil to know what constitutes the beginning. We will notice in the exercises that are to be given how a simple maneuver can be traced back to a primary motion. It will be seen for the start in any long swing that the first movement is the arching of the body well forforward or back. Another thing is the flexing of the thighs. Third, the straightening of the legs and the placing of the feet in position. Attention will be called to this later on. Take one more illustration: The pupil who has leaped to the bar is supposed to perform an exercise of some kind. To do this he must be in one of the three positions, relative to the horizontal bar: (1) Hanging below; (2) The hips even with the bar; (3) Above. He may desire to pass from number one to number two. Of the various ways to accomplish this we will illustrate by the kip, which for analysis will consist, first, of the hanging position, second, of the swing, third, the bending of the body at the hips to bring the feet to the bar, and fourth, the "whip up" to a finish. To do this feat rapidly is a somewhat difficult thing. The teacher should analyze the parts, drill himself well on them, and then putting them together work at the whole. We understand number one, but number two will be new. The swing starts by exaggerating the long curve of the body, from which position both thighs are flexed until the knees nearly touch the bar. Then thrusting the feet quickly forward and up, straighten the body out to a nearly horizontal position. It will now be seen that the curve of the body is parallel to the floor. The action of gravity, together with the impetus derived from the start, gives plenty of force for the long swing. The body should be held perfectly rigid, and permitted to swing back and forth, keeping the chest well arched until the pupil is sure of his swing. At no time is the long curve of the body changed. To digress for a moment, we will see how number two of the kip would be subdivided into a minor exercise. The flexing of one thigh, or both thighs. The straightening of one knee from the flexed position, then both knees. By this method we will be enabled to reach what is called the beginning exercise in heavy work. The third part of the kip consists in the bending of the body at the hips, and the bringing of the toes to the horizontal bar. This is done on the forward part of the long swing. The legs are kept as nearly straight as possible, and also the arms, and the force of the return swing is thrown down to the region of the hips, whereby the body is raised high enough to be pulled against the bar, even with the hips. This part of the trick should be given as an exercise.

These two illustrations, namely, the hanging position, and the kip are given to show that nearly every exercise is made up of parts, which can be used as elementary drill movements.

Form in gymnastics cannot be secured unless the teacher pays strict attention to these details. If an exercise is worth giving it is worth being well done, it cannot be well done unless the teacher is patient in learning and teaching little things, and persistent in practicing, but the pay is worth the labor.

In the class drill on the horse, buck, ladder, ropes, or any piece of apparatus in the gymnasium, the teacher should do what he says he can, well,—very well; not "after a fashion." Avoid the teacher who does his work "after a fashion." There are too many of these men in our American gymnasia. It is one of the serious defects in our American work. The teacher leads; he is the model; as is his example so will be the work of the pupil. Therefore, when a teacher says he can do an exercise and then does it poorly, his pupils lose their faith in him at once. If they doubt him in one respect, they will in another. It is necessary for a teacher of heavy gymnastics to be an expert in certain branches of his work, and it is form in gymnastics that helps make a man expert. One of the greatest aids to this end is light gymnastics. Many men who have made a specialty of heavy work are to a certain extent muscle bound. This is especially true of weight lifters and throwers. The drill in light gymnastics is one of the quickest means of destroying the clumsy, awkward movements that are seen in many of our heavy gymnasts. Beauty in any work is admired. Skill in any performance will give power to the teacher.

How to Teach Form

It will be impossible to dwell upon this part of the article "How to Teach Form" without saying a word on the pedagogy of gymnastics. I know of no books on the subject, at present, which will give the desired information upon the subject of *how* to teach gymnastics. Works on mental pedagogy are legion. There will be on the market within a few years, a number of books upon the subject of how to teach physical training. The teacher of gymnastics should model his methods by the rules laid down for the teacher of mental branches. If he is to start at the beginning, it is necessary for him to place his pupils upon a par with beginners in any mental branch. By watching the method of teaching children we notice that the educator depends a great deal upon pictures. So in gymnastics—do not waste time and words upon describing the exercises which can be *shown* in the fraction of a minute. I should advise any instructor to make his own body by performing a desired exercise the picture of the motion. This will teach and educate much quicker than many words. For example, a man wishes to teach the vault over the buck with the proper start, act and finish. His best method would be to show the exercise, then explain the parts.

The Value of Form

The practical man may ask, and he has a perfect right to ask, what is the value of form? If it is valuable, it is worth acquiring. If it is not, it is a loss of time to argue in its favor. The practical teacher may answer, what is the value of form in writing, or playing any instrument? What does form indicate? The acquiring of form is an important part of education. It is the result of careful training. It indicates perseverance. Apart from the grace and beauty which form indicates, it is also a proof of energy and perseverance on the part of the teacher. It is not to be acquired without application to work and constant drill. The very habit of acquiring form reflects credit upon the pupil. It is indicative of qualifications that are valuable in the teacher of gymnastics. If this is characteristic in his gymnastic work it will be seen in other ways. It will make him more careful in his business and social dealings with other people. The man who is willing to be accurate in gymnastics will not be satisfied to do poor work in anything else.

A valuable book for the teacher who is anxious to improve his form is the Swedish work "Gymnastick," by Balck och Schersten. Its illustrations of work on the horizontal, parallel bar, horse, in free work, with bells, wands and clubs are admirable and full of life.

W. G. ANDERSON.

BASKET BALL

Jas. Naismith
Instructor in International
Y.M.C.A. Training School,
Springfield, Mass.

Basket Ball is not a game intended merely for amusement, but is the attempted solution of a problem which has been pressing on physical educators. Most of the games which are played out of doors are unsuitable for indoors, and consequently whenever the season closes, the game, together with all the benefits to be derived therefrom, is dropped. It is true that some players have been accustomed to keep up a desultory kind of training but it lacked the all-round development that is so requisite, and very frequently failed to give that training for the heart and lungs which is so desirable. A number of gymnasiums have running tracks, but even then it is more or less uninteresting to run around a gallery so many times per day.

There were certain definite conditions to be met by the game which was required, and these had to be complied with before it could be pronounced satisfactory.

1st. It should be such as could be played on any kind of ground,—in a gymnasium, a large room, a small lot, a large field, whether these had uneven or smooth surface, so that no special preparation would be necessary. This is especially necessary in large cities where in order to get a good sized field you must go to a considerable distance, thus rendering it inaccessible to many of the members. Basket ball may be played on any grounds and on any kind of a surface. It has been played in a gymnasium 12 x 20 and can be played on an ordinary foot ball field.

2d. It should be such as could be played by a large number of men at once. This has been fully met, as the only limit to the number of men that can play is the space at command. If a great number of

Jas. Naismith, *Rules for Basket Ball* (Springfield: Press of Springfield Printing and Binding Company, 1892), pp. 3-15.

men wish to play at once, two balls may be used at the same time, and thus the fun is augmented though some of the science may be lost. The men however are required to keep their positions a little more carefully. As many as fifty on a side have been accommodated.

3d. It should exercise a man all-round. Every part of his body should get a share of attention. His legs are used to sustain his body and his arms are exercised in handling an object, which is a normal function. In the bendings and twistings of the trunk and limbs the vital organs receive such exercise as will make them healthy and strong. Thus in a manner it serves the same purpose as the sum total of the apparatus in a gymnasium, while the main development is in strict accord with the idea of unity in man. It should cultivate the different energies of which he is capable. Agility is one of the prime requisites in a game where the ball must be secured before an opponent can reach it, and when obtained he must be baffled in his attempt to take it away. This also gives us grace as the perfection of action. Physical judgment is required and cultivated in handling the ball, receiving it from one of your own side, and eluding an opponent. This requires that a man should keep complete control of himself or his play is more than likely to count for nothing. A wrong pass may give the opponent a decided advantage and an instant's hesitation is sufficient to lose the best opportunity that might be offered. There should also be developed that manly courage which is so essential in every true gentleman.

4th. It should be so attractive that men would desire to play it for its own sake. This is one of the chief points in this game. The thorough abandonment of every thought but that of true sport makes it entirely recreative, while the laughable side of the game may be appreciated by both players and spectators. It is made more attractive by the fact that it is a game into which competition may enter and opposing teams may try their skill, thus giving zest to those who have become proficient in the game.

5th. It should have little or none of the reputed roughness of Rugby or Association foot ball, for this reason, kicking at the ball and striking at it with the fist were prohibited. All running with the ball was done away with because when a man runs with the ball we necessarily have tackling to stop him, and it is at this point that the roughness of Rugby is most severely felt. This regulation has been criticised specially by Rugby men, but the above reasons should appeal to every one who is seeking a game that can be played without roughness. A man's whole attention is thus centered on the ball and not on the person of an opponent, and thus opportunity for personal spite is taken away. If some of the rules seem unnecessarily severe it should be remembered that the best time to stop roughness is before it begins. A gymnasium is bounded by walls, so that a push which would result in no harm on the soft turf may send a player against the wall with force enough to injure him. If the rules are strictly enforced at first the men will soon get accustomed to playing ball instead of trying to injure those who are opposed to them only for the time being, and they will soon realize that it is nothing but a friendly game. The very men who wish to play roughly will be the first to condemn the game if roughness is allowed, for it is generally they who get the worst of the roughness in the end.

6th. It should be easy to learn. Lacrosse, which is considered one of the best all-round games, has this objection, that it requires too much practice in order to obtain even the exercise from the game, whereas any one can learn to play basket ball at a single lesson, and at the same time obtain the exercise which an experienced player gets.

These were felt to be the conditions that would determine the usefulness of a game that might be played summer and winter, in any climate, and under varying conditions.

The object of a player should be whenever his own side has possession of the ball to gain an uncovered position so that his own side may pass it to him. On the other hand, his opponent should see that he does not gain this favorable position. It is at this point that head work and the ability to do a certain thing without letting his opponent know what he is about to do, are valuable. Individual play does not count for much, for very often a man has to sacrifice his own *chance* of making a goal that he may be sure of it from the hands of another. In the gymnasium the ball as a rule should not be passed swiftly in a straight line, but should be tossed lightly so that the one who receives it shall lose no time in passing it to another or throwing for a goal. But on the field, where long passes may be made, the straight throw may be used to advantage.

Nine men make a nice team for an ordinary sized gymnasium, and they may be arranged as indicated by diagram on page 114.

A goal keeper; two guards to assist him; a center; a right and left center; two wings and a home man.

These are arranged in this order from the goal which they are defending. A man does not need to keep strictly to his place, but should be always in his own part of the grounds. It should be the duty of the home man and the two wings to get a favorable position to throw for goal and to assist one another in this matter. These ought to be men who are not afraid to sacrifice their own glory for the good of

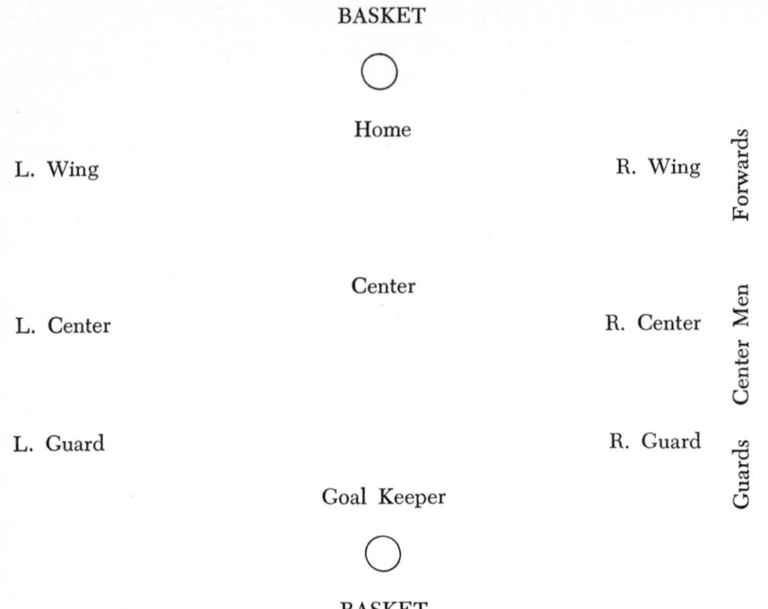

Diagram of Basket Ball—position of players

the team, while, at the same time, they should be cool headed enough to use every opportunity of trying for goal. It is often the unexpected that wins. The center men are placed so that they may assist the forwards or help the guards, as the strain comes on each of these. They should be able to make a good shot for goal and quick enough to stop a good play of an opponent. Their aim should be constantly to feed the ball forward to their own men and keep them in a position to make goals. The duty of the guards is principally to prevent the opponents throwing for goal, by preventing them from getting the ball, and by taking it from them when they are preparing to throw. In this, if anywhere, prevention is better than cure, for when a ball is thrown up so as to alight in the basket there is no goal keeper who can keep it from entering. The goal keeper's duty is to get the ball away from the vicinity of his goal and to stop as many plays as possible, thus he will bat the ball more frequently than is advisable in the case of the other players.

When fun and recreation are desired, as many men as please may play, and they may be distributed according to the captain's own idea, but the best plan seems to be to divide the men into three classes, forwards occupying the third of the ground nearest the opponents' goal;

center men occupying the middle third; guards occupying the defensive third of the ground. This is not a hard and fast division, but merely to let the men know for what part of the field they are responsible. The men ought to be taught to fill every position, as it is intended to be an all-round game, and though each position entails plenty of hard work yet each man is better if he be able to take any part.

The Grounds

These are the gymnasium floor cleared of apparatus, though any building of this nature would suit. If there is a gallery or running track around the building the baskets may be hung up on this, one at each end, and the bounds marked out on the floor just beneath this gallery. The apparatus may be stored away behind this line and thus be out of the field of play. If there is no gallery the baskets may be hung on the wall, one at each end. In an open field a couple of posts may be set up with baskets on top, and set at the most convenient distance. Out of doors, with plenty of room, the field may be 150 feet long, the goal lines running through the baskets perpendicular to the length of the field; the side boundaries 100 feet apart, but the ball must be passed into the field when behind the goal lines. A player cannot run after he has picked up the ball, though he may throw it and endeavor to get it again; by this means he may make progress from one part of the field to another, but his opponent always has an opportunity of gaining the ball without tackling him. Again, he may bat it in front of him as he runs, or dribble it with his hand along the ground, but he cannot kick it with his feet, not even to dribble it. At a picnic

the baskets may be hung on a couple of trees and the game carried on as usual.

Goals

The goals are a couple of baskets or boxes about fifteen inches in diameter across the opening and about fifteen inches deep. If the field of play is large the baskets may be larger, so as to allow of more goals being made. When the field is 150 feet long the baskets may be thirty inches in diameter. These are to be suspended, one at each end of the grounds, about ten feet from the floor. A neat device for a goal has been arranged by the Narragansett Machine Company, by which the ball is held and may be thrown out by pulling a string. It is both lasting and convenient.

The object of the game is to put the ball into your opponent's goal. This may be done by throwing the ball from any part of the grounds, with one or both hands, under the following conditions and rules:—

The ball to be an ordinary *Association* foot ball.

1. The ball may be thrown in any direction with one or both hands.
2. The ball may be batted in any direction with one or both hands (never with the fist).
3. A player cannot run with the ball. The player must throw it from the spot on which he catches it, allowance to be made for a man who catches the ball when running if he tries to stop.
4. The ball must be held by the hands, the arms or body must not be used for holding it.
5. No shouldering, holding, pushing, tripping, or striking in any way the person of an opponent shall be allowed; the first infringement of this rule by any player shall count as a foul, the second shall disqualify him until the next goal is made, or, if there was evident intent to injure the person, for the whole of the game, no substitute allowed.
6. A foul is striking at the ball with the fist, violation of Rules 3, 4, and such as described in Rule 5.
7. If either side makes three consecutive fouls it shall count a goal for the opponents (consecutive means without the opponents in the mean time making a foul).
8. A goal shall be made when the ball is thrown or batted *from the grounds* into the basket and stays there, providing those defending the goal do not touch or disturb the goal. If the ball rests on the edges, and the opponent moves the basket, it shall count as a goal.
9. When the ball goes out of bounds, it shall be thrown into the field of play by the person first touching it. He has a right to hold

it unmolested for five seconds. In case of a dispute the umpire shall throw it straight into the field. The thrower-in is allowed five seconds, if he holds it longer it shall go to the opponent. If any side persists in delaying the game the umpire shall call a foul on that side.

10. The umpire shall be judge of the men and shall note the fouls and notify the referee when three consecutive fouls have been made. He shall have power to disqualify men according to Rule 5.

11. The referee shall be judge of the ball and shall decide when the ball is in play, in bounds, to which side it belongs, and shall keep the time. He shall decide when a goal has been made, and keep account of the goals, with any other duties that are usually performed by a referee.

12. The time shall be two fifteen minutes, halves, with five minutes' rest between.

13. The side making the most goals in that time shall be declared the winner. In case of a draw the game may, by agreement of the captains, be continued until another goal is made.

The position of umpire is a very responsible one, and on his ruling depends, to a great degree, the value of the game. If he deliberately overlooks violation of the rules he is responsible for a great deal of unnecessary roughness and consequent ill feeling, but if he is firm and impartial in his decisions he will soon win the respect of all, even those who suffered at the time.

When a goal is made it does not cancel the fouls made, neither does half time.

Any player has a right to get the ball at any time when it is in the field of play, provided only that he handles the *ball* and not the opponent. He may slap or pull the ball out of another's hands at any time while in the field of play.

A player may stand in front of the thrower and obstruct the ball, but he must not violate Rule 5. One aim of the rules has been to eliminate rough play, and for this reason the umpire must interpret them with this aim in view.

Any side which persistently makes fouls is working against its own interests, as three consecutive fouls count a goal for the other side. This seemed the best way of compensating those who play a good clean game, and it has proved of value already, for many a team has had two fouls called on them, but very seldom do they make the third, for a team is then on its good behavior, and thus shows that it is possible to play without making many fouls. Setting the number at three gives plenty of room for those made by accident.

MODIFICATIONS OF THE SWEDISH SYSTEM OF GYMNASTICS TO MEET AMERICAN CONDITIONS

Educators of to-day recognize that there are certain fundamental principles which must form the basis of all good teaching, whether it be of one branch or another and that we are surely passing out of the era of systems and text books. The methods of teaching now in vogue have been in the light that science has shed upon our conception of the needs and possibilities of human nature; to be a true educator, the teacher of to-day follows no set form, no ready made system, but applies the laws which Nature dictates; his effort is to make men and women, not puppets with a smattering of useless book-learning. His method varies with his classes, and text books become merely tools to assist in making the framework around which mind and character are built.

Since body is the basis of human nature and not least of that portion called the mind, it seems reasonable to assume that the education of the body must follow laws quite as definite as those relating to the mind and that all physical training must be based upon the laws of Nature and not upon any arbitrary or artificial consideration. The principles of gymnastics must of necessity be the same the world over, and the so-called systems must become very similar to each other, if they are built on the same leading laws. Physical education has reached a new era: one where the word "system" with its diverse prefixes of nationality will disappear and where the teacher will cease to feel the handicap of restricting superscriptions. Science and arts are cosmopolitan not national, so the science of gymnastics and the art of applying it must belong to the world at large, even though it happens that its

Baron Nils Posse, M. G., "Modifications of the Swedish System of Gymnastics to Meet American Conditions," *Physical Education,* vol. I, no. 9, November 1892, pp. 169-174.

foremost investigators must claim one section of the earth as their native land.

In Sweden a new science was evolved by Ling and his followers who named it Kinesiology (Kinesis—motion), which in free translation means the science of gymnastics. It embraces the principles which are fundamental to all exercise, whether medical or educational, German or Chinese, and its contents might be best expressed thus:

Kinesiology	The Mechanics The Physiology The Philosophy The Classification	of exercise.

It is based upon the three-fold nature of man, viz: the machine, the organized body, and the thinking individual. It demonstrates how bodily movements are affected by the laws of physics, physiology and psychology and how exercise may influence these laws. Upon the laws of life as described in general kinesiology the Swedes have based their theory upon practical experience. So it happens that when correctly taught, Ling's system is not merely Swedish but it is gymnastic in the broadest sense of the word, and these *Swedish* gymnastics merely stand for *rational* gymnastics.

I have no hesitation in saying that, before long, all gymnasia in this country will have quite a Swedish atmosphere, and that even now, in many, the exercises are already showing symptoms of "Lingœmia," even though the instructors may be unconscious of having been contaminated.

It is true that scientists from everywhere have added material to the general knowledge of the subject of gymnastics, but the quantity and quality of their contributions are disappearingly small when compared to the achievements of the Swedes, and certainly their systems of gymnastics are often and unmistakably at variance with the laws of Nature. To gather a few ideas from Swedish gymnastics, a few from the German, a few from some other source, and shake them up together may be systematic, but it is not rational and certainly can not be any improvement upon these ideas which have been arranged in scientific sequence, the evolution of decades of research. "Science is organized common sense," not systematized nonsense, and those teachers who begin by modifying scientific gymnastics will end by modifying their "own" systems to correspond to the one modified. This might be conveniently expressed like this: John Smith's system! Swedish system!! John Smith's theory! general kinesiology. It is hardly necessary to prove this theorem. The contest to-day is essentially between the empiricism, personal pride and professional prejudice of John Smith on the one side and scientific exercise on the other. Swedish gymnastics contain "the good from all sources," but would cease to be scientific if all the useless *possibilities* of exercise were added.

General kinesiology teaches that movements should be chosen for their effects upon the one exercising, for development or correction to meet his needs; or for classes, to correspond to the requirements of the average of the class. If an exercise violates any of the laws of physics, physiology or psychology as related to bodily movements, it is discarded. These rules are fundamental in Swedish gymnastics and must become so in any gymnastics. It will then happen that all the possible will not be used in physical training, but only such movements will be applied as are distinctly useful; and no gymnast will waste his time on movements of doubtful or indifferent effects, not to mention those which are distinctly harmful as merely pretty.

The Swedes exercise for the sake of the body, not for the sake of the apparatus, hence the latter is made subservient to the exercise; and the system is one of the movements where the chief apparatus is the body itself. When external appliances are needed to produce more volation or more exact localization, they are made to fit the movements not *vice versa*. It was in this manner that the Swedish apparatus was evolved; and it was in accordance with such principles that the movements were classified according to gymnastic effects into arch-flexions, bearing-movements, (not "arm-movements"), balance-movements, etc., embracing the typical forms of all exercise, not in Calisthenics, Apparatus work, Wand Drill, etc., since the latter classification embraces within each group exercises of the most dissimilar effects and hence to an educated gymnast means practically nothing. Whether bending backward with the arms free above the head, or holding a pair of dumb-bells or a wand, or grasping a stall-bar, a pair of breast-bars, the uprights of the parallel bars, or a vaulting bar of Swedish or of German model, the movement, when correctly executed, is an arch-flexion, giving the effects peculiar to that class of exercises, and as such is recognized by general kinesiology; and it has not ceased to be Swedish as long as it applied in its proper place as an evolution of preceding movements.

If you draw yourself up on a machine that you call horizontal bar, heaving-board, boom,* flying rings, high parallels, etc., or if you use a

*A Swedish word meaning thick bar—boom; the thin Swedish bar is called "hät-planka," which literally means heaving-board.

giant pulley in a corresponding manner, you have in each case done a heaving movement, if the form of execution was correct, and even the most rampant Swede will be obliged to admit that there is nothing un-Swedish in any of those exercises. If, in Swedish gymnasia, no flying rings or chest-weights are to be found, it is because the Swedes do not need them. If, on the other hand, a trained Swede has to teach where he finds no Swedish apparatus, he uses whatever is at hand. He can use a school desk of American make just as readily as one of Swedish make without having to Americanize his movement. About the chest-weight a curious fact may be mentioned; it was invented to substitute the operator in giving resistive movements, and this kind of movement is peculiarly characteristic of Medical Gymnastics, as revised in Sweden and exported to America. Whether the chest-weight be an improvement upon the original means of resistance is at least questionable. The machine is American, but the movements done upon it are not necessarily so.

The laws of progression—the kernel of general kinesiology—have been thoroughly elucidated by the Swedes, and if others are tardy in adopting and applying them it is not because of their knowledge of these laws. The principles of progression are direct conclusions from the laws of physics, physiology, and psychology and must necessarily obtain whether exercises are called by one name or another. In accordance with these laws, the Swedes have assigned definite places for all exercises and apparatus, and while some of them may deny the need of chest-weights, Indian clubs and parallel bars, etc., they are careful to affirm their usefulness when handled on correct principles—or Swedish principles, if you so wish. "It is characteristic of Swedish gymnastics to be able to make good use of poor apparatus. The apparatus as such does not thereby lose its bad qualities."—Torngren.

The Swedes maintain that while human nature may be the same the world over, yet different nationalities have distinct characteristics, both physical and mental. Consequently while the leading principles for applying gymnastics will be the same for all, the details of some movements and the progression must vary somewhat to correspond to these differences. Ling, Jr., meant something when he said that "nationality must influence progression," and his idea was somewhat similar to the Swedish rule about gymnastic games, to "select games familiar in your locality, familiar to your pupils, and modify them to correspond to gymnastic principles." Mark well it is *gymnastic games,* not American games, German games or Swedish games; so it should be *gymnastic exercises, not American,* German or Swedish exercises. The Swedes are too progressive to often use the antiquated dumb-bell (the oldest known gymnastic apparatus); they dislike the exercises with Indian Clubs, chest-weights and flying rings, and hence exercises with such apparatus, though used, are not popular in Sweden and never will be—perhaps because as a Boston woman said "those movements seem silly and useless when you have tried the others." But wherever movements or such machines are popular, the Swedish teacher who is thoroughly imbued with the spirit of Ling, the spirit of gymnastics, will use them, letting himself be guided by the law, however, that no movement should ever be used for its own sake, but for the sake of its effect upon the one exercising. This modification according to externalia is inherent in the Swedish system itself, and makes it none the less Swedish; for it certainly is gymnastic and in accordance with Ling.

The Swedes recognize that individuality influences exercise; they do not believe that any one set form will fit all classes, ages and individuals, but maintain, that, before you arrange your movements, you should study your pupils from a psychological point of view. Necessarily the exercises will vary somewhat in different lands, for mental characteristics differ in different nations. Hence gymnastics taught in America may not look exactly the same as when taught in Sweden, even if applied on the same principles.

The following statements may serve further to elucidate our subject of consideration.

Col. Gust. Nyblœus, late Director Roy. Gym. Cent. Inst.; "Gymnastics in itself is neither Swedish, French, English, German or Finnish, it is international in a broad sense. For that reason, in this branch, one should avoid all *chauvinisme,* and boast as little with the name Swedish as abuse the name Ling to shelter one's own more or less correct views." "Since organic life eludes the degree of mathematical precision which one can force upon inorganic matter, the effort, nevertheless, to enforce it upon the former easily becomes pedantic humbug with the name of science. This is especially true of gymnastics, where precision neither of form nor of time of movement can be driven to the extreme."

Capt. V. G. Balck, Prof. R. G. C. I., and *Lieut. O. Schersten,* Teacher R. G. C. I. in their book on gymnastics, referring to the wand: "A good addition to the exercise as a change and a more powerful interpolation in the free movements. The use of the wand has for its object to make the movement stronger by adding weight to the lever;" and referring to the dumbbell: "They may enter with good effect as an adjunct in the ordinary gymnastic lessons. Without doubt this kind of gymnastic exercise is of great value, if good forms are selected."

The late *Prof. Hjalmar Ling* said: "A really ideal conception leads to a constant effort toward and preference for a certain *selection* of the most perfect and complete forms within every important type. But it does not exclude the teacher's duty, out of compassion for the inability of a crowd of little and clumsy pupils, humbly to use all the means which in the shortest possible way can improve the condition."

"Every movement, sufficiently exact as to form and known as to effect, which plainly corresponds to an essential need is beautiful in itself, through its useful purpose."

"It has been said with justice that the stumbling stones of the gymnast are the vanity of the rope-dancer, the affectation of the dancing-master, the rigidity of the soldier."

"No apparatus, not even the most inconvenient, is harmful in itself if it is correctly used; without the teacher's more or less skilled hand for guide, *i.e.* for correction, assistance, resistance, etc., there is no single piece which is absolutely necessary and entirely impossible to substitute under all conditions."

"It is not enough, as has been supposed, that a movement should be *harmless* in order to receive gymnastic consideration."

In conclusion let me state in behalf of Swedish gymnastics, that

1. We believe that the laws of Nature should form the basis of all exercise and that nothing should be introduced (*a*) which is at variance with these laws and (*b*) whose value remains to be proved.

2. We believe that the laws of exercise as evolved by the Swedes are essentially correct for they have been proved by experiment. We shall adhere to them until we have satisfactory evidence that we are wrong; but we can accept no statements which are not borne out by science; all such we are ready to adopt and incorporate into the science of gymnastics.

3. We believe that while the leading laws have been framed correctly, much detail remains to be added—not by arbitration, but by the commands of Nature. As the science of gymnastics grows we propose to grow with it, along the lines of physics, physiology, and psychology. Meanwhile we take pride in the conviction that it was born in Sweden.

4. We do not believe in modifying the Swedish system, for it is in itself a modification—its elasticity is as great as the tenacity which has enabled it to survive three generations of investigation. Neither do we believe in modifying any other system, nor in inventing a new one to meet American or other conditions. Gymnastics is a science and demands to be treated as such. And the scientific world demands that no one attempt to modify anything before he understands the

thing itself. And we beg that those who adopt a few movements, label them "Swedish gymnastics" with various surnames, and inflict them upon all alike, will do us the favor to eliminate the word Swedish, for looks and name do not constitute character.

5. We believe that the demands of the times is not for a particular system or form, but it is one for good teaching. It is demanded that each physical trainer should possess a thorough knowledge of the principles and practice of gymnastics as a science and an art, and that he should know how to teach. What he is to teach let him decide for himself as long as he produces the correct results. Then the rivalry will be one not of factions but of skill, and we may justly look for the best results. The untrained and unskilled teacher has had his day; he has taught us what not to do.

6. We do not ask that anyone adopt the Swedish system, but we demand that all should teach rational kinesiological gymnastics, and that all try to drop personal vanities and narrow prejudices, and by recognition of our own imperfections absorb of the vast infinite to aid us in shaping the definite for which we are working.

Let us vie with one another to produce the best; let it be a peaceful competition where each will delight in the others' success, and improve by it; and let us remember that energy cannot afford to be misspent nor time wasted.

BARON NILS POSSE, M. G.

REPORT OF THE CHAIRMAN OF SECTION ON HISTORY AND BIBLIOGRAPHY OF PHYSICAL EDUCATION

E. M. Hartwell

Read at the Eighth Annual Meeting of the American Association for the Advancement of Physical Education, held at Chicago, July 29, 1893.

This is the first meeting of the Section on the History and Bibliography of Physical Education, which was established by the vote of the A. A. A. P. E., at its seventh annual meeting in Philadelphia. You will find certain questions printed on the program which have been propounded by the committee for discussion by this Section. Aside from the presentation of these questions and a plea for their discussion your committee has no formal report to offer at this time.

As the morning is too far advanced to admit of our devoting a sufficient amount of time to the meetings of the various Sections into which the Association has been divided, I will avail myself of this opportunity to make some general remarks upon the questions placed upon the program, leaving it for the Association to decide whether or not your committee shall be placed in a position to fulfill its proper functions in the future.

Hitherto, beyond the mere providing for the establishment and organization of the Section and Committee on History and Bibliography of Physical Education, the A. A. A. P. E. has made no attempt whatever to collect even the current literature pertaining to any branch of Physical Training, and no system of exchanges with periodicals of any subject in return for our annual proceedings has been instituted as yet. No adequate yearly report of progress in physical education, even if the survey be confined to the United States, can be made by a committee which never receives a book or periodical, or a dollar with which to buy one. Moreover, the pecuniary resources of the Association have been so limited and precarious that no committee would

E. M. Hartwell, "Report of the Chairman of Section on History and Bibliography of Physical Education," *Physical Education*, vol. II, no. 8, October 1893, pp. 127-130.

be justified during the past year in incurring any expense, even the slightest, for the purpose of securing material on which to report.

The list of topics presented for your consideration has been prepared chiefly with a view to calling forth some expression of opinion that shall serve to show how far and in what way the Association is desirous of promoting the work appropriate to this Section. We desire to ascertain whether or not the Association has any vital and genuine interest in the history and literature of the science and art of physical education (or either of them); and what measures, if any, it is willing to take towards providing its members, and the public, with accurate, adequate and timely information regarding the progress of physical education in our own and other countries.

One of the principal obstacles to the advancement of physical education in America, it seems to me, is to be found in the general ignorance of the teachings of science as to the nature and effects of such training and in the prevalent indifference to the plain teachings of experience as to the best that has been done towards making physical education a genuine and efficient department of instruction. It is plainly our duty to do our utmost towards overcoming such indifference and dissipating such ignorance, which is relatively as wide spread and dense among practical educators and educational authorities as in the public at large. Yet if we, who are chiefly concerned with physical training, almost utterly neglect its history and literature, how shall we hope to enlighten those whose influence and aid we desire to secure? If we fail to apprehend and to enforce upon our followers the lessons in strategy to be derived from a study of the precepts and campaigns of those who have displayed generalship in our cause, and content ourselves with mere drill and tactics, any efforts that our Association may put forth for the advancement of physical education will resemble a series of guerilla raids, rather than the prosecution of a campaign in legitimate warfare.

Let us look a little closer at the main features of the situation. Not only have the leading European works on physical training not been translated into English, even in condensed form, but there is no handbook in English that affords a comprehensive historical survey of the rise and development of physical education during the last hundred or even fifty years.

During the last decade the Ministers of Education, in nearly all the leading countries of Europe, have been more or less actively engaged with problems pertaining to the physical side of education. This state of things has stimulated a large addition to the existing literature on the subject. Official reports and regulations, as well as periodical publications, have been multiplied, and the number of books, articles and brochures in German, French, Italian and the Scandinavian tongues, have been greatly increased. Very little of this great body of contemporary literature has been brought to the notice of British or American readers, either in the shape of translations, digests, reviews, or even bibliographical notes. I do not know of any library or institution in America that pretends to collect the books and pamphlets that are published, from year to year, on this subject, or even to subscribe for the principal foreign periodicals devoted to physical training. Unless the schools specially devoted to the training of teachers of gymnastics, and the universities that offer degrees in physical training shall institute a radical reform, in the department under consideration, educated men and women will be amply justified in refusing to recognize our calling as one of the liberal professions.

Though it is manifestly evident that we are not fully in touch with our fellow-workers in Europe, it is not altogether clear whether or not we are willing to make the necessary exertion to become so. Yet, by way of argument, it may be assumed that we do desire to make a beginning in the direction indicated; the question arises as to what can be done towards realizing our desire? Shall we attempt to secure a complete and scientific bibliography for the benefit of the public and ourselves; shall we remain content for the present with less ambitious efforts; or shall we continue to do nothing?

In making a strictly scientific bibliography of any subject, a critical examination of the publications to be classified is indispensable, as it may even happen that titles transcribed at first hand shall prove misleading. For instance, in the case of what is probably the first book published in the United States on physical training, which was published in 1803, in Philadelphia, and purports to be a translation from the German of Salzmann, there is internal evidence that Guts Muths was the author of the original and not Salzmann!

The fact of the matter is that no library in the country possesses a collection of works complete enough to meet the requirements of a scientific bibliographer. No American student could prepare a complete bibliography of our subject without visiting libraries in Europe, or spending more than the cost of a trip to Europe in the purchase of books. Furthermore, no mere list of books and articles would meet the needs of the majority of those who are in course of training to become teachers of physical education, since comparatively few of them have a working knowledge of any but their mother tongue.

What seems to be most needed at the present time, is a handbook printed in English, to serve both as an elementary text-book in the history of physical education and a guide to its most important literature. Such a book in addition to a classified skeleton bibliography, should combine condensed digests of the chief works of the leading writers past and present, with enough of critical comment to indicate their historical or practical value. In lieu of such a handbook, whose preparation would necessarily require a considerable expenditure of time, labor and money, a series of short reviews, or of bibliographical and critical notes on the more important classical and recent works in our department, would undoubtedly prove interesting and valuable to many students and teachers. Such notes could be prepared through the co-operative effort of a well organized committee, and might be made to serve as the nuclei of a series of essays or brochures on special subjects, or as material for such a handbook as is alluded to above. At any rate such of them as related to current literature could be combined from year to year under the form of "Publications of the Year." Doubtless such periodicals as the TURN ZEITUNG, PHYSICAL EDUCATION and THE GYMNASIUM would be glad to publish such notes from time to time, and in their final form they might well be given a place in the proceedings of the A. A. A. P. E.

The resources of the several institutions and interests represented in the membership of this Association are adequate, I believe, for the compiling and publishing a classified skeleton bibliography of the most important works, and of a fairly complete "Annual Bibliography of Current Publications on Physical Training."

The question of organizing a circulating library for the benefit of the members of this Association seems to me, to be worthy of careful consideration. A well ordered scheme for such a purpose if under the control of a committee of this Section, would go far toward supplying your committee with material for its reports at a nominal cost. It would enable individual members to keep posted on matters of current interest, and it could readily be so managed as to provide many members with new books at reduced rates. Every one of us who is in a position to exert any influence upon those in charge of public schools or college libraries should lose no time in urging such persons to begin making collections of books and periodicals that bear upon this subject. Where public libraries are numerous, as for instance, in Massachusetts, it might even be possible to institute a co-operative circulating library on a large scale. Such a system would tend to widen and deepen the interest of the public in physical education, and thereby to strengthen and promote the efficiency of the A. A. A. P. E. To carry into effect the plans that I have roughly outlined, or any of them will entail a very considerable amount of patient, strenuous, co-operative, unpaid, unselfish work on the part of many persons. But is not the attempt worth making for that very reason? Is it not the chief object of this Association to undertake work that solitary and selfish teachers and students would pronounce unpractical and unrewarding? Is not more light our most crying need, at this juncture,—light that shall warm, illumine, and unify ourselves, and through us others who for lack of knowledge are indifferent or opposed to the interests that we have at heart? What better watch-word could we adopt if we purpose to achieve solid and lasting results therein, "Seek light and impart it?"

PRESIDENT'S ADDRESS—THE CONDITION AND PROSPECTS OF PHYSICAL EDUCATION IN THE UNITED STATES

Dr. Edward M. Hartwell

According to a prevalent belief of long standing, the number seven is considered to be ominous and fateful. For instance, the human body is said to be renewed in all its parts once in seven years, and its life is supposed to be divided into seven periods or ages. In ancient Greece the boy was left in charge of his mother and nurse till he became seven years old. He was then handed over to the pedagogue and the pedotribe in order that his course of training, as an aspirant to citizenship, might be begun. Similarly in the days of chivalry, the boy was kept in feminine leading strings till he was seven years old; henceforth his training was directed with an eye single to preparing him to play the part of a courtier and knight. He was removed from the sphere of woman's teaching, to a considerable extent, and was surrounded by influences calculated to make him an adept in manly sports and duties. To become a craftsman, the apprentice served his seven years; and seven years was likewise the period of training and probation for proficients in the liberal arts.

Following ancient usage, therefore, I venture to emphasize the fact that this is the seventh annual meeting of our Association for the Advancement of Physical Education. We may well congratulate ourselves, that though, as a corporate body, we are unquestionably larger and more vigorous than was the case seven years ago, few, if any, of those who were active in the establishment of this association have been cast out or have removed themselves to make way for new material. A glance at our list of members and the programmes of our

Edward M. Hartwell, "President's Address—The Condition and Prospects of Physical Education in the United States," *Proceedings of the American Association for the Advancement of Physical Education,* no. 6, 1893, pp. 13-40.

NOTE—This address has been largely rewritten since it was delivered.

meetings makes it evident that there is little prospect of our being removed from the sphere of woman's influence and suffered or required to run alone.

Having then, in a sense, arrived at a critical point in our history it behooves us to review the course of events within the field of physical education during the first period of our existence, and to forecast, so far as we may, the character and direction of the forces which are likely to be operative and influential in the period upon which we are entering.

Much has transpired during the infancy of this association that is worthy to be recounted in this presence. But, desirable though it be that the annals of physical education for the last decade should be compiled for the benefit of the public and ourselves, my purpose, at this time, is to discuss the significance, relations, and trend of the present movement for the advancement of physical training in the United States. I shall, therefore, content myself, at this point, with a cursory sketch of the principal events that have signalized the history of our cause during the past seven years.

Interest in problems pertaining to the physical side of education has never been so general, so active, or so intelligent in the United States, as it is to-day. Though that interest has continually gained in force and volume since the revival in athletics set in, after the close of the war, its spread has become much more rapid, and its manifesations much more widely diversified since the year 1884. Evidences of its extension are to be found in all parts of the country, under an increasing variety of forms. Within the period under review, the discussion by the general, the religious, the medical, and the educational press of the more superficial aspects of physical training has been notably enlarged. In certain quarters, likewise, a keener and more intelligent interest in questions relating to the scientific, historical, and pedagogical bearings of the subject has been awakened and fostered by publications emanating from the United States Bureau of Education, from this association, and from various other sources. At the same time not a little hubbub has arisen from various groups of would-be reformers and minor prophets, who are quick to scent an opportunity to call public attention to themselves and their crude and inept schemes for hastening the millennium.

In the field of superior and secondary education, the multiplication and improvement of material appliances have gone bravely on, and large sums of money have been expended on gymnasia, gymnastic apparatus, and playgrounds, and numerous colleges and preparatory schools, for both sexes, have established departments or *quasi* departments of physical training and personal hygiene. School boards, here and there, have shown a quickened sense of the need and value of bodily education, and a hopeful new departure has been made in the direction of establishing public education on a really sound foundation. Since 1884 cities aggregating an enrolled school population of more than 300,000 have taken steps towards providing instruction in gymnastics of one kind or another for the children in their elementary schools. In promoting this end, especially in the West, the N. A. Turnerbund has achieved more than any other organization or class of organizations. In the East an independent movement has arisen, with Boston as its center, for the promotion and extension of the Swedish system of pedagogical gymnastics. The battle of the systems has but just begun. Its earnest and prolonged continuance will in the main, I am confident, be productive of good results, as it cannot fail to bring out a large body of principles and facts which our educators as a class have ignored hitherto; and it is also likely to exercise an enlightening and humanizing influence on the too often uncritical and intolerant partisans of the systems and alleged systems of which we hear so much. Teachers that are not teachable are almost certain to prove false guides, and it is *teachers* and not mere gymnasts or expert foreturners that we must have if physical education is to win its proper place in the school and college world. Summer schools and a variety of nondescript "institutes" and "colleges" have shown marked activity in organizing what they are pleased to advertise as normal courses in physical culture. Of much greater consequence is the fact that several prominent normal schools have enlarged their curriculum by the appointment of special teachers of physical training, and other well established schools of the same kind are moving in the same direction. One of the most striking and hopeful signs of the times is the growing conviction that teachers and preachers of physical training require to be carefully and thoroughly trained for their work; and the measure of success attained by a few normal and training schools for the special teaching of the principles and practice of physical education, that have been started or re-formed within ten years, leads us to hope that this indispensable department of our work will in the future be much more adequately organized and supported. In this connection special mention should be made of the Turnlehrer Seminar in Milwaukee, the Physical Department of the International Y. M. C. A. Training School at Springfield, Mass., the Boston Normal School of Gymnastics, and of the extensive courses in physical training that Cornell and Harvard Universities have promised to establish in the near future.

The aims of the Young Men's and also the Young Women's Christian Associations throughout the country have been greatly enlarged, and their activity augmented within the last few years. The associations are to be congratulated on their success in multiplying new gymnasia and playgrounds, and commended for their zeal in striving to secure a higher grade of intelligence and efficiency for the direction of their "physical departments." A marked tendency on the part of public spirited philanthropists to provide the unfortunate and neglected classes with facilities for gymnastic and athletic forms of recreation has also declared itself. For instance, one of the Vanderbilts has built and furnished a gymnasium for the use of certain employees of the New York Central railroad; and a generous lady of Norfolk, Connecticut, has borne the expense of providing a costly and well-appointed gymnasium for the use of the Norfolk townspeople. The Park Commissioners of the city of Boston have taken a step that, I believe, is without precedent in this country, in the establishment and maintenance of a public out-of-door gymnasium for boys, and another for girls, at Charlesbank, a new park near to one of the most crowded quarters of the city. Another innovation worthy of mention is the activity shown by officers and men in organizing athletic sports and gymnastic instruction for the benefit of the rank and file, at several posts of the Regular Army of the United States. The use of gymnastics in retreats and asylums for the insane has also been recently revived. Emphatic acknowledgment should here be made of the wisdom and success shown by the management of the State Reformatory at Elmira, N. Y., in demonstrating the fact that systematic physical training is an essential and potent factor in the mental and moral reformation of criminal dullards. The pedagogical results of the Elmira experiments are of capital importance, and the progressive spirit shown by the government of the state of New York in providing generously for the establishment and maintenance of a department of physical training in its reformatory for felons is worthy of the warmest commendation. Would that even half of our school boards and boards of college trustees were equally progressive!

Being Americans and members of an American association for the advancement of physical education not yet in its teens, it is natural that we should be most interested in the present condition of physical education in the localities in which we are called to labor. The temptation is great to magnify the importance and extent of the present movement for extending the scope of physical training: and to measure our hopes for the future by the achievements of the last few years, in which many of the members of this association have borne an influential and honored part. It is easy to forget, therefore, the part played by our predecessors and to lose sight of the fact that the movement in which we are engaged is a composite and resultant effect of forces that have been operative in this country for nearly three quarters of a century and in Europe for more than a century. In order to adequately measure the advancement of physical training in this country during the last ten years or to forecast the prospects of its further advancement, it is necessary to consider some of the more characteristic features of the general movement for educational reform of which the movement for the advancement of physical education forms a part. Physical training is at most a province in the realm of human training, and the struggle for its advancement is but an episode in a general campaign. The main issues of that campaign were joined in the conflict that arose from the revolt of the Realists and Philanthropists against the Humanists in the revolutionary decades of the last century.

The political, social, and industrial revolutions that have been wrought within the last hundred years have done much to spread and popularize the ideals and methods of the Philanthropists; and have contributed not a little towards forcing the Humanists to abate their somewhat arrogant and exclusive claims with regard to superiority of "discipline studies" over "information studies"; in other words, scientific training has won, or is fast winning, a secure place for itself beside its present rival and former over-lord and master, "classical culture." It is not probable that permanent or absolute victory will be achieved in America either by the devotees of humanism or realism; a much more desirable result is likely to be brought about; viz.: that the parties shall become so far united and reconciled as to work side by side for a complete human training.

In reviewing the history of the rise of physical training as a distinct department of modern education in Europe, five distinct periods are recognizable. They are: (1) the period beginning with the Renascence and the Reformation, and extending to the year 1774, a period in which bodily training aroused the theoretical and critical approval of various humanistic writers and reformers; (2) the period extending from 1774 to 1820, which was characterized by innovation and experiment on the part of the Philanthropists and their followers; (3) a period of comparative quiescence and neglect, as regards physical education, covered by the interval between 1820 and 1840; (4) the period 1840 to 1860, which was a period of revival and expansion; (5) 1860 to the present time, a period of active growth and development on the whole, though a tendency to reorganization and reform has declared itself within the last decade.

The development of physical education in America has taken place along lines that are in general parallel to the course of the development of physical education in Europe. It may be divided roughly into periods as follows: (1) The period extending from the outbreak of the Revolutionary War to the year 1825; this was a period of premonitory criticism and slight theoretical recognition. (2) A period of enthusiastic discussion and of hopeful but short-lived experiments due to foreign example. (3) The period 1835 to 1860 was one of quiescence and neglect, marked by the beginnings of a reaction towards its close. (4) 1860 to 1880 was a period of awakening, revival, and experiment. (5) The period extending from 1880 to the present time has been a time of active growth and diversified expansion.

Let us now consider more closely some of the more salient features disclosed by the history of physical education in Europe and our own country.

The Humanists of the Renascence and the Reformation were inclined, owing to their reverence for the example set in ancient times by the Greeks and Romans, to recognize in a general and literary way the worth of bodily exercises and accomplishments, but they made no strenuous attempt to engraft physical training upon their reformed schemes of education. We might multiply citations from such writers as Rabelais and Montaigne in France, Martin Luther and Melanchthon in Germany, Milton and John Locke in England, to show their enlightened opinions with regard to the fundamental importance of bodily training. But it would be difficult to show that their writings led to any thoroughgoing attempt to realize their generous ideals prior to the last three decades of the last century.

To Basedow, the first of the Philanthropists, belongs the honor of making the first hopeful experiment in combining physical and mental education in the general training of youth. In 1774, he was instrumental in founding an institution at Dessau, which was called the Philanthropinum, for the purpose of realizing Rousseau's "method of nature." Twelve years before, Basedow had attempted to adapt to general educational purposes certain physical exercises that were peculiar to institutions set apart for the education of young men of gentle blood. These schools, which bore the name of schools for the nobility, or "Ritter-akademien," furnished instruction in riding, fencing, vaulting, and dancing. Basedow endeavored to make use of these knightly exercises in his scheme for educating the sons of the burghers. He also introduced certain forms of exercise derived from popular German sports. Simon, one of Basedow's assistants, induced him to make trial of certain exercises copied from the gymnastics of the ancient Greeks; thus arose the so-called Dessau pentathlon, which consisted of running, jumping, climbing, balancing, and carrying of heavy weights. Basedow's immediate disciples and imitators were Campe, Salzmann, and Guts-muths, who labored to extend and perfect the Dessau system of physical training, in which manual training was also given a place. As regards their efforts to promote physical training, Pestalozzi and Fellenberg in Switzerland, Nachtegall in Denmark, Ling in Sweden, and "Father Jahn" and Spiess in Germany may fairly be classed with the men above mentioned as followers of Basedow among the Philanthropists.

Pestalozzi has been called the father of education for the people. He attempted to devise a system of school gymnastics based upon the nature of the human body; and endeavored to combine industrial as well as general bodily training with mental and moral education in his experiments for the amelioration of the condition of the common people. Pestalozzi's attempts in the period 1780 to 1810 were practically failures. What he was unable to accomplish was largely realized by Fellenberg and his successors in the schools at Hofwyl near Berne between the years 1807 and 1848. Not a few of those who were engaged in educational reform, as marked out and attempted by Pestalozzi, became identified with the physical education movement. Among these we may mention Colonel Amoros, who in 1817 opened the first gymnastic institute in Paris. He had formerly been at the head of a Pestalozzian Institute in Madrid; and it is noteworthy that Father Jahn and two of his nearest friends and helpers in the gymnastic movement, viz., Friedrich Friesen and Ernst Eiselen, were teachers in a Pestalozzian institute in Berlin. That gymnastics under the name of Turnen became a popular institution and a potent factor in national life was mainly due to Jahn, whose strong and rugged nature and restless, passionate spirit qualified him for agitation and leadership. During the time of Prussia's deepest humiliation and distress, in the period, viz.: 1806-1813, Jahn seized the idea of making physical training a force in national regeneration and education, and wrote, and dreamed, and plotted for a free and united Germany. He made gymnastics popular as a means of acquiring bodily force and skill; but, though himself a teacher of boys, his aim was not chiefly to develop a system of school gymnastics. He aimed at bringing boys and men together for gymnastic pursuits out of doors and out of school hours. The Turners were active in the successful uprising of the Prussians against the French in 1813, so that turning became more than ever popular throughout Germany during 1813 and 1814. In 1819 a plan was perfected by the educational authorities for the establishment of turning grounds throughout Prussia in connection with the schools for boys; but political troubles arose which caused the suppression of popular gymnastics in Prussia from 1820 till 1842. In 1842 the King of Prussia gave his sanction to the proposal of his ministers that "bodily exercises should be acknowledged formally as a necessary and indispensable integral part of male education, and should be adopted as an agency in the education of the people."

The king also authorized the establishment of "gymnastic institutes" in connection with "the gymnasien, the higher middle schools, the training schools for teachers, and the division and brigade schools in the army." The measures taken to give effect to the king's cabinet order of 1842 need not detain us here. Suffice it to say that not only in Prussia, but also in all other German states, and, indeed, throughout nearly all continental countries, gymnastics, since 1842, have become "a necessary and indispensable integral part" of the school training of boys, and to a large degree of girls also.

Unquestionably, Jahn and his followers prepared the way for the rise of the present widespread system of German school gymnastics, which, in addition to some heavy gymnastic features borrowed from the Jahn turning, includes free movements, order movements, and class exercises in light gymnastics that have been invented or adopted since Jahn's time. The most prominent name in connection with the rise and spread of German school gymnastics is that of the Hessian, Adolf Spiess; whose distinctive work it was to render German gymnastics systematic and scientific, and to adapt them to pedagogical purposes and methods. Spiess was chiefly active and influential as a teacher and writer between 1840 and 1858, the year of his death. The normal schools of gymnastics at Berlin and Dresden were founded prior to 1860, while those at Munich, Stuttgart, and Carlsruhe are of later date.

Although traces of German influence may be found in the early work of Ling, the founder of Swedish gymnastics, he soon opened paths of his own, and some of the most distinctive features of the system of school gymnastics now in vogue in Sweden are rightly accredited to Ling, who held the position of director of the Royal Central Gymnastic Institute in Stockholm from its foundation in 1813 till his death in 1839. Ling worked out the principles of free movements and of class exercises in advance of Spiess.

Since 1840, and more particularly since 1860, Germany has become the stronghold of Volks-turnen or popular gymnastics,—even as England has become the stronghold of athletic sports,—so that now the turning societies of Germany and Austria number nearly 5,000, with an aggregate membership of nearly half a million men and boys over fourteen years of age. Despite the excellence of the Ling gymnastics for school and military purposes, popular gymnastics have remained comparatively undeveloped in Sweden. In Norway, Finland, and Denmark gymnastics are more generally popular than in Sweden and show the traces of German influence and example to a considerable degree. Since 1884 a wide and influential movement has arisen in Germany whose purpose is to utilize popular sports in the physical education of school children. This movement has met with marked favor and active sympathy from the teaching class and the educational authorities. In France a very general movement is in progress to acclimatize British athletic sports; and a strong party exists in Sweden whose aim it is to popularize gymnastics by the incorporation of athletic features and methods that have heretofore found little favor. On the other hand, while school gymnastics in Switzerland, Austria, Denmark, Russia, Italy, England, and even in France have followed or resembled German school gymnastics in the main, a tendency to adopt or approximate Swedish methods has recently begun to declare itself in France, Denmark, Russia, and England, as well as in this country.

Turning to America we find our prehistoric period, or the period in which the literary recognition of physical education began to manifest itself, did not close until the first quarter of the present century. It corresponds, then, in point of time, roughly with the period of preliminary experiments in Europe. During this period Americans were too busily engaged with war and politics to pay much attention to matters pertaining to educational reform. Still, there were not lacking, even before the year 1800, influential and outspoken critics of what then passed for a liberal education. Among such we may mention Benjamin Franklin and Benjamin Rush, both of Philadelphia, and both signers of the Declaration of Independence, and Noah Webster, the founder of the dictionary. It is clear that both Rush and Webster held views decidedly favorable to bodily exercise of certain kinds.

Noah Webster seems to have been the first American of note to propose the institution of a college course of physical training. His proposal was, however, of a rather rudimentary nature. It is found in his "Address to Yung Gentlemen," dated Hartford, January, 1790. He says it should be "the buzziness of yung persons to assist nature, and strengthen the growing frame by athletic exercizes. . . . When it iz not the lot of a yung person to labor, in agriculture or mekanic arts, some laborious amusement should constantly and daily be pursued az a substitute, and none iz preferable to fencing. A fencing skool iz, perhaps, az necessary an institution in a college az a professorship of mathematics." He further recommends running, football, quoits, and dancing as suited to the needs of sedentary persons.

Among Dr. Rush's published essays is one dated in August, 1790, "On the Amusements and Punishments Proper for Schools." In it he proposes that "the amusements of our youth shall consist of such exercises as will be most subservient to their future employments in life." He favored agricultural and mechanical employments as means of diversion and training, and notes with approval that "in the Methodist College in Maryland a large lot is divided among the scholars and premiums are adjudged to those who raise the most vegetables." "The Methodists," he adds, "have wisely banished every species of play from their college." Again he says, "All the amusements of the children of the Moravians at Bethlehem, Pa., are derived from their performing the subordinate parts of several of the mechanical arts." It was in accordance with such notions as these that farm, manual labor, and Fellenberg schools were founded, and societies for promoting manual labor in literary institutions were organized somewhat extensively, in various parts of the United States, during the first third of the present century.

The prominence given to military considerations in many of the earlier and some of the later attempts to make a place for physical education may be noticed here. Bodily accomplishments have ever been assigned a prominent place in the codes of the soldier and the gentleman; and every outburst of military ardor in our history has led to attempts to engraft certain technical forms of military training upon the general training of the rising generation. The War of the Revolution, the War of 1812, and the War of the Rebellion each gave rise to such attempts.

In 1790, President Washington transmitted to the First Senate of the United States an elaborate scheme prepared by Gen. Henry Knox, then Secretary of War, for the military training of all men over eighteen and under sixty. The youth of eighteen, nineteen, and twenty years were to receive their military education in annual camps of discipline to be formed in each state, and a certificate of military proficiency was proposed as a prerequisite to the right to vote. This plan failed of adoption as did also the following recommendation that was urged in the national House of Representatives in 1817 and 1819, *"that a corps of military instructors should be formed to attend to the gymnastic and elementary part of instruction in every school in the United States."* In 1862, Congress made the teaching of military tactics obligatory on all state colleges that should avail themselves of the Morrill Act, whereby certain public lands were apportioned among the several States for the purpose of promoting education in agriculture and the mechanic arts. In 1864, a plan recommended by the State Board of Education for making military drill a part of the public school training of boys throughout the state narrowly escaped adoption by the Legislature of Massachusetts.

Excepting the Military Academy at West Point, in whose curriculum bodily exercises have figured more or less largely since 1817, the "American Literary, Scientific, and Military Academy," founded at Norwich, Vermont, in 1820, by Capt. Alden Partridge, formerly superintendent of West Point, seems to have been the first educational institution of note in America to attempt to connect "mental improvement with a regular course of bodily exercises and the full development of the physical powers." The example of the West Point and Norwich academies proved mildly stimulating, and led to the establishment of perhaps a score of select military schools for boys in the course of thirty years, but, so far as I know, that example had no effect upon the development of the public school system of instruction in any city or state. The impulse which led to the gladsome advocacy and espousal of physical education in the second quarter of this century was distinctly humanitarian in its nature.

The movement for educational reform in Europe made but slight impression upon American thought and endeavor until after the close of the War of 1812. But the United States shared markedly in the exalted and restless mental activity which characterized the first two or three decades following the battle of Waterloo. This period was peculiarly prolific in optimistic schemes for the amelioration of popular ignorance and misery: and American reformers became highly susceptible to the influence of foreign example, and developed a well marked aptitude for laudation and imitation. In the years 1825 and 1826 physical education became a matter of almost epidemic interest in New England; Boston in particular was a focus of infection. Although, as I shall point out, the attempt was definitely made to introduce gymnastics into a number of colleges and private schools for boys, physical education was very vaguely apprehended, as it was often held to include pretty much all that is now relegated to the department of personal hygiene. Physical education fired the imagination of educational reformers for a time,—but so did monitorial instruction, manual training, the propagation of useful information, vegetarianism, teetotalism, and phrenology.

The Round Hill School, established at Northampton, Mass., in 1823, and the High School, founded in New York city in 1825, each introduced many features that were novelties in the education of American boys; but the most striking innovations by which these schools were marked were copied from Lancasterian, Fellenbergian, or Pestalozzian schools in Europe. Physical training was accorded a place both in the Round Hill School and in the New York High School, which schools constituted a sort of *stella-duplex* in the educational firmament, and served for some years to fire the emulation of a host of aspiring and enterprising pedagogical adventurers. As regards physical education the Round Hill School was decidedly the more refulgent. Although a rude attempt at gymnastics was made in the Monitorial School for Girls in Boston early in the spring of 1825, I know of no reason to dispute the claim of Messrs. Cogswell and Bancroft of Round Hill that they "were the first in the new continent to connect gymnastics with a purely literary establishment." The Round Hill gymnasium was established in 1825. It was in reality a *turn-platz* or outdoor gymnastic ground, planned, fitted, and managed in accordance with the Jahn system of turning then prevalent in Germany, and to a much less extent in England. Dr. Charles Beck, who was "Instructor in Latin and Gymnastics" at Round Hill, had been a pupil of Jahn himself, it is said. Gymnastics continued to be a feature at Round Hill for several years.

Harvard College started the first American college gymnasium in one of its dining-halls in March, 1826; and later in the same season a variety of gymnastic appliances were put up in the playground, known as the Delta. Dr. Follen, a German exile familiar with the Jahn turning, was the instructor and leader in gymnastics. The Boston Gymnasium, opened in the Washington Gardens, October 3, 1826, with Dr. Follen as its principal instructor, seems to have been the first public gymnasium of any note in the United States. In July, 1827, Dr. Francis Lieber, who was warmly recommended by his old teacher and friend, Father Jahn, succeeded Dr. Follen. It is said that the attendance at the Boston Gymnasium rose to four hundred in the first year and dwindled to four in the course of the second year. Gymnastic grounds were established at Yale in 1826; and at Williams, Amherst, and Brown in 1827. Did time permit a dozen schools might be named that were established in the period 1825-1828 for the sake of giving effect to the reformed principles of education. Doubtless a much larger list might be made but for the meager and chaotic character of the educational annals of the time in question. As it is, my list comprises only such institutions as have left us printed evidence of their profession of faith. Only one of the twelve was properly speaking a public school. All of them promised and some of them furnished facilities of a sort for the physical education of their pupils. The day of normal training had not come, and, so far as I know, no attempt whatever was made to train up teachers of gymnastics in a systematic, rational way!

The public school system of the country was still in embryo. The current conception of "common school education" was so mean and narrow, and the teaching class, at least outside of the colleges, academies, and better private adventure schools, was so largely made up of inferior and incongruous elements that we need not wonder that the interest in physical education, in the second of our five periods, proved to be illusory and short lived, and exercised almost no influence in the field of popular education. What had been heralded as a new era in physical education in 1825 was practically closed by 1830. What might have been the result if Drs. Beck, Follen, and Lieber had not quit the field it is vain to surmise. Even they were ruled more by theoretical notions of human perfectibility than by scientific knowledge of bodily health and development.

No general or widespread revival of interest in school or college gymnastics occurred between 1830 and 1860; and athletic sports had no standing either as an elective or compulsory branch of education. Still, what was loosely termed "physical education" continued to receive marked attention. A considerable party arose who favored manual labor instead of gymnastics, and a number of enthusiastic attempts were made, prior to 1835, to provide college and seminary students with facilities for gaining health, recreation, and cash by means of agricultural and mechanical labor. Voluminous and curious evidence of this exists, particularly in a report of Mr. T. D. Weld, the general agent of the Society for Promoting Manual Labor in Literary Institutions. The society was founded in 1831, and Mr. Weld's report was published in 1835, or thereabouts.

Among the multifarious and heterogeneous stirs and movements for the regeneration of society which constitute so marked a feature of the first third of the present century, the crusade for popularizing the doctrines of physiology is especially worthy of our notice, since it served to keep alive and in some measure to spread a vague theoretical interest in physical education, as it was then superficially conceived. Indeed, it is not too much to say that the physiology-crusade served to perpetuate the essential spirit of the period 1825-1830 and had much to do with preparing the way for the gymnastic revival that set in just before the war broke out. This crusade had its beginnings as early as 1825, or possibly earlier; it was greatly stimulated by the furor which was created by the books and lectures of the phrenologists Spürzheim and George Combe, who argued in a solemn and taking way that education should be based on the teachings of physiology and ordered in accordance with the alleged laws of their pseudoscience. It may be said to have culminated in the year

1850, when the Legislature of Massachusetts passed a law authorizing school committees throughout the commonwealth "to make physiology and hygiene a compulsory study in all the public schools." Through the multiplication of popular manuals of physiology, which frequently contained much hortatory and laudatory matter on physical education, the general public came to entertain a nebulous notion that serviceable bodies were worth striving for and that school machinery of some sort should be devised for the purpose of securing them. Did time permit, an interesting list might be given of lectures, addresses, and books that helped to propagate this notion. I will content myself with mentioning: Miss Catherine Beecher's "Course of Callisthenics for Young Ladies," published in 1832; "The Principles of Physiology Applied to the Preservation of Health and to the Improvement of Physical and Mental Education," by Dr. Andrew Combe of Edinburgh, a pirated edition of which was published in New York in 1834; and Horace Mann's "Sixth Annual Report, as Secretary of the Massachusetts Board of Education," published in 1843. Miss Beecher was a precursor of Dio Lewis as regards the advocacy of free and light gymnastics and musical drill, and appears to have been the first native American to assert claims to originality as a "system-maker." Her system seems to have awakened some mild and passing attention in the proprietors of private schools for girls. In the preface to her "Manual of Physiology and Calisthenics for Schools and Families, New York, 1856," Miss Beecher professes to be a disciple of Ling; but the body of the book is not written in accordance with the distinctive principles of the Swedish gymnasiarch.

Very little attention was bestowed by Americans upon German gymnastics in the period 1835 to 1860, which period as a whole was one of ground breaking and seed sowing as regards physical education. In the North American Turnerbund we have a genuine and vigorous offshoot from the German stock, but the transplanting of that sapling and its cultivation in American soil failed to excite the interest of American educationists for more than a generation. The beginnings of the Turnerbund, which for many years has been the largest, most widespread, and efficient gymnastic association in the United States are to be found in the Turnvereine established by political refugees from Germany, who found an asylum in this country after the revolutionary year of 1848.

We have abundant evidence that there was a growing interest in gymnastic and athletic forms of exercise in the latter half of the decade ending in 1860. Such evidence is found in the effort to secure funds for the erection of school and college gymnasia; in the increased addiction of collegians and others to rowing and ball matches; in the instant popularity achieved by the Tom Brown books; in the interest excited by the lectures and exhibitions of Dr. G. B. Windship, whose public career as an exponent of heavy lifting began in Boston in 1859; and in the prominence given to topics relating to physical education in general, and school gymnastics in particular, by speakers at teachers' conventions and institutes, by the conductors of educational journals, and by public school officials.

The Gymnastic Revival of 1860 may be said to date from the meeting of the American Institute of Instruction at Boston in August of that year, at which meeting Diocletian Lewis, commonly called Dr. Dio Lewis, took a prominent part in the discussion as to the expediency of making "calisthenics and gymnastics a part of school-teaching." This revival was not a thing apart, but grew out of the crusade for popularizing physiology and hygiene, if, indeed, it be not better described as a phase or continuation of that crusade.

It was wholly natural that Dio Lewis should figure in both movements. He was by nature an enthusiast, a radical, and a free lance. He was born and bred at a time when advocacy of the doctrines of temperance, anti-slavery, phrenology, homœopathy, physiology, and of educational reform savored more or less of ultra-liberalism, or even of "free-thinking." Before his first public appearance in Boston, when he may be said to have stormed the key to the situation, by his capture of the American Institute of Instruction, Dio Lewis had traveled extensively, for some years, in the Southern and Western States, as a week-day lecturer on physiology and hygiene, and as a Sunday orator on temperance. He had given some attention to physical education, withal; and, being well versed in the arts of the platform, was quick and apt in taking advantage of the growing interest in gymnastics. He was unconventional, sympathetic, plausible, oracular, and self-sufficient; and the time was ripe for a gymnasiarch of that sort. The doctrines and methods of the Lewis gymnastics, which were novelties and seemed original to most of his followers and imitators, spread rapidly over the whole country, and, if we may credit certain eulogists of the system, even into "Europe, Asia, and Africa." His skill in securing the aid and backing of educationists and notabilities contributed materially towards making Dio Lewis the most conspicuous luminary, for a time, in the American gymnastical firmament, but failed to make him a fixed star. He was in great demand as a lecturer before normal schools, teachers' associations and institutes, and lyceum audiences; and his contributions to leading periodicals were eagerly read and favorably received. He was medical practitioner, lecturer, editor, gymnasium manager, teacher, hotel proprietor, and preacher by turns. In short, Dio Lewis was a revivalist and agitator, and not a scientist in any proper sense. His originality has been much overrated,—very few of his inventions, either in the line of apparatus or of methods of teaching, being really new. In his book he borrowed lavishly from German sources, so that his "New Gymnastics" were in the main neither new nor his own. The establishment by Dio Lewis in 1861 of the Boston Normal Institute for Physical Education was a really new departure—in America—(unless perchance the *Turnlehrer Seminar* of the North American Turnerbund antedated it), and constituted, perhaps, the most considerable and solid of Dio Lewis's contributions to the cause of physical education. He is also deserving of praise and credit for convincing the public of the utility of light gymnastics, and for his influential aid in popularizing gymnastics for school children of both sexes.

Teachers and school managers showed unexampled interest in the "New Gymnastics," which seemed destined soon to form a part of the curriculum of the public schools of the more progressive cities of the country, as well as in a multitude of private schools and academies. For instance, the School Board of Cincinnati, in 1861, and that of Boston, in 1864, formally adopted schemes looking to the general introduction of gymnastic teaching into their public schools. Owing to various reasons that I will not take time to enumerate, these and similar schemes proved illusory and impracticable. Even to-day we must admit that no important city or town in the United States has succeeded in maintaining for ten consecutive years a genuine and adequate system of school gymnastics.

The War of the Rebellion acted as a check to the spread of the interest excited by the Gymnastic Revival of 1860 in athletic and gymnastic forms of physical education, on the one hand, while, on the other, it served to bring military forms of drill and exercise into prominence and favor. In the year 1860 the colleges of Harvard, Yale, and Amherst erected gymnasium buildings; but their example was not followed to any considerable extent by the other colleges until after the close of the war. Amherst College established a department of Hygiene and Physical Education in 1860. Dr. Edward Hitchcock, Sr., who has served continuously as the professor in charge of that department since August, 1861, was elected the first president of this association in 1885. The example of Amherst, in making gymnastics a compulsory branch of college work, had but little effect upon the other colleges of the country prior to 1880.

The building of college gymnasia was resumed after the close of the war. During the decade after the war the disbanded armies of the republic furnished to the preparatory schools and colleges a large contingent of students who had been subjected to strenuous physical training. The influence exerted by this contingent in reviving and developing an interest in physical training was far more potent in the department of athletics than in that of gymnastics or of military drill. Baseball and rowing developed rapidly and led to the multiplication of intercollegiate athletic contests. The inadequacy of the facilities afforded by the older gymnasia for the indoor exercise and training of crews, teams, and champion athletes, had much to do with inaugurating a new era of gymnasium building, and with improving the organization and administration of the departments of physical education in the leading colleges for both sexes. This era opened in 1879-1880 with the completion of the Hemenway gymnasium at Harvard University. This gymnasium, for whose erection and equipment Mr. Augustus Hemenway of Boston, a graduate of Harvard in 1876, had given the sum of $115,000, surpassed in size, convenience, and magnificence any of the gymnasia then existing in the country. This gymnasium, both as regards its structural features, its fittings, and its methods of administration, has served as the model for most of the gymnasia, whether public or private, that have since been built. To Dr. Sargent, the director of the Hemenway gymnasium, we owe a debt of gratitude for many improvements in the construction of apparatus, for the invention of the so-called Sargent System of Developing Gymnastics, and the demonstration of the fact that gymnastic and athletic exercise on the part of young men and boys can and should be controlled and directed in the interest of healthful growth and normal development.

Thus far the colleges of the country have made no material advance over the method of gymnastic instruction adopted at Amherst thirty years ago, nor upon the Sargent idea of employing physical diagnosis and anthropometrical observations, in connection with the use of developing appliances, in the oversight and guidance of the physical training of students. Here and there the beginnings of forward movements in promoting class-instruction in light and heavy gymnastics have begun to show themselves—in this connection honorable mention should be made of Bowdoin and Haverford colleges for men. Certain colleges for women, which have adopted Swedish pedagogical gymnastics, notably the Woman's College of Baltimore and Smith College at Northhampton, Mass., have taken a step which most of their sister and brother institutions will do well to heed and possibly to follow. As a rule our American gymnasia, excepting those belonging to the Turnerbund and those organized in accordance with the principles of the Swedish system, fall short of excellence as schools of physical training. This, I take it, arises from the fact that the educational worth of physical training has been largely overshadowed in the minds of those who officer and control our schools and colleges by the obvious, but, in many respects, less important hygienic influences of muscular exercise. Whatever the reason for this state of things, the fact is obvious that our colleges and secondary schools, with few exceptions, have shown vastly more skill and energy in the acquisition of mere appliances than they have in developing the science and art of physical education. Indeed, one is tempted to think that those who control our colleges, and our preparatory and normal schools have yet to learn that physical education has a history and is capable of being organized as a genuine department of instruction.

Although the underlying principles of gymnastic exercises and athletic sports are identical, the distinctive aims and methods of the athletic trainer and the gymnastic teacher are divergent and to some extent antipathetic: and one reason, as it seems to me, for the lamentable neglect of genuine gymnastic instruction in the college world is found in the fact that college authorities have been so engrossed by a variety of unfamiliar and perplexing problems, forced upon them by the sudden and rapid expansion of the interest in athletic sports, that they have lacked energy for grappling further problems in bodily training. Quite naturally athletics constitute the most popular and obtrusive branch of physical training, and the athletic movement possesses much greater force and volume than any of the allied movements that have been revived or originated since 1860. Though the athlete belongs to a type that is not new to the world, he is practically a new species of man in America—a species having many varieties. The American gymnasium is a semi-original creation that has been devised mainly by the American architect in order to provide for the expressed or fancied needs of the American athlete. Allusion has already been made to the growth of athletic clubs within the past ten years. All things considered, the athletic clubs constitute the consummate and peculiar product of the athletic movement. There is nothing quite like them outside of America. Their influence, which is not salutary in all respects, is already great among schoolboys and collegians. The athletes as a class, those who aid them and those who bet on them, have had little to do with urging or promoting the educational side of physical training—for the simple reason that their interest in gymnastics is even feebler and less intelligent, considering their opportunities, than that of college faculties and boards of trust. It is chiefly in indirect or negative ways that the athletic clubs have contributed to the advancement of physical education, in its proper sense.

Athletics when wisely regulated afford valuable, I will even say invaluable, means of mental, moral, and physical training for boys and young men; but the element of rivalry and competition is so inseparable from athletic aims and methods, and excellence in the athletic specialties demands so much time and requires such costly appliances, as to preclude the general adoption of athletic sports as the principal means of securing the hygienic and educational ends of physical training for the mass of pupils in our public schools, especially in urban districts.

Gymnastics, if well ordered and properly taught during the early years of school life, afford the best preparation that an aspirant for athletic honors can have. Aside from the question of expense, there is no good reason for prolonging mere gymnastic drill to the exclusion of the higher forms of gymnastics and of outdoor sports after a pupil reaches the age of fifteen years. When the managers of our high and preparatory schools shall have learned their business—as regards bodily training—they will, I believe, institute courses of gymnastic instruction after the analogy of their elementary courses in language and mathematics, so that their pupils, on entering college we will say, will be prepared to choose their athletic and gymnastic electives in much the same way as they now choose their elective studies when the opportunity is given them. When the schools perform their duty in the premises, the colleges can give up the kindergarten and grammar school styles of physical education, and it will then be much easier for them to solve the athletic question. That question will never be satisfactorily solved till it is taken out of the hands of growing boys and professional or semi-professional athletic trainers.

It is the part of wisdom to recognize the fact that athletics and gymnastics are co-ordinate departments rather than hostile camps, and to strive manfully to define their limits and determine their relations and interrelations; inasmuch as one of the weightiest questions confronting us at this time is this: How shall athletics and gymnastics be justly united in the physical training of American youth of both sexes?

Neither our colleges nor our athletic organizations have earned the right to speak with authority on the question of what constitutes a well ordered and practicable system of physical training for elementary and secondary schools. Therefore the successful introduction of school gymnastics, since 1884, by the cities of Chicago, Kansas City, Cleveland, Denver, Indianapolis, and Boston, through the action of their respective school boards, has been chiefly due to the zeal and insistence of the advocates of the German and Swedish systems of gymnastics who were prepared to speak with knowledge and to act with intelligence. In every city named above, excepting Boston, German free and light gymnastics have been adopted, and the directors of physical education are graduates of the *Seminar* or normal school of the N. A. Turnerbund.

The promotion of gymnastic teaching in the public schools has ever been one of the cherished aims of the Turnerbund; but its efforts in that direction met with but little recognition or success prior to 1884. During the last fifteen years the Turnerbund has built up a flourishing system of gymnastic schools for children of school age; and the experience gained in these schools—which should not be confused with the Turnvereine—has at last been turned to some account by the school authorities of several cities where the voting strength of the Germans is great. At first sight, it seems a most extraordinary circumstance that, up to 1885, American educationists and system-makers should have ignored, almost entirely, the practical and efficient system of gymnastic instruction in vogue among the German-American Turners. But the truth is, the Turners were somewhat chauvinistic and inaccessible, while the educational world, in spite of occasional gusts of theoretical enthusiasm, was really apathetic and incurious with regard to the practical side of physical education. Since 1884, at about which time the Turnerbund first made a course in English an obligatory part of its *Seminar* curriculum, the policy of the Turners has become more liberal and their influence and success correspondingly greater.

Unlike their Teutonic kindred, the Scandinavians of this country have made no general or effective propaganda for their national gymnastics. The rise of Swedish pedagogical gymnastics within the last five years has been due chiefly to American initiative and endeavor. The appointment in 1874 of a Swedish teacher for three months' service in the Girls' High School of Boston seems to have been a fortuitous circumstance. Nearly ten years ago Mr. Wilson, the superintendent of schools in Washington, D. C., organized teachers' classes in Swedish gymnastics under the charge of Mr. Hartvig Nissen, who in 1886-1887 gave instruction, with good success, in Swedish "Free-standing movements" in the Johns Hopkins University Gymnasium, of which I was then director. Owing to the lack of support by those in authority these experiments proved abortive.

The gymnasium of the Woman's College of Baltimore, which was opened in 1888-1889, and is in some respects without a rival in the country, was fitted with Swedish apparatus at the outset, and has always been managed in strict accordance with Swedish principles, the class-instruction being intrusted to graduates of the Royal Central Gymnastic Institute only. This was the first successful experiment to adopt Swedish methods on a large scale in the physical education of American youth. The gymnasium of the Bryn Mawr School for Girls, also in Baltimore, opened in 1890, likewise has a Swedish teacher for Swedish work.

But Boston has earned the right to be considered the most influential center, in America, of the movement for promoting Swedish educational gymnastics. This result, which has been brought about within the last three years, is primarily due to the wisdom, generosity, and public spirit of Mrs. Mary Hemenway, and secondarily to the adoption of the Ling gymnastics for the public schools by the Boston school board, in June, 1890.

The establishment, by Mrs. Hemenway, of the Boston Normal School of Gymnastics, which already stands in the forefront among similar schools in the country, is an event of capital importance in the history of physical training in America, and may well be ranked beside the gift, to Harvard University, of the Hemenway Gymnasium by Mr. Augustus Hemenway, her son.

Considered as a whole, the history of physical training, in America, has not been a brilliant one, and physical education is not only less advanced here than it is abroad, but it has not even kept pace with the progress made by most other departments of education at home. Progress in our cause has been materially impeded by the prepossessions and prejudices of the teaching class, which, like the general public, is still largely ruled by ancient and traditional conceptions of mind and body, and has so feeble a comprehension of the new physiology and the new psychology that it is unprepared to acknowledge the just claims of physical education. Progress there has been since 1825, but for the most part it has been sporadic, fitful, and retarded. Too often the experiments, in our field of endeavor, have been characterized by furor, hurry, and failure. He would be a bold man who should venture to predict, in the face of past events and present tendencies, that even the most hopeful experiments of the last ten years will not sink out of sight or lose their identity within the next decade. We are still prone to rash experiment and to uncritical imitation. It is in the comparatively rude and primitive field of athletics that our greatest triumphs have been won. Our originality has been chiefly shown in the improvement of buildings and the invention of apparatus. In the field of superior education, the interest of faculties and trustees in physical training is most usually manifested by costly offerings of buildings or other plant to the unappeasable "animal spirits" of their students and younger alumni. In the field of elementary education, though cheapness is a *sine qua non,* we have succeeded in initiating a number of tentative schemes, a few of which are decidedly promising. In the professional training of the teaching class, bodily training is commonly considered superfluous; and it is only here and there that public normal schools have taken any measures to provide for it. A large proportion of those who are rushing forward to fill the role of apostles and teachers of physical education are self-educated or insufficiently trained.

Since physical training, on its theoretical side, belongs to a class of questions that fascinate doctrinaires and dabblers, it has suffered much at the hands of its vociferous friends. It bodes but little good to the immediate future of our cause that a disproportionate number of those who offer themselves as recruits are women—with bees in their bonnets. Summer schools, Chautauqua methods, and crusades for compulsory legislation are ill calculated to correct this tendency. Agitation, discussion, imitative and uncertain experiment, have been the dominant factors in the growth of the American physical education movement hitherto. We cannot pass to the stage of constructive development, unless accurate knowledge, clear ideas, definite aims, thorough training, and the capacity for sustained effort shall become much more general within our ranks and among our allies than is yet the case.

But our prospect is not wholly dark. I am constrained to believe that there are gleams of promise in the sky. It is a significant and encouraging fact that the question of bodily training is like Banquo's ghost, and will not down. In one form or another it rises and shall rise before every generation of civilized men. For us and our successors it has assumed portentous proportions, by reason of the untoward influences of city life upon the rising generation. Never before have the teachings of medical science been so clear and authoritative as they are to-day regarding the necessity and the means of securing and conserving the health of the student class. Physiology and psychology have been revolutionized within sixty years, and the critics of our educational aims and methods are beginning to use the weapons thus furnished to their hands. The existing systems of physical education and "culture" are largely empirical in their nature; but the time is at hand when they shall be subjected to the scrutiny and tests of disinterested scientists and shall have judgment passed upon them by men who are able to distinguish between claims and proof, between shadow and substance. Our present fashion of lauding apparatus and of multiplying gymnasia, club houses, and grounds is, after all, somewhat of a blessing in disguise, as it tends to force the question as to the real purpose of such appliances and the best means of securing their proper use. That our educational authorities as a class shall continue much longer both deaf and blind to the plain teachings of science and experience as to the nature, scope, and legitimate results of physical education, seems improbable. To my mind, the most hopeful and distinctive characteristic of the present diversified and expanding interest in physical training is found in the growing conviction that trained intelligence must be employed to supplement and re-enforce enlightened enthusiasm, and in the evident desire of a few benefactors and governors of educational foundations to provide ways and means for developing and seconding such intelligence. In various quarters, including two of our leading universities, attempts are in progress to embody that conviction and to realize that desire. These attempts betoken the dawning of a new day. Let us gird ourselves and go forth to meet it!

RUNNING

By Hans Ballin
Southern Illinois State Normal University

Running was much practiced by the ancient Greeks. It held at all times one of the foremost places in their gymnastics. It was part of their pentathlon and Plato was an ardent advocate of running. "Running was regarded as a criterion of athletic superiority, and the characteristic of Achilles in Homer was the quickness of his legs." The Romans had a quite different view of gymnastics from the Greeks; it was less educational with them, than for practical purposes. Running being of great avail in warfare, was at all times diligently fostered by them. Among the ancient Germans running held not a lesser place than with the Romans and Greeks. The sturdy teutonic warrior ran beside the swiftest horse, holding to its mane with one hand and carrying his weapons in the other. He pursued the wild animal and overtook it by the swiftness of his legs.

Present humanity holds quite a different attitude towards this most natural of all gymnastic exercises. Steam, electricity and the pneumatic tire not only take the place of rapid locomotion of the body by running, but also of the more moderate form, walking. Some pessimistic prognosticators describe with some credibility the man at the end of the coming century. His legs, after their descriptions, have a wonderful resemblance to those of the crane, stork and kindred birds. This would be pitiful, indeed. Not only the losing of a marked and beautifying attribute of the human form, but the so utterly giving up of one of the most healthgiving and healthpreserving exercises. That it be not thus, will be the office of the physical culturists who enjoy the exhilarating run. To know some of the nature and conditions of running will certainly be of interest.

Hans Ballin, "Running," *Mind and Body*, vol. I, no. 9, November 1894, pp. 1-3.

The swiftness of locomotion of our body by walking has a fixed limit by its very mechanism. This is partly due to the fact that the space which we span with one leg, while the other is vertical, limits a step to half the space both legs are capable of spanning. To this circumstance is due in part that the number of steps in walking in a given time cannot exceed the number of pendulum motions which the leg could execute in the same time, thereby limiting mechanically the duration of steps to half the pendulous swinging of the leg. Running, however, is quite a different method of locomotion. Its velocity is not bounded by this law. Running is a method of moving the body by the extension power of the legs. Neither the number nor the size of steps is limited by the same law as in walking. The main object of running is the attaining of a greater velocity of locomotion than can be accomplished in walking. This does not suggest that running necessarily involves a greater speed than walking. One may run and still not move any faster than in quick walking.

This main object in running, velocity, is accomplished in flitting the body with each step momentarily in the air by giving it a thrusting motion. During this short period both legs are suspended from the trunk, fleeting with it and each step may thus become larger than the span-width of the legs permits in walking. Children make use of the allotted time of the fleeting body when skipping the rope. In running the extension power of the legs has greater scope than in walking as it is voluntary how far the body shall be moved until one leg is to reach the ground. The body and legs fly and rest alternately and this permits a larger number of steps in a given time than in walking. In both kinds of locomotion, the leg which leaves the ground last must swing forward so far as to permit the support of the trunk vertically on the head of the femur. In the swiftest running or walking the leg swings thus far, but no farther. If the leg performs this motion by its own gravity, it requires a fixed time for it, which is the limit of a step's duration in walking. In running the same time is required. Nevertheless is the duration of the steps in running of shorter time, because a part of the swinging of the leg has been performed in the preceding step. This is the peculiarity of running which distinguishes it from walking. In running a man flies periodically in the air. Both legs execute simultaneously a part of their pendulous motion, the leg which is to be placed on the ground presently, as well as the one which will touch the ground at the end of the next step. The latter leg, having performed at the beginning of the next step a part of its necessary course and continuing to do so in the whole duration of it, does this by making the time of its swinging greater than the time of this step. Therefor, is the duration of a step in running always smaller, than in walking and never greater than half the duration of the swinging of the legs. In walking both legs never swing at the same time. A leg begins and ends its swinging during the same step which it just then executes. It rests on the ground while the other leg performs the next step. In walking, each step must last as long as is necessary for the stepping leg to begin the execution of its swinging, till the requisite moment that it steps down again. In slow walking each step must even last longer, for there is a period in this kind of movement when both legs are on the ground at the same time.

Experience has proved the above. At different velocity, measurements have shown that one makes in running steps as large again as in walking and that the number of steps in running and walking in the same time is in the average as two to three. This is conducive to the fact that man can cover approximately threefold the space in the same time by running as by walking. The speed that he attains is very great and may be six to seven meters in a second.

Wilhelm Weber who was professor in Göttingen and his brother Eduard Weber who was prosector in Leipzig, have given us the most elaborate investigations on the mechanism of running and walking. Their work has been fundamental in all later researches on this subject. They also give some accurate data regarding the speed in a second relative to the duration of a step and the length of each step.

Duration of step.	Length of step.	Speed in a second.
0.326 seconds.	0.934 meters.	2.862 meters.
0.301 "	1.209 "	4.021 "
0.268 "	1.542 "	5.745 "
0.247 "	1.753 "	6.66 "

If man was able to continue to run at the same speed he would cover a geographical mile, or four and six-tenths. English miles, in eighteen minutes. The best trained runner, however, can cover only a short distance at his utmost speed. This is observed in all exercises of human effort. The velocity decreases gradually after a certain time. An exception to this rule can only be observed in distances less than about 100 meters. This distance can be run in about 10 seconds. The following table best illustrates the above. It gives the best records made by experts on English and American race-tracks.

Highest Record.			Average Speed.
45.7 m.	in	5.5 seconds.	100 m. in 12.0 seconds.
68.5 "	"	7.75 "	" " " 11.3 "
91.4 "	"	9.25 "	" " " 10.12 "
201.0 "	"	22.5 "	" " " 11.19 "
402.0 "	"	48.5 "	" " " 11.5 "
804.0 "	"	1 min. 53.5 seconds.	" " " 12.0 "
1609.0 "	"	4 " 16.2 "	" " " 14.0 "
3218.0 "	"	9 " 11.5 "	" " " 15.9 "
6436.0 "	"	19 " 36.0 "	" " " 17.1 "
12872.0 "	"	40 " 20.0 "	" " " 18.2 "
25744.0 "	"	1 hr. 28 min. 6.0 sec.	" " " 22.8 "

We learn from this table that it takes a man twice the time to cover a geographical mile than it would if he could continue running at the same velocity he attains in a short distance.

REACTION-TIME AND TIME-MEMORY IN GYMNASTIC WORK

E. W. Scripture, Ph.D. (Leipsic)
Yale University

(Owing to the illness of Dr. Scripture, the experiments here described were performed by Dr. C. B. Bliss, Yale University.)

The objects of gymnastic work are, or should be, two: (1) Bodily health and development; (2) mental development and health. In actual gymnasium work the latter remains practically unrecognized. The general statement, that gymnastic work benefits the will and the moral character, is too vague to be of any practical worth. Modern science and modern psychology demand that definite facts and figures shall be given.

You do not say in an off-hand manner that exercise is good for the health or develops the body in a general way. Quite the contrary—you measure the chest and the muscles, you carefully notice any spinal curvature, any defects of bodily development; then you prescribe appropriate exercises. That is the only correct way of managing gymnastic work, and is the way you ought to do in psychological matters, also; you should test and measure the mental powers of your subject and prescribe just the appropriate kind of exercise to correct his mental faults, to develop the weak parts and to maintain a sound mind in a sound body. You ought to know just as much about the mental processes involved in gymnastic training as about the names and sizes of the different muscles. Nevertheless, no one has yet investigated the influence of various exercises on the various mental processes; no one has even pointed out how the mental acts and conditions of persons in training differ from those of other persons. The reason for this is clear. Although the two branches of the new psychology, experimental and clinical psychology, have abundance of methods and material which can be applied to gymnastic work, yet there is no teacher of physical

E. W. Scripture, "Reaction-Time and Time-Memory in Gymnastic Work," *Proceedings of the American Association for the Advancement of Physical Education*, Ninth Annual Meeting, no. 2, 1894, pp. 44-49.

training, I think, who has ever entered the psychological laboratory to learn its methods and applications.

You might ask me why we psychologists do not work out the psychology of exercise. I must answer that we are far too busy investigating the fundamental laws of mental life to have any time to spend on practical applications. We are scientists, not technologists, and our duty ends when we have invented methods and discovered facts. It is your business, as practical people, to take up the matter where we leave it; we will furnish the rough metal, but you must shape it for practical service. To illustrate this I shall here not attempt to go over a multitude of applications, but will choose only two factors of mental life and will try to show how they are or may be developed by gymnastic work. These are reaction-time and time-memory.

(1) By reaction-time we mean the time that actually elapses between a signal to act and the execution of the act. I will show you an example of reaction-time as exhibited by persons starting for a race. This has never before been measured; we have been able to do so by the invention of an electric-contact for the starter's pistol and a break-contact for the runner.

The end of the barrel of the pistol with contact is shown in Figure 1.

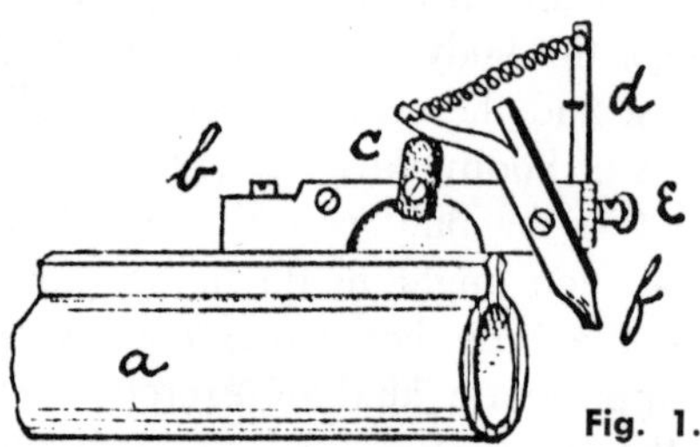

Fig. 1.

The blast from the pistol moves the small fan projecting down near, but not in front of, the mouth. A spring makes it fly back immediately. This interrupts an electric circuit for a moment.

The runner's key is shown in Figure 2.

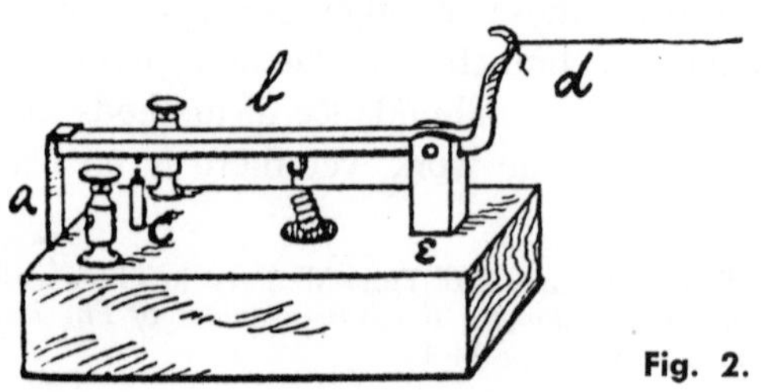

Fig. 2.

A thread is stretched from the hook of the key to a pin in the clothes of the runner. When the thread is pulled, the circuit is broken.

There are various methods of measuring small intervals of time. The one we generally use is accurate to 0.001 of a second, and gives us less labor than any other equally accurate method. Simpler and less accurate methods can be readily substituted.

Our method is to have a surface of smoked paper on a revolving cylinder passing under a metal point vibrating 100 times per second. The pistol and the key are arranged electrically so that whenever the circuit is broken a spark flies off the metal point to the drum. The vibrations of the point make a wavy time-line on the drum, and the sparks put dots on it. The number of waves and tenths of a wave between the two dots will give the elapsed time.

To perform the experiment the runner is placed at "set" and the pistol is fired; the starting of the runner jerks and breaks the thread. The firing of the pistol breaks contact for an instant and makes a dot; the jerking of the key likewise makes a dot. The number of tenths of a wave between the two give the elapsed time in thousandths of a second.

No experiments having been made, I cannot give you any definite results beyond the fact the runner loses from 0.1 to 0.5 of a second on account of his reaction-time. Persons with long reaction-time cannot succeed as sprinters. Moreover, we know from analogous cases that it makes a difference whether the person is attending to, or thinking of, the expected sound or his legs. To attend to the wrong one may mean loss of the race. I might also point out that loud sounds, such as a pistol shot, lengthen a person's reaction-time. All cases of response to a signal are cases of reaction-time. Simple reaction-time is to a great degree a psychological phenomenon depending on mental conditions that have been extensively investigated in the laboratory.

Let us turn to a more complicated form of reaction involving two additional processes, discrimination and choice. I have here (Fig. 3) an arrangement for giving two different signals, to which the person

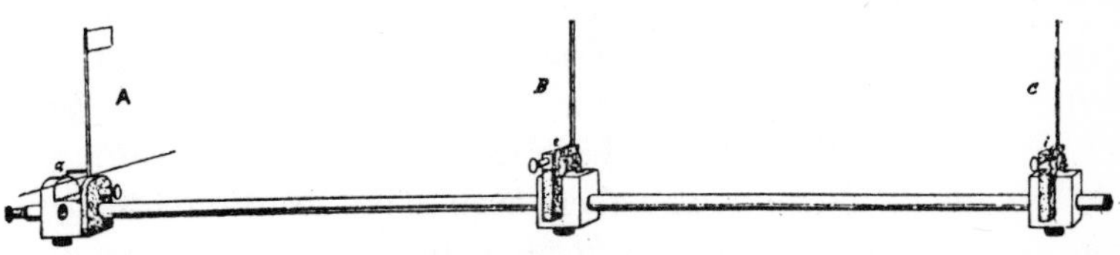

Fig. 3.

is to react. For example, I place a pugilist with his fist just touching the vertical rod *C*. When the signal *A* moves, he is to strike a blow. The moving of *A* makes a record and the moving of *C* makes a record; the time between the two records gives the simple reaction-time as before. Now I give him a more difficult problem. When the signal *A* moves to the right he is to strike a blow; when to the left he is not to move. He thus has to be sure of what he sees and has to choose between moving and not moving. His reaction-time will be found to be much lengthened. If it is desired to know just how much of the whole time is taken by the mental processes of discrimination and choice, the result for simple reaction-time is subtracted from the complex time; the remainder will be due to these two processes. If a fencer place his foil against the rod, his discrimination and choice-time can likewise be measured. You yourselves can furnish countless examples where you discriminate, choose and act; each of these processes takes more or less time.

I will mention that a second rod *B* can be placed at any desired distance from *C* in order to measure the rapidity of the blow or the lunge after it has once started. I might go on to more complicated forms or might show other means of measurement. But if you will agree with me that the proper cultivation of quick and accurate discrimination and quick and certain choice are probably the most vital points in the mental life of a man,—points on which have hung defeat or victory of an army as depending on its general, the safety of a ship on its captain, the fall of a ministry on the leader of the opposition, or the winning of a foot-ball game by the skill of the eleven,—I shall not need to urge you to have a little more psychology in the gymnasium.

As no one else pays any attention to the cultivation of a rapid and reliable reaction-time, the task of developing a youth in this respect falls into your hands. By simple methods you can determine which kind of reaction, muscular or sensory, needs cultivating. If the youth has a long, simple reaction-time, you can select games and exercises that will make it shorter. If his discrimination and choice are too slow you can set him to boxing or playing tennis.

(2) Time-memory, or the accuracy with which we can remember intervals of time, forms, in connection with reaction-time, the basis of rhythmic action. Rhythmic action is keeping time to some repeated sound or sight. If we actually wait till the sound be heard we are simply reacting; in such a case there would be no difference between regular and irregular sounds. In keeping time, however, we anticipate the moment the sound is to occur and generally plan the act to

occur at the moment of the sound. We cannot keep time to irregular sounds, but with regular sounds we are sometimes ahead, sometimes correct and sometimes behind.

Let us see how we can measure a person's regularity and accuracy in keeping time with his foot to a sound. I have here a specially made stop-watch which not only indicates fifths of a second, but can also be made to write seconds or fifths of a second on the smoked paper of a revolving cylinder, and can further be made to break an electric current at seconds or fifths. An ordinary telegraph-sounder is connected electrically with the stop-watch, so that a sharp click is heard at every beat. An electric contact is placed on the heel of the person, and is so arranged (in our method) as to make a spark on the drum whenever the heel hits the floor. The watch is set to beat seconds. At each beat a click is heard and a mark is made on the drum. The person keeping time with his heel makes sparks that are supposed to coincide with the sounds. The record on the drum shows you that they do not coincide, and, moreover, that each person has his own peculiar fault.

By putting the contact on the toe of the shoe and letting the watch beat fifths of a second, the rhythmic time of running can be also investigated.

By running the current through a pair of iron dumb-bells the accuracy and regularity of the person can be tested with front and back movements, the rataplan, etc.

With a little ingenuity such connections could be made with all gymnastic apparatus with which regular movements are to be made, e. g., Indian clubs, wands, oars in the practice tank or in the shell, etc.

Defective time-memory and consequently irregular or inaccurate or irregular-inaccurate rhythmic action are exceedingly common. Proper exercises and games can, however, greatly improve most cases.

I have thus called your attention to two out of the countless number of mental processes that enter into gymnastic exercise and might be developed or corrected in the gymnasium. In conclusion, let me impress upon you the fact that the most valuable part of a man's mental development comes not from schoolrooms and colleges, from geography and Latin, but from his games and plays as a child and from his gymnastic training and sports as a youth. To have a sound mind it is not sufficient to have a sound body; the mind itself must be attended to. To the Greek the gymnasium was the central point of a man's life, and I sincerely hope that with a broadened conception of the scope of a gymnasium our youth will obtain in it the full *mental, manly* training that now finds no place in school or college.

SOME RELATIONS BETWEEN PHYSICAL AND MENTAL TRAINING

G. Stanley Hall, Ph.D., LL.D.

(This was delivered without notes, and is taken from the stenographer's report.)

My impression is this: that intellectual development ought always to be based upon physical, and that it is liable to be abnormal or unhealthy unless it is. In fact, this has become almost a cardinal axiom with me. In the first place, we ought always to give only one subject precedence to physical training, as it is generally understood, and that is the matter of regimen. We are very prone to forget that there is a nutritive and trophic background to every function and activity of life. If the brain or muscles are imperfectly nourished, if we have not the power to convert food into blood, if we have not the power to convert it into not merely so-so, but tolerably good human meat, we have not any right to educate the brain very much, and there is disaster liable, if not inevitable, if we do.

The first thing, then, is digestion—those processes, so infinitely complex, by which food is transmuted into brain. There is a vast difference in the power of men and women to make that transmutation. We ought to think on the basis of the most perfect human tissue that digestive apparatus can produce; but when you see flabby muscles, and bad complexions, and the other signs of dyspepsia or imperfect nutrition, it is certain to infect the thought. There is not a man or woman who would not do more for science, for literature and everything that is good, if they could make better blood and better tissue, and I think physiological chemistry is coming to show that the difference in blood is very great, so that the first thing of all which gives us justification for intellectual and for athletic training, I believe, is a good digestion. Of course, we cannot have the best without exer-

G. Stanley Hall, "Some Relations Between Physical and Mental Training," *Proceedings of the American Association for the Advancement of Physical Education,* Ninth Annual Meeting, no. 2, 1894, pp. 30-37.

cise, but what I am attempting to assert is, that digestion must be put in the foreground and other things subordinated, as means, until that is secured.

I do not believe it is possible to lay too great stress upon this. We know that a great majority of nervous diseases, and a very large number of other diseases that are not known to be of neural origin, begin in imperfect nutrition. A great many begin in that kind of nutrition that affects chiefly the brain. There is every reason to believe that the molecule of the brain and nervous tissues raises matter to the very highest complexity of which it is capable of being raised; and God and nature designed that our thinking should be done upon that platform. That is the physical basis of science and literature, the highest degree of nutrition. Therefore, the regimen of sleep and food,—plain food, abundance of sleep, and a wholesome and unconstraining regimen, which is so difficult to achieve in this country, where everything is always fiddling on the nerves, where our cities are getting to be biological furnaces that burn us out to the socket,—that is the first postulate; and when you come to the harvest home of this great cause of physical education, that is to say, when the final verdict of the race is made up to date, I believe that the basis upon which judgment will be pronounced will be the standpoint of regimen.

Does physical training tend to make us habitually take more wholesome food, sleep better, and perform these other functions that may, perhaps, be called regimen, as distinct from physical training? That is the question. A distinguished doctor said a little while ago that if it was his duty to pick out the wife of the future king of England, he would first ask what she ate, what her habitual diet was, whether wholesome or fantastic, of the sweetmeat order, that laid great stress upon desserts; second, he would ask whether she slept well nights, and he would be very glad if she took a wholesome amount of physical exercise; but if all these were secured he would thank God for all other extras.

Of course physical exercise addresses itself to the great muscle tissues which make up half the average adult male body, I suppose, by weight; their culture is very important. The muscles have done all man's work in the world. They are especially the organs of will. You cannot have a firm will without firm muscles; and there is nothing so dangerous for morals as to have the gap between knowing what is right and proper and healthy and the doing of it, yawn; and it always yawns if the muscles get weak. If they are flabby it is a great deal harder to do things. I believe that the temptations that assail young people nowadays are, to quite an extent, those that would not overcome them if their muscles were strong. They are of that insidious, corroding, undermining kind that are, somehow or other, so prone to creep in as the contractile tissues become relaxed and habitually flabby. So that I should place, as the second, muscle habits, because that is another criterion by which a nation is judged, in the long view. Those nations persist, survive, that have good muscle habits that exercise in a proper and normal way.

There is one subject that is fundamental, and yet often ignored. One of the most important bases for intellectual training is the muscle habits, because they give us what I call rhythm. Rhythm is a subject which it is hard to discuss, and one of the most hopeful signs of the laboratory has been that we have been able to control its complicated conditions to some extent and experiment upon it. It is an old saying, that the man who writes the songs for a nation does more for it than he who writes the laws. Plato's dictum was, that if he had any of these Lydian poets,—and if he lived now he would have said these writers of cheap opera music, that is exciting, stimulating,—he would crown them with fillets of wool and lead them to the boundary of his ideal republic and tell them not to come back. He would cultivate the Doric hymns, and perhaps the Phrygian hymns, as being perhaps more allied to the mood of the gymnasium.

See how one moves, walks and talks, and you will see a great deal about him. The habitual rhythm of motion, I believe, is fundamental for full intellectual development. I do not believe it is easy to overestimate the importance of it. There is a profound and close relationship between our muscle habits in that respect and thinking. Who of you would ever expect to see one of those light young fellows that you see on a chilly morning always standing on the street corners, perhaps doubly shuffling, with a large idea in his head? Take the girls who love a neurotic machine, which, I have been told, in Germany has been banished from the few retreats for insane patients in which it ever found entrance,—the American rocking-chair,—the instrument that increases that tendency that nervous people always have when they get fidgety to move about, to get an accelerated rhythm. I wonder how much of a revolution it would make if we could banish the rocking-chair from America? One distinguished alienist says the American rocking-chair is the cause of Americanitis. We know, now, enough about the development of children and adolescents to know that the powers of activity are always developed before the powers of control. The powers of reflex action, of responding to things, come first, and later comes the power to resist this tendency—the power to inhibit, as we say. First, the powers that are spontaneous, then the power to control and rest. A great many people live and die undeveloped. They have no control; the last, highest story has not been put on. They have not, you may say figuratively, that last layer of the brain where association, which connects one part with another, crosses, and that is a thing of very slow rhythm. We are coming to believe now, in the study of physiological psychology, and it is no materialistic notion of the specialists, that, besides all its other functions, that serves a very important physiological function in this: it mediates in the brain; it is that which acts on fibers that have been called, perhaps prematurely, the association fibers, the distributers of energy in the brain. There are some parts of the brain that are liable to suffer from overpressure—there is more energy generated than they use. There are other parts of the brain, where men spend all their time doing some little thing, that suffer and decay; and it is, therefore, a point just as important for the economy of the brain that there should be thinking power in it as that there should be commercial exchange, clearing houses. This function mediates between the points of the brain that are overcharged with energy and those which are undercharged. It allows us to draw upon our resources; and if intellectual discipline had no other functions, education would be worth all it costs, and more too, because it is the generalizing function—it communicates between parts of the brain. Jean Paul Richter said he had seen a great many men who had in their brain charcoal, and saltpeter, and sulphur, which are the three ingredients of gunpowder, but they never made an atom of gunpowder in their lives, because these elements never got together—they had not been associated.

This is an aspect of things from which we are judging intellectual training, from your standpoint, the standpoint of athletics. Possibly a man who can do a little thinking can summon his physical and mental powers more readily, bring himself to a slow, long, hard, concentrative focus, so that all the resources in his brain can be heard from. He will not always suffer from after-thought, as some people do, but will bring all of himself to bear upon all things. It seems to me that the old Turner adage, "frisch, frei, fröhlich, fromm," points in that direction. Your ideal athlete is a man of heartiness and genuineness, with good, earnest, serious, large, steady thoughts.

We are finding from very careful study made this year on school children, one very important thing, and that is this: that physical training ought to be based on the child, like everything else. We have tried hundreds of school children, to have them make simple movements with the shoulders, hands, arms, fingers, and the result, I think you will all see when it is published, is amazing with regard to the inability of children. Previous child studies have shown an amazing amount of ignorance; this showed inability to make simple common movements, on the part of the children, from the time they enter school on. In more than sixty or seventy movements, we took the children and subjected them, with the utmost caution, to eliminate all sources of error that we were able, to these tests, and are now figuring up the results, and this in general appears very distinctly: that the power to move the hand well comes late. They can move the trunk, shoulders, hips, legs, but the power to make fine movements with the hand comes much later. And another result is this: that the child, in growing, passes through almost all the stages of motor diseases. It has been said, and it is pretty well accepted now among those who study from the physiological standpoint, that the child suffers all forms of speech diseases in learning to speak. But it seems also true that a child shows symptoms of about all the motor diseases in learning to walk and use its hands and arms. We are amazed to find that if we diagnosed severely we could convict almost every child, of some paretic or motor disorder, which, of course, most outgrow without a trace. That shows how very important motor education is in the schools, and we must go slowly.

And not only that, but the last thought is this: we must not invert the order of nature. The great crime of wrong education, the danger into which it is always falling at every point, cannot be better designated than by the word precocity. We are always inverting growth and letting children begin where adults ought to begin, and working down, instead of working the other way. I read lately that a committee of the British Association for the Advancement of Science found the science teaching was decreasing in the schools. Why, nobody knew; nobody knows now. But I believe one reason for it is this: that we begin with too modern methods. The country child not only has a totally different motor habit from the city child,—the city person's motion is limited at every point,—but the city child cannot have a complete physical development; it cannot come to full maturity. Perhaps that is strong language, but it cannot perhaps be put too strongly as a mere exclamation point to call attention to the subject. The city child to-day is not only totally different in all its motor habits from the country child, but the city child is liable always to imperfect muscular development, and therefore to precocity. The city child has no chance to get at nature, and therefore science, which deals with nature, he approaches in an abnormal, rather inverted way. Take a child and give him a microscope when he gets into the high school or college; is not that an inversion of the natural order of things? He ought to have been introduced to nature in the way the old naturalists were introduced. He does not know nature at first hand, he has not been brought up close to it, he has not served an apprenticeship to that old-fashioned paganism, with a little fetichism in it, that the race has passed through, and which the child ought to pass through. If you do not give a child an experience of paganism that way you are building your Christian character on sand; and just so, if you do not give a child a basis for science in free contact with nature, but introduce him to science through the microscope or through any technique of the laboratory, he cannot have a deep, strong love of nature. We tested many years ago Boston children on entering school. I think it was 23 per cent. of the children had never seen growing wheat or any of the cereals, didn't know where they came from. I think it was something like 52 per cent. didn't know what was inside of them, whether bone or stick. A great many had never seen a robin, never seen a blue-bird; and I think it was 71 per cent. of these six-year-old Boston children that didn't know beans, even in Boston. Now what can you expect of a love of science built without a foundation? There must be some acquaintance with nature first, and you cannot get acquaintance with nature sitting down; you have got to get out of doors. We must bring children in contact with nature, and that works for physical development.

Now I must add one more thought, and it is this: I spoke of rhythm; perhaps I can finish what I began to say about it. Rhythm underlies poetry, music, our gait, everything. There is in man what is called a psychic constant; for instance, in most it is about .76 of a second, regular time; it varies a little with different people. That psychic constant is the time toward which we approximate if we close the eyes and attempt to beat time. That this "leg-time" is the constant toward which one gravitates, that is shown by a great many experiments. The power of rhythm and its effect upon the genesis of Americanitis is shown in this: that if you accelerate that rhythm you produce a state of tension; if you retard it you produce a state of rest. What mother would ever think of putting her child to sleep by patting its shoulder in this way? (indicating irregular, accelerated motion). On the contrary, the motion grows slower and slower, and lighter and lighter. I am told it is now being introduced into neurasthenic retreats. Try it sometime when you are sleepless.

Another thing laboratory experiments show: let a drop of water fall on your hand, or any other part of your body once, two seconds, three seconds even; you will be surprised to find what an effect it has; nobody can stand it very long. It has the power that repeated stimuli always have; it exhausts to the very last degree. Now, wherever we can substitute a more moderate and a stronger movement for a more rapid and lighter, I think we are doing a good thing. What is the matter with the kindergarten? One thing is this: they illustrate the same precocity, the children handle little toothpicks, and very small things that require finger movements. If they would deal with objects twenty-five times as large and heavy, if they would work with rods laid a foot long, so that it would throw the strain from the fine muscles back to the shoulder muscles,—for we know that the cells connected with them have been traced directly to the large fundamental muscles, which develop first,—they would throw the strain where it belongs. Everything depends on exercising the trunk, which gives poise and motion, and wherever you can substitute a more deliberate motion or rhythm of work and speech you are substituting a healthy for a morbid nervous diathesis. A person whose rhythm is established, and at a rate which gives poise, can have large ideas, and others cannot. The power of it is everything. I think if we had the assembly of our daily efforts registered and recorded we should see what has been shown in the study of the daily rhythm of children of late—that they accelerate as the day advances, that the movements are likely to be a little faster when they begin to be a little tired. In order, therefore, to be earnest and serious the muscle habits must have a deliberate rhythm and forceful rhythm. There has been a careful study of the hand in the last year, which shows that range of motion and intensity are inversely to each other. The main thing is this: that all thought, I will not say is, but is connected with, the innervation of muscles. Many go so far as to say that there is no thought possible without a corresponding change in muscle tension. This is, as everybody knows, the basis of these slight movements that constitute mind reading, which is really muscle reading. That shows us that the two are connected; localization shows the same thing. So we are educating the brain when we educate the muscles.

A complete system of education will begin with regimen and digestion, with the habits that give strength, and end with the education of those very slight, subtle, complicated movements which, I will not quite say constitute thought, but which it is a pre-requisite to teach first, which must be taught upon the basis of the solid, all-round education of that half of the body which is made up of muscle tissue.

HISTORY OF ANTHROPOMETRY

Jay W. Seaver

There can be no study of more interest than that which pertains to human life and development. It is the center around which all thought and all energy crystallizes. Youthful ambition, parental solicitude and mature counsel all aim at the elevation of life to a higher standard and more complete form; the child is to be better than the parent, the race is to evolve toward perfection.

The highest ideal of art has been to portray life in its most perfect form, whatever may have been the vehicle of the thought: stone, color, tone or word. The outward form and its action has also become the test of the inward man; the thoughts, the impulses, the feelings, are recognized as having a physical basis that can be measured in some way and thus serve as a partial guide to the possibilities and probabilities of the future. Psychology looks for its material in the physical data that can be gathered, and no longer has its roots in speculation and personal opinion but in physiology. A determination of the law of physical growth for the human animal has done more to correct educational methods than any other influence in pedagogy. Keen observation had made great teachers before but their method was never reduced to law. The nearest approach to this was the establishment of the Kindergarten by Froebel. But even here the establishment of the fact of a normal development of the control of fundamental muscles before the accessory has introduced vast improvement into the method.

We must study then to "know ourselves" physically if we are to train ourselves into the highest type of mental development as well as into the perfection of health and bodily vigor. In studying the law of organic growth it became necessary to record in definite terms the

Jay W. Seaver, "History of Anthropometry," *Anthropometry and Physical Examination* (New Haven: O. A. Dorman, Co., 1896), pp. 7-16.

changes that characterized the various periods of life, and measurements of size and weight were made. Thus the knowledge of modern human proportions has been derived from the measurements of living persons of all ages and of both sexes. For this process Quetelet coined the apt word—Anthropometry.

In considering the science of anthropometry it may be worth our while to glance somewhat briefly at its history. It is old as compared with other sciences, but it was developed primarily for purposes of art, rather than for those of physiology or anthropology; and art, which is said to be "the daughter of the imagination," did not consider originally the true proportions of the human body, but tried to represent an ideal that corresponded closely to the modern conventionalized forms, or so-called fashion. We see this in Egyptian art, where both hands were made right, and where a peculiar facial type is given which certainly did not represent the ordinary beautiful face of the race, but an idealized face. The development of art called for a closer adherence to the normal type of body, and probably the greatest incentive to imitate life came through the Greek admiration for the athlete, it being a law that the successful competitor at the Olympic games should have his statue carved in marble. The influence of this custom undoubtedly modified Greek art favorably, and brought it to the highest standard that sculpture has ever attained. We know that certain artists, who were celebrated for the excellence of their work, left as their masterpieces statues that undoubtedly represent victors at these games. Polycleitos is said to have made five statues of victors at Olympia, and a head of Hera that was "like a verse from Homer."

The study of human proportions as related to art expression was carried to a high degree of perfection by Polycleitos, who, after mature study, sought to fashion a model that represented the ideal man. While this statue, called the Doryphoros or Spear Thrower, has been lost, undoubted copies of it in fair condition of preservation are extant.*

The Doryphoros, "*viriliter puer,*" was, in intent and by general consent, the representation of absolute perfection in human proportion. It was the canon followed by succeeding schools in portraying the highly developed figures while the companion figure, the Diadoumenos, "*molliter juvenis,*" constructed on the same proportions of length became the model of younger types. As a result of his minute study of human proportions this artist left a large number of statues, all of which are considered by art critics to be of a high standard of excellence.

*See Reber's "History of Art," Waldstein's "Essays on the Art of Pheidias," Collignon's "Histoire de la Sculpture Grecque," and Sybel's "Weltgeschichte der Kunst."

The Roman sculptors to a certain extent followed the Greek canons, and at the same time developed original lines of thought in connection with human proportions. We do not know, however, that they derived these ideals from many measurements of proportion, but have reason to believe that they were the result of the study of graceful forms and of ripened judgment in regard to physical beauty. The table of proportions given by Vitruvius does not give evidence of actual measurements taken and compiled but he probably drew on older canons—the Egyptian or the Greek.

Among more modern artists the same effort to secure some law of proportion, that should apply to all artistic productions, has been made, and with comparatively little advance from ancient canons. The failure in these methods has been from the attempt to find some one part of the body that should be a common measure of all the other parts; as in the ancient Egyptian canon (Fig. 1), where the length of the middle finger was considered a common measure of all the other proportions, five fingers being the height of the knee, ten fingers the height of the pubic arch, eight fingers the length of the arm to the tip of the fingers, three fingers being the length of the head and neck, and the total height being nineteen fingers.

The physiologist Carus, of Dresden, conceived the vertebral column to be the unit of measure and this he divided into twenty-four parts, according to the number of vertebrae, assigning to each the same value, as in embryonic life.

The great German artist, Albert Dürer, of Nuremberg, worked on a canon of proportion, considering the total height to be unity. The length of foot was one-sixth of this total, the head one-seventh, the hand one-tenth, etc. Dürer made the ratio of height between men and women as 17 to 18, while among English people the ratio is as 12 to 13. This showed his method to be that of the artist rather than of the anthropologist. The artist Schadow of Berlin, saw the failure of Dürer's canon and drew up tables of proportions derived by averaging the measures of various models, carrying the investigation to the time of birth.

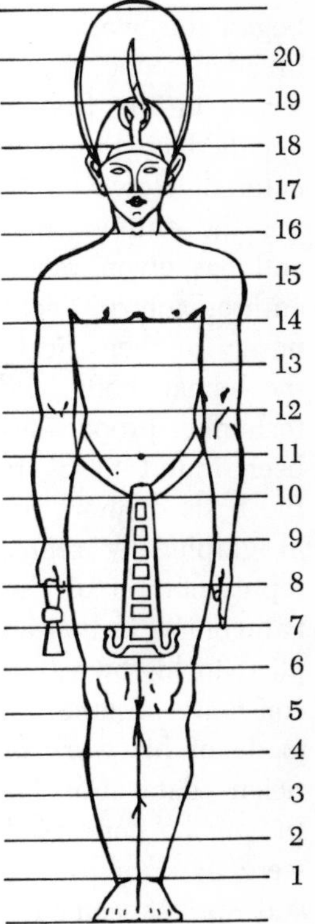

Fig. 1.

Later artists have in general endeavored to follow the classic canons or to educe a new modulus after the Egyptian type and perhaps the most successful effort toward this end has been that of Story, whose method is based on the mathematical relation of certain geometric figures.

In the early half of the present century the strong trend of study toward the *natural sciences* led to the more thorough investigation of the natural history of mankind, and we find that more or less valuable treatises were published on anthropology. This gave a new impulse to the study of human proportions, for in studying different races of men it was found that they had marked peculiarities of physique, as well as marked mental peculiarities and customs. In 1870 Quetelet, who was at this time director of the Royal Observatory at Brussels, and a leading mathematician of his day, conceived the idea of assisting anthropology in its classification of human races by the determination of their physical proportions, believing that each race had such peculiarities as should constantly serve as a means of identification. He began this work with much zeal, and soon found that it had a much broader scope than he anticipated when he began his research. He writes in the first chapter of his book on anthropometry that he is appalled by the magnitude of the field of research into which he has entered. However, being accustomed to deal with numbers, and having the enthusiasm of the true scientist, he proceeded in his work, and has given valuable material for all students of anthropology and anthropometry since his day. He was the first investigator to apply purely mathematical methods in determining the physical constants of the human body, and he demonstrated the "law of chance" as applied to human proportions. This so-called law of chance, or probability, has been found to be true in its general application. It has been made the basis of more recent investigations, and has been specially applied in graphically representing the racial type; as, for instance, in the representation of the difference between tall and short races, as the Patagonian Indian and the Chinese. After establishing this law as applied to his own countrymen, he endeavored to determine the physical constants of other races, and perhaps the only criticism that can be made of his work is that he sometimes drew conclusions from insufficient data. For instance, in determining the size of the American Indian, he concluded from the measurement of a few specimens that were on exhibition in Brussels that the Indian is of excessive height and size as compared with the ordinary European—which conclusion has been found by more recent investigators to be not in accordance with the facts. He did determine the fact that various races follow special laws in their growth and development, as do the various organs, and the discovery of this fact has led to important results, not only in anthropology but in physiology, as we find that those types having comparatively long trunks and short limbs possess higher resisting power than the opposite types. We also find that the size of certain physical organs, like the chest, has a direct relation to the working power of the individual when considered as a machine. The relation of total size to the respiratory power is an important physiological factor, as is also the relative length of different levers when the adaptability of the individual for special occupations is considered. It may be said that in more recent years the incentive to anthropometrical investigation has not lain in artistic or anthropological lines, but in pedagogical, psychological and hygienic.

By far the greater part of anthropometrical work that has been done in the last twenty-five years has been done in connection with educational institutions and for educational purposes, and it may be truly said to-day that the investigators who are most active are the ones connected with departments of psychological study. The reason for this may be clearly seen in the fact that the racial type having been considered, the study of the individual for the sake of bringing him up to a high degree of excellence becomes the next important duty of the educator. In this country especially it may be said that the work has tended in this particular line, while in England the research has been devoted to such departments as tend to the determination of general anthropological laws. In 1884 Francis Galton established in connection with the Health Exposition of London a bureau of anthropometry, for the purpose of gathering material that should determine the physical constants of English men and women, and serve as a check on work done before on the Continent, and that might possibly lead to the discovery of new laws. A preparation for this work had been made by Charles Roberts of London when, in 1878, as secretary of the British Association for the Advancement of Science, he published the report of the Committee on Anthropometry, and presented some interesting material gathered by himself. The material gathered by Mr. Galton was extensive and was studied by a new method, which has been quite generally adopted during the last fifteen years and which has a high utility in showing the distribution of proportions. His plan, in brief, was to group all the measurements of any particular item, as height or weight, into percentile groups, or into such groups as could be represented by integral parts of one hundred. These measurements being grouped in this particular way made a determination of the mean easy (*l'homme moyen de Quetelet*), and showed that the proportions, when so grouped, followed Quetelet's binomial law of chance. This method enabled him to say of any given individual that he excelled a certain percentage of other persons, or that he was excelled by such a percentage of individuals in any item recorded. This, therefore, became a valuable method of graphically representing the size of any person, for, after having determined the distribution of the sizes of any particular item, the position of the individual in this distribution was easily determined. If, then, we group all the items of measurement of a similar class of persons, according to the percentile form, and have a table prepared that shows this distribution, we have an easy form of graphic representation. This method has been followed out most completely in this country as applied to the student classes of the community, no one as yet having undertaken the general measurements planned by Galton in England. The nearest approach to this English standard for mature individuals is probably found in Gould's Sanitary Commission Memoirs, gathered from recruits who were examined during the Civil War. This memoir is a fairly comprehensive study of the actual and relative proportions of over a million men between the ages of sixteen and forty-five years.

In our educational institutions we have largely followed the example set by Dr. Hitchcock of Amherst thirty-five years ago, in making a physical examination of the students who were admitted to the gymnasia connected with our colleges. In connection with this physical examination a measurement of some of the more important items has been made. This method has resulted so satisfactorily that it is now applied, not only to the students of the leading colleges and universities throughout the land, but in very many of the better class of secondary and private schools. This work has also been extended by the investigations of persons who have been interested in physiological or experimental psychology, and large numbers of school children of various ages have been measured and tested in order to determine, so far as possible, what relation might exist between physical condition and intellectual activities.

In this connection we must mention the very thorough study of the growth of American school children made by Dr. Bowditch in 1877. The result of his investigations determined for the first time the law of growth for Anglo-Saxon children between the ages of five and sixteen years. This investigation had been preceded by a somewhat similar one, made by Dr. Fahrner of Zurich, Switzerland,* al-

*Das Kind and der Schultisch.

though his results never received the attention accorded to the work of Dr. Bowditch, because that of the latter was far superior in accuracy and extent. Dr. Geo. W. Peckham of Milwaukee, Wis., in 1880-83, made a study of the growth of school children, and a like investigation has been made in 1892-93, by Dr. W. T. Porter, upon children in the public schools of St. Louis, Mo., which confirmed the conclusions of Dr. Bowditch and established several new facts pertaining to the physical and mental growth of children.

In 1893-4 Dr. E. M. Hartwell made a study of the relation of the nervous phenomenon of stuttering to growth and to the "specific intensity of life," among the school children of Boston.* The term specific intensity of life is used to express the ratio between the number of children living at any age and the number dying at that age. Incidentally he demonstrated the direct relation between the specific intensity of life and acceleration of growth.

The study of the nervous phenomena of school life and its relation to growth has been most thoroughly planned by President Hall of Clark University, and the results so far as published have given a basis for a critical discussion of pedagogical systems that is already bearing fruit. In the same field of inquiry are found some papers by Dr. E. W. Scripture† of Yale, and Dr. J. Allen Gilbert.‡

Dr. G. W. Fitz of Harvard has also called attention to some of the nerve reactions that help to declare the condition of a person,§ and has invented some instruments that record the time of reactions. In foreign countries the study of physical data obtained by anthropometric tests has been carried to a high degree of perfection along physiological lines. Axel Key of Sweden has studied the relation of growth to temperature and climate, as marked by the seasons of the year, and to the pubertal period. Bertillon and Demeny of France, Mosso and Livi of Italy, Schmidt and Voigt of Germany, and many others have made additions to our knowlege of the human body and its development. The problems of the future will lie in a determination of the influences affecting the neuro-muscular mechanism and its dominating center, the intellect; the exact values of heredity and nurture as the determining factors of a large part of life; and the evolving of a pedagogical system that shall train the young to the highest possibilities of their faculties.

*School Document, No. 8, 1894, Boston.
†Ninth Annual Report Am. Asso. for Adv. of Phys. Education.
‡Studies from the Yale Psychological Laboratory, Vol. II.
§Tenth Annual Report Am. Asso. for Adv. of Phys. Education.

VOLLEY BALL

During the past winter Mr. W. G. Morgan of Holyoke, Mass., has developed a game in his gymnasium which is called Volley Ball. It was presented at the Physical Directors' Conference, and the general impression seemed to be that it would fill a place not filled by any other game. It is to be played indoors, and by those who wish a game not so rough as basket ball and yet one in which the same degree of activity is demanded. The complete report as given to the Conference by W. G. Morgan is as follows:

* * *

Volley Ball is a new game which is preeminently fitted for the gymnasium or the exercise hall, but which may be played out of doors. Any number of persons may play the game. The play consists of keeping a ball in motion over a high net, from one side to the other, thus partaking of the character of two games,—tennis and handball.

Play is started by a player on one side serving the ball over the net into the opponents' field or court. The opponents then, without allowing the ball to strike the floor, return it, and it is in this way kept going back and forth until one side fails to return it or it hits the floor. This counts a "score" for one side or a "server out" for the other, depending upon the side in point. The game consists of nine innings, each side serving a certain number of times, as per rules, in each inning.

Rules of Volley Ball

1. Game. The game consists of nine innings.

2. Inning. An inning consists of: when one person is playing on each side, one service on each side; when two are playing on each side,

W. G. Morgan, "Volley Ball," *Physical Education*, vol. 5, July 1896, pp. 50-51.

two services on each side; when three or more are playing on each side, three services on each side. The man serving continues to do so until out by failure of his side to return the ball. Each man shall serve in turn.

3. Court. The court or floor space shall be twenty-five feet wide and fifty feet long, to be divided into two square courts, twenty-five by twenty-five feet, by the net. Four feet from the net on either side and parallel with it shall be a line across the court, the Dribbling line. The boundary lines must be plainly marked so as to be visible from all parts of the courts.

Note.—The exact size of the court may be changed to suit the convenience of the place.

4. Net. The net shall be at least two feet wide and twenty-seven feet long, and shall be suspended from uprights placed at least one foot outside the side lines. The top line of the net must be six feet six inches from the floor.

5. Ball. The ball shall be a rubber bladder covered with leather or canvas. It shall measure not less than twenty-five inches nor more than twenty-seven inches in circumference, and shall weigh not less than nine ounces nor more than twelve ounces.

6. Server and Service. The server shall stand with one foot on the back line. The ball must be batted with the hand. Two services or trials are allowed him to place the ball in the opponents' court (as in tennis). The server may serve into the opponents' court at any place. In a service the ball must be batted at least ten feet, no dribbling allowed. A service which would strike the net, but is struck by another of the same side before striking the net, if it goes over into the opponents' court, is good, but if it should go outside, the server has no second trial.

7. Scoring. Each good service unreturned or ball in play unreturned by the side receiving, counts one score for the side serving. A side only scores when serving, as a failure to return the ball on their part results in the server being put out.

8. Net Ball. A play which hits the net aside from the first service is called a net ball and is equivalent to a failure to return, counting for the opposite side. The ball hitting the net on first service shall be called *dead,* and counts as a trial.

9. Line Ball. It is a ball striking the boundary line; it is equivalent to one out of court and counts as such.

10. Play and Players. Any number may play that is convenient to the place. A player should be able to cover about ten by ten feet.

Should any player during play touch the net, it puts the ball out of play and counts against his side. Should any player catch or hold for an instant the ball, it is out of play and counts for the opposite side. Should the ball strike any object other than the floor and bound back into the court, it is still in play.

To DRIBBLE the ball is to carry it all the time keeping it bouncing. When dribbling the ball no player shall cross the Dribbling line, this putting the ball out of play and counting against him.

Any player, except the captain, addressing the umpire or casting any slurring remarks at him or any of the players on the opposite side, may be disqualified and his side be compelled to play the game without him or a substitute or forfeit the same.

Helps in playing the game

Strike the ball with both hands.
Look for uncovered space in opponents' field.
Play together; cover your own space.
Pass from one to another when possible.
Watch the play constantly, especially the opponents'.

THE MOTOR ELEMENT IN EDUCATION

D. F. Lincoln
of Boston

The distinction between studies pursued for the sake of "information" and those whose end is "training" is a familiar one. Among the latter class certain are distinguished for their objective and concrete character; they are eminent for their direct, first-hand contact with facts, for the attitude of self-reliant observation they cultivate, and for the responsibility in regard to data and inferences which they place upon the student.

The sciences of biology, chemistry, physics, and their allies, are well understood to represent these qualities. In the present paper it is maintained that a claim of similar purpose and function may justly be made on behalf of the motor studies called "manual training,"—including under this name work with tools on wood or metal, modeling in clay, scissor work, weaving and color work, dressmaking, and cooking.

The economic value of many of the "manual training" studies is so obvious that there is a temptation to overlook their educational side. It cannot be too frequently stated that the work of the public school is essentially education and not instruction in a trade; and manual training is no exception to the principle. A source of misapprehension occurs in the very name used to denote these studies. It is made to seem as if the working hand were the object developed rather than the working brain,—which is the reverse of the fact. It is unfortunate that the term "Sloyd," which conveys the desired meaning, and is certainly elastic enough to cover all kinds of manual study, is so foreign to our language. It is unfortunate that so good a word should have been at the outset so narrowed in popular appreciation

D. F. Lincoln, "The Motor Element in Education," *American Physical Education Review,* vol. II, no. 2, June 1897, pp. 65-72.

that it has been taken as equivalent to "knife work"—in reference to a feature which has already been greatly modified in American usage, and which is in fact entirely secondary to the main idea of educative tool-work.

Gymnastics, including the training of the voice for singing and speaking, is so closely allied to manual training on its motor side that we are tempted to believe that the analogy is deep enough to justify our classing them together. Both are marked by the application of attention to physical facts,—on the one hand, the qualities of steel, wood, clay,—on the other hand, the laws of force, weight, balance, motion. The ideas in both cases are objective, incorporated, visible, and tangible. In short, there exists a rational basis for uniting these studies into a single group, which is motor, and therefore objective in essential character, and employs the motor faculties to a similar end.

But what is that end? In a word, it is *plastic activity* (building or making something; the exercise of the constructive faculty) *as an agent in mental training*. The function of gymnastics embraces all this, and is not understood without it. In some form gymnastics is an essential basal part of the mental and moral education. In the higher forms, as systematized for school use, gymnastics is a sculpturing or building of the visible bodily form, a consciously plastic operation.

The sciences of observation train the faculties of the intellect in a way equally objective; and from this point of view they deserve to be associated with the strictly motor studies of which we have spoken. But they are unlike the latter in possessing no plastic tendencies. The materials studied are analyzed and destroyed; sectioned, burnt, stained, teased. The result of analysis is the generalized fact or law, not a new plastic object; further generalization only carries forward the results of previous analysis, raising the abstraction to a higher grade, but not rebuilding in the concrete.

This is, however, a point of view which enables us to group these three sections (observational science, manual training, gymnastics) under one head.* They are the studies in which the student makes his own text-book out of the objects studied. The contrary is implied in literary and humanistic work in general; not that scientific study is impossible in history or philology, but that, for children, language and history work must be for the most part based on imitation, memory, and repetition.

It is worth inquiry, as a matter of relation, whether the motor studies (gymnastics, voice-training, manual training) do not deserve

*Which we may designate as "Objectivistic" studies.

a collective appellation, designative of the predominance of the motor element. They are "kineto-paideutic" studies; the word is offered as a hint.

Our motor experiences serve two entirely different educational ends, since they may either form a basis or a reinforcement of ideas.

First, as a basis: The mass of perceptions, recollections, comparisons, which compose the contents of our minds, is very largely made up of movement ideas, in origin either external and objective, or volitional. Few thoughts can be entertained without recalling some associations of movement, seen or felt. Beginning in earliest infancy there is a very large volume of mental experiences founded upon the movements of our bodies; they are associated inextricably with the sensations of movement, and often are directly acquired by the aid of these movements. We will consider some of these.

1. Perceptions of physical properties.—Weight, tension, velocity, momentum, inertia, are appreciated by the amount and intensity of the muscular effort required in producing or counteracting them, combined with a variety of sensations of touch. These are learned as facts of experience, in childish play, long before they are analyzed in the class-room as data of science, and as a matter of fact they form the basis of physical science.

To the sense of touch a large variety of perceptions are assigned. But it is of prime importance in our study of the motor element to observe that the sense of touch is practically helpless without the aid of muscular action in placing the fingers aptly, in giving suitable movements of stroking and palpation, and in regulating the degree of pressure. It is worthy of deep attention that the parts which are best provided with tactile sensibility (hands, lips, tongue) are eminent for the delicacy and variety of the movements they execute, owing to the possession of a complex and highly co-ordinated scheme of muscles. The uses of their movements are accordingly not limited to the purposes of holding and handling, and of speech; they are through touch of prime importance in forming the mental impressions which we denote by the words rough, smooth, polished, prickly, bristly, wooly, downy, silky, thready, velvety, sharp, blunt, angular, hard, soft, pulpy, pasty, fluid, plastic, flexible, compressible, elastic, clean, sticky, and many others.

The importance of this series of adjectives in a literary and ethical direction is noteworthy. It furnishes such phrases as "a hard man," "the plastic age," "elastic spirits," the rough side of his tongue"; a sort of metaphorical usage without which language would be robbed of half its force and beauty. It deserves to be placed parallel with the series of ocular and other sensory epithets so frequent in literary use,—"bright" thoughts, "sweet" charity, "fragrant" memories, "bitter" experience, "harmony" and "discord" between neighbors, and a crowd of others. Such words have, further, a moral value, superimposed on their æsthetic quality; they enable us to feel the character described more vividly by associating it with memories of strong impressions of sense.

2. Perception of number.—In teaching a child to count he is called on to pick up and arrange a series of sticks, beans, coins, etc. In grasping the idea of two or three, it is quite as much the notion of doing the act (of moving the object) twice or thrice that impresses the mind as the fact that there are two or three objects present. Three beans or sticks on a table may present by their arrangement a number of rival ideas—triangle, vertical line, horizontal line, angle or broken line, heap, etc.—which must be put aside as confusing the notion of pure number; at the same time the notion of moving the hand twice or thrice is offered to the mind as an extremely simple fact to which attention and memory cling while the idea "two" or "three" is being mastered.

3. Perception of geometric form.—Here the ocular impression needs to be paired with that of touch or motion. Neither is complete by itself. The edges and angles of solid bodies give room for delicate discriminations of acute and obtuse by muscular tact. It is a beautiful sight to observe the seeing hand of a blind workman directing his tools by a keen sense of position; and testing with inquisitive fingers the symmetry of some graceful outline in wood which those fingers have just fashioned from the same material.

4. Perception of position, motion, distance, direction.—Fundamental notions of this sort are developed so early in life that we forget how they come to us. We acquire the notion "a mile" rather painfully by the sense of time and tiredness associated with a walk to a given point. The visible shape of the nursery is associated in the mind of the creeping child with the efforts made to reach different parts. For the infant in arms the distant is that which is beyond the grasp of the hands. A child in the lap observing a ball on the floor finds that very considerable changes in the position of the eyes, head, and neck are required in keeping the rolling object in view. As for the size and position of near objects it is his constant habit to go for them with his hands as soon as he sees them; the motive of these acts is largely the alimentary one, but the movements none the less aid in fixing ideas of position.

The distinction between right and left has to be acquired. It is learned at the time when a child begins to differentiate in the use of his two hands for different purposes. The power of recollecting which is the right hand may be based on recollection of the special uses to which he puts it, as writing or shaking hands. The value of this simple acquisition, in geography and astronomy, for instance, is beyond calculation; but in its beginning it seems to be based on a memory of special muscular acts, the impulse to which is related to a single hemisphere.

In young children almost every idea or perception produces a motor reflex act,—a muscular act. Emotion is expressed by a cry. A word thought is a word half spoken. What is longed for is reached for. This abundance of motor impulses is one of nature's chief means of educating little children in the essentials of living. The gratification of these impulses is as strong a tendency in children, and gives them as much pleasure, as the act of eating. The desire for locomotion and for eating constitute the two leading impulses of that peculiar age.

In the conduct of the kindergarten a wise use of this motor trait has been made. The minor and more delicate muscles of the fingers, which at that age are not under perfect control, are entrusted with a few very simple operations. I do not wish to offer a criticism upon a subject which others are better prepared to discuss, but would note that the adaptation of the kindergarten "gifts" to the children's age and muscular powers is not closed for discussion.

In regard to the "mother-plays," which form the real back-bone of the kindergarten, they are in the closest harmony with child nature, from the point of view of the physiologist. They are movement-plays, emotional, realistic, histrionic, with much song and descriptive action. The large groups of muscles, chiefly those of the legs, those of breathing, and to a moderate extent those of the arm, are called into frequent use in the mother-play of the kindergarten.

The aching void in our present school system appears to be the want of union between kindergarten and primary schools. Children are started on the road of normal activity in the kindergarten; they fail to find a thoroughfare in the primary school. I am most hopeful that the spirit of progress, of which I have seen evidence in recent inquiries among public schools, will soon find means of supplying the want.

I have now illustrated somewhat at length, though not exhaustively, the way in which motor experiences serve as the *basis* of ideas. The converse relation, in which ideas are *reinforced* by motor expressions or associations, remains to be explained.

Under this head I would first mention a special application of the motor idea in primary teaching set forth in a recent article in the

Popular Science Monthly (November, 1896) by Professor Edward R. Shaw. The author of the scheme is a German named Heusinger. The idea, which is expanded in a variety of ways, consists in associating various movements of the parts of the body with exercises on the blackboard. While spelling a word aloud a motion is made with the arm for each letter, pointing as many times as there are letters pronounced. As a way of securing variety, the pupil when he has read his sentence goes to the blackboard and writes it, then to the table, picks out the printed or script letters according as he has been directed, forms on a tablet these letters into the sentence, and then takes them to the teacher for her approval. If it seems necessary to have the child write the same sentence several times, the mere matter of going from one board to another, in order to write it in a new place, gives him pleasure, enhances the interest, and strengthens his power to make effort. Thus much orderly activity is combined with all reading exercises. The result of this systematic motor scheme is that during a child's first year at school he is kept in his seat less than one-fourth of the time.

The same principle seems to have been discovered a few years ago by a Boston lady then a teacher in a public school. She found herself in charge of a very stupid class of girls of about the age of thirteen. They were equally dull in gymnastics and in spelling; and it occurred to their teacher that a combination of the two subjects might be made helpful in both directions. She accordingly prepared a list of a convenient number of words of a given number of letters, which she wrote on the blackboard. Certain simple gymnastic movements were chosen and so arranged that they could be performed, a movement for a letter, while the girls were spelling aloud. This original plan succeeded admirably, the interest became vivid, and the spelling improved notably for the period of six weeks, during which the experiment continued.

These considerations are not out of place if they assist us to assign a just rank in the educational scale to a class of operations which, until very lately, have been regarded as entirely subordinate to what are popularly termed intellectual acts. In the words of the late illustrious Dr. Bois-Reymond, "It is easy to show that such bodily exercises as gymnastics, fencing, swimming, riding, dancing, and skating are much more exercises of the central nervous system, of the brain and spinal cord," than of the muscular system. He points out that a high degree of guiding skill must be present in order to direct a numerous group of muscles in consentaneous performance of a task which in appearance is most simple, but in reality is most complex; this skill, moreover, is not situated in the muscles; "the peculiar mechanism of the composite movements resides in the central nervous system, and consequently exercise in such movements is really nothing else than exercise of the central nervous system. The bodily exercises we have mentioned above are not mere muscle gymnastics, but also, and that pre-eminently, nerve-gymnastics, if for brevity's sake we may apply the term nerves to the whole nervous system."

The motor studies, of which gymnastics is the more pure kinetic, and manual training the more applied form, should be regarded as constituting a part of a liberal education in the broad sense, equally with the study of geometry or Latin.

Each of the two applications has its special value; each its defects. Manual training is of necessity very defective as an instrument of general physical development; it even has special dangers in the way of possible deformities, although it must be added that these dangers are fully foreseen by the prominent leaders of the department, and are provided for. Gymnastic training is somewhat defective in a direction in which the other is strong, namely, in attractiveness, and in the presence of an immediate appreciable motive. Do not misunderstand my import. I am convinced that gymnastics is an indispensable means, and I do not see how a boy or girl can be called educated who has not passed through its training. But there is a certain lack of sense of *something done* about it; a consciousness that what is done is preparatory work, fractional work, rather than distinct, namable acts. Remedies for this psychical defect are being sought in various directions,—by the partial substitution of games, by the freer use of apparatus, etc.

We all appreciate the value of the principle of "learning by doing." The words are a motor aphorism. But in one respect they fail to explain themselves. We do *not* learn by "doing" per se, but by doing *something;* and motor activity as such, however well incorporated into our habits, however skillfully mechanized in our subconscious life, is not educative, except as it leads towards a conscious intellectual goal of performance. We want not so much a *fine* machine as a machine that *thinks.*

REPORT OF THE FIRST STANDING COMMITTEE ON THEORY AND STATISTICS*

MR. PRESIDENT:—

Your committee on Theory and Statistics in presenting its report, wish to take the opportunity to express its thanks for, and appreciation of, the work of their predecessors (the members of your committee of last year), who have collected much of the material which has been compiled for this evening's discussion.

As you know, the American Association for the Advancement of Physical Education at its tenth annual meeting held in New York City in 1895, voted to adopt a revised Constitution and By-Laws. Under the terms of the new constitution, your Executive Committee appointed committees on Theory and Statistics, Publications and Bibliography, and on Technical matters pertaining to the practical side of physical education, and have set apart one monthly meeting for each of the committees named.

In offering for your particular consideration this evening the subject—"Physical Education as Taught in Some of the Normal Schools of This Country"—the committee wishes to state that it has found the subject broad, and one in which there was much difficulty in obtaining full statistics, and that the object in presenting it is to obtain as accurate a knowledge as is possible of some of the fundamental principles as taught in a few of the leading schools; and we wish to ask in the discussion which is to follow, for the correction of any mistakes which have been made in consulting old catalogues, where

Walter Truslow *et al.*, "Report of the First Standing Committee on Theory and Statistics," *American Physical Education Review,* vol. III, no. 4, December 1898, pp. 295-298.

*Delivered before the Physical Education Society of New York and vicinity, March 16, 1898.

new ones were not obtainable, and for any further information which the members may be able to give.

The theory and practice of physical education is taught in this country in independent Normal Schools of Gymnastics, also in Departments of Gymnastics connected with State Normal Schools, as at the Cook County Normal School at Chicago, and the Westchester State Normal School of Pennsylvania, or as a part of the curriculum of colleges, as at Cornell, Oberlin and Vanderbilt University—or connected with other organizations, as the departments of Physical Training at the Training Schools of the International Committee of the Y. M. C. A. at Springfield, Mass., and Chicago, Ill. Important work is also done in the Summer Schools of Gymnastics, the best examples of which are the Summer Course in Physical Training at Harvard University, under the direction of Dr. D. A. Sargent, and the Chautauqua School of Physical Education, under the direction of Drs. Anderson and Seaver, of Yale.

This report will deal with only six of the leading Normal Schools of Gymnastics, the choice being based upon the list furnished the committee by the Bureau of Education at Washington; we therefore ask your attention to some of the lines followed in the training of gymnastic teachers as taught at—

The Normal School of the North American Gymnastic Union, Milwaukee, Wis.

Dr. Sargent's Normal School of Physical Training, Cambridge, Mass.

The Anderson Normal School of Gymnastics, New Haven, Ct.

The Boston Normal School of Gymnastics, Boston, Mass.

The Posse Normal School of Gymnastics, Boston, Mass., and

The Physical Department of the International Young Men's Christian Association Training School, Springfield, Mass.

The history of the origin and growth of each of these is both interesting and instructive. Each was started to meet a definite need and each has proved by its progressively enlarging field of work its ability to supply the requirements. The first five named have for their object the training of men and women to fill the positions of teachers in any field of gymnastic work, but with special reference to the gymnastics of the schools and colleges of the country, both public and private. The Training School at Springfield fits young men only and for positions mainly connected with institutions of a purely philanthropic character, particularly the Y.M.C.A.'s in the cities, towns and colleges throughout the country.

Requirements for admission to the schools are more or less rigid. At Milwaukee, the candidate is first examined by a committee from the Turnverein of his own district, and then at the school he is given a thorough physical and mental examination.

The catalogue of the Y. M. C. A. Training School states of the applicant: "If a graduate of a college or high school, he shall upon entering show his certificate of graduation; if not, he must before he can be accepted, pass a preliminary examination. * * * He will also be required to undergo a physical examination."

The Posse catalogue says: "Applicants must be high school graduates or prove by examination or certificate from reliable authority that they possess a corresponding education."

Students entering Dr. Sargent's Normal Course "should be at least eighteen years of age, have good health, a sound physique, and a high school education or its equivalent."

It is understood of the candidates entering the Boston Normal School of Gymnastics that he or she is to remain during the first two months on probation.

Requirements for obtaining a diploma are practically the same in all the schools: the student must take the full course and must satisfactorily pass a written examination in all the theoretical work. These examinations are usually given at the completion of each course of lectures; the student must also stand a test of his practical, or floor work.

The length of the course in all the schools is two years and there is a tendency to increase the time to three years; several of the schools offer a post-graduate course of one year in Medical Gymnastics.

The theoretical work in the schools embraces the following subjects: Physics (Pure), Inorganic Chemistry, Biology, Anatomy, Physiology, Hygiene, General and Special Kinesiology, Psychology, Science and Philosophy of Teaching, History of Gymnastics, Study of different systems of gymnastics, Anthropometry, Lectures on First Aid to the Injured, Symptomatology, Gymnastic Therapeutics and Required Reading of Literature on Physical Education. In regard to the practical work, we may say that one system only is taught in but one of the schools, and that is at the Boston Normal School of Gymnastics, where all the attention is given to the Swedish System.

At the Posse School the system taught is essentially the Swedish, but some time is devoted each week to instruction in German and Æsthetical gymnastics.

Also at Milwaukee, although the system taught is distinctly the German, some time is allowed for instruction in Swedish gymnastics.

At the schools of the Y. M. C. A., they have a method of their own, which is founded mainly on the principles laid down by the Germans.

At Dr. Sargent's school, "no rigid system is adhered to," and instruction is given in Swedish gymnastics, Delsarte movements and Military Drill, in addition to a general training in gymnastics, including free movements, calisthenics, work with light and heavy apparatus, and individual instruction in the use of Dr. Sargent's developing appliances.

According to the Anderson catalogue, three kinds of gymnastics are taught in that school,—American, Swedish and German. Some time is also given to Delsarte movements and Æsthetic gymnastics.

Daily drills for all students are given in all the schools. Special work for individual development is given in all the schools mentioned except at the Normal School of the North American Gymnastic Union, where the student is required to pass a physical examination, and is expected to be well developed before beginning his normal work.

Under the head of Applied Gymnastics we have placed Dancing, Fencing, Boxing, Swimming and Boating. Dancing is taught in some form in all the schools except at the Y. M. C. A.; Fencing, in all; Boxing, at Milwaukee and Y. M. C. A.; Swimming, in all except the Anderson and the Posse; Boating, only at the Y. M. C. A. Gymnastic games are taught in all of the schools.

An opportunity is given to the students in all of the Normal Schools mentioned to do actual teaching during the second year, so that they not only get the theory but the practice as well. At the Anderson School, the students in their Senior Year instruct in the public schools of New Haven, and at the Boston Normal School of Gymnastics, the students instruct public school children who come to the gymnasium Saturday mornings.

Respectfully submitted,
WALTER TRUSLOW, Chairman,
JOSEPHINE BEIDERHASE,
HERMAN SEIBERT,
Committee.

EFFECT OF COLLEGE WORK UPON THE HEALTH OF WOMEN

Delphine Hanna
and Nellie A. Spore
Oberlin College

In Oberlin, young women of the college and academy are given their first physical examination soon after entering school in the fall, their second in the following spring, and their final examination in the spring of the junior year, when they complete their required gymnasium work. The required work for the year is four half-hour periods a week for four months.

The following table shows the relative strength of one hundred young women as taken at their first and second examinations. The table is arranged according to percentages; the strength expressed in pounds, the lung capacity in cubic inches.

Of these one hundred young women, forty-eight report their general health the same as on entering, forty-three report a decided improvement, the health of nine is not so good, forty-two had no colds or the same number as the previous year, forty-eight report fewer colds, and ten more colds. Only twenty had needed the services of a physician, and none of these for serious illness; eighty-eight had gained in muscular strength and twelve had lost; ninety-eight had increased in lung capacity and two had decreased.

Of the thirty juniors examined, twenty-five report their general health better than during their high school course; two had never been ill; the remaining three report themselves in a more nervous condition than when in high school; twenty had gained in muscular strength, and ten had lost, the loss being largely in strength of legs, probably due to the level country; twenty-seven had increased in lung capacity, and three had decreased.

Delphine Hanna and Nellie A. Spore, "Effect of College Work Upon the Health of Women," *American Physical Education Review,* vol. IV, no. 3, September 1899, pp. 279-280.

	Back		Legs		Chest		R. Forearm		L. Forearm		Lung Capacity	
Per Cent	First	Second	First	Second	First	Second	First	Second	First	Second	First	Second
1	232.6	243.6	277.8	369.3	86	90.4	68.3	83.8	59	67.2	202.5	217.5
2.5	222.9	238.7	271.2	333.5	77.8	81.1	65	73.1	57.3	66.5	196.125	211.25
5	218.3	226	265.7	303.1	73.9	78.3	61.7	67.2	55.5	62.8	183.185	197.5
10	196.2	214.9	240.3	281.1	70	76.9	59.7	62.8	53.3	56.2	179	187.75
15	191.3	208.9	226	254.6	66.6	75.2	54.9	59.2	50.1	54.7	175.525	184.1
20	185.2	200.6	219.8	241.4	65	71.6	52.7	57.3	47.8	53.6	171.485	180.12
25	179.7	198.4	214.9	238.4	63.2	69.4	49.6	55.4	45.6	52.5	169	178.5
30	175.3	196.2	207.2	232.1	58.4	67.8	48	53.7	44.4	50.7	163.85	176.01
35	171.6	193.8	200.6	226	57.2	66.3	46.3	52.3	43.4	48.8	160.94	173.525
40	166.4	186.3	194.6	219.4	56.1	64.5	44.9	52	41.4	47.4	159	171.45
45	160.9	181.1	178.6	206.5	54.7	62.1	44.1	49.6	40	45.8	157	169.7
50	157.6	177.5	174.9	202.8	52.9	60.4	43.7	48.5	39	44.1	152.1	165.85
45	154.9	174.8	171.6	199.1	51	59.4	43	47.4	37.7	42.6	149.875	162.5
40	152.1	172.6	163.4	196.7	49.6	58.4	40.1	45.2	36	41.4	144.9	160.33
35	144.4	168.7	157.6	185.2	47.4	57	38.8	44.1	34.2	39.7	141.745	158
30	136.7	163.1	153	174.2	46.3	55.9	35.3	43.6	32.6	38	139.75	153.85
25	131.2	157.3	147.7	162	45.2	54.5	33.9	42.3	31.3	36.9	137.15	148.5
20	124.6	150.3	133.6	155.6	42.1	53.1	32.3	39.5	30	34.2	131.65	143.5
15	110.2	141.1	128.3	150.5	40.8	51.3	30.5	37	26.9	32	128	138.165
10	99.2	129	115.2	138	37.9	47.4	28.5	33.5	24	29.8	120.65	131.485
5.5	75.4	117.9	93.7	115.7	34.2	45.2	23.1	30.9	20.9	26.1	110	129
2	70.9	113.2	90.4	104.7	28.7	39.7	20.4	28.2	17.6	23.7	97.525	123.025
1	68.3	99.2	88.8	91.5	27.1	36.4	14.3	24.3	13.2	22	82.5	112.5

From so small an amount of data one must not draw too broad conclusions, but for these young women there certainly was an increase in vitality.

If college directors would publish more of their data, we might in time settle the question about which there seems to be so much doubt in the public mind, and know that under proper conditions, a college course increases the physical as well as the mental strength.

PHYSICAL TRAINING IN THE EDUCATIONAL CURRICULUM

President C. W. Eliot
Harvard University

The question which we are discussing is "What measures are best calculated to secure a dignified and influential place for Physical Training in the Educational Curriculum?"

"I suppose from the phrasing of the question that the educational curriculum meant the whole length and breadth of education from the primary school up; and I infer from the quality of this audience that physical training in the elementary school and the secondary school is quite as interesting to you as that in the college or university; so what I am to say will relate to the whole course of education, and will not be particularly concerned with the college period. Indeed, I should like to throw out at once from all consideration here the whole question of college athletics, so-called. They do not seem to me to be a part of what we should understand by physical training. They are an enormous exaggeration of anything desirable in the form of physical training; they result for a period more or less brief in the almost complete devotion of a young man's time to his body, necessarily at the sacrifice of his intellectual interests. I therefore put those highly competitive sports aside altogether, as having but little to do with the special subject before us.

"We mean by physical training the systematic side in the long course of development of the body from four or five years of age to full maturity; and the measure which seems to me best calculated to secure a 'dignified and influential place for physical training' in that sense is to get rid of the word 'physical' altogether, or, at any rate, to materially qualify its meaning. The Greeks had a far better con-

C. W. Eliot, "Physical Training in the Educational Curriculum," *American Physical Education Review*, vol. 8, no. 2, June 1899, pp. 230-233.

ception than we have of the relation of the training of the body to that of the whole man. In this part of the country, at least, we inherit from our Puritan ancestors the conception that the body is something noxious and degrading, to be mortified and subjugated, and we carry this view of the body into education. I remember that, a dozen years ago or more, I made to our Faculty the modest proposition that the young men who were applicants for scholarships should first, as a necessary preliminary, submit to a physical examination, just as young men going into the military and naval schools submit to a physical examination. I thought it reasonable that we should know that young men, in whom we were to invest anywhere from $200 to $1,000 a piece, had at least a fair chance of possessing the health and strength necessary to usefulness in the community after they had received their training. This proposition, however, commanded but small support in the college Faculty. It was denounced as the most materialistic proposition the speakers had ever heard made in that room. That illustrates what I mean by saying that this word 'physical' is an incumbrance to us, that we should be better off from the point of view of this Association, if we got rid of it. As Dr. James has pointed out, the child is an intricate complex of physical, intellectual, and moral qualities, and all his qualities go together in education. Not that there may not be exceptional cases in which moral force triumphs over physical weakness; indeed, we know there are such cases. We know there are emergencies in life and in death when physical weakness is momentarily mastered by moral force—by the will power. But that sort of exception is not what we talk about in education. What we want in education is a harmonious, symmetrical development of the whole being, physical, intellectual, and moral, taken together. As Dr. James has already said, there are in this development certain parts of the body very important in their relation to the mind and the will. They are the nervous centres; and I am more and more persuaded that our particular care, in what we now call physical training, should be directed to the training of those nervous centres, rather than to the training of the muscles. Of course, we cannot train the muscles without training the nerves, nor can we train the nerves without training the muscles. We are dealing with an intricate problem; we must affect simultaneously the whole human system.

"This tendency to separate in our thinking bodily training from mental and moral training is in many ways deceptive. I have already spoken of the difficulty I encountered in proposing that candidates for scholarships should be tested physically before we invest in them. Now I am happy to say that, as the years have gone on, and we have provided in Harvard bodily exercises of all sorts, we have learned that the good physique, and particularly the good nerves, generally goes with the good mind and the steady, controlling will. As a rule they all go together. For example, we now have a physical examination of the holders of scholarships. We try to have them all examined twice a year. It has turned out, after a good many years of experience in these matters, that the holders of scholarships are physically, as well as mentally, superior to the average student. That illustrates what I think we see afterwards in the active world,—that the men who succeed in business, in professions, or in any strenuous occupation involving responsibility and hard work, are greatly superior physically to the average man. I think the present Faculty of Harvard College is a remarkably tough set of men; they have the bodily qualifications for prolonged, strenuous attention; and there is no better evidence than this of physical toughness. It is too much to expect that a child attend intently to any one thing for more than a few moments; and when you find men and women who are capable of prolonged and intense attention, you may be sure that they are persons of decided physical merit. Now it is this combination of powers that the prolonged courses of education should aim to develop; and when we advocate physical training for little children, youths, or grown-up people out in the stress of the world, let it be understood that we mean the harmonious, general development of body, mind, and will together; and that we are not thinking especially of the development of the muscular system, or even of bodily strength in the ordinary sense.

"Let me add a few words of encouragement with regard to the present position in the educational curriculum of what we call physical training. The propounding of this question suggests that we are somewhat discouraged about the present situation. Now I see no ground for such discouragement; but, on the contrary, I think this Association has the greatest reason to rejoice in the rapid progress of the educational interests with which it is specially concerned. When I look back on the condition of things in our schools and colleges thirty years ago, it seems to me that the progress has been in the highest degree satisfactory. I have no doubt what is true of Harvard is true of a multitude of colleges and schools as well; and here, on this ground, we have made extraordinary progress in the average well-being of the student and in his bodily strength. We have demonstrated also that the student class, as a whole, is physically superior to any other class of young men of the same age, whether mechanics, shopmen, clerks or farmers. The student class, I say, is physically superior to the mechanic class, the farming class, or the clerical class. Is that not an encouraging result of only twenty years' systematic attention to your subject? I believe, therefore, that this Association should look back with utter content at the progress already made, and with the clearest conviction that the near future will show greater progress still.

"Before I close I want to say one word about what seems to me an essential element in every profitable form of physical training. It is the element of enjoyment. I should say precisely the same thing of mental training—that kind of mental training is best, whether for the individual or for the community, which is invariably associated with enjoyment, with enjoyment at the moment and in reminiscence,—with the great enjoyment of achievement. I know that in my own case the reason why I have persisted during life in taking a reasonable amount of physical exercise is that I have always enjoyed it. I enjoyed my ride on the wheel for an hour this very morning. I am afraid I should not take open-air exercise if I did not enjoy it; and I think that is good sense,—good sense for a child, or for a youth of eighteen, just as it is for an old man. In every systematic physical training we should always seek this enjoyable quality. Therefore, sports are best,—sensible, moderate, unexaggerated sports; therefore those exercises are best, which always have in them an element of enjoyment, and which give a sense of achievement, the satisfaction of attaining skill, and a feeling of exhilaration.

"I look, therefore, with great satisfaction on what seems to be a distinct tendency just at present to develop in every possible way interesting and enjoyable sports as means of physical training, sports which can be followed throughout life. The development of yachting, horseback-riding, bicycle-riding and golf illustrate this. It is the enduring things that are best, the things that will last through life for man or woman, and that are thoroughly enjoyable for child or man."

THE VALUE OF ATHLETICS TO COLLEGE GIRLS

By Miss Harriet I. Ballintine
Vassar College

In the physical training of girls, and especially with older college students, it is most important to arouse in them an interest in their work. While recognizing that individual exercise is absolutely necessary to bring about certain results, and that nothing can take the place of prescribed individual work in correcting physical defects, we must do more than this if physical training is to have its proper place in the college. It is necessary to secure the interest of the student if we wish to inculcate fixed habits of exercise and train girls to look upon their physical work as a matter of course. The therapeutic value of exercise does not appeal to the majority of college students, already overburdened with duties. They demand, and need, recreation and relaxation, and, if the work offered does not meet these requirements, it will fail in its purpose.

In the training of college girls we must satisfy, as far as is consistent with the ability of the individual, the demand for interesting work. We must first endeavor to arouse the interest of the girl; and after that is accomplished, it ought not to be difficult to turn her attention to her individual development, if necessary.

What, then, are the forms of exercise best adapted for this purpose?

Basketball has already an established place in the majority of girls' schools and colleges, and has done more perhaps than any one game in arousing an interest in out-of-door work among girls. But in a college with hundreds of students, basketball does not fulfill all the requirements. We must have more than one form of sport in order to benefit and interest all. Unfortunately, unless our students play well enough to gain a position on the regular team, they are apt to lose

Harriet I. Ballintine, "The Value of Athletics to College Girls," *American Physical Education Review*, vol. VI, no. 2, June 1901, pp. 151-153.

interest and will not practise simply for the sake of the exercise, if there is no prospect of competing in the match games.

In every college there are certain conditions relative to the work of physical training that must be met by only that college. The line of work laid down in one place cannot always be carried out in another. The demands of the place and time must be met. Shortly after the introduction of basketball at Vassar College the students asked permission to institute track and field athletics. It may be of interest to give a short resumé of our athletic sports and to show what is being done in this line of work at present. Athletics were introduced with some reluctance, it is admitted, because of the demand. It was an experiment and so far has been most satisfactory.

Training for these events has added greatly to the interest in all out-of-door sports. The attitude toward the whole question of physical training has changed in a marked degree since the introduction of our field day. The sports have been running, hurdling, the fence vault, broad and high jump, throwing the basketball and putting the shot. The shot is only eight pounds, and those who enter for this event are the stronger girls. The students in training practise regularly at least three hours each week and sometimes more, for from four to five weeks, and out-of-doors whenever the weather permits. All required work in the gymnasium is over the last of March, and the out-of-door work is optional. There is no forcing of the students to induce them to take up this kind of exercise, but it is left entirely to their inclination.

Last year over eighty students took the out-of-door training, while only thirty cared to enter the field day. There must be something in active sport of this kind that meets a want, when girls will train systematically for several weeks simply for the pleasure they find in it. The out-of-door practice is under the direction of the gymnasium director and the assistants in the department; but the students have the management of the field day in their hands and they have instituted the rules governing those in training.

Regulations in regard to diet and sleep are strictly followed. Confectionery, afternoon teas and all eating between meals are prohibited, and for several weeks those entering either for the sports on the field day or training only lead a most hygienic life. The good results from this alone are not to be underestimated.

Since the introduction of athletics the interest among our girls in their physical development has been greatly stimulated. If a girl finds that another excels her in some favorite event, because of greater strength and endurance, she has been known to devote hours to her formerly slighted prescription work. At the present time and during the past winter there has been a greater interest in the coming field day than ever before, and there has never been a year when the developing appliances in the gymnasium have been so popular.

Thus far only the advantages of active and vigorous sports have been considered. What are the objections to girls engaging in athletics? The question will at once arise, Are they strong enough and can such a line of work be of benefit to them physically? In taking up the question of athletics for women, only those in a normal physical condition are to be considered. Girls who are physically weak in any way, or those for whom the excitement of competitive sports would be detrimental, should be prohibited from taking part in this branch of physical training. Fortunately, there are hundreds of girls in our colleges who are well and strong, whose vigorous and normal conditions demand a certain amount of healthful excitement and really *hard* physical work. These students will not be satisfied, either mentally or physically, for any length of time, with the milder forms of gymnastics.

Is there not danger of forgetting that we have this class of students to train, as well as the weaker ones? The opinions of some physicians and teachers, especially those engaged in the practice of corrective gymnastics, cannot help but be somewhat biased by the abnormal conditions with which they come in contact.

The ability and needs of the healthy girl should not be determined by that of the neurotic or orthopedic subject, who requires the advice and treatment of the specialist. In all cases the physical condition of the individual should be determined, the exercise prescribed. The question of athletics for girls should be carefully considered and, where introduced, the work should have the most constant supervision. In colleges for women, where there is always more or less control over the students, it ought not to be a difficult matter to regulate the management of athletics and eliminate the objectionable features. If women are to enter into athletics it should be for the purpose of recreation and maintaining health. The making of records, while of some interest to the competitor, should be only secondary in importance. Those who advocate a more radical form of physical training for women realize that there is a growing demand for it among the stronger class of college students, and that it is necessary to meet this demand. If the standard of health is to be raised, it is of importance to gain the co-operation of the students by giving them work that will act as an incentive to induce them to practise habitually active, out-of-door exercise.

A SELECT BIBLIOGRAPHY OF THE HISTORY OF PHYSICAL TRAINING

Fred. Eugene Leonard
Oberlin College

The following bibliography was prepared primarily for use in connection with a series of ten lectures which constituted one of the Harvard University Summer Courses in Physical Education in 1902. Its incompleteness is largely due to this fact, but even in the present imperfect form it may serve a useful purpose in the case of persons interested in the subject to which it refers. Titles bearing exclusively upon physical training have been carefully selected after examination of the best libraries in this country and on the Continent, and first-hand acquaintance with the sources. Books and articles of a more general nature are the best with which the writer is familiar, but doubtless others of equal or greater value have escaped his notice. Suggestions with regard to such omissions will be welcomed. Works in English are usually mentioned first, and those most generally accessible to students. Foreign titles are restricted to German and French sources as being the only ones open to the majority of readers. In sections where the literature is abundant, the most reliable, complete, or recent authorities are mentioned.

It is fitting that even so slight a contribution as the present one should contain more than a passing reference to the invaluable pioneer services of Dr. Edward Mussey Hartwell. His classic writings, backed by his scholarly and commanding personality, have been among the most potent forces in arousing interest and disseminating right conceptions of the nature of physical training. In this country he was the first to reveal the rich history and literature of the subject, and it is with the respect and affection due from a pupil to his master that the writer acknowledges here his own indebtedness for the im-

Fred. Eugene Leonard, "A Select Bibliography of the History of Physical Training," *American Physical Education Review,* vol. VII, no. 1, March 1902, pp. 39-48.

pulse to enter what has proved to be a fascinating and fruitful field of investigation.

1. *General Works.*

Hartwell, E. M.—Physical Training in American Colleges and Universities. Circulars of Information of United States Bureau of Education, No. 5 for 1885. Washington, 1886.

——— Report of the Director of Physical Training. School Document No. 22, Boston, 1891.

——— Chap. XII in Report of Commissioner of Education for 1897-98. Washington, 1899.

Boykin, J. C.—Chap. XIII in Report of Commissioner of Education for 1891-92. Washington, 1894.

Schaible, C. H.—The Systematic Training of the Body. 2d ed., London, 1892. Part I.

Carl Euler and others—Encyklopädisches Handbuch des gesamten Turnwesens. 3 volumes. Vienna and Leipsic, 1894-96.

Euler, Carl—Geschichte des Turnunterrichts. Gotha, 1891. Pp. XXIII, 520.

Hirth—Das gesamte Turnwesen, 2d ed. by F. R. Gasch. 4 volumes. Hof, 1893 and 1895.

Angerstein, E.—Geschichte und Entwicklung der Leibesübungen. 2d ed. Vienna and Leipsic, 1897. Pp. VIII, 156.

Rühl, Hugo—Entwicklungsgeschichte des Turnens. 2d ed. Leipsic, 1897. Pp. *c.* 150.

Brendicke, Hans—Grundriss zur Geschichte der Leibesübungen. Köthen, 1882. Pp. VI, 175.

2. *Greece.*

Smith, Wm.—A Dictionary of Greek and Roman Antiquities. 3d ed., 2 volumes. London, 1890-91. Articles "Palæstra, Gymnasium, Olympia, Olympias, Athletæ," etc.

Harper's Dictionary of Classical Literature and Antiquities, edited by H. T. Peck. New York, 1897. Articles "Athletæ, Education, Gymnasium, Olympia, Olympias, Nemea, Isthmia, Pythia," etc.

The Life of the Greeks and Romans, by E. Guhl and W. Koner, translated by F. Hueffer. New York, 1875. Sections 25, 29, 50, 52, etc.

Marquand, Allan—The Old Olympic Games. Century Mag., April, 1896, p. 803.

Plummer, E. M.—Am. Phys. Educ. Review, II:97; III:1, 93, 157. Issued as reprint with title "Athletics and Games of the Ancient Greeks."

Mahaffy, J. P.—Old Greek Education. New York, 1882. Chap. III, VII, etc.

Laurie, S. S.—Historical Survey of Pre-Christian Education. 2d ed. New York, 1900. Pp. 230-235, 264-267, etc.

Krause, J. H.—Die Gymnastik und Agonistik der Hellenen. Leipsic, 1841.

Grasberger, L.—Die liebliche Erziehung bei den Griechen und Römern. Würzburg, 1864.

Jaeger, O. H.—Die Gymnastik der Hellenen. Stuttgart, 1881. (1st ed. 1850.)

Bintz, J.—Die Gymnastik der Hellenen. Gütersloh, 1878.

Fedde, F.—Über den Fünfkampf der Hellenen. Leipsic, 1889.

Juthner, J.—Über antike Turngeräthe. Vienna, 1896 (Heft XII in "Abhandlungen des Archäologisch-Epigraphischen Seminars der Universität Wien").

3. *Rome.*

Smith, *l. c.* under (2)—Articles "Amphitheatrum, Circus, Gladiatores, Ludi, Balneæ."

Harper's Dictionary, as under (2)—Articles as above.

Guhl and Koner, *l. c.* under (2)—Sections 80, 83, 85, 99, 104, 105, etc.

Lecky, W. E. H.—History of European Morals. New York, 1870. I:287-308; II:37-41.

See also Sienkiewicz, "Quo Vadis," Chap. 55 (Coliseum); and Wallace, "Ben Hur," Book V, Chap. 12-14 (Circus).

4. *Asceticism.*

Lecky, *l. c.* under (3)—II:107-132.

Painter, F. V. N.—A History of Education. New York, 1896. Pp. 93-99.

See also Tennyson's "Saint Simeon Stylites" (1842), and Kingsley's "Hypatia."

5. *Early Teutonic Life and Customs.*

Weinhold, Karl—Altnordisches Leben. Berlin, 1856.

Bintz, J.—Die Leibesübungen des Mittelalters Gütersloh, 1880. Chapters I-V.

6. *Monastic Schools.*

West, A. F.—Alcuin and the Rise of the Christian Schools. New York, 1892. Introduction, Chap. I, etc.

Painter, *l. c.* under (4)—Pp. 99-102.

7. *Chivalry and Knighty Education.*

Schultz, Alwin—Das Höfische Leben zur Zeit der Minnesinger. Leipsic, Vol. I, 1879; Vol. II, 1880. 2d ed., 1889.

Lacroix, Paul—Military and Religious Life in the Middle Ages. London, 1874. Chap. V (Chivalry), etc.

Bintz, *l. c.* under (5)—Chap. VI.

Painter, *l. c.* under (4)—Pp. 107-110.

See also Tennyson's "Idylls of the King" (Elaine, Enid); and Scott's "Ivanhoe," Chap. 8-12.

8. *The Humanists.*

Painter, *l. c.* under (4)—Pp. 119-121, 154-164.

Woodward, W. H.—Vittorino da Feltre and other Humanist Educators. Cambridge (Eng.), 1897.

Krampe, W.—Die Italienischen Humanisten. Breslau, 1895.

Karl von Raumer—Life and Educational System of John Sturm (translation), in Barnard's Am. J. Educ. IV:167, 401 (1857).

Bintz, *l. c.* under (5)—Chap. VII.

See also Mercurialis—De Arte Gymnastica. Venice, 1569, etc.

9. *The Reformers.*

Boykin, *l. c.* under (1)—Pp. 471-483.

Milton's Tractate on Education, edited by Oscar Browning. Cambridge (Eng.), 1890.

Locke on Education, edited by R. H. Quick. Cambridge (Eng.), 2d ed. 1889.

Rousseau's Emile, translated and edited by W. H. Payne. New York, 1896.

10. *The Philanthropinists and their Followers.*

Am. Phys. Educ. Review IV:1-18 (1899). Leonard, The Period of Philanthropinism.

On Basedow see Barnard's Am. J. Educ. V:487 (translated from von Raumer); and Quick's Educational Reformers, New York, 1896, Chap. XV.

Guts Muths—Gymnastik für die Jugend. Schnepfenthal, 1793. 2 volumes.

———Gymnastics for Youth. London, 1800; Philadelphia, 1802. A translation of the above. On the title page the work is wrongly attributed to Salzmann.

———Spiele zur Uebung und Erholung. Schnepfenthal, 1796.

Vieth–Encyklopädie der Leibesübungen. Vols. I and II, Berlin, 1794, 1795; vol. III, Leipsic, 1818.

Krieger, G.–Zur Erinnerung an G. U. A. Vieth. Dessau, 1885. Pp. 55.

Clias–Anfangsgründe der Gymnastik. Bern, 1816.

——— Gymnastique Élémentaire. Paris, 1819.

———An Elementary Course of Gymnastic Exercises. London, 1823.

———Kalisthenie oder Uebungen . . . für Mädchen. Bern, 1829.

Amoros–Gymnase Normal, Militaire et Civil. Paris, 1821.

——— Manuel d'Éducation physique, gymnastique et morale. Paris, 1830. 2 volumes and atlas.

——— Nouveau Manuel d'Éducation physique, etc. Paris, 1848. 2 volumes and atlas.

Nachtegall–Lehrbuch der Gymnastik für Volks- und Bürger-schulen (translated from the Danish by C. Kopp). Tondern, 1831.

——— Lehrbuch der Gymnastik . . . für die gelehrten Schulen (translated as above). Tondern, 1837.

11. *Jahn, and Popular Gymnastics in Germany.*

Am. Phys. Educ. Review V:18-39 (1900). Leonard, Jahn's life up to the publication of "Die Deutsche Turnkunst" (1816).

Jahn and Eiselen–Die Deutsche Turnkunst. Berlin, 1816.

(Chas. Beck)–Treatise on Gymnastics . . . from the German of F. L. Jahn. Northampton (Mass.), 1828.

F. L. Jahns Werke, edited by Carl Euler. 3 volumes. Hof, 1884, 1885, 1887.

Euler, Carl–F. L. Jahn, sein Leben und Wirken. Stuttgart, 1881.

Schultheiss, F. G.–F. L. Jahn, sein Leben und seine Bedeutung. Berlin, 1894.

Handbuch der Deutschen Turnerschaft. 6th ed., Hof, 1899.

See also the files of the Deutsche Turn-Zeitung, Leipsic.

12. *Ling, and School Gymnastics in Sweden.*

Hartwell, in Am. Phys. Educ. Review I:1-13 (1896), reprinted in Report of Commissioner of Education for 1897-98, pp. 539-546.

Leonard, in Am. Phys. Educ. Review V:301 (1900) and VI:1 (1901).

P. H. Ling's Schriften über Leibesübungen, translated by H. F. Massmann. Magdeburg, 1847.

Ling, par une Moscovite. Paris, 1900.

Demeny–L'Education physique en Suède. Paris, 1892. Pp. 105.

Balck, in Revue Encyclopédique Larousse, 2. Sept. 1899 (p. 747). Paris.

Törngren, in Proceedings A. A. A. P. E. VIII:50 (1893).
See also the files of the Tidskrift i Gymnastik, Stockholm.

13. *Spiess, and School Gymnastics in Germany.*

Hartwell, 1899, as under (1)—Pp. 532-539.

Spiess—Kleine Schriften über Turnen, edited by J. C. Lion. Hof, 1877.

——— Die Lehre der Turnkunst. 4 volumes. Basel, 1840, 1842, 1843, 1846. 2d ed. 1867, 1871, 1874, 1885.

——— Turnbuch für Schulen. 2 volumes. Basel, 1847, 1851.

Leitfaden für den Turnunterricht in der Preussischen Volksschulen. Berlin, 1895.

Maul—Turnunterricht in Knabenschulen. 3 volumes. Karlsruhe, 1893, 1895, 1897.

——— Turnunterricht in Mädchenschulen. 4 volumes. Karlsruhe, 1892, 1885, 1888, 1890.

See also the files of the Monatsschrift für das Turnwesen, Berlin; and volumes of the Jahrbuch für Volks- und Jugendspiele, Leipsic.

United States

14. *Beck, Follen, Lieber.*

Jahrbücher der Deutsch-Amerik. Turnerei I:5-19 (1890). New York. Drei Pioniere deutsch-amerik. Turnerei.

Charles Beck—Translation of Jahn's Turnkunst, as cited under (11).

Follen, (Mrs.) E. L.—The Life of Charles Follen. Boston, 1844.

Francke, Kuno—Karl Follen and the German Liberal Movement. In Papers of the American Historical Association, 1891, pp. 65-81.

Perry, T. S.—The Life and Letters of Francis Lieber. Boston, 1882.

Harley, L. R.—Francis Lieber. New York, 1899.

Hinsdale, B. A.—Foreign Influence upon Education in the United States. In Report of Commissioner of Education for 1897-98 (see especially pp. 614-620). Washington, 1899.

(Ticknor, A. E.)—Life of J. G. Cogswell. Cambridge, 1874.

Griscom, John—A Year in Europe (1818-19). New York, 1823.

Barnard's Am. J. Educ. VIII:325-347 (1860), on John Griscom.

Am. Phys. Educ. Review II:22 (1897), on Lieber in the United States.

Consult files of the American Journal of Education, Boston, 1826-1829.

15. *The Manual Labor Movement.*

First Annual Report of T. D. Weld, General Agent of the Society for Promoting Manual Labor in Literary Institutions. New York, 1833.

16. 1830-1860 (*Various*).

Beecher, Catharine E.—A Course in Calisthenics for Young Ladies. Hartford, 1831.

——— Physiology and Calisthenics for Schools and Families. New York, 1856.

Henry de Laspée—Calisthenics. London (1856).

Windship, Dr. G. B.—Autobiographical Sketches . . . Atlantic Monthly IX:102 (1862).

Higginson, T. W.—Out-Door Papers (Atlantic Monthly, 1858-1862). Boston, 1863; New York, 1894.

17. *Dio Lewis and his Work.*

Eastman, Mary F.—The Biography of Dio Lewis. New York, 1891.

Dio Lewis—The New Gymnastics. Boston, 1862.

Tyler, M. C.—Brawnville Papers. Boston, 1869.

18. *Introduction of Military Drill in Private Schools and in Colleges.*

Barnard's Am. J. Educ. XIII:49, 683 (1863), on Capt. Alden Partridge. Reprinted in XXIII:833 (1872).

Hartwell, 1886, as under (1)—Pp. 95-105.

19. *Dr. Sargent's Work, and Physical Training in the Colleges.*

Sargent, D. A.—In Report of Physical Training Conference, Boston, 1889, pp. 62-76.

Hartwell, 1886, as under (1)—Pp. 29-82.

Pop. Sci. Mo. 52:622 (1898). Leonard, Physical Training in the Colleges.

Am. Phys. Educ. Review VI:14 (1901). Phillips, Credit for Physical Exercise.

20. *German Gymnastics in the United States.*

Metzner, H.—Jahrbücher der Deutsch-Amerik. Turnerei. 3 volumes. New York, 1890-94.

Jahres-Bericht des Vororts des Nord-Amerikanischen Turner-Bundes. Milwaukee.

Charles Bary—The Turners' Organization. Milwaukee. (Pamphlet.)

Report of the Special Committee on Observation, 26th National Festival of the North American Gymnastic Union, Milwaukee, 1893.

Report of Committee of Observation, 27th National Festival, St. Louis, 1897. In Mind and Body V:75, 102, 121 (1898).

Illustrated Souvenir of the 27th National Festival. St. Louis, 1897.

Das 28. Bundesturnfest des N.-A. Turner-Bundes, Philadelphia, 1900. Milwaukee, 1900.

German-American System of Gymnastics, edited by W. A. Stecher. Boston, 1895.

See also the files of the Amerikanische Turnzeitung, Milwaukee.

21. *Swedish Gymnastics in the United States.*

Posse—In Report of Physical Training Conference, Boston, 1889, pp. 42-51.

——— Special Kinesiology of Educational Gymnastics. Boston, 1894.

——— Handbook of School Gymnastics. Boston, 1892.

Enebuske—Proceedings A. A. A. P. E., V:21 (1890).

——— Progressive Gymnastic Day's Orders. Boston, 1892.

Hough—Review of Swedish Gymnastics, in Report of Commissioner of Education for 1898-99, I:1209-1226. Washington, 1900.

See also the files of the Posse Gymnasium Journal, Boston.

22. *The Young Men's Christian Associations.*

Gulick—Proceedings A. A. A. P. E., VI:43 (1891).

Files of "Association Men" (monthly), New York. (March, 1902, is a Physical Training number.)

Year Books of the Young Men's Christian Associations of America. New York.

Catalogues of the International Y. M. C. A. Training School, Springfield, Mass.; and of the Secretarial Institute and Training School, Chicago and Lake Geneva.

23. *Physical Training in the United States Army.*

Greenleaf—Proceedings A. A. A. P. E., VI:58 (1891).

Butts, Lieut. E. L.—Manual of Physical Drill. New York, 1898.

Luscomb—Am. Phys. Educ. Review IV:111 (1899).

24. *Physical Training for Criminals and Dullards.*

Wey, H. D.—Physical and Industrial Training of Criminals. Monographs of the Industrial Education Association, I, 3. New York, 1888.

——— Proceedings A. A. A. P. E., IV:17 (1888) and VIII:34 (1893).
Year Books of Elmira (New York) State Reformatory. (1892, 1893, 1895, 1897, etc.)

25. *City Playgrounds and Open-Air Gymnasia.*

Proceedings A. A. A. P. E., VIII:29 (1893) and IX:125 (1894).
The Bostonian, June, 1896, p. 258. Charlesbank Gymnasium for Women.
Am. Phys. Educ. Review III:133 (1898). Playgrounds in Boston.
The Outlook, January, 1900, p. 47. The Outdoor Recreation League of New York.
Harper's Monthly, June, 1902, p. 22. Vacation Schools and Playgrounds.
Harper's Weekly for September 11th and December 25th, 1897.
Chap. XV in Report of Commissioner of Education for 1899-1900 (I:895-904). Washington, 1901.

26. *"Delsarte Gymnastics."*

Durivage, F. A.—Atlantic Monthly 27:613 (1871). A Visit to François Delsarte.
Delaumosne and Arnaud—Delsarte System of Oratory. New York, 4th ed. 1893.
F. H. Sargent and others—Proceedings A. A. A. P. E., VII:74-96 (1892).
Bishop, Mrs. E. M.—Americanized Delsarte Culture. Washington, 1892.

27. *Military Drill in the Public Schools.*

Moore—In Report of Physical Training Conference, Boston, 1889, p. 121.
Sargent, D. A.—Effects of Military Drill on Boys. Reprint, Boston, 1886.
——— In Am. Phys. Educ. Review I:50 (1896).
Boyer and others—Proceedings A. A. A. P. E., X:124-135 (1895).
Boston Committee—Am. Phys. Educ. Review I:43 (1896).
Ballin—Militarism, a Symposium. Mind and Body II:210, 234; III:18 (1896). Reprinted.
MacCracken—In Report of Commissioner of Education for 1898-99, I:479-488. Washington, 1900.

28. *The American Association for the Advancement of Physical Education,* and *The Society of College Gymnasium Directors.*

See Proceedings of A. A. A. P. E., I-X (1885-1895), and files of the American Physical Education Review, Boston and Brooklyn.

29. *Reports and Periodicals.*

Proceedings of the American Association for the Advancement of Physical Education, as above. Brooklyn.

American Physical Education Review, Brooklyn. Since 1896. Quarterly.

Report of Physical Training Conference, Boston, 1889.

Physical Education, Springfield, Mass. I-V (incomplete), 1892-1896. Monthly.

Mind and Body, Milwaukee. Since March, 1894. Monthly.

Posse Gymnasium Journal, Boston. Since December, 1892. Monthly.

Amerikanische Turnzeitung, Milwaukee. Weekly.

The Gymnasium, London (early volumes at Cardiff, Wales). Since 1889. Monthly.

The Gymnast and Athletic Review, London. October, 1890-January, 1899. Monthly.

Jahrbücher der deutschen Turnkunst, Dresden (vols. 1-27) and Leipsic (vols. 28-40), 1855-1894. At first bimonthly, and later monthly.

Deutsche Turn-Zeitung, Leipsic. Since 1856. Weekly.

Monatsschrift für das Turnwesen, Berlin. Since 1882. Monthly.

Jahrbuch für Volks- und Jugendspiele, Leipsic. Annually since 1892.

Tidskrift i Gymnastik, Stockholm. Since 1874. 2 numbers a year.

EDITORIAL

from *Basketball for Women*

Senda Berenson

Basket ball was invented by Dr. James Naismith, about January of 1892. It was invented particularly for the Y. M. C. A. Training School, at Springfield, Mass., and in all probability, Dr. Naismith had no idea it would ever be played by women.

However, directors of gymnasia for women saw at once that it was, perhaps, the game they were eagerly seeking—one that should not have the rough element of foot ball, yet should be a quick, spirited game—should cultivate strength and physical endurance, and should be interesting enough to become a part of physical training for women as foot ball and base ball are for men. They saw at once that it had many elements of success required for such a game, and forthwith attempted it as part of their gymnastic work. Its success proved far beyond their expectations. It was only necessary to try it to have it become most popular wherever it was played. The colleges for women found it a boon. The physical training schools took it up, and their women graduates spread it all over the country. Today there are few gymnasia for women where basket ball is not a part of their curriculum, and hundreds of basket ball teams are formed yearly in all our cities by women who play the game at regular times during the winter. It is by far the most popular game that women play.

Experience with the game, however, soon proved that its one great fault is its tendency to roughness, and that in order to overcome this tendency some modifications would be necessary. Nothing is more conclusive of this than the fact that the majority of women who play the game, do so with more or less modifications. Dr. Sargent made some changes and had his rules printed. His Normal School pupils play the

Senda Berenson, "Editorial," *Basketball for Women* (New York: American Sports Publishing Co., 1903), pp. 7-11.

game with his rules and it is natural to infer that the pupils teach it with his modifications. The Boston Normal School of Gymnastics has printed modified rules of its own, and its graduates teach it with these rules. Miss Clara Baer, of Newcomb College, made many changes, and had her rules printed, calling the game "Basquette." Lewis, Drexel, and Pratt Institutes play the game with modified rules. Vassar, Radcliffe, Lake Forest University, University of Wisconsin, and Smith play with more or less modifications. At Smith College the game was played with modifications as early as the autumn of 1892. The preparatory schools and normal schools who play with some changes are too numerous to mention.

One has a natural antipathy against making changes in rules previously established. The fact that the majority of women find it necessary to change the rules of basket ball to suit their needs seems significant.

All this has brought about a great cause for dissatisfaction; namely, that scarcely two institutions of education for women play with precisely the same rules. Most of them play with changes of some sort, but each institution uses the changes it has made for itself.

At the Conference of Physical Training held at Springfield, Mass., from June 14 to 28, 1899, a committee was appointed to investigate this matter and to draw up rules which should voice the different modifications used all over the country as much as possible.

This committee consisted of Alice Bertha Foster, Director of Physical Training for Women, Oberlin College, Chairman; Ethel Perrin, Instructor of Gymnastics, Boston Normal School of Gymnastics; Elizabeth Wright, Director of Physical Training, Radcliffe College; Senda Berenson, director of Physical Training, Smith College.

The committee offered the following report:

The Committee respectfully recommends

First—That the Conference give its approval to the publication of a set of rules for the Basket Ball for Women, based on the official rules, but with such modifications as seem desirable.

Second—That these rules be offered for publication either with the Spalding Official Rules, or by the Spalding Athletic Library, together with some articles discussing the use of the game by women.

Third—That the leading institutions wherein the game is played by women be consulted, asking suggestions as to modifications thought necessary.

Fourth—That this guide be edited by Miss Senda Berenson of Smith College.

Fifth—That the changes made in the rules be as follows: * * *

The report and rules were read for approval before the Conference and discussed. The Conference voted unanimously that the report be accepted and rules adopted and printed.

The rules offered in this pamphlet seem to the Committee to voice the wisest changes of those used all over the country. On the other hand, they are not put forth as final, and the Committee will be glad of suggestions from any one who thinks further changes necessary.

THE PLACE OF AUTOMATISM IN GYMNASTIC EXERCISE

Jessie H. Bancroft
Director of Physical Training
Public Schools
Borough of Brooklyn
New York City

The only extended treatise we have had upon the relation of automatism to gymnastic or athletic exercise is that by Lagrange in his "Physiology of Bodily Exercise," a work which in this and many other ways marked an epoch in literature upon physical training. Lagrange's application of this particular aspect of his subject, however, is very much in the large; he discusses automatism in its relation only to running, walking, dancing, etc., with very little reference to the kinds of exercise taken exclusively in the gymnasium, and none whatever to methods in gymnastic instruction. That a further extension and closer application of the study might be made, Lagrange clearly recognizes and plainly states. He says: "The subject has not been as yet methodically studied, nor has any one hitherto endeavored to deduce from this curious phenomenon of automatism the practical conclusions which would be valuable in considering the hygienic applications of muscular exercise."

In this paper we attempt a contribution to such further study. The subject involves the entire question of mental work in connection with physical exercise. When the issue is raised as to whether gymnastic exercise should require attention and effort from the pupil, thus placing it in the category of work, or whether it should be in the nature of relaxation and rest, giving physical activity without mental strain, one should be able to discuss the question with at least as much definiteness as inheres in applied psychology. We believe that every method employed in gymnastic instruction has a distinct place in an ascending scale of demand upon the mental powers, and that automatism,

Jessie H. Bancroft, "The Place of Automatism in Gymnastic Exercise," *American Physical Education Review,* vol. VIII, no. 4, December 1903, pp. 218-231.

in which nature reduces to a minimum the mental work involved in muscular exercise, aside from having its place in this scale, affords a standard, or basis, for comparison and judgment of the various methods. We shall select for discussion but a few of the most salient topics offered by the subject.

Our point of departure will be taken from Lagrange, with a brief review of the ground which he covers and of the conclusions reached in his discussion. We shall then attempt an analysis, from the viewpoint of automatism, of some of the prevailing methods of the gymnasium. In this connection we think it will appear that some of the controversies that have waged over methods in gymnastic teaching—for example, as to the value or worthlessness of drills; as to whether or not a teacher shall lead a class in the performance of exercise; as to whether work shall be taken to musical accompaniment or without music, etc.—are referable for partial solution at least, to this principle of physiological psychology.

Part VI of Lagrange's "Physiology of Bodily Exercise" is devoted to the general topic, "The office of the brain in exercise." Here automatism is defined as "the faculty, possessed by certain nervous elements, of putting the muscles in action without the intervention of the will," an office performed by the spinal cord. The author makes very clear the difference in nervous expenditure between movements guided by the nerve centers in the brain—or consciously directed movements—and those directed automatically by the spinal cord, and selects as the pivotal point of his argument the fatigue which accompanies the mastering of new co-ordinations, or the conscious direction and control of old ones, by these higher centers, as contrasted with sub-conscious or automatic work. "Dancing," he says, "is an amusement; learning to dance is mental as well as physical work." He attributes the fatigue from this work largely to the toxic products of mental activity, and concludes that exercise which calls for work of the centers of consciousness merely adds to these toxic products, and therefore to the fatigue, and should not be used by one who is mentally overworked. Mental overwork is a term which he employs to express so normal a condition of fatigue as that of the usual school child, and which he would presumably apply to the tired business man, or brain worker in any line. He concludes—to quote from the text—that there is "great hygienic superiority in exercise which can be performed automatically. Economy of nervous energy, complete repose of the brain, absolute inaction of the psychical faculties, such are the conditions in which automatic exercise is performed." And such exercise he would prescribe for the class of gymnastic pupils mentioned.

For the sake of clearness we may visualize this plan in a rough diagram, in which a line may be drawn to indicate the demarkation between the nerve centers of conscious movement and those of automatic movement. Any exercise once mastered by the higher, or conscious, centers above this line is handed over by nature to the lower or automatic centers below the line for after performance. To quote again from the text, "We cannot regard automatism as a character which will serve to mark off a particular group of exercises. It is rather a mode of performance which most known exercises may assume under certain conditions." These conditions include familiarity, frequent repetition, and rhythm, including music. Types of such automatic exercise are walking, dancing and rowing. Lagrange plainly states that exercises automatically performed have less tension and effort than others, and consequently have less effect upon circulation, respiration and related functions.

With this condensed statement of Lagrange's definition of automatism and of the value he places upon it as a means of avoiding fatigue in exercise, we may proceed to an application of the subject to various methods common to gymnastics.

Learning New Exercises

Is the mere process of learning new exercises—mastering new co-ordinations—so difficult as to be harmfully fatiguing? We believe that this is largely influenced by the methods of teaching used. New exercises may be taught in a way that will reduce the work of the pupil in mastering them very close to the plane of automatism, or, on the contrary, so as to make a maximal, artificial and fatiguing demand upon the centers of conscious attention.

Imitation is one of the great economic agencies for the mastering of new co-ordinations. The person who sees another perform an exercise has that exercise already partly co-ordinated in his own nervous system, so closely related are the motor and sensory powers. Imitation, in other words, is very close to the plane of automatism; it is related to that class of movements called conscious reflexes.

At the opposite extreme in methods of teaching is the presentation of work wholly by verbal description. This method requires a tense and artificial effort on the part of the conscious centers to comprehend, or think out, co-ordinate and execute the movements described in words. No other form of neuro-muscular work is taught in this way. Drawing, for instance, is not taught by requiring pupils to give expression to something verbally described; on the contrary, the motor

	Lagrange's Outline	Methods of Mastering New Co-ordinations	Forms in Which Exercise May Be Taken	Rhythm (Music)
Conscious direction of movements	Mastering new co-ordinations.	Teaching by verbal description. Corrective gymnastics. Exact co-ordinations ("good form.") General or gross co-ordinations ("poor form.")	Methods of conducting work which unnecessarily call for conscious attention to co-ordinations. Type—analytical commands.	Slow time.
	Imaginary Line Dividing the Automatic from the Conscious Centers		Middle plane. Volitional effort conscious, co-ordinations automatic. { Well-known separate exercises, as on apparatus or to command. Methods of teaching which employ urging, correction, etc.; applicable to drills or separate exercises.	Rapid tempo. { Volitional effort conscious—co-ordinations automatic.
Automatism	Repeating old co-ordinations. Automatism favored by { Familiarity. Frequent repetition. Rhythm (music). Types of automatic exercise. Walking. Running. Dancing. Rowing.	Objective effort. Imitation.	Wholly automatic drills.	Normal tempo.

Chart Showing the Relation to Automatism of Various Methods of Gymnastic Instruction and Procedure.

activity is a direct reaction to the object itself; and such should be the reaction in learning gymnastic exercises. We do not believe that so artificial a method as teaching from verbal description could be too strongly condemned. Indeed it is hard to understand how anyone familiar with the laboratory experiments made by Dr. Anderson in 1893 can fail of such a conclusion. These experiments showed that greater fatigue followed the verbal method of learning exercises than the imitative method, and that a longer time was required in the process. A great deal might be said on this subject of imitation in gymnastic teaching; but suffice it here to note the fact that because it is a semi-automatic process, it reduces to a minimum the work of learning new exercises. To continue this imitation after an exercise is once known may reduce a pupil to the level of a reflex machine, echoing the teacher's movements. Whether or not that would be desirable would depend upon the objects sought for in the work.

Another great economic agency for both the mastering of new exercises and their after performance we believe to lie in some objective interest—some apparatus outside of the body to which the body conforms, rather than to have the bodily movements themselves the sole object of attention. Many have noted this before, but an impressive experience with light apparatus as compared to free gymnastics for school children, has convinced us overwhelmingly of the greater ease with which even corrective co-ordinations are mastered when the technic is subordinated to an objective result. This principle lies back of achievement in all of the arts. When Paderewski literally carves great masses of emotion and thought out of sound, he conforms his manual skill to the idea to be expressed: he does not concentrate his attention upon the manual skill. When Michelangelo's chisel bit into the marble from great, ringing strokes, which no other sculptor of his time or ours has ever dared to imitate, he adapted his bodily movements to a creative vision so intense that it became an objective reality. We cannot afford to disregard in our work this principle of nature, by which the body accommodates itself to objective interests, when it would stumble and halt if thinking solely of its own processes.

Whether exercise be with or without apparatus or other objective interest, we believe that for the mass of normal pupils the learning of new exercises by a rational method is one of the great elements of pleasure and one of the chief means of interest in gymnastic work. Pupils continually wish to learn something new, and often the only resource of a young and inexperienced teacher for holding interest is the presentation of new material. We doubt if there would at this time be in existence one summer school of physical training if teachers did not feel this natural and healthful need for new exercises. No one thinks of confining his or her reading to two or three books, or even to the "best one hundred." Why should the novelty of a new book be a rest or stimulus, and new exercises prove an exception to the rule? To see boys swarm at recess around an overhead ladder, or a horizontal bar, each taking his turn at trying new and most difficult feats, does not give one the impression that such exercise is "instinctively repugnant." Indeed, the college gymnasium director will tell you that the freshman's complaint of the gymnasium is, "Oh, we learned to do all of those old things at 'prep'!"

Pupils who have passed an age of motor facility, or who do not belong in some degree to the motor type, may find the mastering of new co-ordinations harmfully fatiguing under any conditions; but it is safe to assume that for normal pupils new exercises taught without excessive demand for conscious co-ordination, need not be a cause of fatigue, but quite the contrary.

Corrective Gymnastics

In a distinct class by itself is to be considered that mastering of new co-ordinations called corrective gymnastics. By corrective gymnastics, we mean that class of exercise which aims to correct the habitual standing posture of the body. We believe that this work requires the greatest effort of the higher centers of any class of gymnastic exercises, for in it one seeks, not only to form new co-ordinations, but to change old ones. For instance, in a position which shows a depressed chest and rounded shoulders, there is an habitual disproportion in the tension of the anterior and posterior muscles over the chest and shoulders: the one is unduly contracted, and the other unduly relaxed. This habitually disproportionate tension is manifest in all exercise that calls these muscles into action. To alter this habitual relation, the co-ordination must be dragged up from the realm of automatic adjustment where it has been long fixed, to that of conscious direction. The higher centers have not only to inaugurate a new adjustment, but to resist an old one—a doubly difficult task. Corrective work, then, is utterly beyond the sphere of automatic exercise; it is a function exclusively of conscious co-ordination. As Dr. White said in his "Elements of Pedagogy," "Automatic exercises may increase the mechanical facility with which pupils repeat processes, but such practice never corrects errors or suggests improved methods or processes. They beget the habit of non-attention to conditions of right activity." We may, therefore, put corrective work on our chart at a level of decidedly conscious effort.

The Execution of Gymnastic Exercises

Returning from corrective to general hygienic gymnastics, there are, on the part of the pupil, degrees of exactness in co-ordination which demand varying degrees of conscious effort, or, to reverse the statement, certain methods of performance are nearer to the automatic plane than others, and require less mental effort. It is a common experience that in teaching a new exercise, all pupils except the few who have reached a high state of motor education, will at first master the general form of the movements without the finer adjustments of finished execution. For example, a pupil raises the arm sideways. The gross movement involved in moving the arm is accomplished; but the exact height and direction and bend of the joints—all of these finer adjustments of finished execution—are neglected. Or, we will say, a pupil vaults over the horse; he gets over—he places his arms and lifts his legs, and performs the gross adjustments; but for all of those finer adjustments in what we call good form—as the erect chest and head, so important for economy of effort—all of these finer and more exact co-ordinations are utterly neglected, and the pupil has to make a later and a distinct effort to master them. In other words, there are degrees of muscular adjustment, ranging from the vague and general, which are very close to automatism, to the definite and finished and precise, and the finished work requires more mental effort than the vague and general.

We do not believe that this exact problem has been covered by any of the hypotheses that have been advanced to account for the facility with which some co-ordinations are mastered, and the difficulty with which others are achieved. Dr. Gulick long ago advanced the theory that certain co-ordinations which are racially old, being more firmly established in the nervous system, were comparatively easy of performance, and that other co-ordinations, being of later acquirement, were more difficult to master. Dr. Hartwell, emphasizing Ross and Mercier, looks upon muscular control as ranging from the fundamental muscles, through the intermediate to the accessory; that is, from the large muscles of the trunk, and those which attach the limbs to the trunk, and which were earliest to develop in the biological series, to the muscles of articulation, of finer manipulation, etc., which were later to develop. We do not think that either of these theories covers the particular phase of muscular control involved in finished work. Whether the co-ordinations be racially old or new; whether the muscles involved be fundamental, intermediate or accessory, the co-ordination goes through this development from an approximate to an exact adjustment. It is a question of degree, not of the muscles involved or of the general character of the movement made. Generally speaking, then, the exact co-ordination is not mastered at the first effort, and a later, and distinct, and special effort is necessary for it.

Whether or not it is desirable to demand this amount of mental work from a gymnastic pupil would probably depend largely upon the age of the pupil and the objects sought for with the exercise. We believe that these different degrees of motor power, in a young pupil at least, mark stages of development from the vague and general to the definite and exact, which he goes through in all other powers of the mind and of the will. One cannot observe, over and over again, the mental responsiveness, the power of concentration, the ability to think clearly and to answer questions in clear, intelligible language, possessed by classes of children capable of finished co-ordinations, and compare it with the mind wandering, the dull, irresponsive intellects of those who control only the gross adjustments, without believing that there is a close and vital relation between this motor ability and the mental acumen. It may not be a relation of cause and effect, as has been often stated; but we believe that both are expressions of the same plane, or level, or zone of development, and that each may help the other. To raise the child's power of thought and expression from the vague and general to the definite and exact is one aim of every other subject in the school curriculum. Such clarity and definiteness of thought power is one object of arithmetic, of manual training, of grammar, and of all other branches of English; and it is recognized as closely allied to the training of the will and character. Matthew Arnold, in speaking of Keats' remarkably clear thought, says: "Lucidity is in itself akin to character and to high and severe work."

When we exact good form and definite finish of execution in gymnastic work, we are using a degree of power in the pupil that is on a plane with this that is highest and best in his development. Such finish undoubtedly requires greater mental work on his part for its first mastery, and whether or not that is harmful to him we shall discuss later. It also means greater work for the teacher. Probably for both of these reasons an enormous amount of gymnastic work is never raised to the point of good form or finished execution. Work which lacks that finish may undoubtedly produce maximal effect upon the heart and lungs and general physiological processes; and for a great many pupils all of the time, and for all pupils some of the time, that may be the only result necessary from exercise; but it is doubtful if we yet fully appreciate the enormous significance which may lie in the training of motor ability to the point of finished execution. This is not to say that those of us who are working for good form in gymnastics do not appreciate that it has a close connection with good mentality and developed wills; and we have data, such as that of Wey and Seguin, proving the development of the abnormal mind through motor training; but we have not, that I know, any scientific data as to the relation between the normal mind and the power for finished muscular co-ordinations of gymnastics, as distinguished from the large, gross adjustments. This offers an interesting field for laboratory experiment.

We may, then, put the gross or general and vague adjustments down near the border line of the automatic, as they require comparatively little effort from the mind; the exact co-ordinations of good form may be placed higher in the scale. Whether an exercise partake of one of these degrees of co-ordination or the other, once it is mastered, nature asserts one of her great economic functions and hands over the direction of these co-ordinations to the spinal cord. After that a nervous impulse, conscious or unconscious, is all that is necessary to start the exercise and the automatic centers take charge of how it is co-ordinated. It is to be noted, however, that as soon as co-ordinations are handed over to the automatic centers they have a great tendency, except in pupils of advanced motor education, to revert to large adjustments only, and to lose finished execution. We have probably all been surprised at some time in our experience to be told that some old, familiar exercise, which we thought we were performing perfectly, was being done inaccurately. A teacher must, to still get finished execution from pupils, by frequent admonitions and corrections lift the co-ordinations back to the plane of conscious attention, until these final adjustments shall become more thoroughly established.

Various Forms in Which Gymnastic Exercises May Be Used

New exercises once having been mastered, and the co-ordinations handed over to the automatic centers, there are possible three methods of repeating them. They may be repeated so that both the co-ordination of the muscles, and the nervous impulse that sets them in motion, are automatic; or the co-ordinations may be automatic and the impulse to movement a conscious volitional act of the will; or the automatic tendency may be wholly resisted and the co-ordinations and volitional effort both held to the plane of conscious effort.

Wholly Automatic Exercise—Drills

A large class of gymnastic work, in which many repetitions of an exercise, or a long series of exercises are taken without pause, tends to the wholly automatic. Drills may be taken as a type of such work, as dumb-bell drills, Indian club drills, free-hand drills, etc. The psychological work in such a series may be explained by Professor James's illustration for an habitual series of movements. This illustration is a zig-zag line, each section of which represents a movement which produces a sensation. "When a series is being learned, each sensation is the object of a separate perception by the mind. By it we test each movement—we hesitate, compare, choose, revoke, reject, etc., by intellectual means; and the order by which the next movement is discharged is an express order from the ideational centers after this deliberation has been gone through." "In action grown habitual, what instigates each new muscular contraction to take place in its appointed order, is not a thought or a perception, but the *sensation occasioned by the muscular contraction just finished:*" Then only the beginning and the end of the series may be matters of conscious attention.

To apply this to gymnastics: When exercises are repeated a usual number of times on one side of the body and then on the other, these repetitions may come to be made with a minimum of conscious effort or even with none after they are once started. When several exercises follow one another in an habitual order, as in drills, it is quite conceivable that even the change from one exercise to the next might be made while the mind was intently engaged upon something else. Many of us who have taught for years have such automatic material in our repertoires. It is therefore safe to make the general statement that long connected series of exercises, such as those in drills, if frequently repeated, tend to reduce the work entirely to the automatic level.

Value of Automatic Drills

Here we have gymnastic exercise with a minimum of mental work. What can such exercise accomplish and what can it not do? Obviously it cannot master new co-ordinations or correct old ones, and is therefore useless for postural correction. Undoubtedly it can produce some of the effects upon the heart of the continuous work of exercises of speed or endurance. We believe, however, that as soon as conscious volition is withdrawn, the muscles tend to contract more feebly—the contractions do not reach a maximum limit as when one consciously puts force into them: the exercise becomes less vigorous. Lagrange, it will be remembered, noted this fact. It would be very valuable if the laboratory workers in physiology would ascertain for us if the effect of weak or partial contractions upon the heart, say in free-hand exercise, are not less than those of vigorous or maximal contractions.

We are inclined to think that this question is not entirely covered by experiments as to the effect of external resistence upon heart action. It is also probable that when exercise reaches the automatic plane, the heart becomes inured to it and the effect is lessened. Empirical observation certainly would lead one to believe that automatic drills have less effect upon the heart than those in which volitional effort is exerted. Indeed, a good teacher of drill work, by vigorous example, and by admonition and urging, seeks continually to lift the work back to the level of conscious volition.

Partly Automatic Exercise

Where such a method of leading drills is used as that just mentioned, it raises exercise from the automatic level to the middle plane, where the subconscious processes of co-ordination and initiative alternate with effort of the higher centers.

Types of this class of exercise are feats of strength or skill on fixed apparatus, or exercises to command, as in free-hand gymnastics; in short, any separate exercises in which the co-ordinations are familiar. When a distinct effort is made to put vigor into a well-known exercise it belongs to this class.

Consciously Directed Movements

There is a method of command used in which not only each exercise, but each component movement, is made an object of distinct volition—a method whereby the co-ordinations of even very well known exercises are not allowed to be directed by the automatic centers. This analytical method places exercise at the farthest remove from automatism and makes an excessive demand upon the centers of conscious volition.

Rhythm—Music

One other element common in gymnastic practice has so direct an influence upon these different psychological processes that it must be considered. This is the tendency of even rhythm, especially when reinforced with musical accompaniment, to reduce work to the automatic stage. It seems to us that this effect of rhythm is beyond dispute as regards what may be called normal rhythm. One reason why many repetitions of an exercise, or long series of exercises, as in drills, tend to the automatic, is because of the even rhythm in which they are generally taken. To break the time into uneven intervals, either by counts or commands, is to raise the work instantly to the plane of conscious effort. We wish, however, to advance this proposition: that the automatic tendency in rhythm or music for gymnastic exercise is related to *tempo*—the normal, fast, or slow time in which it is taken. Each individual has a natural or normal rhythm; for one person time would seem to be very slow which for another would seem quite rapid; yet for a large number of persons taken together there is an average which may be called the normal rhythm. Let the orchestra play too fast or too slow, and the dancers complain. We believe that the rhythms which may be called normal in time, those which are easiest and most natural for the largest number, are the ones which have the greatest tendency to automatism, and that by quickening or slowing the time psychologic changes are involved. It would seem that in quickening the time, as in jig steps, or in rapid drills, co-ordinations become more surely automatic, but volitional effort has to be increased beyond the limits of automatism for all save the few who may become inured to it. We know one gymnastic teacher who exhausts her pupils by the rapid time in which she takes all exercises, irrespective of the pupils' nervous condition and irrespective of whether or not they know the exercises so thoroughly as to render the co-ordinations automatic and rapid. On the other hand, if the time be made slower than the normal, as in long, stretching, æsthetic gymnastics, we believe that both the impulse to movement and the co-ordinations are of necessity raised to the plane of conscious attention. This slow time is at first very fatiguing, but eventually becomes soothing in its effect. The slow work would seem to be favorable to the changing of co-ordinations required by corrective gymnastics, and experience has shown its efficacy for that purpose. We believe that this form of exercise—the æsthetic stretching movements—is emerging from the sentimental, unscientific and faddish atmosphere in which it was first introduced to us, and that it will come to be valued more widely for some pupils as one of the most useful agencies for corrective work, aside from its æsthetic values.

Is Mental Work in Gymnastics Necessarily Fatiguing?

We take issue with the proposition that wholly automatic exercise is restful to the mind, because it gives "complete repose of the brain," and "absolute inaction of the psychical faculties." The fact is, that such a mental state is psychologically impossible. At no time during life, sleeping or waking, at work or at play, is the mind absolutely inactive; the attention must fasten upon something during all waking hours. Wholly automatic exercise leaves the mind free to wander back to the subjects which have tired it and so loses its power for mental recuperation.

We believe the crux of the entire subject of mental activity in gymnastic work lies, not in whether or not the mind shall be employed upon the exercise, but in the way in which it is employed and the character of the attention demanded of it. This brings us to one of the great battlefields of pedagogy. If the interest in what is being done be so great that attention is involuntary, then fatigue from this element could be no more harmful than in play, for even in play the mind is intently concentrated. If, on the other hand, gymnastics demand voluntary attention, which requires an effort of the will to hold it to the subject in hand, that effort may become an element of harmful fatigue. This is generally the kind of attention required for conscious co-ordinations, or the kind of work in which an automatic tendency is resisted. The circumstances of gymnastic exercise offer no occupation for the mind, except various phases of the exercise itself, as do walking or rowing, or other outdoor activities of an automatic character. To eliminate the attention, therefore, from all phases of the body's activity is to reduce the mind to the necessity of vacant wandering, to cultivate habits of careless, unfinished and half-hearted work, with their demoralizing effect upon character, and, in school classes, at least, to put a premium upon disorder. Pupils do not enjoy such work; the teachers who have the most enthusiastic following will be found every time to be those whose work is of the thorough, forceful kind that demands and holds attention.

Conclusions

It is apparent that vigor in gymnastic exercise, the mastering of new co-ordinations (especially of the finer adjustments and of corrective work) require the conscious co-operation of the brain; and on the other hand, that automatic work, done without such attention and effort, while it may produce some effect upon the heart, is comparatively weak in execution, continues old habits of co-ordination, and, save in exceptional instances, lacks the definite finish which marks motor work on a plane of mind where dwells power of definite thought and developed wills.

Applying this to some phases of gymnastic exercise, it would appear that in the learning of new exercises the methods that partake of automatism—imitation and objective effort—may reduce the fatigue incident to the artificial process of consciously mastering new co-ordinations. The changed co-ordinations of corrective work, however, may probably never be achieved without conscious effort, though certain methods of teaching may render them easier of acquirement than others.

For most pupils, any new exercise, however taught, is at first performed only in its gross or general features which are near to the plane of automatism and which receive comparatively little conscious attention. The fine adjustments of correct or finished form require conscious effort on the part of the pupil. The psychological value of exact co-ordinations may be placed very high. Their physiological and corrective value is equally high.

After exercises are "learned"—i. e., after the co-ordinations have become easy, rapid and automatic—the nervous impulse needed to inaugurate the movements may be a matter of conscious effort, as in separate exercises on fixed apparatus or to commands; or it may be unconscious or automatic, as in automatic drills.

The tendency of the automatic process being to reduce both the vigor of muscular contraction and the extent of the movements, to continue old co-ordinations, and to reduce new ones to the gross adjustments only, we may say of the wholly automatic drill that while it may stimulate the circulation and respiration, it will do these in a slighter degree than methods that call for volitional effort; and that it is wholly inadequate for corrective work as it continues old co-ordinations. Drills, however, need not of necessity be automatic. A teacher may, by comment, correction, suggestion, and urging, continually lift the work back to a plane of conscious effort, where it may become both vigorous and corrective. What a drill accomplishes, therefore, may depend upon the way in which it is conducted. The correction, urging and effort require so much of a teacher, and the elements in a drill that tend to automatism are so strong, that the chances are against its having the vigor or accuracy of separate exercises.

Any kind of work, as in analytical methods of execution, in which well known co-ordinations are not allowed to be governed by the automatic centers, makes an unnecessary, excessive and fatiguing demand upon the conscious centers of the brain.

Music as an accompaniment to gymnastic exercise favors automatism, if in normal *tempo,* and automatic co-ordinations only if in rapid *tempo.* Very slow time lifts the entire work to the plane of conscious attention and is favorable to the correction of co-ordinations.

We believe that mental work in gymnastic exercise is necessary for vigor and accuracy of execution and for the pupil's interest in, and enjoyment of, the work; we believe that the proportion which this mental work shall bear to physical activity is dependent upon methods of teaching and adapting exercise, which may reduce it to a minimum, or raise it to a maximum, or vary and mingle these extremes in a happy medium; and we believe that complete automatism, while it has some utility for gymnastic purposes, is there possible only within very narrow limits, and ranks low as a mode of gymnastic exercise. We have endeavored to show, however, that it furnishes a standard by which to judge of the amount of mental work in some of the most important methods of gymnastic procedure.

INTRODUCTION

to *Athletics and Outdoor Sports for Women*

Lucille E. Hill

"Truly, an embarrassment of riches," an enthusiast in physical exercise will delightedly say while turning over the pages of this proof of women's interest in health, strength, and beauty.

Not until one's attention is thus directly attracted to the variety of gymnastic exercises, sports, and pastimes now enjoyed by women, does one realize how much has been done in a very few years to interest us in physical activity as a curative agent and a recreation.

And the list could be even longer with all honor to the pioneer services of the bicycle. Hand-ball, squash, racquets, lacrosse, and cricket have their devotees, and fisherwomen, campers, canoeists, and gardeners believe the most attractive forms of activity in the open have been omitted.

How contagious, too, is the enthusiasm of each writer for his or her favorite sport, making the novice long to taste the joys of all in one day!

This awakening of girls to the delights of athletics, together with an aroused intelligence in the desirability of possessing a strong and beautiful body for both use and ornament, makes imperative a corresponding knowledge of the practical laws of health and the relation of proper food, sleep, bathing, and clothing, as well as exercise, to the welfare of the body. Otherwise, through ignorance and lack of self-direction and control, a great power for good will become a source of evil.

Our ever present ideal should be Health and Beauty; and during this early stage of our experience in athletics our watchword should be "Moderation." Already we have shown our incompetence in self-

Lucille E. Hill, "Introduction," *Athletics and Outdoor Sports for Women* (New York: The Macmillan Company, 1903), pp. 1-15.

control and judgment by meriting the following statement in one of the papers in this book: "If the advocates of athletics for women are ardent, their *opponents are equally strenuous.* Their chief objections are based very naturally on health considerations. They say, with reason, that all instructors are not wise and that most girls are overzealous. Few women can work or play moderately, and if they once become absorbed in athletics, they will be prone, in their excitement, to go beyond their strength and do themselves lasting harm."

The only possible way in which we can change our strenuous opponents to ardent advocates is to conduct our athletics, both social and organized, on such a high plane of intelligence and control that there can be no ground for this disfavor. We hear constantly of the "*abuse* of men's athletics"; we should hear nothing but the "*use* of women's athletics."

It is always a pity to see a good thing so misused or overused that the majority of people lose sight of its true mission and recognize its superficial popularity only.

As a means to an end, the value of athletics is as great—and greater—for women as for men; but while we enthusiastically seek the health and recreation which comes with natural play, we must avoid the evils which are so apparent to thoughtful people in the conduct of athletics for men.

Women should be exponents of the "New Athletics," whose platform is largely idea at present, but with unity of effort it can be made very real.

And the first plank is this,—Underneath the gayety of physical activity we must acknowledge that *Health of Body and Mind* is the moving and governing principle.

And the second is this,—That all associated efforts must secure the greatest good to the greatest number; not the greatest good to the smallest number, which is one of the evils of the "Old Athletics."

And the third is this,—That competition in organized athletic sports is desirable so far as it strengthens the first two planks of the platform.

Dean Briggs said in his Commencement address to a graduating class at Wellesley College: "The girl of to-day has more independent manners, and, happily, has along with them a freer life. She may ride a horse without an accompanying groom; she may bestride a horse; she may row and run and swim and take part in a hundred athletic exercises without being one whit less a woman,"—he forgot to add, but a great deal more of a woman,—"but some things she had better leave to men. Fiercely competitive athletics have their dangers for men, but they develop manly strength. For women their dangers are greater, and the qualities they tend to develop are not womanly." There are many people having the interests of women's athletics deeply at heart who are anxiously watching the signs of the times and asking each other, "The Lady or the Tiger?"

Women, engaging in some form of athletics for one reason or another, can be roughly divided into five big classes, exclusive of the large number in normal schools of physical training.

First, women of leisure who make golf, riding, skating, and other sports fashionable pastimes, and a means of gaining physical beauty and sound health. Second, business and professional women, who tramp, skate, and use gymnasia in the winter, and their vacations on hill farms or by the sea in the summer, with the serious object of keeping themselves in condition for their daily work.

Third, women who are—or think themselves—more or less out of sorts from neglect of the laws of hygiene, and whose physicians prescribe some form of exercise as a remedial agent.

Fourth, young girls in secondary schools, both public and private; and fifth, the great class of college girls.

Now we are all, in different ways, responsible for the good or ill repute of athletics for women, and it behooves us to work together in our various classes to win public and private respect and confidence in our management. We are in honor bound to do this unselfishly and seriously.

I am sure we all agree that as yet most of us are too untrained in stability of purpose and in keeping up a sufficiently sustained interest in any special form of exercise to attain a high degree of strength or skill. We are quickly enthusiastic and as quickly discouraged. When we become accustomed to regularity of daily muscular activity, as we are accustomed to taking food and sleeo regularly, an invaluable habit will be formed.

The first thing to be considered by a woman whose physical condition does not demand a prescribed exercise, is the selection of some form of physical activity which will bring her keen enjoyment and mental stimulus. The element of joyousness is strong for health. For this reason a game is desirable for many women who find it difficult to change the trend of serious thought without a strong "counter-irritant."

Dancing, under favorable conditions,—as an athletic costume, abundance of cool fresh air, day or early evening hours, and gay music,—need fear no indoor rival as a source of physical and mental refreshment.

It is a thousand pities that woman's good comrade, the bicycle, has felt our fickleness. Its extensive banishment has sadly decreased life in the open for great numbers of women who have not the strength of wish or will to defy fashion for the sake of a partially developed conviction. Golf, the aristocrat, cannot fill the place of the bicycle, the democrat.

Most of us are so situated that much freedom of choice of a physical recreation is denied us, for as yet comparatively few towns have links, and rinks, and gymnasia, swimming, riding, and fencing schools, bowling alleys, athletic fields, tennis courts, playgrounds, and play-sheds for women. Perhaps sometime the city fathers will realize that the city mothers must be strong, and provide more extensive means for physical, as well as mental, education.

But no woman can beg off from a splendid, daily athletic exercise because the above attractions are unavailable, unless she is destitute of shoes and a short skirt. Cross-country tramping—not just "taking a walk"—for an hour or more, the body well set up, the heart and lungs working hard, is a glorious, health-giving exercise, and all the finer if one has the sympathetic companionship of a dog or some other jolly friend.

It seems to me that the first class of athletic women mentioned, with plenty of money or leisure or both, may have to watch out that they do not exaggerate the importance of athletics and, by drawing an excess of public attention to themselves, spread abroad the false impression that women are becoming "sporty" as a type, whereas it is well-nigh impossible to induce the average woman to walk a few miles a day in all kinds of weather. With abundance of time at their disposal in which to "train," they have a fine opportunity to prove the value of right living as a means of gaining physical beauty and health.

The second class, of very busy women, perhaps, forget that rest and nourishing food, with exercise in the open air, are of prime importance, supplemented by gymnasium exercise. Women whose nerves are under constant tension, and whose brains are very active, need a variety of physical recreation, bringing with them gayety and relaxation. Business and professional women should have big, airy club buildings for dancing, tennis, hand-ball, squash, rackets, basket-ball, bowling, fencing, and swimming. How delightful it would be if every large town and city had great wooden structures which could be made semi-outdoors by drawing back or pulling up shutters, in which nerve-tired women could play!

The third class, of women who are endeavoring to regain their health through some prescribed form of exercise, diet, bathing, and rest, can easily become discouraged and not persist in the new régime long or regularly enough to prove the efficacy of the training.

But most women in the foregoing classes are practically engaging in unorganized athletics and are subject to no recognized control in training beyond technical instruction, therefore the responsibility lies entirely with the individual to achieve good results from the exercise through the exertion of her intelligence and self-control.

The greatest menace to the good repute of athletics for women is at present found in the secondary schools, and it is so striking that promoters of the cause of health for women have grave reason for anxiety.

Doubtless, we can truthfully quote that "all instructors are not wise" and that a great deal of the trouble comes from "over-zealousness," ignorance, and thoughtlessness on the part of the young pupils, who should be strictly disciplined and trained. But I believe the greatest responsibility lies with the school authorities who permit young girls to engage in games of the athletic grade without *any* recognized examiner or competent instructor.

The "play instinct" is so keen in all healthy young animals, that a girl's active or latent interest in games suited to her age and strength should be encouraged and developed.

It is of special importance that direction and instruction should be given at the age when childish play is outgrown and the need of more difficult and vigorous games is apparent, the period extending to the age of the college freshman.

We believe the college girl has a right to expect guidance and instruction in the recreative branches of physical training,—the sports,—as in the gymnastic courses. How much more does the younger, less-experienced girl need competent supervision!

The initiative in the introduction of games should be taken by the school authorities, not by the pupils, as a part of the scheme of education; a playground, and, if possible, a playshed for use in bad weather provided, and an instructor of games appointed. Where this cannot be done, games of the severity of hockey and basket-ball should not be permitted to exist as school organizations, and inter-scholastic matches should be prohibited. Where the conditions are favorable for the development of school games, matches between class teams in the school will insure a larger number of entries in the sport and less danger from over-excitement than inter-scholastic matches, where a school furnishes but one team and more intense nervous strain accompanies the keener competition.

The conduct of athletics in women's colleges will naturally be criticised to our advantage or disadvantage, by persons who believe physical training to be a part of a girl's education, and we should take so firm a stand for the highest ideal and direct the development of the subject so wisely that our example can be followed with confidence.

This youthful work will require, for some time yet, more or less experimental administration in the various colleges, but we labor with a common end in view, and athletics are a means only to that end.

College women are beginning to recognize the true relation of the body and mind and to value physical training as an aid to the best intellectual activity. There is also an increasing appreciation of physical beauty to be found in abounding health, grace of motion, and dignity of bearing.

Women should also recognize the need of perfect organization in all parts calling for teams, crews, or champions. The ethical value of "athletics for women" may be placed side by side with the physical value. The necessary submission to strict discipline, the unquestioning obedience demanded by the officers, the perfect control of the temper and sensitiveness under coaching, together with the fact that she must be absolutely unselfish in order to become a loyal and valued member of her organization, develops a young girl's character while she develops her muscles.

The word "training" as applied to the extreme care of the body preceding an event requiring a high degree of physical and nervous effort, has not the man's interpretation in the woman's college. We believe that "training" is simple, practical "right living." That the "training" need never be so extreme as to make it desirable to "break training." The interest in an organized sport is a legitimate and effective cat's-paw in establishing hygienic habits of living, and we hope that the common sense and improved health of the girl will encourage her to continue in her abstinence from sweets, her eight hours—or more—of sleep, her cold-water baths, and her daily exercise in the open air.

Too despotic, mechanical "training" should be discouraged, as an appreciation of the intrinsic value of right living must be acknowledged by the individual if permanent benefit is to be gained.

The "event" for which women should train is a long and happy life of usefulness—with no "nerves."

The influence which we are all consciously, or unconsciously, exerting over athletics is inevitably placing the subject on a permanently high or low plane of development.

Those who believe physical training in all its branches to be a vital part of the scheme of education will treat it with the dignity such a position demands.

Those who look upon athletics as a fad or pastime only, will take no serious interest in its growth or decline.

I believe, too, that unnecessary publicity tends to cheapen the efforts of an individual and an organization; therefore those of us who labor for the success of physical training as a powerful health factor in the lives of American women will esteem reserve as womanly and notoriety as unwomanly.

LUCILLE EATON HILL
Director of Physical Training,
Wellesley College

A STUDY OF HARVARD UNIVERSITY OARSMEN FROM 1852 TO 1892

By Dr. Geo. L. Meylan

Dr. George L. Meylan of Columbia University read a paper recently before the Boston Physical Educational Society on "A Study of Harvard University Oarsmen from 1852 to 1892, Inclusive." He presented some facts in the much disputed question of the effects of athletics upon the college student, principally with reference to possible injury to the health and vitality in later life. His general conclusion was that rowing, at least, even in races, effected no injury that could be detected.

There were during the 40 years in question, 152 Harvard "varsity" oarsmen, of whom 32 have died. The remaining 120 were interviewed in one way or another, about 75 personally by Dr. Meylan, and certain facts regarding their present physical condition and their status in the community were gathered and tabulated. The first question considered was the value of their lives as an insurance risk. The ages of the oarsmen are known and the insurance mortality tables give a forecast of how soon they should die. On this test the oarsmen averaged 7½ years more than the average insurance risk, in point for longevity, for the same number of men.

Contrary to the usual accepted notion, there was a higher marriage rate; and their families averaged larger, than the Harvard students generally and also the average Massachusetts man. On applying the "who's who" test, to see whether Harvard oarsmen were sufficiently successful to get mentioned among the 8000 prominent Americans in the book, the oarsmen were found to be more largely represented than either the students generally or the Phi Beta Kappa men at Harvard or at all the large eastern universities. In the matter of general condition and health, they were markedly above the average

George L. Meylan, "A Study of Harvard University Oarsmen from 1852 to 1892," *Mind and Body,* vol. 2, no. 121, March 1904, pp. 21-22.

citizen. In none of the statistical tests thus applied, of which there were over a dozen, such as would occur to a skilled physical director, were the oarsmen found wanting, or indicating that rowing in college races hurt them.

Only one of the 120 believed that he was injured by his college rowing. He suffers from dyspepsia, but is an active professional man nevertheless. He attributes his dyspepsia to his rowing experience. His surviving associates point out, however, that the modern physical examination to which crew candidates are subjected would prevent his rowing, in races at least, and he also rowed during the period when trainers forbade all liquids with food, a notion now abandoned.

About a dozen old Harvard oarsmen were present, the oldest one having rowed in the 1865 and 1866 'varsity crews. Brief remarks were made on the paper by Drs. Charles Williams and H. L. Morse, both ex-'varsity oars of many years ago. Drs. Sargent and Leavitt spoke briefly in the ensuing discussion, the former pointing out that 'varsity oarsmen were a specially selected class, but that it was a gratifying result to find that their early exertions in races had not hurt them. Dr. Morse said he believed his rowing, at least, was distinctly beneficial. Dr. Meylan argued, by way of finale, that the results ought to strengthen the case for regulated athletics in colleges.

Dr. Dudley A. Sargent was chosen a delegate to represent the society in the international conference at Nuremburg April 4 to 9, 1904, on school hygiene.—BOSTON HERALD.

OUR NATIONAL GAME AS A FACTOR IN EDUCATION

By Arthur J. Arnold

Base ball! The great national game of the American people! Which one of the many outdoor sports so well known to us can be compared with it? It is the greatest joy of the small boy; a source of honor to the young man of the high school or university; the bread of life to the professional. And it serves all purposes admirably, not only to the player, but to the spectator as well, for no other game is so fascinating and so wholesome at the same time. No matter where you may go at this time of the year you will see boys of all ages playing base ball. Almost every vacant lot has its quota of embryo players. You see the joyous little fellow of five or six playing with an old yarn or cord ball, or you may see the older brother, who fields his position with all the ease and grace of the professional. If you wait until a little later in the season you may, some fine day, go out to Fairview Park and watch the doctors play the lawyers. Notice how they seem to enjoy the game and you cannot fail to realize that it is the one that suits all ages; which all enjoy with equal pleasure. This is the reason why it has such a hold on the hearts of the American people.

And this very American game is so well known to each and every one of us that we seldom give a thought to the good resulting from it, or to the lasting part which it plays in the education of the American youth. The fact that the game is so interesting is always uppermost in our minds; we are so susceptible to its excitement that we fail to realize what good it really brings to us.

The first thing the little chap of six or seven, who wishes to follow in the footsteps of his elder brothers on the ball field, learns is to obey.

Arthur J. Arnold, "Our National Game as a Factor in Education," *Mind and Body*, vol. 2, no. 123, May 1904, pp. 64-66.

He knows that the older boys understand more about the game than he does. So when they tell him to do this or that he obeys their instructions to the letter. Until he attains his full size he will always play, more or less, with older and better players than himself. He values the instruction which they give him and almost consciously learns to obey them. He learns to obey without realizing the fact, but he learns it all the same. As he grows into manhood he will continue to follow the advice of those who know better than he himself does, not only in base ball, but also in whatever business he may pursue.

Control of his temper is an essential requirement of a ball player. Realizing this, he strives to avoid any display of temper, especially during a game. Instead of getting angry and indulging in unkind remarks should one of his team make an error, he is always ready to stand by him with his "All right, old boy! That was not your fault," or some other saying which will cause his unfortunate colleague to resolve then and there that he will not make such an other misplay. Should he get angry, he knows that he will be the target of cutting remarks of the opposing team, to avoid which he must retain his temper at all times.

And self-reliance, one of the most important and lasting benefits to the boy who has played ball ever since he was able to throw one, must not be forgotten. Practice brings self-reliance. The more he plays and the older he grows the more confidence he has in himself. And as he acquires this reliance in himself, this confidence that he can hit or catch the ball at all times, a resulting benefit comes with it. When he goes to the bat with the chances decidedly against him and some one yells, "Hit it, old boy!" he answers in his mind, "I will!" This perseverance, this "I will," will stay with him throughout his life. No matter what business he may take up, no matter what profession he may pursue, nothing will prove more valuable to him than his "I will" in connection with the self-reliance which he has in himself. He will always be ready when an opportunity comes.

And so we might go on naming the various benefits which he receives and acquires. But of all others what one can be compared to that most important of all, a healthy body? The fresh air, the exercise, the enjoyment which comes from playing ball, all combine to give the player the best of health. We cannot expect the boy accustomed to indoor life, who is constantly complaining of headaches and sicknesses of all descriptions, to be very healthy in manhood. Can we then expect the same work, the same success, from him as from the man who has had the benefit of fresh air and pleasant exercise during his entire boyhood and youth? If he be a lawyer, can we expect him to carry on a trial, which may last for two or three months as do some of them, with the same zeal, with the same power and ability as does his opponent who does not know what sickness is and who is just as fresh and anxious at the end of those several months of hard work as at the beginning? If he be a physician, can we expect him to stand the continuous work, which he may sometimes be called upon to do in the case of the general prevalence of some dangerous disease, as well as does that physician who has always the best health? If he be an engineer, whether mechanical, mining or otherwise, can we expect the same work, the same results, from him as from his brother engineer who possesses the healthiest of bodies, and who is capable of performing his work, whether it be in the shops or in the mines, day after day and year after year with the same energy and ability? He may have the confidence in himself, but his "I can" is lacking.

With good health, with confidence and reliance in himself and the will to do a thing, with control of temper, with the power to make and carry out immediate decisions, what cannot be expected from the youth who has all these qualifications of a successful business man? And every one of them can be learned from the great American game which we all love. Since all real education of the American youth must tend toward producing these traits of character which contribute so materially to a successful life, the game which gives so much enjoyment at the same time that it is bestowing these benefits on the player will always be a most important factor in his education.

THE ACADEMIC STATUS OF THE GYMNASIUM*

Thomas A. Storey, Ph.D., M.D.

Associate Professor and Director
of Physical Instruction
College of the City of New York

The first conclusion which I wish to advance is that the work done by the student in the gymnasium is not academic. The academic value of a subject in the curriculum is measured by its intellectual qualities. Thus languages, philosophy and science are intellectual. They are therefore academic. Dancing, swimming, singing, the mechanical technical procedures in laboratories, and physical exercise are not intellectual. They are therefore not academic.†

The gymnasium has been brought into the academic community from the outside. Yesterday it was entirely distinct. To-day there is hardly a university, college, preparatory school, or high school of truly modern proportions that does not support a gymnasium. Coming from a distinctly unacademic source it has secured an unquestioned and permanent position in these academic institutions. But this close relationship is not the result of any intrinsic academic qualities possessed by the gymnasium.

It has been brought about by a wise appreciation of the fundamental value of a healthy body and its essential relation to a healthy mind. The pedagogical farmer has found that his harvest is best when his seed falls on fertile ground. And for these reasons universities, colleges, preparatory schools, and high schools build, equip, and man gymnasiums, and in one way or another encourage the student to use the advantages thus provided. In one case the student is cordially in-

Thomas A. Storey, "The Academic Status of the Gymnasium," *American Physical Education Review*, vol. XII, no. 4, December 1907, pp. 303-306.

*Presented in a slightly different context before the Society of College Gymnasium Directors, Springfield, Massachusetts, December '06.

†The writer separates the meaning of the term "academic" from the term "educational." A subject must be intellectual in order to be academic. An educational subject need not be intellectual and may not therefore be academic.

vited to come at will; in another he is required to attend during a certain portion of his academic life; in a third he is given credit on the registrar's books for the time spent in regular gymnasium courses.

For these same reasons Y. M. C. A. gymnasiums have spread from the Atlantic to the Pacific; for the same reasons churches, factories, social clubs, and municipalities spend large sums of money on gymnasiums. Healthy bodies and the consequent healthy minds mean as much socially, politically, commercially, and religiously as they do academically.

My second conclusion is that the work done by the director is fast becoming truly academic.

The work done by the student to-day is fundamentally the same as that done thirty years ago but the work done by the director has changed vastly. To-day his preparation requires years of intellectual and technical work. There is no profession that in its ideal requires more. Law requires less time and medicine is rapidly becoming only a part of the director's equipment.

The college gymnasium director is now usually appointed to a position of academic dignity ranking him on an equality with the professors in and heads of other departments. He enjoys the rights of academic franchise; serves on committees; and enjoys privileges of equality with other members of the faculty. He often gives lecture courses on academic subjects occupying unchallenged positions on the curriculum.

We then have in the modern gymnasium a situation in which the director with an academic preparation holding an academic appointment and giving some academic courses has for the major quantitative portion of his supervision gymnasium classes in which the student is not doing academic work.

There is in this situation nothing to be ashamed of. No professor on the academic faculty has a larger opportunity to influence the health, happiness and character of the student. No one has larger possibilities, I believe, for affecting the health habits of the general public through his influence on the student body which is each year scattered to the four corners. This I maintain gives the director a powerful, far reaching influence toward all that is good in our social system. For good habits, good health, happiness, and good citizenship are in strong and natural sequence.

But regardless of the value of these possibilities the fact remains that the students coming to our confreres on the faculty are doing academic work and those coming to us are not. And we are too likely to be standardized academically from this viewpoint not only by the pardonably thoughtless public, but even by our sometimes unpardonably thoughtless confreres.

Without the slightest diminution of my high regard for the ideals of my profession I have for several years considered seriously the possibility of developing academic qualities in student work in the gymnasium. With this in mind I have watched the correlation of personal hygiene with gymnasium work and have had an opportunity to observe the fate of several attempts to add intellectual features to the work. I have found that where hygiene and gymnastics were given concomitantly but as separate courses they remain entirely dissociated in the average student mind and it is not legitimate to claim for the one course any of the qualities possessed by the other. In another scheme the Physiology of Exercise was given as a lecture course one hour each week and gymnastic work, two hours. The three hours counted for one hour of credit on the registrar's books. It was planned to make the lectures directly applicable to the floor work in the gymnasium and to teach the student something about what he was doing and what his work would do for him. The plan seemed theoretically to be sound. Practically we were disappointed. We failed to secure any general realization of the fact that the lectures and the floor work were part of a whole. They remained distinct in the student mind. The students' work in relation to the lectures was academic: that in relation to gymnastics was not academic.

In another scheme we devoted the first few moments of the drill period to the discussion of some point bearing upon personal health. The men were seated cross legged on the floor, uniformed, and in their regular class formation. It was a unique situation and was peculiarly appropriate for such a purpose. It seemed to be the psychological moment for securing concentrated attention; for the association of hygienic precepts with their practical application and for making persistent memory impressions. I was greatly pleased with the success of the method for its effect was made known to me in various ways.

Finally I discovered that the men whom I used from time to time as subjects in physiological experimental work always became much interested. They seemed to be attracted by anything that showed them something about their own functional activities.

These two experiences—one with the short discussion preceding the drill and the other with gymnasium students as subjects in physiological experimental work related to physical education—have led me to the hope that by such methods we may be able to add an academic quality to general gymnasium work which would add to its dignity and what is far more important would add to the possibilities of its intelligent use.

I have formulated in a general way a hypothetical gymnasium course on this basis. At the beginning of each class period throughout the year I would spend from five to ten minutes discussing subjects related to personal health. The body of the hour with its medical examinations, variety of interesting and approved exercises, and opportunities for bathing, would give occasion for the fulfillment of a number of the fundamental laws of health. In addition each student would be assigned practical experiments to be done in the gymnasium or at home, which would bring him into more intelligent relationship with some of the simple fundamental phenomena of human physiology. Then I would assign appropriate references to standard related literature. Finally I would require reports on the experiments performed with logical deductions from the same; examinations on reading assigned; and a reasonable evidence based upon examination that each student had made an average gain in strength and co-ordination.

Such a scheme if properly carried out would certainly give each student an intelligent conception of his own problems of personal health. It would give him a practical working knowledge resting on an intellectual basis which would, I think, lay just claim to academic qualities. I cannot say that the drills and apparatus work would differ under such a plan from what they now are. Such work can never be intrinsically academic but the student would exercise more wisely and he would evolve an intelligent working scheme for the government of his own physical habits.

THE EVOLUTION OF ATHLETIC EVILS*

Wilbur P. Bowen
Professor of Physical Education
Michigan State Normal College
Ypsilanti, Michigan

The growth of student athletics has been very rapid for twenty years. From small beginnings in a few eastern universities the movement has not only grown to enormous proportions where it started, but it has spread to nearly all the colleges and high schools in the country. This rapid growth has brought about some serious athletic problems that have compelled the attention of teachers, and for several years past the educational press has brought out many able discussions of these problems. As a result of the chance afforded to study the growth and development of various phases of athletic life and custom, and the illumination given in these discussions, we can now see clearly some things that were formerly rather hazy and of doubtful significance.

One notable change within the last few years has been the gradual falling away of athletics as a part of education. It is practically admitted by everybody nowadays that the athletic games and sports have come to stay, and that there is a good reason for their staying. The general public is just beginning to recognize for the first time that the occupations of everyday life in the future, and especially with the more intelligent classes, will not afford enough bodily exercise and training to maintain the physique of the race. Leading educators are seeing for the first time that something like athletic training is necessary to the highest mental development. Physicians are urging as never before the universal practice of bodily exercises as one great means of health, instead of relying solely on the taking of medicine. So strong

Wilbur P. Bowen, "The Evolution of Athletic Evils," *American Physical Education Review,* vol. XIV, no. 3, March 1909, pp. 151-156.

*Reprinted from *The Western Journal of Education,* December, 1908.

has this sentiment become in all directions that there no longer exists any practical opposition to the general advisability of athletic sports.

Along with the growing recognition of the hygienic and educational value of athletic practice has come the realization that high school and college sports, as now carried on, do not even remotely approach the accomplishment of what they can do along these lines. They are apparently conducted for the benefit of the few who least need such training, rather than for the good of the mass of students; their main purpose seems to be spectacular, rather than hygienic and educational; they frequently lead to various forms of dishonesty and brutality, and to all degrees of excess. How can we account for such an amazing inconsistency? What motive can there be strong enough to induce a college or a high school, purporting to stand for all that is highest and best in Christian civilization, to secretly hire trained athletes to play on its teams? What advantage can there be in such an institution's making a false showing in athletics? Why should our educational institutions, the country over, sacrifice the best interests of 90 per cent of their students in order to promote a series of shows given by their few best athletes?

A brief study of the evolution of American college athletics and athletic customs clears the mystery and shows exactly how such misuse of athletics has arisen. A century ago, when the foundations of our educational system were being laid, American life called for no special means to secure bodily training. Fully 95 per cent of the population lived in the country. Pioneer life in the midst of a new country had developed a hardy race. In the past of the race the work necessary to secure the necessities of life had always provided all the bodily development that was necessary. No one in those days ever dreamed of the complete revolution that the invention of machinery has since wrought in the occupations and life habits of the American people. Those who attended the colleges and academies of those days went there, in most instances, from the active outdoor life of the farm, and looked forward to a life of considerable bodily activity afterwards. The educational system was moulded to meet the needs of these people as they saw them. In a sparsely settled country, with very limited opportunities for reading and for social intercourse, and with a democratic form of government, education was planned to give students a liberal culture, a more scholarly and polite use of the mother tongue, and the opportunity to acquire useful knowledge, especially along lines pertaining to industry and politics. When, as time went on, college men began to take up athletic sports, no one thought of them as having any serious importance, either educationally or otherwise. Since they were considered simply as forms of amusement which certain persons chose to follow, it was naturally expected that those who took part in them should pay whatever it cost to carry them on. Even after they assumed great proportions, and after it began to be seen that they had great educational value, still the college authorities everywhere adhered to the tradition that the colleges were intended to provide intellectual culture only, and considered it entirely outside the province of a school or college to provide the funds to carry on athletic work.

As the attention given to athletics increased, the need of money to provide the maintenance of the sports increased along with it. The students interested in the sports, failing to secure from the funds of the institution any allowance for their maintenance, saw that the existence of any such training depended upon their putting on the market a kind and quality of sport that would pay. Working along this line they soon found that financial support depended upon their putting out a winning team. They found that the average individual likes to be on the winning side of everything, and that while people have a moderate desire to see games and contests, they have an immensely greater interest in the team or the man who can beat all competitors. They found that the average community will give liberal support to a team that can win all its games, but that it will not give much financial or moral support to a team that loses.

As soon as the promotors of athletics clearly grasped this principle, they at once set about making athletics pay. The old idea of athletics for health and for discipline was discarded; that of athletics for revenue took its place. What had been sport now became business; what had been friendly competition became war. "The team" existed but for one purpose: to defeat and humiliate the teams of rival institutions; only in that way could it swell the gate receipts. The mass of students, lacking unusual physical ability, merited consideration only in so far as they would aid in the enterprise by paying the admission fee and "rooting" for the team. With a zeal and shrewdness seldom surpassed in the world of finance, many a genius of the college world has invented schemes that have been used in every college and high school. Professional coaches have been employed; famous athletes from the alumni have been brought back to help the coach whip the team into fighting trim; students, coaches, and alumni have been set at the work of inducing promising athletes to come to the institution; athletes have been enticed and even hired to leave rival institutions and play against their old associates; newspapers have been induced to give large space and attention to the games and to individual players of certain institutions; players have been given extra inducements in the form of expensive uniforms and equipment for the sport, free board at the "training table," long and frequent railroad trips, and an amount of hero worship seldom equalled in the days of chivalry.

The system has worked well for what it was intended. The success of athletics as a commercial venture has been phenomenal, even in this commercial age. Single games sometimes bring in gate receipts amounting to more than a thousand dollars apiece for all the men on both of the competing teams. Several of the largest student associations spend more than $100,000 annually for the expenses of teams. Several have an equipment, paid for by earnings and by gifts of loyal alumni, approaching half a million dollars. The athletics of smaller institutions have also met with prosperity on a smaller scale.

The financial success of student athletics has given them a standing and prestige with the general public that they could not have gained in the same time in any other way. Business men appreciate financial success, and are apt to measure success in dollars and cents. As a consequence, many who looked upon athletics a few years ago as a piece of student foolishness are now enthusiastic supporters of the games. College men, formerly held in little esteem in the commercial world, won the respect of the public when they demonstrated that they were able to make money. Coming to have an interest in athletics in this way, the general public naturally thinks of the matter as a financial proposition and accepts the commercial idea of athletics as the correct one.

A great many people, both students and citizens, viewing the matter from this standpoint, have little patience with the disposition of faculty committees to frame rules of eligibility and to discourage the custom of offering inducements to good athletes. What harm is there, they ask, in hiring good men, if by so doing you can pay them and realize a profit? That is good business. If a college may hire a good teacher in all propriety, why not a good athlete? No one ever demands that a doctor be an amateur, then why a ball player? Why should a college faculty discriminate against its own teams by requiring all the players to keep up in their studies to the same standard as those students who have no athletic work to do? What sense is there in hampering a system that works so well by a lot of rules and restrictions that have nothing to do with the case?

As long as the commercial basis of the present system is accepted as the correct one by the college authorities, there is no answer to these questions. The trouble with student athletics is not on the surface, but in the principles on which the system is founded. Athletics promoted, as most student athletics are today, chiefly in the interest of their earning capacity, are essentially professional. What matters it whether the proceeds go to benefit the system as a whole or the players individually? The distinction is a mere matter of words. The whole train of athletic evils against which the faculty committees and the intercollegiate boards have been battling are the natural and inevitable results of the false principles on which the system rests. As long as we expect the athletics to support themselves, we must expect the managers to plan to draw a crowd; since this depends on winning, winning will be considered the thing of supreme importance; as long as athletics are carried on between teams and before crowds who look at it from this standpoint, the temptations to dishonesty, brutality, and excess will be too great for many to withstand. As long as the purpose of athletics is commercial, the spirit will not rise above the spirit of the stock exchange, no matter what rules the faculty committee try to enforce. Efforts to reform have met with only partial and temporary success, because they have been mainly attempts to remove certain evils while retaining the system and the spirit from which they inevitably spring.

In the great schools for boys in England and in a few schools and colleges in this country the institution has furnished room and equipment for athletic sports, and has provided for the organization and practice of such sports irrespective of physical ability. In these institutions the percentage of students engaging in some form of bodily training is two or three times as great as in those that are most famous for their athletics, the sports are more uniformly beneficial to the participants, and the evils are much less evident. In a few institutions the fund is raised by a subscription or voluntary assessment paid by the members of the school, no admission fees being charged at the games. This is a great improvement over the usual system, as shown by the greater numbers benefited and the general spirit of the student body. The students of such institutions have a healthy interest in taking part in real sport, rather than in taking it all by proxy, and they are more apt to be loyal to the team at all times, whether it wins or not. The man in a paid seat in the bleacher is not the best exponent of college spirit; he has paid for the satisfaction of seeing his side win, and he wants his money's worth; he is gleeful and noisy as long as his team is ahead and gaining, but subsides into sullen and silent gloom when it is losing. This is a cheap brand of loyalty, but it is the kind that has been developed by the system.

The school and college authorities who wish athletic reform can get it at any time when they are ready to provide the funds; then they can dictate the method of expenditure and the system will be free from the commercial spirit and the moral and educational evils that go along with it. Some fear that to divorce commercialism from sport will take away all vim, but the instinctive desire to excel, possessed by every normal individual, is a sufficient incentive to make everyone anxious to win. This is natural and right, and gives to all plays and games the zest that makes them so great a force in education; the influence is bad when the desire to win is exaggerated out of all reason by making financial support and the existence of the sports depend on winning.

It is not surprising that coaches, students, and citizens should see in athletics a commercial instead of an educational problem; they are not students of education, and they have been driven to their point of view by the failure of faculties, principals, and governing boards to provide the funds for this branch of education as they provide for all others. It is surprising that the leaders of education in America, those who dictate or advise the apportionment of funds among all branches of education, should have for two decades failed to grasp the educational value of this work and have left it to go off on a tangent; it is still more surprising that the teachers, the great band of wide-awake and progressive people who handle the educational destinies of the nation, should have but yesterday passed by the golden opportunity of a lifetime and permitted the playground associations, made up chiefly of outsiders, to inaugurate the greatest educational movement of modern times. There is hope that in a time not too far in the future the high schools, colleges, and universities will learn from observation of the playgrounds what games and sports are for. Of all things, let us hope that the playgrounds will not be commercialized.

THE FOUNDATION OF AMATEURISM

Clark W. Hetherington
University of Missouri
Columbia, Mo.

The amateur problem is one of those discussions that is always with us. It began with the dawn of athletic rivalry between groups. It existed among those people we are wont to think ideal in sports as in art. It arose with the rise of sports in England. It has grown in prominence with the development of American athletics.

Our present situation is the result of social conditions. With the rapid rise of American athletics without traditions to guide us we have gone on many by-paths of athletic adventure. Neglect in proper leadership brought on corruption, which authorities met with drastic legislation. Those hit, countered with a voluble attack on the traditional ideals of amateur sport. Having no deeply rooted public opinion on athletics as an educational and social force, there has developed through lack of information and insight a widespread doubt of the wisdom of amateurism. In the attack, Anglophobia has taken its part. Even intellectual leaders have been heard to say that the amateur law came from England, from entirely different social conditions, that it had no place in American democratic life, etc., without once pausing to consider whether the law had any foundation in human needs or any necessary significance in human relationships. It is surprising the number of college men that have dropped like plums into the apron of the opposition over the college summer baseball controversy, because the arguments are seductive and hard to meet by the layman and because we have no strong background of national ideals in play or sport.

We need some constructive criticism. Amateurism can no longer stand on its traditional legs. Public faith in its justice is tottering. We

Clark W. Hetherington, "The Foundation of Amateurism," *American Physical Education Review,* vol. XIV, no. 8, November 1909, pp. 566-578.

must either modify our law or show that amateurism is a necessary element in human playful relationships. If amateurism wins public confidence, it must be demonstrated that the law is rooted in human nature and social forces, and essential for a healthful boy's play life. To consider this phase of the discussion will be the purpose of this paper.

To understand our problem we must analyze, first, the primary interests that create athletics, second, the factors controlling the development of these interests in participation and, third, the place and effect of the professional motive among these factors.

In considering these points, I shall assume that we are all agreed on the functions and values of athletic sports for boys, i.e., the values for organic development, motor development and character discipline, that all recognize athletics as the natural physical-social education of boys, that they are especially important in the later adolescent years, and that we want *all,* fitted physically, to take part in them. As educators and social workers, this must be our viewpoint.

We shall first analyze the primary impulse, pleasure, interest, motive, that leads to participation in play or athletics; then the impulses that create the professional.

At the foundation of all motor play there is a satisfaction in the motor discharge exhibited by the young of all animals; a satisfaction of the primitive hunger for activity, together with the sense stimuli which are intensely pleasureable. Closely associated are other sensuously agreeable stimuli most strikingly illustrated in adult life by the pleasure in watching a thrown object.

To these fundamental pleasures in play there are added a long series of pleasurable emotional states appearing more or less in all motor plays from infancy to adulthood. There is the conflict of daring and fear in feats, the pleasure in accomplishment and success, the pleasure and pride in overcoming difficulties and encountering risk or danger with all its emotional tension, the exaltation that comes in the rebound from fear through relief, the tension of expectation and shock of surprise, the pleasure of enduring hardships and suppressing pain, the pleasure in the feeling of mastery of self, the inspiration of being a cause, and all the emotional content that holds attention and heightens the reality of life which is opposed to ennui and which for the adolescent is a neurological necessity.

Then there are the impulses which influence the form of play. The combative, social and egoistic impulses, appearing in play from early childhood, become especially prominent with adolescence. Simple running for its own sake soon loses its charm and must be turned into a contest, thus satisfying the combative impulse. Rolling about on the floor is changed into a tussle. Destructiveness is sometimes prominent. Through all childhood there is intense pleasure in being chased and chasing, hiding, being sought and seeking.

The egoistic impulse combines with the combative to give keenness to do something as well as, or better than, some one else. This tendency becomes peculiarly strong in the adolescent period. So out of rivalry we derive all the fighting games and contests of youth. These are perpetuated and emphasized by imitation.

The social impulses, with perhaps some sexual elements, add their force. The desire to be noticed leads to showing off, especially by boys. A desire for social applause and approbation leads often to self-exhibition and a display of skill and courage. Especially keen is the pleasure of achievement in competition under social conditions, perhaps the highest stimulus and satisfaction in youth to the egoistic impulses and emotions. Cravings for self-testing, self-evaluation, the determination of one's social status, superiority or inferiority, become prominent. Where these impulses come in contact with developed or traditional play activities as in athletics, there arises spontaneously a craving to gain one's place in the social system, to become a member of the team, to represent one's fellows, to support the honor of the institution and to win the satisfaction and applause of achievement. Public interest intensifies these expressions. To be in the swim is the most general of social motives.

In this brief summary of the impulses, pleasures, interests and motives that create play and playful athletics, we see revealed all the meaning and significance of play and athletics. They are Nature's means of securing organic, motor, mental and social education, which comes from strong motor social activities. The motives and the normal results are purely educational. The boy's aim is pleasure; Nature's aim is education. Educators and social workers are interested in the motives and the activities because of their educational and moral meaning. *In the activities boys have inherent rights; parents have rights in the boy's rights, and in protecting these rights educators and social workers have rights.* The boy who takes part in athletic contests purely in obedience to these impulses and for the pleasure derived is an amateur. His interest in the satisfaction of the impulses and in the pleasure derived reveal the content of those motives we commonly call "sport for sport's sake"; this is amateurism. It is the attitude of mind that determines the root of amateurism. Whoever exhibits this attitude in all his play is psychologically an amateur, no matter what the man-made law or definition of amateurism for social control may be. Here we make a sharp distinction between the principle of amateurism and the law formulated for its administration in practice. Like all human law the principle may be sound, the law enacted may be defective. The principle of amateurism is the concept of the natural mental attitude in play; the law is an enactment for social control. This analysis shows further that Nature's aim in play, the boy's pleasure, amateurism as a principle, and educational athletics as an administrative endeavor, have at the root one and the same purpose.

Usually the professional interest in athletics is contrasted with the amateur. The amateur motive, however, is the flower of a primary human need and interest; the professional interest is not. This is a secondary interest derived from the spectator's interest which is primary.

Glance for a moment at the spectator's interest and see how deeply rooted it is in human nature. Human interest in contests is as broad as the struggle of nature and man. A storm, ants at work, men blasting rock or launching a lifeboat excites interest. Especially strong is the interest in fighting contests. Human nature loves to see a fight. A dog fight excites even the refined. The emotional extremes to which the indulgence of this impulse will lead is best illustrated by the world's great fighting spectacles: the gladiatorial contest, the chariot race and the bull fight of earlier times; the horse race, the prize fight and the professional baseball contest of modern times. From out of this primal interest in any struggle comes the spectator. As indicated in the social elements of the players' motives, the spectator's interest in witnessing contests has had a profound influence on the higher development of contests. He supplies the social setting, the approbation and the applause which stimulates development. He has also supplied most of the money for the support of highly organized contests. This fact has given him his power in the development of contests. Still to make his status clear, it should be understood that the spectator is not essential to highly organized athletics and the educational ideal that all should participate.

Our interest in the spectator, however, centers in his influence in creating the professional and professional motive. It is impossible to conceive of a professional athlete without the spectator. There would be no reason for his existence. The professional is created by the spectator's interest acting as an economic demand on those who have interesting feats to exhibit. The economic needs of those having personal skill and physical prowess impel some to supply this social demand resulting from the general human interest in feats and contests. The interest is satisfied for a consideration. Interesting stunts and contests are held at a price. Often the large rewards and the social applause or notoriety are intense stimuli for effort. Historically this is the origin of all professional performers in sporting spectacles. The spectator's influence does not stop with the creation of the pure professional. He creates in athletics the petty money motive which is expressed in irregular and intermittent demands for reward. The process is simple. The spectator becomes a partisan. He wishes one side or the other to win. Where one social group is organized for contests with another social group the rivalry becomes intense. It is play war. Group pride enters into the contest. The group partisan's craving to win exerts pressure on contestants for skillful performance. The effort to supply the skill makes training severe, the time consumed the maximum. Fun is often replaced by work. As a natural result there develops in some athletes the question, What is there in it? This the spectator tends to meet by extra encouragement and rewards. The play motive is replaced by the petty money motive. The motive is perpetuated by custom.

The concept of professionalism complements that of amateurism. The athlete who caters to the spectator's interest and holds his participation in contests at a value, or who desires a reward for such participation, is a professional. It is the attitude of mind that determines the root and motive of professionalism. Whoever exhibits this attitude is psychologically and in social motives a professional, no matter what the man-made law of professionalism may be. The professional may have all the interests of a pure amateur but he adds something to the amateur motive which has no direct or indirect connection with the biological, psychological, sociological, or educational purpose of play. Producing this attitude of mind was the point emphasized by educators a few years ago in their bitter denunciation of our "commercialized and professionalized" college athletics.

To make our discussion unbiased the social status of the professional should be clearly stated. It has been said many times that there is no objection from the standpoint of play or the amateur propaganda to professional athletics or the professional athlete. There is no objection to earning money or to making a living by the use or exhibition of one's skill in any physical feat. Accepting money for playing baseball or teaching boxing or coaching a basket ball team, are not acts that in themselves are immoral. These are economically legitimate methods of making money or one's entire living. These acts become immoral when and only when the individual commits them while pretending to be something that he is not, or when he violates a social or educational law enacted on the theory that it protects the natural rights of the many in play.

In summarizing this analysis of the interests and motives in athletics we make a distinction, clear and decisive, between the concept of amateurism and the concept of professionalism on the one hand, and the law of amateurism or law of professionalism on the other. The concept in each case is based on fundamental impulses which are as deep as human nature. The law of amateurism is man-made and subject to all the limitations and defects of human laws. It is our problem to search into the need and justice of the law.

In passing it should be noted that our analysis of the influences of the spectator indicates the line of future struggles in education concerning amateurism.

We turn to the second division of our analysis, the factors controlling participation. Those personal and social factors which control a boy's participation or non-participation in sports give the background for our ultimate question, the effect of the money motive in play. For convenience we will divide these factors into four groups: (1) The strength of the native impulse to vigorous activity and competition; (2) the personal and social influences affecting this impulse; (3) the special influence of other interests; (4) the effect of what we shall call the law of competition.

The first two of these we may consider briefly together.

Individuals differ radically in the strength of the spontaneous impulse towards strong motor play. This begins early in childhood and continues through youth. Some temperaments are active, alert, and eager for experience, enjoying keenly every sensation; other temperaments are inactive, even sluggish. This does not necessarily signify a less degree of undeveloped capacities. Early in life these differences in impulse are emphasized by differences in physical vigor or nervous vitality. Social aggressiveness or timidity add their quotum. To these personal tendencies in the development of efficient play habits, social conditions determining opportunities carry the divergence between individuals to the limit of possibilities in human developmental variation. Some children have every opportunity and encouragement to play; others lack every opportunity in point of time, space, equipment, the examples of social usage, the stimulus of organization, information or instruction, or even parental sympathy. Hence there begins early in childhood a divergence between individuals that increases with each successive year of youth in strength, skill, adaptability, resourcefulness, the play habit with its enthusiasm, the play appetite and a feeling of need for its satisfaction. Consequently, the *developed* in each little group initiate and organize the strong motor plays; others are drawn in; but the less developed or enthusiastic are progressively eliminated to milder games, and there often results in them a lack of that development to secure which the play impulse was probably created. In the first case the play impulse has been efficient; in the latter it has been thwarted in its purpose, its biological and social ends. Therefore the motor-play impulse is not always certain of its purpose; it is easily overpowered, sidetracked, perverted, or satisfied with activities that do not achieve its end. The bearing of these facts for social workers and educators is clear. They give us the bedrock principles necessary in the organization of play and athletics. Educators dealing with play must realize the folly of leaving children and youth to their own devices in play. They must have proper opportunities, stimuli, examples, sympathy and guidance. Each child must be taken where he is in the process of development and led on to a higher realization of his powers. This means organization based on a classification of children by age, sex, height, weight, strength, vitality, experience, habits, etc. All education and social endeavor is based on some classification of individuals or groups according to capacities. In schools this grading is conspicuous. For strong motor plays, play educators are separating sharply the girls from the boys; and classifying the boys by weight rather than age or school grade. Recent experiments on physiological age as compared with age by years indicate a more scientific classification in the near future. The more complex the social conditions the greater is the need for a classification of children that will recognize temperament, strength, and habits; and for organization that will give stimulus, opportunity, encouragement, and sympathetic guidance. Otherwise Nature's chief educational force will fail. In the special need for classification in contests lies the root of our problem.

The third factor influencing participation is peculiar to the later adolescent years and increases further the tendencies to divergence between individuals. We refer to the rise of social and intellectual interests and ambitions. Being motor, athletics are among the most primary and fundamental of play activities. They are, therefore, open to all grades and classes of people, the ignorant, trifling, worthless, as well as the intelligent, earnest, ambitious. Through public interest they give great opportunities for personal achievement and social approbation. Social standards, however, tend to class them in a social scale of activities as merely physical. This tends to influence interest according to social ambitions. On the one hand, many boys and men with large physical energies and low intellectual capacities seek through athletics the only means open to them of gaining a continued social approbation. Athletics tend to become the activities of boys and men who have limited mental powers other than motor. As a result, they are stigmatized socially as worthy only of the individual who is motor inclined and limited in mental powers or ambition. On the other hand, men with strong intellectual, artistic or moral inclinations and men with strong social pride, strive for development in higher fields of culture and social achievement. Intellectual and social impulses swamp the athletic impulse. Ambitious boys tend to withdraw from motor activities even as a means of healthful recreation, especially where the influences surrounding athletics are unfavorable to the individual's pleasures or desires. This process begins in its most intensive form in the later adolescent years, the period of intellectual and social awakening. The process is most striking where strength, skill and the play habit are equal among individuals, but intellectual interests and social ambitions most unequal. It, therefore, plays an important part in our discussion.

The fourth factor determining participation is the effect on classification through what we shall call the *law of competition.* This is rooted in the very soul of the impulse to compete. It enters athletic competition through the prominence of social rivalry. The pleasure in the contest is centered largely in the emotions connected with the chances of winning. Human nature demands a fair or equal chance to win, and no hunger in human nature is more insistent on its rights.

In boys' fights the law of competition finds its elemental expression. In boy society the fighting impulse is governed by it. Fighting ability is determined by age, height, weight, strength, skill and disposition. By this power, groups of boys often tend to grade themselves. Boys fight within the groups to determine social superiority. The boy who will fight with a superior is considered unusually gritty. A boy that will not fight among his equals when the code demands it is considered a coward. A boy who fights only his inferiors is a coward and a bully. The code requires a boy to fight within his own class. This is the law of competition.

A sharp distinction must be made between play, the issue of which is not serious, and play charged with rivalry. The law of competition operates in proportion to the seriousness of the contest as a test of powers and therefore is particularly important in our discussion.

There is often play *at* a contest where a serious contest could not exist.

A boy of six, one of eight, a girl of nine, two young ladies, a judge, a physician, a banker and his wife, a college professor and his wife played "baseball" on the front lawn. For the boys it was a contest; for the adults it was a rollicking good time with laughter in proportion to the comic elements present. The judge suddenly exhibited rivalry and lined out a ball which passed just over the head of the six-year-old boy on second base. Instantly the *play* vanished. The boy wiggled, looked disappointed and mumbled, "pshaw, that isn't fair." The parents realized the "close call" and tactfully changed the entertainment to refreshments. The game was *play* until rivalry and skill came in. Serious competition could not exist in such groups.

A boy will tussle with his father with all his energy or a girl again will wrestle with her older brother, but should the father or the brother use more than just enough power to neutralize the efforts of their struggling antagonist and so keep the struggle interesting, or exhibit rivalry and use the tactics they would use against equals, immediately there comes the complaint, "Oh, you're rough." Either there must be reform or the play ceases. Here again there is play at a contest where there could be no contest. Similarly a young lady or an inexperienced gentleman will play at a contest in tennis or golf with a champion but they will refuse to compete against him.

Often real contests take place between individuals or teams that are unequal in strength, but the inequality is recognized and an inequality in score expected. Inexperienced individuals, ambitious to learn, often enter the inconspicuous preliminaries of tennis or golf tournaments. High school football teams often play against superior college teams, and small college teams against great university teams. Rivalry enters and the score is a serious item, but the balance of the score is recognized beforehand or there could be no contest. The weaker team does its best, the stronger sometimes does also, but the outcome is preordained and there is no disturbance of social feelings. Such contests can exist so long as the spectators and the public recognize the natural inequality and make allowance for it in the score. Unrecognized, the contest would not exist, because of the workings of the law of competition.

In contests between individuals or teams that are supposed to be equals the law of competition has full sway. The law is emphasized by the rivalry of partisan backers. The desire for fairness in an equal opportunity becomes insistent. The sharper the rivalry, the more closely are the lines drawn. Nowhere in life does the demand for a square deal so promptly assert itself. Unfairness ruins the contest.

Here we come to the core of our problem. We are concerned chiefly with the upper end of play, the contest, in the later adolescent years, when rivalry is most keen. This is the contesting age. It is here that the law of competition becomes peculiarly important in determining any classification for participation.

This brings us naturally to the last division of our analysis and the ultimate question in the amateur discussion. What place and influence has the professional motive among the factors controlling participation? To put it another way: What effect has the professional motive on participation when brought in contact with the playful or amateur motive?

The effect of the pure or regular adult professional is seen at a glance, is recognized by all and gives no cause for discussion. He eliminates the amateur under the law of competition. Given partisans with money and no amateur regulation and he would eliminate the amateur from all highly organized contests representing a group. The extent of this elimination, if allowed, down the years into boy life, is limited only by the living wage and the financial capacity of partisans. If we are to have highly organized contests to satisfy the amateur motive it is clear that pure professional activities must be kept separated from the amateur by an effective law of classification. Over this there is no dispute.

Our difficulty is not with the pure professional but with the petty professional who has irregular or intermittent professional experience. The money motive in the petty professional is linked with desires for a little extra spending money, a trip, a pleasant summer outing or a means of making expenses in school, etc. Our first interest in these experiences is not in the moral nature of the acts themselves but in the results which they have on participation in contests when the actor is brought in contact with the pure play motive. *The meaning of play in boy life demands that the amateur motive and the participation of the majority be conserved.*

It is clear that professional experience makes more expert performers. Practice gives skill; practice among the devotees of an art gives superior knowledge. No one denies this; it is one of the stock arguments used by those opposing the amateur law. Other things being equal the boy with professional experience will always have greater chances of making a place on the team of his group than the boy who has had no professional experience. This means that among the typical mass of boys the professionally experienced is a special or exceptional case. Against him in the contest the typical boy is handicapped. He is defeated; the professionally experienced wins. The two parties are not equally matched; the contest is unfair. By the law of competition the typical boy is deprived of competition. This undemocratic influence alone establishes the place of the money motive as represented by the petty professional among the influences controlling the participation of the many and explains the necessity of a law fixing a classification, separating the money motive from the amateur.

But the results do not stop with the majority. This is only the first step. A little experience in athletics and contact with the petty professional, teaches the typical boy interested in athletics why he is handicapped. He is outclassed because of his competitor's superior experience. If his athletic impulse is strong and he craves to make the highest team of his group, the incentives to gain skill by the methods of his competitors will be strong. He is denied the pleasure of participation until he gains superior skill either by a large expenditure of time or by professional experience. He must accept defeat, or do as the Romans do.

In this connection there are two points to be noted. First, the time element controls those with the higher ambitions even if they have no scruples against professional experience. To the ambitious, time is valuable; a disproportionate amount of time cannot be spent on things purely physical and recreative. Among college men the influences here are striking. College athletes, even under present conditions, have little time free from routine studies and athletics. They must forego other recreative and culture activities. Ambitious men refuse to make the sacrifice. They tend to withdraw from athletic participation in proportion as the administration disregards their higher interests. They not only lose the benefits of athletics but athletics lose the influence of them. *What these boys want is not money but their athletic rights.* They have a right to education of athletics without a loss of culture life. They have a right to enter an athletic organization that gives the hope of achieving athletic honors without sacrificing their higher ambitions. *A custom that either discourages general culture or the education contained in athletics must be condemned.* In so far as the petty professional tends to create a situation requiring an excessive expenditure of time in sports, he must be legislated out of existence.

The second point concerns the generally unwholesome influences of professional experience. Making an exhibition of one's self for money before a miscellaneous crowd of pleasure seekers who supply the money is not calculated to develop the best type of character or intelligence for American citizenship. The appeal is to impulses low in the scale of character and social values. However much professional sport may be elevated in essential elements, it will always remain low in the scale of human occupations. The trend of its influence is low. Manners and customs, especially the gambling, language, and humor, are not refining. There is plenty of time for loafing, usually with sporty associations. The occupation and environment emphasize the sporting news habit. The sporting page, the most licensed and unwholesome page in the modern newspaper, is the literature of the professional. An experienced professional once said that it took only about four years of professional summer baseball to make a man "nutty."

While there are many "good fellows" and many intelligent men in professional athletics, this does not alter the status of the occupation nor the trend of its influences. It is not the atmosphere in which educators and social workers wish boys to be educated. Earnest parents, as they see the growing importance of athletics in the lives of their boys and realize the moral influences of professionalism, will insist that their boys be guarded from professional experience. Boys without earnest parents must also be protected. Therefore educators and social workers must condemn professional experience for the typical mass of boys. Inasmuch as the money motive breeds the money motive, and professionalism breeds professional ideals, we must legislate against both.

As a final product of all these tendencies the status of athletics as play is lowered in public esteem. Among the serious classes social sentiments develop that are dangerous to the physical and social welfare of boys. The boy of good social training conceives of athletics as something foreign to his life and education. Athletics are for those other fellows, the motor specialist, the material. He tends to lose all sense of the meaning of athletics for himself. The public tends to lose sight of the distinction between athletics as a spectacle for the pleasure of the spectator and athletics as play for the pleasure and education of the boy.

It is clear, therefore, that if we are to have any highly organized interesting athletics that are strong in wholesome rivalry and that will appeal to the average intelligent, self-respecting boy in the later adolescent period, and also command public esteem, the athlete with the money motive must be eliminated from the contest with the athlete with the amateur motive. This we have shown can be done only by a classification that separates sharply the money or professional motive from the play or amateur motive. *This classification is the law of amateurism.*

It has been our purpose to search for the roots of amateurism in human nature and the need of an amateur law in social forces. We have shown that amateurism is a concept of the motives in play which is as necessary to the life of youth as air. We have shown that a law of amateurism is necessary if athletics, as the play of the later adolescent years, is to achieve its biological and social ends.

There are many moral problems, many questions concerning the nature of the law, and many administrative difficulties which we have not touched. We have been after the foundations of amateurism, and have dealt only with ultimate problems to which all arguments must resort in final appeal. What we need is conviction of the soundness of the law.

In closing we might call attention to the fact that amateurism as a principle and as a law in the administration of athletics is democratic. It aims to conserve the natural rights of the many as against the privileges of the few. The selfish seekers after personal profit, in addition to social applause through pleasant and exciting activities, will always oppose it. Thoughtless and short-sighted partisans who gain a cheap pleasure from the selfish privilege seeker will also oppose the law. The amateur law and the administration of the law must seek to eliminate the few seekers after special privilege for the benefit of the many. Administrators must teach the public that professional athletics are for the pleasure of the spectator and that amateur athletics are for the pleasure and benefit of the participant.

THE "ALL OR NONE" PRINCIPLE AND ITS IMPLICATIONS

Percy G. Stiles

Simmons College

NOTE.—The ideas contained in this article were briefly sketched by the writer in *The American Journal of Public Hygiene,* May, 1909, Vol. XIX, p. 420.

Next to the wonder of coördination there is, perhaps, no feature of muscular activity more remarkable than our constant and precise grading of contractions to suit their purposes. An anticipated resistance is overcome by an application of force just sufficient for the work. When one raises a book from the table one does not jerk or fling it upward with an excess of energy nor does one lose appreciable time in preliminary efforts too weak to lift it. We are usually quite unconscious of this quick and perfect adaptation of the means to the end. Its failure is brought vividly to our attention when we attempt to pick up a bottle of mercury or when we move a large empty box which we were prepared to find heavy. What is the intimate mechanism of these graded responses?

Many years ago it was found that such gradations were not observed with cardiac muscle. If the ventricle of a terrapin heart is separated from the auricles it remains quiescent but ready to contract when stimulated. If repeated induction shocks are brought to bear upon it, the stimuli increasing or, better, diminishing in intensity, the fact appears that any stimulus which initiates a visible response develops a full-sized and typical beat. This is known as the "All or None" principle. A skeletal muscle similarly treated gives small contractions in response to certain stimuli and greater ones as the shocks are made stronger through a long range of stimulation. This contrast between the behavior of cardiac muscle and that of the skeletal type has usually been regarded as a fundamental one. Recent work makes it possible if not probable that it is quite superficial. The chief contributor to

Percy G. Stiles, "The 'All or None' Principle and Its Implications," *American Physical Education Review,* vol. XV, no. 1, January 1910, pp. 1-5.

our knowledge of this matter has been Keith Lucas, an English physiologist.*

Underlying the dynamic differences between skeletal and cardiac muscle are differences of structure. The fibre of striped muscle is an isolated unit. Around it is the sarcolemma, broken only at the point of entrance of the nerve-fibre. The single fibre may contract in response to stimulation without communicating the katabolic process to its neighbors. The cell of cardiac muscle is so linked with its fellows that a decomposition started in it will usually sweep through the entire contractile fabric of the organ.

We have been accustomed to assume that when a muscle such as the biceps shortens, the movement is the expression of the simultaneous contraction of all its fibres. If the movement is small we have imagined that each fibre has shortened by a little, if it is large we have supposed that the percentage of shortening has been greater in all its fibers. It has never been easy to see how graded stimuli can give graded responses in this sense. How could we conceive of a katabolic process initiated within the fibre which should not itself become a stimulus and precipitate a maximal discharge of the mechanism? If the fibre is like a magazine rifle in which a new portion of explosive, representing a definite amount of energy, is made ready after every contraction, how can we use any less than the whole charge available at a given moment? Dr. Lucas maintains that we cannot. It is his belief that the individual striated fibre obeys the "All or None" law—that it makes none but maximal contractions, varying of course, with its condition but not influenced by the intensity of stimulation provided only that it is above the threshold value. The gradations between the minimal movements of a muscle and its utmost shortening—or tension—are held to be merely the expression of the varying proportion of the units employed. The muscle is capable of many degrees of contraction because it is composed of a great number of elements, any fraction of which may be contracted while the rest are passive. Dr. Lucas has shown that a smoothly graded series of contractions is not obtainable from a very small collection of fibres. When a slender slip of frog's muscle is subjected to a succession of gradually increasing shocks the records show that several responses in a series may be of equal height and that an abrupt leap to a new level may follow. This is interpreted to mean that a fixed number of fibres coöperate to produce all those contractions which are of the same height and that the augmented response comes when the increased stimulus first

*_Journal of Physiology_, 1905, XXXIII., 125; 1909, XXXVIII., 113.

affects certain additional fibres which were less easily excited. The reasoning is ingenious and the technique of the research is exquisite. The characteristics of the records remain the same whether the stimulation is direct or applied to the nerve.

It is too soon to say whether this view of the working of the neuromuscular mechanism will be fully accepted, but its implications are of great interest. It introduces the idea that *a muscle is really a musculature* with no necessary unity of functioning parts and that the central representation of it is probably multiple and diffuse. It seems to the writer that the conception of the fractional use of muscles is helpful in clearing up many difficulties. Take for example the question of training. When an individual improves his condition by exercise we know that his gain in efficiency is greatly in excess of any sheer increase of muscular tissue. The advance may be due in part to a betterment of quality in the muscle substance coincident with a freer circulation and lymph-flow. But we usually assume that much of the gain is due to more effective innervation. In terms of the Lucas theory it is the result of control acquired over more and more fibres. The conception of the untrained muscle is that of one in which there are always many idle elements. In such a muscle under stimulation the unused fibres might be expected to lie in curves among the shortened and thickened members.

If training increases the proportion of units under voluntary control we may attribute the result to increased command over cortical motor cells, to extension of synaptic diffusion at lower levels, or to increased facility of end-plate transmission. Cerebellar reënforcement may also be gained. In any case the improvement may be founded in part upon the development of reflexes. If for example, we suppose that one half the fibres in a muscle are so connected as to respond to what we call the action of the will, while the remaining fibres can be reached only by impulses from spinal centers, it is plain that the contractions will grow powerful in proportion as an afferent flow of impulses is secured to spur these centers. Such an auxiliary reflex action probably results from practice.

By a similar assumption we can throw light upon the postponement of fatigue through interest in an occupation. There is no better instance of this than the surprising endurance displayed by slight women when dancing. How can they maintain such a degree of activity for a period of hours which they enter upon at the end of a normal day's work and which would be intolerable as a matter of routine? The matter becomes intelligible when we suppose that their strength as usually estimated is merely that of a fraction of the musculature under strictly voluntary control. A larger proportion of the fibres may be utterly removed from direct command but may be brought into play through concurrent reflexes, due in the specific case to light, music, and tactile stimuli. Indeed emotion itself may operate on the motor cortex in the fashion of a reflex stimulation. For if we suppose that the efficiency of motor discharge is determined by the number of paths bearing impulses to the cortical motor region, this number will be increased when emotion seconds volition. If the peripheral state is the essence of emotion, we have a definite source for such afferent impulses; if the state is central, the association paths are emphasized. According to older views emotional reënforcement means a more intense process in the same motor elements and a more intense resulting katabolism in the same muscle-fibres. According to the Lucas theory it means the development of parallel streams in the motor channels and the response of muscular units previously unstimulated.

If we adopt such views, subject no doubt to a good deal of revision, we can accept Dr. Lee's contention that every-day fatigue is chiefly peripheral, and still we can emphasize the importance of central factors. A muscle which appears—subjectively—to be fatigued is a muscle containing a group of fatigued fibres or end-plates, these being the ones normally most accessible to cerebral excitation. A much greater number of its fibres may be quite unfatigued but out of the range of unemotional, deliberate volition. The muscles of a fever patient may in this ordinary sense be very much fatigued, yet with a trifling rise of temperature or deepening of toxæmia the unused fibres may suddenly become responsive to central stimulation and an amazing display of energy result.

Thus we have presented to us a new picture of the conditions which may underlie the powerful contractions of muscles in delirium, hypnosis, strychnia poisoning, etc. Instead of assuming an abnormally intense process in the musculature we should perhaps simply assume a more general participation of the fibres than is usually obtainable. Back of this must lie the lowered synaptic resistance characteristic of these conditions, giving a widespread distribution of stimuli within the muscles. Under these circumstances the untrained subject may approach an athlete's strength because for the moment he possesses an athlete's extended innervation. The athlete himself when burning with fever may also show unexpected strength, but in his case there will be less margin of increase over his normal power than with the untrained person. For he has previously acquired something approaching a full command of his resources. The fibres which have been beyond his ordinary control must have been relatively few.

Dr. Lucas, we must bear in mind, has observed simple contractions in arriving at his conclusions. Human muscles are usually so stimulated as to give tetanic responses. This fact somewhat complicates the problem of analysis with which we are dealing. Sub-maximal contractions may, on his theory, be due to the tetanizing of limited numbers of fibres or to the alternating responses of distinct groups. The tremulous character of human contractions has been taken to indicate incomplete tetanus but it might result from the alternate action of sets of fibres.

NOTE.—Since the above was written an article has come to hand in which the author shows that simultaneous stimulation of two afferent nerves gives a greater reflex response from a muscle (which answers to each separately) than can be obtained by the strongest separate excitation of the paths. His interpretation is like my own. M. Camis, *Journal of Physiology,* 1909, XXXIX., p. 228.

HISTORY OF THE ADMINISTRATION OF INTERCOLLEGIATE ATHLETICS IN THE UNITED STATES*

D. A. Sargent, M.D.
Harvard University
Cambridge, Mass.

The earliest record of a regular Harvard team contesting in intercollegiate sports is a reference to a boat-race with Yale in 1852. Soon followed the first organized game of intercollegiate baseball in 1863, and in 1873 the formation of the football association with a game against Yale in 1875. The athletic association was formed in that same year, while the first meet between Harvard and Yale was held in 1879.

A quotation from the President's report of 1873-74 will show that, even at that early date when conditions were comparatively simple, the evils which have caused agitation in more recent times were recognized and guarded against. After stating that "The corporation was well satisfied that the moral and physical effects of such sports as were then practiced on Jarvis and Holmes fields were alike salutary," the report continues: "that while the corporation desired to foster manly sports, they felt compelled to discourage by every means in their power the association of the students with the class of persons who make their living by practicing or exhibiting these games; and to dissuade students from making athletic sports the main business instead of one of the incidental pleasures of their college lives; and to prohibit altogether the taking of money for admission to witness the sports upon the college playgrounds." This last limitation was shortly removed.

Before 1882 the faculty had imposed only one regulation over athletics at Harvard, which was that "No match games, races or athletic exhibitions should take place in Cambridge except after the last recitation hour on Saturday or after four o'clock in the afternoon.

D. A. Sargent, "History of the Administration of Intercollegiate Athletics in the United States," *American Physical Education Review,* vol. XV, no. 4, April 1910, pp. 252-261.

*Read before the Athletic Research Society, New York, December 29, 1909.

In the spring of 1882, alarmed by the number of baseball games to be played, away from Cambridge, by the Harvard team, the faculty appointed a committee to consider the subject of athletic sports. After their examination, they recommended (1) that a standing committee on the regulation of athletic sports be appointed, to consist of three members, including the director of the gymnasium, which committee should report to the faculty each year; and (2) that the President of Harvard address other colleges and secure the passing of regulations that baseball clubs of their respective colleges be forbidden to play with professional clubs. Brown, Dartmouth, Princeton and Amherst were willing to do so, Yale was not.

This committee of three constituted the first committee on the regulation of athletic sports at Harvard. The regulations they introduced tended to restrict college sports within the limits of amateur athletics.

Their articles were: (1) No college club or athletic association should play or compete with professionals. (2) No person should assume the functions of trainer or instructor in athletics upon the grounds or within the buildings of the college without authority in writing from the committee. (3) That no student should enter as a competitor in any athletic sport, or join as an active member any college athletic club including baseball, football, cricket, lacrosse, and rowing associations, without a previous examination by the director of the gymnasium, and his permission to do so. (4) That all match games outside of Cambridge should be played on Saturday, unless permission to play upon other days was first obtained from the committee. These regulations remained in force six years.

This committee endeavored to secure the joint action of various colleges to remedy the "brutal and dangerous" elements that had developed in football, and to that end called a conference on intercollegiate regulation, in New York, December 28, 1883. Eight colleges represented by twelve delegates responded. These resolutions were presented:

1. That every director or instructor in physical exercises or athletic sports must be appointed by the college authorities, and announced as such in the catalogue.

2. That no professional athlete, oarsman, or ball player shall be employed either for instruction or for practice in preparation for any intercollegiate contest.

3. That no college organization shall row or play baseball, football, lacrosse, or cricket, except with similar organizations from their own or other institutions of learning.

4. That there shall be a standing committee, composed of one member from the faculty of each of the colleges adopting these regu-

lations, whose duty it shall be to supervise all contests in which students of their respective colleges may engage, and approve all rules and regulations under which such contests may be held.

5. That no student shall be allowed to take part in any intercollegiate contest as a member of any club, team or crew for more than four years.

6. That all intercollegiate games of baseball, football, lacrosse, and cricket shall take place upon the home grounds of one or the other of the competing colleges.

7. That no intercollegiate boat-race shall be for a longer distance than three miles.

8. That the students of colleges in which these resolutions are in force shall not be allowed to engage in games or contests with students of colleges in which they are not in force.

At a second conference these resolutions were discussed and sent to twenty-one colleges, stating that if they were adopted by five they would become binding. Princeton adopted them unanimously and Harvard by a faculty vote of 25 to 5; none of the other colleges did so, and this attempt to exercise joint control of athletics was abandoned. A later report said of these resolutions: "If it (joint control) had been successful, the evils would probably never have arisen which now cause the friends of the University great anxiety, prompting some of them to propose strict limitations upon intercollegiate contests, and inducing others even to urge their abolition."

The faculty then, through the athletic committee, prohibited all intercollegiate football games for one year. They nominated to the corporation the assistant in the department of physical training, to act as an officer of the college, and to train the students in track and field athletics. The committee was active in checking evils which had risen in regard to rowing, and maintained the policy of keeping in touch with the students by holding weekly open meetings, and frequent conferences with representatives of the various athletic organizations.

But many of the faculty looked upon the rapid growth of interests in athletics with alarm and disapproval, and this, with the growing demands of regulation, led the committee to propose that a new committee of five be appointed, to consist of the director of the gymnasium, a physician resident in Boston or Cambridge, a recent Harvard graduate interested in athletics, and two undergraduates.

This committee was significant because it recognized the principle of student representation. Its members were appointed by the President, and it was responsible to the faculty. A report of the policy of this committee says, "They have dealt resolutely with the evils attaching to football, securing finally such changes of the rules under which the game is played as will probably rid it of its most objectionable features: they have excluded professional attendants from the floor of the gymnasium during public contests; they have considered means of lessening the evil of betting at intercollegiate contests, they have promoted the formation of class organizations in the different sports; they have aimed to lessen the number of games played by the teams with other colleges and with amateurs; they have secured the appointment of a committee to audit the receipts and expenditures of the five principal athletic organizations."

In 1888 the Board of Overseers were again alarmed at the growth of athletics represented by a large increase in the number of intercollegiate and other contests, and at their instigation a committee of three of the faculty was appointed to investigate the state of "athletic exercises, and alleged abuses, excesses, and accidents incident on the same."

The extensive report of this committee was submitted to the faculty June 12, 1888. It contains (1) a short historical account of previous attempts at control, (2) minute statistical tables tending to disprove the charges of the abuse of sports in lowering scholarships, interfering with the students' academic work, etc., and (3) recommendations as to changes in the athletic committee, its number, powers, responsibility, etc. These recommendations were such as to remove the control of athletics from the college faculty to the Board, therefore the faculty rejected them and substituted the following, which were adopted by the corporation as the authority under which the committee was appointed:

"A committee for the regulation of athletic sports shall hereafter be annually appointed and chosen as follows: Three members of the college faculty, and three graduates of the college . . . these six to be appointed by the corporation with the consent of the overseers; and also three undergraduates to be chosen during the first week of the college year by the majority vote of the following students: the president of the senior, junior, and sophomore classes, and a representative from each of the following athletic organizations: the boat club, the cricket club, and the athletic, baseball, football, lacrosse, and tennis associations, who shall be called together for the purpose of making this choice by the President of the University.

"This committee shall have entire supervision and control of all athletic exercises within and without the precincts of the University, subject to the authority of the faculty of the college as defined by the statutes."

The regulations of this committee, published January 23, 1889, were substantially the same as those adopted by the first committee in 1882, enlarged, but with the first regulation (games with professionals) omitted.

The suggestion to this athletic committee by the corporation that "further restriction should be placed upon intercollegiate contests in regard to the places where and the days when they should be played, and the teams that should take part therein," led to the formation of the New England Rule—"That Harvard athletic organizations hereafter shall engage in intercollegiate contests only in New England."

Restrictions were also put on freshmen intercollegiate contests and the committee declared "they would recognize no arrangement or agreement entered into by freshman organizations without the sanction of their respective university organizations." The meaning and limitation of what was implied by the term freshman was clearly defined.

In 1889 the students of Harvard, in a mass meeting withdrew from the Intercollegiate Football Association. At the football convention rules were passed to suppress the evils of admitting to membership on teams those who were not *bona fide* students of colleges, and not amateurs. The Intercollegiate Association was unable to enforce the rules, therefore the Harvard Association withdrew and subsequently adopted the rules and made them the standing rules of the committee.

An attempt about 1890 to form a dual league with Yale was unsuccessful, since Harvard would not consent to but one football game a year, that game to be played in New York, and Yale would not withdraw objection to special students on teams except on that condition. There were in the proposed articles of agreement valuable restrictions as to professionalism and amateurs; time limitation; playing rules; number, time and place of contests, etc.; and there can be no doubt that their adoption would have furthered the true interests of sports at both universities.

In 1890 the athletic committee, believing that expert advice was needed on many matters coming under their charge, formed a plan for the organization of permanent graduate advisory committees to advise the officers of the various athletic organizations. Some of the members of the graduate advisory committee acted as coaches to the teams.

The committee, realizing the necessity for a coach fitted to give time and thought to the work, offered to secure the appointment of trainers in other sports, as it had in track athletics, who should be assistants in the department of physical training and officers of the college. Their offer was refused by the boat club in 1891.

As far back as 1882 the first committee had tried to secure better financial management of college athletics, but the attempts were not wholly successful. In 1889 articles of agreement were drawn up establishing a graduate treasurer. His reports are published, and an endeavor is made to have all funds put into his hands promptly to prevent their careless handling by treasurers of the athletic associations.

About 1890 the evils connected with athletics which had been rife in the East, penetrated to the Western Colleges, and in the rapid and vigorous growth of those institutions these abuses seemed to find fertile soil in which to flourish.

In 1903, at a meeting of the Association of Colleges and Preparatory Schools of the North Central States, the athletic situation was thoroughly discussed. The glaring abuses of the system of hired coaches; the recruiting of "strong men" for the college; the inducements offered to keep good "material" on the teams; and the subterfuges practiced in regard to evading college requirements as to scholarship, etc., all seemed to call forth more open and ardent criticisms from western authorities than appears in the reports of investigation in the East.

Mr. C. A. Waldo of Purdue University said, "The faculty began drastic action against professionalism, their motto being 'Amateurism or nothing.'" Their regulations were:

Against non-students or "ringers."

Against direct or indirect pay for athletic services.

Against coach or professional trainer on the field.

Against playing under assumed name.

Against migration from college to college for athletic purposes.

Against non-genuine student representation.

Against lack of faculty control over games and grounds.

Against salaried outside coaches of questionable morals and influence.

Against undergraduates handling large sums of athletic money.

Against bad moral effects of games when rules are broken, evaded, etc.

Control by suppression of athletics is a confession of defeat by the faculty and few colleges are ready to adopt that method. Control by revolution is a radical departure from established methods, and difficult to bring about. The suggestion of an endowed department of physical training and consequently the removal of the necessity for gate money to pay expenses is the remedy advocated by the Dean of Washington University, St. Louis.

Control by regulations with the development of a spirit of reform from within the student body is the best means of eliminating present evils. Such regulations embrace:

Absolute business probity.

Year's residence, good college standing for candidate intercollegiate team.

Graduate and amateur coaching.

Lower limit to gate money.

Socializing intercollegiate athletics.

Disarmament.

No recruiting agencies, etc.

Legislation against betting.

In 1901 the professional coach was abolished at Leland Stanford University. The situation there (in 1903) was much simpler than in the colleges nearer the East. There was only one big game for which to prepare, and after which to calm down. President Jordan said, "It is the absolute duty of the faculty to see that no one is in the institution for football alone." He also expressed a desire to abolish gate money "as soon as they could get around to it."

President Butler heartily approved the action which prohibited intercollegiate football in Columbia. His arguments were: That the game had become a profession, not a sport; that the prolonged training absorbed time and interest from studies; that it was participated in by a few unrepresentative athletes; that it was an academic nuisance; that the gate money was a temptation and a commercial enterprise.

The Intercollegiate Athletic Association of the United States

In 1905 a convention of delegates from all the leading colleges was called to consider the advisability of football reform. Sixty-eight colleges sent delegates and a committee was chosen who were to amalgamate with the old rules committee on football, if possible; if not possible, to act alone; and in any case to formulate rules to correct certain evils and to secure an open game, elimination of rough and brutal playing, definite and precise rules of play, and organization and control of officials in order that the rules should be strictly and impartially enforced. Their committee met with the old rules committee consisting of representatives from Harvard, Yale, Cornell, Princeton, Chicago, Pennsylvania and Annapolis, and the necessary reforms in the playing rules of football were adopted.

At first the Association proposed "stringent eligibility rules and methods for enforcement," but this idea was abandoned in favor of "an educating and supporting body for the betterment of collegiate athletics." It endeavors "to make sport for sport's sake the controlling spirit in all institutions of learning; it discourages commercialism and encourages true amateurism; it believes the use of intercollegiate athletics for advertising purposes should be frowned upon; it strives to coördinate, in their proper relations, athletic and academic work; it cultivates high ideals of conduct on every field of sport."

Principles of amateur sport

Regulations.

Each institution which is a member of the Association agrees to enact and enforce such measures as may be necessary to prevent violations of the principles of amateur sport such as:

a. Proselyting.

1. The offering of inducements to players to enter colleges or universities because of their athletic abilities, and of supporting or maintaining players while students, on account of their athletic abilities, either by athletic organizations, individual alumni, or otherwise, directly or indirectly.

2. The singling out of prominent athletic students of preparatory schools and endeavoring to influence them to enter a particular college or university.

b. The playing of those ineligible as amateurs.

c. The playing of those who are not *bona fide* students in good and regular standing.

d. Improper and unsportsmanlike conduct of any sort whatever, either on the part of the contestants, the coaches, their assistants or the student body.

In 1909 there were 57 Colleges and Universities enrolled in the Association. These included all the large institutions except Harvard, Yale, Princeton, Cornell and Columbia.

Harvard's policy had remained about as defined by the regulations of its athletic committee of 1889, the committees of succeeding years endeavoring to support the athletic organizations in their attempts to maintain the standard of sports, while the general direction of teams was still left to undergraduate managers and captains. The evils still existing, such as abnormal interest in and prominence of intercollegiate contests, the expenses and extravagances incident to athletics were questions requiring careful consideration.

In 1905, before the formation of the new rules committee with the Intercollegiate Athletic Association of the United States, the Harvard committee had adopted new eligibility rules debarring freshmen and graduates from Varsity teams.

Some of the old rules such as the "New England Rule" were modified and the Harvard teams played against Cornell, Pennsylvania and Princeton, outside of New England.

The formation in 1891 of a nine years' agreement for an annual Harvard-Yale contest for the University Track Athletic cup, involved a constitution which was clear and strict in its rules, and the adoption of which "was a long step in advance in the effort to put intercollegiate athletics on a sound basis."

The question of professional coaching was one which had confronted athletic managements since intercollegiate contests became a feature of university life. The attitude of the authorities, East and West, has been unanimously against the professional coach. Some Western colleges went so far as to attribute the majority of the evils in the athletic situation to the influence of the high salaried outside coach, who was at liberty to use his money in securing undesirable men to attend college to make his team a winning one and thus insure his position.

The sentiment of Harvard's athletic committee was to "cling to amateur coaching even if it caused defeat." But the policy of the great body of graduates and undergraduates advocated professional coaching for the sake of a more continuous policy in methods and training of the teams than could be secured by graduate coaching.

In regard to track athletics, as stated before, a regular officer of the college had been appointed in 1884, who served until 1900, and whose skillful training won success for the team in intercollegiate contests. The various athletic associations representing the different sports, hired professional coaches. In boating, the Weld Club hired Coach Donovan 1896-97, Wray in 1901, Rice in 1904; the Newell Club hired O'Dea 1899, Vail 1900, Stephenson 1905. In June, 1905, Wray was appointed coach for the university crew on a contract for five years.

Dartmouth College took the lead in 1907 by limiting coaching to the employment of alumni. That the Harvard authorities are in sympathy with this movement appears in the college report of 1907.

In that year a joint committee of the two governing boards on the regulation of athletic sports presented to the President and Fellows a report which contained these recommendations:

a. That hereafter the Dean of the Faculty of Arts and Sciences, the Dean of Harvard College, and the Dean of the Lawrence Scientific

School be the faculty members of the committee on the regulation of athletic sports.

b. That certain changes be made in the mode of selecting the three undergraduate members of the committee.

c. That the committee be recommended to secure the services of some man, who can give his entire time to the work, to act as graduate manager and the administrative officer of the committee.

d. That the expenses connected with athletic contests be reduced by diminishing the cost of training tables, and reducing the number, distance, and duration of trips of athletic teams away from Cambridge.

e. That the number of intercollegiate contests be reduced.

f. That the athletic committee use every effort to get concerted action with other colleges to abolish professional coaches.

g. That the athletic committee be instructed to apply the entire surplus of athletic receipts over the sums needed for current athletic expenses to the extinguishment of the debt on the Stadium until that debt is paid, and then to reduce the gate receipts in such manner as it shall decide, so that there shall only be sufficient surplus each year for the gradual development of the athletic buildings and grounds of the university.

These recommendations were adopted, but the following year a return was made to the form of the committee as it was constituted in 1888, with three members of the Faculty of Arts and Sciences representing the faculty members, instead of the Deans of three departments of the university.

The recommendation to reduce the number of intercollegiate contests had no appreciable results the first year, but some reduction in the winter schedule was secured later. Nor has the attempt to diminish the exaggerated interest in and importance of football contests, both with the public and the students, been successful. The evils of extravagance, betting, excitement and publicity have remained to demoralize the game and its effects on the universities.

FIELD HOCKEY—GIRLS

By Helene Saxe MacLaughlin
Coach of Field Hockey
Girls' Branch of the Public Schools'
Athletic League
in Greater New York

The popular young lady of the time of our grandmothers was she who could manage her gown well, who could trip with dainty precision and grace through the figures of a minuet, and whose lack of independence and self-reliance were assets in her favor rather than to her discredit. To-day the athletic girl has prominence, not the loud, masculinely dressed, man-apeing individual, but the whole-hearted, rosy-cheeked, healthy girl who exercises because she loves it and who plays for the joy of the playing.

Among the games which have recently begun to gain position on this side of the Atlantic, is the English game of field hockey. It was introduced in this country in 1901 by various women's colleges—Vassar, Wellesley, Smith, and Bryn Mawr being among the first.

During the autumn of 1907, the author introduced field hockey in the Day Public School District of New Haven, Connecticut. About thirty girls, ranging in age from twelve to sixteen years, reported twice a week for practice. Later, a group of girls from the New Haven High School organized into two teams and played field hockey during the fall of 1907 and the spring of 1908. Each year since, there has been a hockey team maintained in connection with the higher grades of the grammar schools in Day District.

The Girls' Branch of the Public Schools' Athletic League had organized various after-school activities. Folk dancing had been introduced and, since music was necessary for this, the meetings were held indoors except in time of exhibition. Basket ball was played both indoors and out in many high schools, but there was yet a need for

Helene Saxe MacLaughlin, "Field Hockey—Girls," *American Physical Education Review,* vol. XVI, no. 1, January 1911, pp. 41-43.

outdoor athletics, some game which would afford exercise for a number of people at the same time.

In the spring of 1910 field hockey was introduced by the Public Schools' Athletic League at Erasmus Hall High School. Here it was received with great enthusiasm. The girls were chosen under three conditions. First, they were required to have rank in scholarship which is ordinarily necessary for participation in any of the school athletics. That is, a mark of at least 60 per cent in studies aggregating fourteen hours of prepared work. Second, only girls who were known to be sportsmanlike in work and play could join a team. Third (an unusual requirement), *high standing in regular school gymnastics* was considered.

On the first day there were about twenty girls on the field with sticks, and ready to play. The necessary arrangements had been made with the Park Commissioner and a splendid field of perfect dimensions was marked out in Prospect Park.

Before the next practice day the other players had obtained sticks and the girls had organized into three teams, each having an elected captain. There were two blue teams and one buff—buff and blue being Erasmus colors—and the teams had voted on and wore costumes appropriate to their chosen color. Those of the buff team were dressed in khaki skirts—six inches from the ground—stout shoes and white sailor blouses with collars of khaki. The girls of the other two teams wore short blue skirts, white sailor blouses with blue collars, and stout shoes. Gloves, too, were worn quite generally. At first, there was the usual wild race up, down and across the field, so common to beginners who have not yet learned that they must keep on their own half and that the whole responsibility of getting the ball and making a goal does not rest entirely with them. Right here lies one of the lessons of the game. If a player on the right sees a clear space to the left and undertakes to send the ball there, the girl who should receive it must be ready, for no one can play on the left side of the field except those who belong there. The first lessons of the game are, be always watching the ball and, when it comes your way, know what to do with it.

It is soon realized that twenty girls can't very well play "on" the same small ball at the same time, though at first, when the game is new, they often attempt it. And then another truth is discovered. Let someone else get the glory of a goal but each one do her share toward getting the ball nearer.

This fall, which opens the second season of field hockey at Erasmus Hall, there are fifty girls out for practice, each one anxious and willing to "play the game."

Two field hockey teams of eleven members each have started practice at Newton High School. The Boys' Athletic Association of the school furnished the funds for the twenty-two sticks and the ball. None of the girls on either team had ever held a hockey stick before her first practice.

No one can stand still when attempting to take part in a hockey game. If one doesn't "move" others soon go running past and you are knocked aside. It is a game of constant and vigorous action. The slow are taught agility and quickness of perception. They learn to hit the ball at which they aim, and to hit it with sufficient force to land it exactly where it should go. They soon are able to think ahead and plan very quickly to meet the play the opponent is most likely to try next.

Our main object is not to teach field hockey but to teach girls to *play*. Girls who report for first practice with hair fixed in the latest fashion and with various extreme modes of dress, soon appear in the regulation costume and with hair dressed simply. Selfishness cannot prosper and those who want to be the chief players soon learn that every girl is a cog in the wheel and that that cog in its place and doing its part conscientiously is necessary for every revolution. Anyone who doubts the good accomplished should see the forty girls who leave the hockey field these glorious days, after a strenuous play-time; tired from their exertions and hair hanging in disarray, no doubt, but framing faces happy, smiling, and simply radiating good health. Who can say that their fun is not worth while?

THE INTERCOLLEGIATE ATHLETIC ASSOCIATION OF THE UNITED STATES*

Captain Palmer E. Pierce
U.S.A.
Leavenworth, Kansas

The formation of The Intercollegiate Athletic Association of the United States was due to a condition of collegiate athletics, the agitation concerning which finally culminated in a largely attended meeting of representatives of institutions of learning in this city in 1905. It seemed to those present at this first gathering that there was a real necessity for a national organization to direct, and in a measure to control, athletics in the universities and colleges of this country. For this purpose this Association was formed.

The ideals of this organization are authoritatively and explicitly set forth in Article II. of its constitution, namely: "Its object shall be the regulation and supervision of college athletics throughout the United States in order that the athletic activities in the colleges and universities may be maintained on an ethical plane in keeping with the dignity and high purpose of education."

The method of control is as set forth in Article VIII. of the constitution, namely: "The colleges and universities enrolled in this Association severally agree to take control of student athletic sports as far as may be necessary to maintain in them a high standard of personal honor, eligibility and fair play and to remedy whatever abuses may exist."

From the above articles it appears that the basic ideas of this society are, high standards of personal honor, eligibility and fair play, and home rule.

Palmer E. Pierce, "The Intercollegiate Athletic Association of the United States," *American Physical Education Review*, vol. XVI, no. 2, February 1911, pp. 75-78.

*President's address before the Fifth Annual Convention of the National Collegiate Athletic Association (formerly the Intercollegiate Athletic Association), New York, December 29, 1910.

It is a great pleasure to report that, as time passes this Association meets with growing approval. In 1906, 39 universities and colleges were members; 1907, 49; 1908, 57, and 1909, 67. This year the membership has grown to 76.

Among the institutions that have joined during the past year are: Grinnell College, Mount Union College, Connecticut Agricultural College, Carnegie Technical Schools, Alabama Polytechnic Institute, Manhattan College, University of Wisconsin, Western Reserve University.

The number of students represented here today then is well over the 100,000 mark.

We welcome the coöperation of our new members, and trust that the delegates present for the first time will become our most ardent partisans.

On account of its really national character and, incidentally, to secure a more distinctive name, it is proposed to call this organization in future "The National Collegiate Athletic Association."

As our purposes and methods become more widely known it is thought that every institution in the country having any athletic influence will become either a full, joint or associate member. It does seem that the importance of proper direction and control of athletics in and among our colleges should be patent to every educator. Some are slow, however, to accept the idea that a national organization is necessary, but it is believed that within a few years all will join in this effort to make the best of the educational features of college athletics. Without a doubt it will be a great thing for this country, when all the boys and young men are filled with a love for personal participation in pure athletics, and play sports *knowing that it is better to lose fairly than to win unfairly.* If we can encourage the great mass of youth of this land to take part in manly games in a rational and gentlemanly manner, we will have done much for their moral and physical being. Since over 50 per cent of the successful men are college graduates, what a wonderful field this is in which to work for the national welfare!

If we succeed in eradicating the "*win at any cost spirit*" on college athletic fields, the civic life of this country undoubtedly will be wonderfully benefited.

Work of the Association During 1910

Your executive committee held meetings January 2 and December 28, 1910. Its labors have been carried on largely by correspondence. The proceedings and the addresses of the last annual meeting were duly published and widely distributed. The delegates present assisted in getting our ideals before the student bodies after their return to college duties, by word of mouth and by articles in the college papers and periodicals. I cannot urge you too strongly to continue this advertisement of our aims and ideals. The National Association must largely depend upon you to act as independent agents to carry on the propaganda for sane and well-controlled college athletics. Please say or write a word whenever opportunity offers in explanation of our purposes and methods or in favor of our ideals of purer, more rational, and more widely participated in college athletics. The Sage Foundation published Chancellor Day's excellent address to the Association last year.

The importance of the work done by the Football Rules Committee cannot be overestimated. This Committee had a difficult situation to face and it is a gratification to know how well they accomplished their task. The playing rules for the past season were not perfect by any means. The game, however, was very much improved and we hope to see the work perfected before another season. Our thanks are due to all those who gave so much attention and time to this most important formulation of play rules.

Your Basket Ball Rules Committee has also progressed towards a better code for this sport. The game has developed in the right direction during the past two years and the gentlemen who are on the Basket Ball Rules Committee are urged to continue their efforts toward a cleaner, less rough and better controlled game.

We again emphasize the necessity of careful faculty control of this sport. College teams should play only college teams and avoid contests under different rules than those of this Association. This Association should assist all organized and well-directed efforts to enforce the rules of amateurism.

Your Committee on Amateurism has been struggling with this important subject during the past year in conjunction with one from the Amateur Athletic Research Society. The importance of the subject of amateurism is becoming greater on account of the complexity of modern life and the close relations that now exist between athletic loving people. It is especially evident that England and her Colonies are struggling with this important question as well as ourselves. It might seem to most of us an easy thing to define an amateur but it appears a satisfactory definition has not yet been discovered.

An important report was submitted at the last annual meeting on the proper control of collegiate athletics. Decided steps in advance are being made by many of our allied institutions. The trend seems to be more and more in the direction of thorough faculty control. Without it the best results seem impossible. Careful attention to the reports of the district representatives to be made this afternoon is requested. The athletic trend among our colleges will be clearly indicated by them.

The summer baseball question is still with us. As shown by the investigation made under the direction of this Association some three years ago, this is a matter that calls for most serious thought and effort. This Association does not frown upon the playing of this game for money by students, but it does object to such students concealing the fact in order to take part in intercollegiate contests. It is better to permit the practice openly than to half-heartedly attempt to enforce the rules of amateurism, knowing that the attempt causes subterfuge and deception. The moral side of this issue is undoubtedly most serious because the temptation to conceal professionalism is so great and so prevalent.

The Committee on Track Athletics will submit recommendations this afternoon. The necessity for uniform track rules and for some satisfactory method of keeping official records seems apparent. It may be thought wise for this organization to invite the Intercollegiate Association, which has been controlling the annual track meets, to affiliate with it. By doing so uniform track rules could be secured, records made could be officially kept, and the selection and control of the college athletes to take part in the great Olympic contests could be influenced by an authoritative body.

The effort to form local conferences is slowly succeeding. One has been formed in the Southwest, including the state of Texas, and another is forming in the South Atlantic states.

The Future of This Association

This Association will last so long as the necessity for an organized national effort to benefit college athletics exists, and so long as it is run on unselfish, common sense lines. It seems apparent that the necessity will persist for many years to come in this not fully developed country of ours, and it is hoped that its affairs will continue to be run along the same lines that have proved so successful in the past. With its every member imbued with a desire to help others as well as himself a long future filled with possibilities of useful, practical work is assured.

THE TWO KINDS OF PLAY*

Joseph Lee
Boston, Mass.

Mark Twain, in responding to the toast of "The Babies" at a reunion of the Army of the Tennessee held in honor of General Grant, said: "Fifty years ago our honored guest was giving his whole attention to a single problem—how to get his toe into his mouth; and if we may judge by passages in his subsequent career with which the civilized world is now familiar, I think we may conclude that he kept on trying until he got it there."

The great humorist is often a great philosopher: Mark Twain in divulging the above historical secret indicated a most important truth not only about the babyhood of General Grant but about all babies and their pursuits. His statement shows an understanding not only of what babies do and of why they do it, but of why there are babies. It is a condensed exposition of the whole modern theory of infancy, and of play as its essential element.

There are many lessons concerning growth and education to be drawn from this early enterprise of General Grant. But the specific lesson I wish to derive from it is as to the mental attitude involved. (The physical attitude also might be worthy of illustration but time and circumstances prevent my yielding—except metaphorically—to the obvious temptation in that respect.)

The essential point to be noted, and the one point we may be absolutely certain of, in regard to the General's mental attitude upon that momentous occasion, is his exclusive concentration on results. He was concerned, not about the manual training secured, about developing his biceps, or even about pulling his own leg; he cared nothing

Joseph Lee, "The Two Kinds of Play," *American Physical Education Review,* vol. XVI, no. 7, October 1911, pp. 439-446.

*Read before the Public School Physical Training Society, Boston, April 12, 1911.

for the motions involved in approaching his toe toward its chosen destination; what he wanted was to get it there. It was the end on which his heart was set; and his whole mind and body were dominated by the end alone.

And Mark Twain was right in presuming that the hero of Appomattox had kept on trying until he got there—even if it took all summer. You cannot go so deep in a man's character but what you will find some childish exploit as the forerunner of whatever he may have accomplished in later life. It is not merely on the football fields of Harrow and Eton (which have always to be mentioned in this connection) but further back than that, in the nurseries of England or of any other country, that the destinies of nations are being shaped.

And a principal reason why play is the best preparation for later life is in its characteristically purposeful attitude, its absorption not on the means but on getting the thing done.

That such concentration on the end is the characteristic of the commonest and most important kind of play, anyone can verify who will watch a child when he is playing. Watch him making his first cake of mud or sand, and see how the miracle of production takes possession of him. Watch him as man's old enemy, the desire to make a better one, asserts itself. You will see him utterly lost in his attendance upon the result, absorbed into it, asleep to all outer circumstances.

Or watch him building a tower of blocks. Note his increasing anxiety as its equilibrium becomes more unstable, the sublime daring required in adding the last block. He is not thinking about himself, not conscious that he is there at all. His whole being is absorbed into the work in hand. It is not he that is building the blocks; the blocks are building him. The tower rules; the child is utterly subordinate. He hardly breathes until the thing is done. He is all builder. There is nothing over, not enough even to know that he is doing it.

Or observe any of the hunting games and note the utter concentration on the purpose to catch or to escape. These games are good for the arms and legs and for some of the fundamental nervous correlations. They develop the heart and lungs. But these are not their object from the children's point of view. The thing is to get away. Run till you drop, if running seems the best expedient. But climb, swim, hide in the coal cellar, roll down the bank, or jump from the second-story window—any way to get off. That is the way they look at it; the terror of capture is the motive. And the passion of pursuit, with the one object to capture the quarry by whatever means, is correspondingly fierce and concentrated.

And so in the later team games the attention is always on the end—making the hit, putting the man out, getting the ball over the line. I do not now refer to the spirit of "anything to win." Where this involves going outside of the game and winning by means not contemplated in the rules, it constitutes a special manifestation of one particular play instinct, namely, that of fighting or competition. What I am here emphasizing is the fact that subordination to an end is the one essential characteristic of the play spirit itself in all its more important manifestations.

It is true that there are often special means prescribed. The familiar tendency toward destructiveness, for instance, is not the result of a pure disinterested desire that things shall be smashed. When not a symptom of the scientific spirit it is usually a manifestation either of the instinct to throw at a mark or of that to strike with a stick or weapon of some sort—the two impulses upon which our ball games are largely built. But even in these cases it is from the child's point of view the end that governs. The boy wants, it is true, to throw with his right arm, but when he does throw, it is not his right arm that interests him, but the friend, window, or other convenient and satisfying object that he is throwing at. He wants to strike with a stick, but when the time for action comes, it is not the flourishing of the bat that governs, but the hitting of the ball—even beyond that, he cares a good deal where he hits it to. Often, indeed, he will express himself as wholly dissatisfied when he has made a very pretty and vigorous motion with the stick but has not connected with the ball. He may want to do the thing in a certain prescribed way, but it is the doing of the thing, not the method used, on which his mind is bent. All his faculties are focused on this end. Every tissue, every drop of blood, prays and travails that the end shall be attained.

That the instinct for the end lies deeper than the prescription of the means and is even independent of such prescription, seems to be directly proved by the instinctive satisfaction in kicking goals, or in throwing a goal with both hands, as in basket ball, instead of with the right alone. People find about as much joy in hitting a mark with an arrow or with a bullet as with a stone or snowball. The man who used to paint with his toes in European galleries illustrated the possibility of another issue of the manipulating impulse than the first instinctive one. So men will satisfy the instinct of song by means of a hollow reed, or by strings of wire or catgut. They will sing even in stone and wood or through colors spread on canvas. Conversely they will find building materials in musical sounds, in poetry, in institutions, as well as in clay or stone.

So the characteristic of this first most important kind of play is subordination, subservience to an end. It is not that the child chooses to play, but that the end prescribed in play chooses the child and adapts him to itself. He is given up, absorbed into its purposes.

* * * *

Play is not for the sake of pleasure. Pleasure results from it and may in the sophisticated become a conscious motive, but it is not the play motive. It is distinctly extraneous, a by-product. It does not in any way account for the play attitude or the direction of the play instincts. In play the motive of the act is the doing of it. The child will know afterwards that he was having a good time, and may choose to play again partly for that reason; but pleasure will never be the present motive in the play itself. In successful play a child does not know that he is having a good time. He does not know that he is having any time at all. Time, in fact, has ceased along with self-consciousness. He is not a receiver of impressions but a doer, pure and simple, and exists for nothing else. The pursuit of pleasure is an egotistic, self-conscious, almost a morbid state of mind, notoriously self-defeating. Play implies the opposite, contrasted attitude, that of self-forgetfulness, subordination. The man who goes out to have a good time is usually disappointed. The one who goes out to play the game, and does play it for all it is worth, is never wholly so.

Play involves pain. You cannot become lost in the achievement of an end, without some disregard of the sacrifice involved. You cannot play the game unless you learn to ignore the kicks and the fatigue. Young men even kill themselves in games; and readiness for such sacrifice as the end may call for is fundamental in the moral attitude of play.

And the ends to which play demands subordination are ideal ends. The child who has made his first cake will look at it a moment very seriously. Then some improvement suggests itself. We all know the rest of that story; it is the story of mankind. We know that he will never achieve that perfect sand cake. But we know that whatever makes life worth living, whatever lends it interest or satisfaction or nobility, will lie in the pursuit.

The human soul is like a magic lantern. The light of a great instinct shines through it from within and casts its picture on the mists ahead. As the child or the man perfects his nature in the likeness of that image, the image itself becomes clearer and more defined. But the copy he makes will never equal the original—not while the man is still alive.

The ideal ends that play prescribes are the ideals that dominate our later life, the ends for which men and women in all ages have gladly died and been praised for doing so. Building, creation, rhythm; nurture, curiosity; hunting, fighting, citizenship,—these are the play instincts and these are the abiding sources of the ideals of mankind. The mother who sacrifices her life for her child, the poet facing poverty and death for the sake of art, the scientist for his discovery, the patriot for his country, testify to the moral sufficiency of the same instinctive motives which govern children's play. The fighting instinct itself, which to some people seems the least ennobling, is the basis of the great ideals of chivalry which alone have shown power to capture not merely the reason but the imagination of our western world.

Of course we all know, since Herr Groos has taught us, that it is no mere coincidence that the play ideals are identical with those of the grown-up world—the whole purpose of play and of the great phenomenon of infancy itself being, as he has shown, to prepare the infant for the work of life. Nature sends her purposes on ahead to form the child for what she later will require of him. She makes him builder, poet, scientist, fighter, nurturer, citizen, because those are the things that he must be in order to succeed,—because it is in those capacities that man has won himself a place in the world she superintends.

It is for this reason—to prepare for real life—that Nature has so insisted on the purposeful attitude of play. We are all of us trying in one way or another to get our toe into our mouth. (Sometimes perhaps we have succeeded in doing so further than we have dreamed.) Nature cares something for the means, but much more for the end. She is of a very Philistine or get-there temperament. Her constant precept is, "Thou shalt arrive." Get the thing done, get the ball over the line—gracefully, pleasantly, politely, if you can, but get it there. To succeed in life we need to get results and it is therefore on results that Nature focuses mind and emotion from the first.

So both in its moral attitude and in its specific aims play prepares for life. And as play instincts are simply those of real life, it is in real life alone that they find their complete and satisfying fulfilment. It is when the phantom stag that he has pursued all through his youth becomes a real one, now actually visible to his waking eye, that all the voices of the young man's nature open in the pursuit; the full passion of the chase is aroused only in contact with reality. Work is the fullest and most satisfying form of play.

All the best work has in it the play motive, of seeking an end for its own sake. Work that is not also play is that which we distinguish as drudgery, meaning work that no longer carries its own motive with it, that is no longer lighted up in the doing of it by the end it serves. Such work as this is done from a motive that is external or, as we say, ulterior. It includes that which is done in obedience to the hunger motives, or for the avoidance of pain,—and not for the joy of doing it. It may be for the sake of the useful, for the thing that can be used for something else, that is not worth making for itself. Or it may be done in obedience to conscience, that is to say, to the human faculty of remembering ideal ends and acting on them even when they are hidden by a cloud and cease to illuminate the path that we are treading. Play is always for the ultimate, for the eternally worth while, the thing that is worth getting for its own sake. It is play so long as this motive of serving the eternally worth while is directly present. In work we must sometimes keep on after the motive seems to have died within us, when only its memory remains—by what we call "grit" or a kind of bull dog obstinacy. Even this grit, however, seems partly to consist of the fighting quality that enables the football player to buck the line when he feels faint and sick and, except for the memory far down somewhere in his spine, would rather go home to bed, or at least let up a little in the fierceness of the attack.

Play supplies what we call the professional element in any kind of work. Standing beside the practical, the useful, the utilitarian end, there is in all such work this other glorified presentation of the same object in its eternal relations as a thing of beauty, as something worth serving for itself. Beside the useful tool, there stands the ideal efficiency; beside the shelter from the cold and rain, the temple not made with hands; behind the serviceable invention, the mystery still unsolved, challenging to new adventure the mind; behind the practical improvement in the public service, the Zion of our dreams.

But not all play is purposeful. Observe a group of children at recess, hear them yell; see them throw their arms up and jump as though they were trying to fly; watch them rush, dodge, chase, thump each other, and generally act like a swarm of flies or a drove of young colts; and you will see that there is another sort of play. This is play of what may be called the exuberant or blowing-off-steam variety. Here the motive seems to be not toward an end but outward from a center. Indeed, the very bodily attitude, with arms and legs, and, even fingers, out-stretched in the likeness of a starfish, seems to suggest the radial nature of the force at work. The phenomenon is more in the nature of an explosion than of a purposeful pursuit. The vital force instead of being turned into the cylinder, there to work toward some desired end, shrieks through the safety valve. Action is squeezed out by an excess of pressure from within rather than drawn forth by a desired end without.

Play at recess or immediately after school is, indeed, a case not so much of action as of reaction. It is the straightening out of the young tree that has been bent rather than the putting forth of new growth. Play at such times should not, as a rule, be of the more formal kind. It should not be of a sort to require too much order or attention. Mental effort of any sort should not be asked at times when nature calls for this especial form of compensation.

But this exuberant form of play is valuable not only at recess; it has an essential function to perform; and opportunity should accordingly always be allowed for it. Even the yelling is an important and necessary experience and should not on all occasions be suppressed.

A characteristic service of all play, and especially of play of this letting-off-steam variety, is as an expression of personality. I have spoken of the great impulses common to all children as representative of the child universal, of the common elements in human life. But there is a different blend and combination of these elements, a peculiar voice and resonance, in every individual. An essential part of what play does for us is the finding of this voice. Play should proceed outward from the depths. It should not only reach the end but start from the beginning. All, from the spinal marrow to the roots of the hair, should be engaged. It should let out the very last link of personality. It should be to the individual spirit what the uninhibited sneeze is to the vocal chords.

A recognized symptom of neurasthenia, present to a greater or less degree in all of us, and the greatest source of failure and ineffectiveness, is that of divided personality. A mind and body made and instructed from the first by thoroughgoing action, proceeding from the very core of being and thrilling out to the circumference—a personality created by authentic acts and only such—would show no such rifts. It would be wholly integrated, strike in a solid mass, be all there, wholly present and alive to our occasions. It is the shallow, what we call half-hearted action, beginning halfway out—factitious motives, semi-enlistment, that create the unfused, unconsolidated self. Life should be radial from the very first, proceed from the very heart as well as toward a self-justifying end.

Life is the appropriation by the spirit of the body and material it needs,—in all creatures essentially the same process as that by which the acorn constructs the oak. But no two acorns are alike; and even if they were each of them would have to work from the inside, on its own law, in order that the product might be not an assemblage of parts or tendencies, but a tree. That the oak may be sound and whole, have one bent and accent through all its infinite variety, it must grow wholly outward from the center, each twig and leaf vibrating to one idea.

I saw the other day some remnants of the Iroquois tribe doing a war dance. Evidently the psychological value of the process consisted in somehow shrieking or agonizing out the very ultimate ego in the man. Each was trying to body forth in one lucky spasm the crude material of which his personality was composed.

The yelling, leaping, expressive play of childhood has this peculiar function, to fetch the voice from the deepest spot, to be sure that it shall be, this once at least, the very boy himself who acts. The rough talk and braggadocio of street boys is an important extension of the same idea.

Finally, these two kinds of play, the purposeful and the exuberant, are not in truth so wholly separate as I have found it necessary for the sake of the clearness to pretend. Exuberant play is not often purely and exclusively exuberant. It will seldom remain without an object for very long. One leap into the air stirs the wish to make a higher one. One good yell arouses the ambition to give another even more satisfying. "The fiend that man harries is love of the best"—even in the matter of letting off steam.

On the other hand, even the most purposeful play has in it the quality of exuberance. Just because the child or man does lose himself in it, just for the very reason that he serves another and a higher will,—a will impersonal, that seems external to himself—such play contains the highest possibilities of self-fulfilment. It is in such humble service of a purpose that we find the highest, the completest, and even, in the end, the most exuberant, expression of personality. True action, true expression, must, like a violin string, be fastened at both ends; otherwise there will be no thrill, no sounding of the depths; no rearrangement to the law of the music, no reconstituting of the individual. It is the function of exuberant play to make certain of the inner connection, to link up action indubitably with the very root of present personality. The function of purposeful play is to extend the personal frontier of existence forth into its prophesied and infinitely elaborated forms.

PRESIDENTIAL ADDRESS*

George L. Meylan, M.D.
Columbia University

This city is a fitting place to hold our convention because Boston and Harvard University have played a conspicuous part in the development of physical education in America. More teachers of physical education have obtained their professional training in the normal schools of Boston and vicinity than in all other normal schools in the United States.

This convention marks the beginning of a new epoch in the history of the American Physical Education Association. Organized in November, 1885, under the name of American Association for the Advancement of Physical Education, the Association has grown steadily from the beginning. In 1897, the *American Physical Education Review,* a quarterly magazine, was founded as the official organ of the Association. In 1903, the name of the Association was changed to American Physical Education Association and in 1908 the *Review* was changed from a quarterly to a monthly published during nine months of the year.

The growth of the Association in twenty-five years, from 1886 to 1911, is shown by the increase in members from 49 to 929; the annual income from $34 to $5532 and the publication from an eight page pamphlet to a monthly magazine of 725 pages in 1910.

The growth in members, income and amount of published material is an index of the activity and importance of the Association, but the success obtained in accomplishing the ends for which the Association was organized is of far greater importance. Through the papers presented, the discussions, and the intercourse between members at con-

George L. Meylan, "Presidential Address," *American Physical Education Review,* vol. XVI, no. 6, June 1911, pp. 353-359.

*Eighteenth convention, American Physical Education Association, Boston, April 11, 1911.

ventions, and through its publications, the Association has exerted a potent influence in bringing about the remarkable development in physical education which has taken place in the United States during the last 25 years.

In 1885 physical education was not generally recognized as an essential part of the educational curriculum. The emphasis in formal education was placed on mental training to such a degree that the psychomotor training needed by the individual for the conscious control of his body was almost entirely neglected and little effort was made to counteract the evil tendencies of the school itself upon the health and normal physical development of the youth. The fundamental principle that "education secured at the expense of health is too costly" was not given due consideration in the general scheme of elementary, secondary and higher education.

The influence of the American Physical Education Association and the activities of its leading members during the period from 1885 to 1895 were directed to the introduction of physical education in educational institutions, in the Young Men's Christian Associations, and various other philanthropic institutions. The meetings of the Association provided a forum for the discussion of principles and methods for the conduct of physical examinations and physical exercises.

A very striking result of the Association's influence during that early period was the clearing up of the bitter controversies that had been raging between the exponents of the various systems of gymnastics. The broad-minded and progressive men and women in the profession, after mature deliberation and experimentation with the various systems, gradually worked out principles and devised methods based on the sciences of anatomy, physiology, education and hygiene, and adapted to American conditions. The Swedish and German systems contributed much that is valuable in the various schemes devised by leaders in physical education. There are those who deplore the fact that we have thus far failed to secure any considerable degree of uniformity in our plans and methods of teaching, but this lack of uniformity and absence of centralized direction has, on the contrary, stimulated individual thought and research, and resulted in more rapid progress than would have ensued from the early adoption of a uniform system.

The period from 1895 to 1905 was marked by a rapid and widespread extension of physical education in all kinds of educational and philanthropic institutions. Other characteristics of this period are: first, the assigning of physical education to a regular place in the academic curriculum with examinations and credits as in other branches of study; second, the extensive development of athletics, plays and games in educational institutions and in municipalities; third, the addition of dancing to the forms of exercise used in the physical education of children and girls; and fourth, a very large increase in the number of professional schools for physical education teachers with an even greater increase in the number of students fitting themselves for the physical education profession.

The last period, from 1905 to the present, has been characterized by considerable progress in various directions; first, the raising of standards in the professional schools of physical education. Six years ago, less than 10 per cent of the graduates in physical education received the bachelor's degree at graduation, whereas now over 30 per cent complete courses leading to the first degree and an increasing number pursue graduate studies for the master's and doctor's degrees; and, second, during this period has occurred a phenomenal growth of interest in all matters pertaining to the conservation of life and health, and the normal physical development of children, public and personal hygiene, and all matters pertaining to health and healthful living. All these interests are related more or less closely to physical education in its broadest sense. Of these new interests those which are most directly related to physical education are the playground and school hygiene movements. The leaders in these two movements are nearly all members of our Association and much of the practical work in these activities is carried out by physical education teachers. Two national associations, the American Playground Association and the American School Hygiene Association, were organized and magazines founded to advance these interests.

The suggestion was made by some of our members that these two new associations should be affiliated with the American Physical Education Association in the interests of coöperation and economy, but after careful and deliberate consideration of the matter the project was finally abandoned because it was found to be impracticable. Coöperation has been secured to the mutual benefit of all concerned, but organic affiliation is not feasible, at least for the present.

The growth of interest and activity in playgrounds, hygiene instruction, school hygiene and all matters pertaining to community and individual health places new and important responsibilities upon all directors and teachers of physical education. It is not feasible nor desirable to dissociate those activities concerned primarily with physical education from those having to do with play, hygiene and supervision of the student's health. In many colleges and preparatory schools and in some public schools the director of physical education is held directly responsible for all these interests, with the result that in institutions where the director is competent and possessed of high ideals, strong personality and human sympathy, he exerts a strong and wholesome influence on the whole life of the institution. On several occasions, college presidents and head masters of preparatory schools have told me that the director of physical education in their respective institutions was the most influential and valuable officer on the staff. One college president said that if he were a young man he would fit himself for the vocation of college physical director because it offers larger opportunities for service in moulding the lives of young men than is afforded by any other position.

That the value of physical education is now fully recognized in American colleges is shown by some figures obtained last year from 124 of the leading colleges and universities.

Ninety-five per cent offer regular courses in physical education and in 87 per cent these courses are prescribed.

The prescription applies to freshmen only in 27 per cent of the colleges, to freshmen and sophomores in 44 per cent; in the other institutions the courses are prescribed for more than two years or only to students who are below a certain standard at entrance.

In more than half of these colleges the courses in physical education were prescribed later than the year 1900.

The standing of these courses in the college curriculum is shown by the fact that positive credit towards the bachelor's degree is given in 58 per cent of the colleges and the students are marked for proficiency as in other courses in 63 per cent of the institutions.

Ninety-eight per cent of the colleges have gymnasium facilities, 96 per cent have athletic fields, and 37 per cent have swimming pools.

The academic standing of the directors of physical education in colleges is steadily increasing. Seventy-six per cent have seats in the faculty, 25 per cent have the title of professor, and out of 58 per cent who have the title of director of the gymnasium or physical director many have professorial rank.

There are no recent figures on the present status of physical education in private secondary schools. Nearly all have some form of physical education and many of them have a well-organized department in charge of a competent director.

Dr. Gulick has secured valuable statistics showing the status of physical education in normal schools, public high and elementary schools.

Seventy-six per cent of the normal schools have regular instruction in gymnastics and 43 per cent in athletics. Courses in gymnastics are prescribed in 68 per cent of the normal schools and 48 per cent give credit for these courses.

In the public high schools only 8 per cent offer regular instruction in gymnastics, 5 per cent prescribe this work and only 3 per cent give academic credit for it.

The figures for public high and elementary schools show a very small percentage of schools with regular instruction in physical education, but that is due to the very large proportion of small rural schools included in the compilation. General observation would lead one to believe that the majority of schools in cities of 10,000 population or more have some form of regular instruction in physical education.

It was my privilege during the past two months to visit schools and universities in several European cities. In London, Paris and Brussels, the Ling system of gymnastics has been adopted officially. The instruction is given in the elementary schools by the regular class teachers, who vary over wide limits in their ability to teach a good gymnastic lesson. There are several reasons for the indifferent work done by many teachers; the present plan was adopted very recently, the teachers did not have adequate training for the work in their normal course, and there is as yet very little inspection and supervision by special teachers. In the classes where the instruction is excellent, it is because the teacher has made a special study of the subject in some private class or society outside of the school system. France has recently adopted an admirable plan for the training of elementary and secondary school teachers. Every male teacher in France is sent during his two years' military service to Joinville-le-Pont for a ten weeks' normal course in the theory and practice of physical education.

In Germany and Switzerland, where physical education has been in the elementary school curriculum for many years, the instruction is far better than in London and Paris. In Bonn, Germany, and in Lausanne and Geneva, Switzerland, the gymnasia are equipped with German and Swedish apparatus and the lessons include German and Swedish gymnastics.

In the secondary schools of England, France, Belgium, Germany and Switzerland, physical education receives considerable attention. There are very few organized departments of physical education with complete equipment and a staff of trained teachers such as we have in many of our preparatory schools, but physical education has a place in the curriculum and the instruction is given by special teachers. The public secondary schools in London have gymnasia and special teachers. The well-known preparatory schools in England devote much attention to all forms of sports and athletics, but Eton has the distinction of being the only school with an organized department of physical education. It has a splendid new gymnasium equipped with Swedish apparatus, and two instructors.

One of the most striking differences between Europe and the United States in the status of physical education is the total absence of organized departments of physical education in European universities. The English university students devote considerable time to athletics and sports, but the universities do not furnish equipment, instructors or courses in physical education. On the continent, the conditions are the same except that only a very small proportion of students interest themselves in athletics.

Several professors and students in English, French and German universities expressed admiration for the high standing of physical education in American colleges and universities and the earnest hope that a similar development would take place in their own institutions.

Upon my return home from Europe I read the program for this convention, and reviewed the main points in the development of physical education in the United States during the last quarter of a century. I was impressed with the progress already made in providing a sound physical education for every American boy and girl.

But the growth and extension of physical education have enlarged the horizon of the physical educator and brought forth new and larger problems for solution. On the scientific side, we must ascertain many facts yet unknown concerning the effects of the various forms of exercise upon heart rate, blood pressure, respiration and metabolism; we need more accurate methods for measuring functional capacity, vitality and endurance; and we need further light concerning the influence of mental states upon physical conditions. On the educational side, we need a more complete correlation of physical education procedure with the educational curriculum; and there is still a large work to be done in the organization and correlation of play and athletics with other forms of physical education before we shall realize the full benefits of these most valuable activities as agents for organic and moral training. Finally, the increasing importance and complexity of physical education demand a higher type of teachers and directors. We must continue the raising of standards for admission and graduation in our professional schools of physical education.

Our Association has lost by death during the past year three honorary members. Professor Angelo Mosso of the University of Turin, who died last November, was one of our most eminent foreign members. As a physiologist he carried on most important studies on exercise in high altitudes, on fatigue and on physical education.

In December, we lost another honorary member in the death of Sir Francis Galton, the eminent English scientist. His pioneer work in methods for the measurement of physical efficiency and his papers read before conventions of the Association have influenced and helped those who seek to advance physical education along scientific lines.

In February of this year our Association suffered a great loss in the death of Dr. Edward Hitchcock, who was one of the founders of the Association, serving as president during the first two years, and completed almost fifty years of most eminent service as Professor of Hygiene and Physical Education at Amherst College. Dr. Hitchcock was very active in the field of anthropometry and published many valuable papers and statistics on that subject. But those of us who had the good fortune of knowing Dr. Hitchcock personally, feel that not only has the profession lost one of the leaders in the physical education movement but we have lost a friend. While his contributions to the scientific and technical development of physical education are exceedingly valuable, the name of Dr. Hitchcock will be remembered and his influence felt because of the man himself and the noble work that he accomplished in combining physical development, health, education and character building. This is the largest problem confronting physical educators to-day. The didactic teaching of ethics is a mere intellectual process, it often fails to affect the ethical habits of the individual. We have in play and athletics, agents capable of affecting the ethical habits of children and young people if the achieving of this end is held up as the chief aim in the conduct of these activities. May I venture to express the hope that the members of this Association will strive earnestly through the various agencies of physical education to achieve this chief aim, the development of character. By so doing we shall pay a high tribute to the memory of Dr. Hitchcock who held that as the chief aim of his life.

Part III

TOWARD MODERN CONCEPTS

1912 - 1930

THE QUEST FOR ELDORADO*

R. Tait McKenzie, B.A., M.D.
Professor of Physical Education
University of Pennsylvania

To the Spaniards of the sixteenth century who lived under Ferdinand and Isabella, the dread mystery that had so long veiled the unknown waters of the western sea had been lifted at last. The new and boundless continent of America spread out before their astonished eyes and into it poured soldiers and merchants, cavaliers and monks, ruffians and priests, adventurers all. Strange tales were told of its marvels by returning travelers who brought back as proof, bars and vessels of gold, rubies and emeralds, in such abundance as to disturb the currency values of all Europe. It is little wonder that the legend of Eldorado, the golden man from whom unlimited riches were to be got, was accepted implicitly by their excited minds. Accounts of the balmy climate of Florida and Mexico gave rise to the story of that fountain in which one had but to bathe, when immediately the infirmities of age would fall off and disappear and the bather would be clothed in the strength and vigor of perpetual youth.

What could be more natural or compelling than the search for these two greatest gifts to an impoverished and suffering humanity—*unbounded wealth* and *perpetual youth*? The search for these boons has not been confined to the sixteenth century Spaniard; it is world old. The wandering nomad of the Arabian desert or the Egyptian in his stone temple brooded over it, and according to his condition set up his ideals. The Greek artists and philosophers carved it in stone or discussed it in their schools. To them wealth was of but secondary

R. Tait McKenzie, "The Quest for Eldorado," *American Physical Education Review*, vol. XVIII, no. 5, May 1913, pp. 295-303.

*Presidential address, 20th Annual Convention American Physical Education Association, Newark, N. J., March 26, 1913.

importance. Commerce to them was an occupation for the slaves who supplied them with all their needs. But into the discovery of perfection of body they threw themselves with passionate fervor, and it was to the hero of the battlefield and the palestra that they looked for the materialization of their gods. *Their gods they created in their own image.* Five hundred years before Christ the Argive sculptor toiled in this quest, searching in the fragmentary remains of the Egyptian wall paintings or legends of his people for the unit on which to construct the perfect, godlike man. Was it the length of the Egyptian high priest's middle finger, the finger of Saturn as it was called, or the foot with which Hercules stepped out the stadium at Olympia, making it 600 feet long? Was it the cubit or length of forearm and hand by which the Arabians still measure their cloth? Sometimes they threw in a hand's breadth for good measure (and with us the hand, now standardized to four inches, is still used in measuring horses). Was it the fathom or span of arms, the yard or girth of waist, was it the face contained ten times in the total height or the head less than eight?

Through laborious days he modeled and wrote and at last was completed the canon of Polycletus, a written book and a bronze statue, and students flocked to Argos to see this broad-shouldered, thick-set and square-chested youth stepping forward with his spear over his shoulder, the unsurpassable ideal of manly beauty. Here was the athlete and fighter, his neck thick and column-like, his body long and his chest deep, his sturdy legs built to support the fatigue of the long march in heavy armor, his brawny arms fit to wield with tireless skill the spear, the sword and the shield. For nearly one hundred years this canon or law of physical perfection was undisputed and widely copied, but as the arts of civilization became more gentle the desire for a more slender and elegant type became greater. The scenes of the palestra replaced the fields of war. Wrestling, jumping and running, flinging the diskos and javelin, had become part of the daily education of every Athenian boy. It was grace rather than strength that began to appeal to the Greek, grown more fastidious, and so was modeled by Lysippus, or one of his school, a standing youth. He scrapes with a strigil from his smooth, lithe body the dust and dirt got from rolling in the soft earth of the palestra. He has not the heavy solidity of the earlier spear bearer, but in his light and graceful form, his long legs and neck and his small round head, he illustrates the change in the Greek ideal from strength to elegance and from power to skill, a passing from the pioneer struggle for national existence in which brute force must be dominant, to the keener and more intellectual conflict of a closer community life.

The same evolution had taken place in Egypt hundreds of years before, where the heavy type predominated from the thirty-fifth to the twenty-second century B. C., when it was replaced by one lighter and less robust.

The peril of all civilizations, including our own, is *high specialization* and *physical decadence,* and with the fall of Greece from these causes the record of these two most efficient types of their day disappeared. We have lost forever the wax tablets on which Polycletus recorded his measurements and calculations. His original bronze has long since been beaten into Persian spear heads or recast as Turkish cannons. Only imperfect marble copies of both works remain to hint at the perfection of these two young Greeks who seemed to have drunk of the waters and bathed in the mythical fountain of perpetual youth, the object of the eager Spaniard's quest.

The physical envelope must give some indication of what it contains. The strong and virile body must harbor a quick and active intellect and a courageous spirit. So held the Greeks, and in the free and untrammeled life of Hellas this was perhaps truer than it is to-day. The type of body to be worshiped by the young and relied upon by the aged must be strong and agile, graceful and hardy. Their whole educational scheme reflects this belief and was planned to cultivate these qualities. So great an impress did they leave on the thought of the world that the search for the laws of physical perfection has been carried on ever since.

Albrecht Dürer, in his four ponderous volumes of bewildering calculations and his anatomical drawings, bespattered as they are with measurements, was on the same hunt with German thoroughness. (His critics claimed that in it he never by any chance deviated into beauty of line or form.)

Leonardo da Vinci, after commenting on the canon of Polycletus, adds the fourteenth verse of the 139th Psalm, "I will praise thee, for I am fearfully and wonderfully made."

Michael Angelo searched for it in the dissecting room at Florence.

Pierre Camper threw light on the laws of beauty in his study of the facial angle. He showed that the Greek had suppressed the heavy prognathous jaw and emphasized the high arched forehead beyond the possibilities of nature in depicting his gods and goddesses.

Professor Carus, the Dresden physiologist, constructed an anatomical figure neither male nor female from which he could calculate and model the ideal man and woman.

Cousin and Gerdy, Audran and Dewit, Schadow and Paul Richer, the present professor of artistic anatomy in Paris, all have sought the laws of the perfect form in terms of proportion until it seems now as if the last word had been written and the volume complete.

The scientist has, however, pursued quite another path in his search for the laws of physical perfection. He has patiently accumulated the facts, he has classified and tabulated them for reference. Whether or not we are willing to admit that whatever *is* is right, the importance of finding out what *is* cannot be questioned. The wise merchant keeps in his books a record of his buying and his selling, that he may know accurately his financial standing. From time to time he takes stock.

Forty years ago Lambert Adolphe Jacques Quételet, director of the Royal Observatory at Brussels and secretary of the Royal Academy of Belgium, in his ambitious work on man, "Sur L'Homme," set himself doggedly to the task of measuring soldiers and sailors, students and laborers, criminals, imbeciles, doctors, lawyers and fellows of the Royal Society. English, French and Belgians, Indians, Negroes and Patagonians, young and old, male and female, all came under his tapeline and yardstick. Time-honored fallacies were knocked in the head and new gods set up. The binomial curve swelled with importance and the percentile chart easily replaced the primitive average, for it allowed us to consider not only the peaks of single facts like the average itself, but to explore the hillsides and valleys of variation on either side. From them the science of anthropometry was born, that the ideal might be found by scientific methods.

Surely the man whose measurements registered 100 per cent on the chart would be the perfect man, and the other whose modest proportions kept a middle course would be but the mediocre, average man. Experience soon showed that no man came up to the high expectation and that the point at which the greatest number of any measurement occurred, the 50 per cent line on the chart, represented the type that *had* after all *actually* survived. Can he not then be justly called the physical *ideal* for our conditions of life?

As our mode of living differs radically from that of the Greeks, our type should differ also from theirs. Instead of the free outdoor life of muscular activity, untrammeled by tight clothing, we now live our days hemmed in by acres of brick. We sit for hours on hard seats and cramped at desks during our most precious growing years. We cultivate myopia by constant reading and starve the great muscle masses that feed our growing frame in the petty movements of writing, instead of strengthening them in the great and free actions of the open. We dry out our mucous membranes in the furnace-heated air of our houses till they become weak and inflamed. How sadly inadequate at their best are our school games and recreations condensed to combat the worst of these abuses, when performed by a hundred children in a single room, or by a large class in a small school yard.

Is it not shameful to think of a big, well-built man, brought up on the farm, maybe, spending his days pushing a small pen or whispering into a dictaphone? It makes one agree with the riveter, sitting astride the iron beam of a new building just hoisted in place opposite an office window on the twentieth story, who called his mate's attention to a man sitting hunched up at a desk, by the remark, "There do be queer ways of making a living now, don't there?"

It is to the fifty years of continuously kept measurements, taken at Amherst, we must look for a record of the physique of the young American and it is from Hitchcock and Phillips that we can claim authority to say that the great revival of physical education and outdoor life, in which this Association has always been the leader, has added an inch to the height of the modern student and increased his weight three pounds. And from the measurements at Smith College we can gain similar encouragement about the modern young woman. The classic charts compiled from the thousands of measurements of college students, arranged according to age and sex, by Sargent, give us a permanent standard with which to compare communities, classes and individuals, and should lead us to cultivate those habits and practices that will bring the race nearer to the ideal of physical perfection. The names of Bowditch, Galton, Porter, Hastings, Gulick and Seaver (our own members), stand out among those whose work remains as a permanent contribution to this science, and already the determining of specialized types, like the sprinter, the speed skater, the strong man, has made some progress.

The Society of Directors of Physical Education in Colleges have sought, in the average proportions of 400 picked

"The Ideal American College Athlete"

athletes, a statue whose measurements would represent the ideal American student athlete. His proportions follow closely the 65 per cent line on a college student's chart and his type comes about midway between the two extreme ideals of beauty held up to the sculptors of Greece, the thickset, powerful warrior and the graceful, agile athlete.

In a general way, members of the learned professions, merchant kings, captains of industry and finance, are taller and heavier than the inmates of our houses of correction and asylums for the insane. It can be proved that brightness of intellect keeps pace with height and weight among growing school children.

But other important considerations should not be overlooked. One of the most magnificent specimens of muscular development I have ever seen was easily surpassed by lighter and smaller men in the application of his muscular power to definite tests. It is more important to find a man's capacity for work than his size alone. If an inventory of the whole muscular system could be taken group by group the total ability to apply effort would be shown by the simple process of addition. This must be of greater practical value than any information given by the tapeline alone, and if correlated with height and weight, what more could be desired?

Instruments were modified or designed, tests were devised to try the power of lifting and grasping. The ability to repeat a comparatively easy feat, like chinning the bar, was tested (a very different kind of power from that of a single maximum effort). In taking these tests the importance of the mental attitude of the pupil soon showed itself. With spectators to encourage or stimulate, the test will be high; if unwillingly taken, the results will sometimes suggest temporary paralysis, for we are not working with the unchanging materials of a machine, but with that perilous stuff of which our body is made, and to find out its limitations and possibilities we must venture farther and farther into that ill-defined and uncharted hinterland that lies between the domains of body and of the mind. Power of concentration, muscular balance and judgment, accuracy, rapidity and steadiness of movement, resistance to fatigue, all these give important indications of efficiency. Already psychologists have made great explorations into this fascinating country. Binet and Simon in France have estimated the mental age of children to a year by tests partly mental and partly muscular. Goddard has modified and proved it in thousands of American school children. By this discovery in the charting of the human consciousness the backward, the normal or the precocious child can be inexorably catalogued and put in just relation to his fellows. (Is there not here an opportunity for some one of our members to devise a series of tests to determine the muscular ability of the child as accurately and as completely as Dr. Goddard can place the mentality?)

And when the proportions of the perfect man have been found, when his muscular strength is calculated and his faculties measured and weighed, can we then know the ideal, the Eldorado of efficiency, the individual in whom youth will tarry longest?

I fear not—for lurking in the socket there may be a distorted eyeball, the dulled hearing may give no outward indication of its presence, in the thorax there may be the crumpled heart valve or the fertile soil for tuberculosis, the abdominal wall may be breached, the foot arch fallen or the spine awry. The journey is short from the land of physiology into realms of the pathologist, and so in our examination we must be prepared to take stock of soundness of wind and limb, as well as of beauty of form or muscular strength.

This is the bookkeeping of physical education. We must know the actual facts if we are to improve the conditions. Too much tuberculosis in a community means bad housing, bad feeding and bad habits of exercise, and the excess can be proved only by comparison with other communities in which these bad conditions do not exist. A low strength test in the arms of a whole class shows lack of sufficient exercise of these muscle groups and can be proved only by comparison with measurements of other classes compiled through laborious years. The girth of the normal chest has first to be known before we can tell if an individual must take special means to bring himself up to his fellows.

The business man of to-day may not need the muscular development and strength of the Greek who lived when the sword and spear were the arbiters in all disputes, but in intellectual as in physical work a sound heart and lungs, a good digestion, and a vigorous, well-developed physique are as great assets as they were then. The soldier and sailor need to-day the same clear eye, enduring frame and dauntless courage as when Leonidas, with his handful of 300 Spartans, crippled the Persian host at Thermopylæ and when in our search for the ideal of physical beauty, of muscular strength, of functional vigor, and of mental power we have marshalled our facts and established our standards, we will have gone farther than did the Egyptians, the Greeks or the adventurers of Spain toward finding "Eldorado"—the man whose touch transforms the crude ore of opportunity into the fine gold of achievement, and toward discovering in America, if not the mystic fountain of perpetual youth, at least those springs the drinking of whose waters will make youth linger and retard the inexorable decadence of age.

BASKET BALL*

Doctor James Naismith
University of Kansas

It appears to be generally conceded that no paper on physical education is quite orthodox unless it traces its descent from the period of Greek culture, but I assure you that I shall not follow that precedent, for basket ball, unlike the great majority of our games, is not the result of evolution but is a modern synthetic product of the office. The conditions were recognized, the requirements met, and the rules formulated and put in typewritten form before any attempt was made to test its value. These rules, as typewritten in the office, which are now in my possession, are identical with the rules as first published and remained unchanged for almost two years. Their first appearance, in print, was in the *Triangle*, the school paper of the Y. M. C. A. College at Springfield, Mass., in the issue of January, 1892, under the heading, "A New Game." In the twenty years of its existence the game has been carried to the ends of the earth, and it is to-day in all probability one of the most widely known and played of all games. Its popularity and extensive introduction are due primarily to three factors: first, there was an absolute need for such a contribution; second, it was founded on fundamental principles; third, it was produced in an international institution, which gave it a world interest.

Physical education, in the early nineties, was confined almost exclusively to gymnastics, derived from a twofold source, the apparatus work of the German, and the free work of the Swedish systems. Athletics as we know them to-day were little used in the work of a department of physical education, games hardly at all. About this time there was a growing interest in games because of their human interest

James Naismith, "Basket Ball," *American Physical Education Review,* vol. XIX, no. 5, May 1914, pp. 339-351.

*Presented at the Eighth Annual Convention of the National Collegiate Athletic Association.

and their adaptability to intercollegiate contests. There had been a steady growth in these since the seventies when intercollegiate sports really began, but they were largely outside the scope of physical education. Those individuals who in the fall season were interested in and took part in football, found that, in the winter, apparatus work was more or less tiresome and uninteresting, while the influence that it might have on the individual did not appeal to the youth who did not know that he had a stomach, save as a receptacle, nor a heart, save in a figurative sense. This left a period of physical inaction for a great many persons who enjoyed participation in a wholesome form of competition. Basket ball was introduced as a deliberate attempt to supply for the winter season a game that would have the same interest for the young man that football has in the fall and baseball in the spring. There was a place that ought to be filled and that apparently was filled by basket ball.

The first principle on which the game was based was that it should demand of, and develop in, the player the highest type of physical and athletic development. This type in the mind of the writer was the tall, agile, graceful, and expert athlete, rather than the massive muscular man on the one hand, or the cadaverous greyhound type on the other. This necessitated that every player should have approximately the same kind of work; that it should demand of him that he be able to reach, jump, and act quickly and easily. Lacrosse was the ideal game to develop this type, but it was impossible to use it or adapt it for an indoor game. But the sport that we sought should embody the same factors.

The second principle was that it should be so easily taken up that any individual could make a fair showing without a long period of practice. It was necessary, therefore, to have very little apparatus and that so easily handled that anyone might make a start. The conclusion was that it should be played with a large, light ball. The only ball that answered that description was the Association football, and the first rules said that the game should be played "with an ordinary Association football."

The third principle was that, on account of the size and varying conditions of the gymnasiums of that time, it should be possible to play the game on any ordinary gymnasium floor. It is interesting to note that it was first played by two teams of nine men each, on a floor 35 x 45, equipped with apparatus, and having a running track in the gallery.

The fourth principle was that it should be capable of being developed to such an extent as to hold the interest of the player when he had become expert in the fundamentals of the game. In other words, it must be capable of being played as a team game. It has been thought that this element is being overemphasized, but the game must have this quality in order to succeed. Indeed, it is the phase that is most interesting to this Association, as the scope of our work is intercollegiate athletics. That the game has the power to hold the interest of the expert makes its use as an intercollegiate sport possible.

With these principles in mind the several games were passed in review or tried out on the floor, but none of them seemed to meet the requirements. Football was too rough, so was Association football; baseball, lacrosse, and tennis were impossible at that time of the year. Track athletics lacked the element of personal competition with a moving competitor, while the gymnastic games lacked the team element. It was plainly evident that there was need for a new game.

The confident assertion that a game could be devised to meet these requirements was met with incredulity and a quiet assumption that the ideal could not be realized. At the same time ample opportunity was given to demonstrate the possibility of such an accomplishment, and the opportunity for testing it was supplied by a class of young men who were compelled to take gymnastic work one hour per day, and whose frame of mind was such that a strike was the only outlet for the natural feeling—and basket ball was the result.

A simple process of reasoning gave the clue that introduced a new element into the game and marks it from all others. This was so simple that the results are surprising. The roughness in football is due largely to tackling. This is necessitated because the opponent is permitted to run with the ball in his possession; therefore, if we eliminate the running, we eliminate the tackling and its consequent roughness. The first step was therefore to prohibit a player from running with the ball in his possession, but he was permitted to throw it in any direction, either to make a point or to pass it to a team mate. This at first sight seemed to take away the possibilities of the game, but when the individual was permitted to move about anywhere, so long as he did not have the ball, the game became spirited and kaleidoscopic.

Association football was rough because of the fact that the ball is kicked through a goal, and the more forceful the kick, the greater the probability of scoring. This would be equally true if the ball were thrown through a goal. To eliminate this form of roughness, it was necessary to so modify conditions that in order to make a goal the ball should be thrown with care rather than with force. A change in the position of the goal solved this problem, for if the opening of the goal were horizontal and above the head the ball would have to be thrown with a curve and this source of roughness would be disposed of.

On asking the janitor for a box of about eighteen inches in width, he informed me that he had a couple of large peach baskets. These were fastened to the gallery for goals and from these the name basket ball was derived.

Another difficulty remained unsolved, how to start the game without kicking or scrimmaging. A solution came from Rugby, where, when the ball goes out of bounds, it is returned by throwing it in between two lines of players. Then in order to avoid the scramble for the ball, which generally ensued, it was decided to throw it up between two men selected for this purpose. Kicking and hitting the ball with the fist were prohibited from the first. With the elimination of running with the ball, there was no excuse for any personal contact, so that all manner of holding or handling the person of an opponent was absolutely prohibited. This has been a point of conflict ever since, but, according to the fundamental idea, there should be no doubt as to the proper attitude toward this feature of basket ball.

In two weeks from the time that the task was undertaken, the game was ready for its trial, and it was with a good deal of anxiety that I anticipated the outcome. The first exclamation by a bystander upon seeing the baskets was far from encouraging—"Huh, a new game!"—and under this caption it appeared in the *Triangle*. It was not until some time later that, in a conference with this same man, it was decided to call the game basket ball, and in the first issue of the "Guide" it was so called.

Its Development

The development of basket ball has been along three main lines. First, the rules were adapted for amateur teams, in an attempt to make the game beneficial to the players, while encouraging legitimate competition for the interest of the men and the organization, rather than for the benefit of the spectators. For this class there have arisen two sets of rules, the A. A. U. and the Collegiate, differing only in one essential, namely, that in the latter the player may make a play after dribbling, while in the former he is restrained. There was need for a divergent set of rules so long as there was a difference in the size of the courts, but as soon as the fields are large enough to admit of the dribbles, there will be no reason why there should be two sets of rules covering the same field.

The second group is that of the purely professional, where the rules are made for the spectator rather than for the player. This has been developed in and around Philadelphia, which is the home of professional basket ball. The professional game was developed through the reluctance of the Y. M. C. A.'s to give time and space to the sport, in the regular work of their gymnasiums. The players who had become expert and were enthusiastic over the game organized teams outside of the Associations, and thus the professional teams began. The aim of their rules was to make the game as fast as possible, for the sake of the spectators; the players are enclosed in a cage so that the ball never goes out of bounds, at the same time giving more space for the spectators. However, this has had the effect of slowing the game, as there are so many occasions for a held ball.

A third line of development was the introduction of changes to adapt the game to the characteristics of girls. The game was played at first according to the rules used by boys; but a misinterpretation of the diagram, illustrating the floor, by some of the Western institutions, gave them the idea of dividing the court into three parts. This avoided the danger of overexertion and exhaustion, which would naturally result when running from end to end of the field was permitted.

A second change was one intended to prevent any opportunity for a struggle over the possession of the ball. Therefore, a rule was formulated that whoever first got possession of the ball with both hands was allowed three seconds in which to dispose of it.

Thus at the present we have these four sets of rules. It seems to me a good provision that the different classes of players should have a game adapted for their own needs; but where the condition of the players and the grounds is similar, there seems little use for more than one set.

Its Distribution

The distribution of basket ball has been along several lines. The first organization to take it up was the Y. M. C. A. This was natural since it originated in their Training College, and it was carried by the students to their home Associations, thus attaining an international scope. One of the players on the first team went to India, another to China, another to Japan, while others carried it over the United States and Canada. The first team was scattered over the world, carrying the game with them. The drawings for the first copy of the rules were made by a Japanese, who later went to his home country. Ever since, the Associations have been the great exponents of the game, and to-day it is played in most of the Associations of the world.

According to statistics supplied by Mr. Ball, one of the international secretaries, there are in the United States 1037 representative teams playing the game. There are a total of 5773 organized teams reported, which would make about 40,000 persons playing organized basket ball. And, if we include the Associations that use basket ball as an adjunct to the regular physical work, the estimate of Mr. Ball is 150,000 members who play the game.

In February, 1892, just one month after the first appearance of the game in the school paper, we find that it had been adopted as a part of the physical work in the Elmira Reformatory, and was used as a recreation and development for the inmates. It is, to-day, recognized as a useful adjunct to the physical and moral education of the youth in these institutions. Hon. H. W. Charles, of the Kansas Industrial School, writing of the game says: "Inasmuch as the inmates are usually lacking in physique and control, much stress is laid on those exercises which will correct these defects. I do not hesitate to commend basket ball as one of the most valuable factors in remedying these conditions."

The first educational institution to introduce basket ball was Carroll Institute, of Washington, D. C., as it was played there in February, 1892, or less than one month after it appeared in print. Cornell was the first college to use the game as a recreation, and there also it was first prohibited. So many men were playing on each side that, in their efforts to get the ball, fifty men would rush from end to end of the gymnasium, and the apprehension that it would do damage to the building led to its prohibition as a class recreation.

Yale was the first college to send out a representative team, as the Yale team played when they had to meet other institutions than colleges. In 1896, Pennsylvania, Wesleyan, and Trinity were playing the game and had representative teams. The University of Iowa was the first of the Western colleges to make it an intercollegiate sport. About the same date Nebraska University was playing the game. Kansas sent out its first representative team in 1898. Since then the spread in the colleges has been rapid, until to-day there are few colleges that do not have a representative team.

In the Army there are teams at the different forts, Leavenworth having twelve teams, Fortress Monroe nine, and others having representative teams. In the Navy, thirteen ships have teams which play whenever they have an opportunity, and this is encouraged by the Y. M. C. A.'s wherever possible. In the Canal Zone, there have been teams playing inter-city games, and last year there was a league of five teams playing the intercollegiate rules. In South America it is obtaining a foothold, and leagues are being formed in the different countries.

The spread among the high schools has been very great, especially in the West, where the state universities have encouraged it by holding an annual tournament. Nebraska University had a tournament in which there were fifty teams; Kansas held one in which there were thirty-three boys' teams and seventeen girls' teams; Washington, one with ten; Montana, one with twenty-nine; and Utah, one with thirty-three teams. These figures do not represent all the teams that played the game, but only those that felt that they had a chance of winning the tournament.

Basket ball is especially adapted for high schools, as it develops those traits which should be developed at that time of life. It is individualistic and at the same time it encourages coöperation; it develops the reflexes which must be developed at that time, if at all, in the ordinary individual. It can be played with few men and is inexpensive.

Another phase of the work is in the Sunday school leagues, chief among which is the league in Springfield, Mass., managed by the Training School. This phase is extending to other cities: Kansas City has a league of sixty-five teams.

In the playground, it has found one of its most fruitful spheres, as it interests more individuals, with less oversight, than any other game. In the New York Park Playground there are 300 teams organized. Foreign countries are organizing teams and playing the game either in connection with the Y. M. C. A.'s, schools, or colleges.

The game had hardly been well started before the girls saw its possibilities for their use. A company of school teachers in Springfield, Mass., organized two teams and played the game in Armory Hill Gymnasium. The game was illustrated at a convention in Providence, R. I., and it was carried to some towns of New England. Smith College early took it up and played it as an interclass game. The students going out from that institution spread it over the country, and in 1894 it was used in Wolfe Hall, a ladies' seminary in Denver. From this institution it spread to the high schools of that city, and soon there was a league organized. In 1896, the girls of Leland Stanford met a team from the University of California.

The schoolgirls of the Philippines are using it as a class game, and it is recognized by the authorities as one of the school interests.

In a recent work on the customs of Japan, basket ball is mentioned as one of the forms of recreation and development for the Japanese girls. The girls of China, even some of them with their crippled feet, play the game in that country. Australia has a league of girls' teams playing a series of contests. In England the girls of Oxford University play it as an outdoor sport.

In our own country the game is popular with the high school girls, and it forms one of the few games that they can use for recreation and competition. There is objection to the game when used as a spectacle for girls' teams, but it is rapidly assuming its true place in the education of the girls. In one high school of Brooklyn there are thirty-two teams playing interclass games, and they are given a definite time on the day's schedule. Smith College has consistently used it as an intramural sport. The game as played by these institutions is the modified game for the girls, and this adds to its permanence and usefulness.

To see how basket ball appeals to and encourages the type of athlete set up as an ideal at the inception of the game, it is interesting to note the charts of the basket ball players. For this purpose I have introduced a chart showing the average measurements of the men who have earned their letter in basket ball at the University of Kansas. The player is about a 70 per cent man, symmetrical with the exception of the left arm, which is slightly smaller than the right. When compared with the ideal athlete of McKenzie, he is one-tenth of an inch taller and ten pounds lighter. The chest is not so muscular, but is flexible. This was to be expected as a development from a game that demanded so much from the lungs and heart. It is impossible to show the development in physical judgment, skill, and control, and those attributes which go to make up the ideal athlete.

	(A)	(B)	(C)
Height	69.1	72.9	72.4
Weight	149.0	168.0	149.0
Neck	14.1	14.5	14.3
Chest (con.)	33.7	34.2	34.8
Chest (exp.)	36.8	38.8	38.7
Waist	29.9	31.6	29.0
Right Arm	10.5	10.9	10.2
Right Arm up	11.9	12.3	11.4
Right Forearm	10.5	11.3	10.5
Left Arm	10.2	11.0	10.1
Left Arm up	11.4	12.4	11.2
Left Forearm	10.2	11.1	10.0
Right Thigh	21.2	21.8	21.0
Righ Calf	13.9	14.8	13.3
Left Thigh	21.0	21.9	21.0
Left Calf	13.9	14.9	13.3

Column A. The average of basket ball players of the University of Kansas.

Column B. The measurements of the captain of the University of Kansas basket ball team.

Column C. The measurements of the best all-round athlete of the University of Kansas (football, basket ball, track, baseball, and gymnasium).

Basket Ball as the Type of a College Game

It is intrinsically an open game, and exhibits skill rather than science. Audiences must expect to appreciate an exhibition of muscular activity, grace of movement, and immediate response to varying conditions rather than to see their team defeat the other. The game is enhanced by clean, rapid play, for it is then that skill can be shown, both in handling the ball and in intercepting passes by the opponent, so as to get the ball into the possession of the quicker team. It is not in a class with football, where the ball marks the progress of the game, and a partisan can become enthusiastic over a game, the science of which he knows nothing about. The main interest in basket ball lies in watching the activity of the players and the kaleidoscopic changes which take place. Every moment of a game is full of thrills, when expert players handle the ball. The instantaneous action of the reflexes, when a ball is caught, in deciding where it shall go, demands a great amount of coördination. There is not time to think out a play, but reflex judgment must control, and the action must be performed with lightning rapidity. No prettier sight can be found in athletic achievement than in a game where the ball, without any preconceived plan, passes from man to man in a series of brilliant movements and lands in the goal, or is cleverly intercepted when a goal seems inevitable. We watch such a game with an increasing admiration for the wonderful capacity of the human frame for accomplishing the seemingly impossible. No amount of rough work, even if it should result in a goal for our side, can compare with such a spectacle. It is indeed a narrow mind that puts goals before grace, scores before skill, or marks before manhood.

Institutions must sooner or later learn to judge the success or failure of a team as much, at least, by the manly attributes exhibited, as by the score. The problem of team games to-day is to discover some method of scoring that will include the attributes of skill and self-control.

One of the conditions that was thought necessary for the best kind of a game was that it should be capable of team work. This feature has been developed from the first, but there are two kinds of team work; *coöperative team work,* in which each player uses his team mates at the right time, and to the right extent, and has become so accustomed to doing this that he does not stop to think, but acts reflexly; *machine team work,* in which every man does that which he has been told to do and does it the same way every time.

Games differ in their capacity for one form or the other; e.g., Rugby is coöperative, American football, machine-like; lacrosse is coöperative, baseball, machine-like. Each of these has its own advantages. Coöperation develops the individual, machine play, the game; the former develops the general reflexes, the latter specializes; the former makes the player broad and independent, the latter makes him a cog; the former develops initiative, the latter, subordination; the former makes him depend on his own resources, the latter makes him dependent on the coach.

Basket ball has possibilities for both forms, but up to the present the former has been emphasized. There is a tendency to develop the machine type, but the effort of the Rules Committee has been to minimize this and to lay the main stress on the development of skill and initiative, the result of which will be the development of the spectacular rather than the partisan form of competition.

Games are instinctive, and intended to develop the individual for the business of life. The educational value of a game, therefore, should be judged by its effects on the powers of the participant. If it makes him better able to master the circumstances of life it is a benefit; if it hinders this, or if it is of negative value in this respect, then it cannot justify its place in a college program. The sports of early times developed brute strength and physical endurance, but neither of these is necessary for the college man after his graduation. But there are many factors that can be developed that would make him a better man and a better citizen. The attributes that are demanded in the life of the twentieth century are initiative, activity, quick judgment, adaptability to conditions, self-control, perseverance, and concentration. These are the attributes developed by basket ball. It is therefore a means of education.

Basket ball is one of the games that attract the player, apart entirely from the competitive element. It is one of the games in which a small group will work trying to make goals. There seems to be an attraction in endeavoring to put the ball in the basket, a desire to acquire the skill necessary to make goals, aside entirely from the feeling that you are doing better than someone else. Of course, the added interest that comes from a good contest makes it all the more attractive. It is this factor that makes it particularly adapted for interclass games and for the development of the individual. It is unnecessary to adapt the rules to suit the spectators, for it will be played wherever a goal and a basket are found. Even should it be put aside as an intercollegiate sport, it still has a part to play in the education of man. But the intercollegiate element is necessary to get the best out of the sport.

The Future of the Game

The future of the game lies in the hands of the coaches and officials. The rules of the intercollegiate game are as nearly perfect as can be under the present conditions. Every safeguard against roughness has been introduced, in order to make the game as clean as possible. It is clearly within the power of the official to so enforce the rules as to make the game an ideal one, for the spectator as well as for the player. It is absolutely necessary that the game be kept free from objectionable features: first, because every play is right before the audience, and every act and even every word is within the range of every spectator. Any roughness therefore is immediately detected and becomes the subject of audible criticism. This is, in turn, heard by the players, and they feel that, if the official does not enforce the rules, they must themselves retaliate or be considered cowards, so that further roughness occurs and mars the game.

Second, the attitude of audiences towards the game is different to-day from what it was several years ago. Now everyone is looking for a square deal, and the official who does not give it is likely to hear from the audience. The official who does not rule as they think he should is condemned and brings the game into disrepute.

In a recent criticism of the rules there was a statement that it is impossible to play a defense, without playing the man rather than the ball. This is a shortsighted policy, as it is not necessary to keep the score small, for the scoring of goals is one of the interesting features to the spectators, and any score around thirty is not too large. In football there are from eight to twelve minutes of actual play, while in basket ball every minute, from the start to the pause for a goal or foul, is one of intense activity. Playing the ball does not mean that the opponent should be ignored, but that, instead of trying to keep him from scoring after he has obtained possession of the ball, a guard's object should be to prevent him from getting the ball at all. The latter calls for more skill than the former, for if the guard were allowed to hold the forward, it would be impossible to make points; but it would then be a tug-of-war, not basket ball.

Those who complain of the roughness of basket ball surely do not interpret the rules aright, for there is not a single provision that allows of any personal contact between players. How anyone can make a rough game of it and follow the rules is hard to understand. If any individual game is rough, the blame cannot be laid on the rule makers, for everywhere is emphasized the fact that the game should be kept free from personal contact in even the slightest degree. It is easy for an official to let fouls pass unnoticed for a time at the beginning of the game, and then endeavor to make the rulings strict after complaint has been lodged. It is infinitely better to be strict from the first, then the players will know what to expect, and will play accordingly. The officials should know the rules of the game and enforce them according to their letter and spirit, rather than according to the desire of any coach, manager, or audience.

In those sections of the country where the game has been kept clean, open, and free from roughness, it has grown in popularity and in esteem. But wherever the officials have been lax, or indifferent about the enforcement of the rules, the game has lost in popularity, and in some cases has been dropped because of its reputed roughness. In the Middle West, players and audiences have commended the work of the very strictest officials, while they have uniformly condemned the work of those who were lax, and allowed roughness to creep in.

The *responsibility* of the coaches is even greater than that of the officials, as many of the latter are influenced by the attitude of the coaches. When the coach lacks the knowledge or ability to perfect a team in individual skill, he is willing to permit holding, in order that his men may keep the score down. He may even request that fouls be overlooked; thus roughness is introduced, for which the rules frequently get the blame. Or the coach may refuse to accept an official who is known to rule strictly and in accord with the spirit of the game. Thus the official to retain his popularity frequently officiates as the coaches ask. I have been asked by members of this Association if there was not some way to change the rules so as to eliminate roughness. There is apparently only one way to meet this difficulty, namely, to have the officials responsible to a Central Board, to get the information from impartial sources rather than from coaches and managers. At the same time dissatisfaction on the part of the coaches could be weighed, and a just estimate of the work of an official could be obtained.

Responsibility of This Association to Basket Ball

While the Y. M. C. A.'s were the early pioneers who carried the game into many countries, this body is now largely responsible for its growth and development. Formerly, it was recognized as a factor in recreation and physical development, and later, as having a value as a means of inculcating ethical instruction. To-day, without losing any of its powers, it has become a part of our educational systems, and in many cases is being introduced into the school program. The teachers in the elementary and secondary schools are graduates of our normal schools and colleges, and the attitude towards the game which they have acquired from their *alma mater* is likely to be the one which they will bear to it when they are responsible for its conduct, whether professionally or incidentally. That college men have an important part in the development of basket ball is seen in such instances as that of Goodhue, who introduced it into Syria; Exner, who organized it in one of the districts of China; Alford and Overfield, who made it popular in Alaska; Gray, who gave it an added impetus in India; the engineers in the Canal Zone, and the multitude of college men who are controlling the game in our high schools and academies.

Therefore, while the immediate responsibility of this organization is primarily with intercollegiate contests, yet it should use every means to put basket ball, as well as every other sport, on such a basis that it will be a factor in the molding of character, as well as to encourage it as a recreative and competitive sport. This organization should take such measures as will result in a rigid enforcement of the rules as formulated, and encourage a manly respect for the rights of others. So much stress is laid to-day on the winning of games that practically all else is lost sight of, and the fine elements of manliness and true sportsmanship are accorded a secondary place. One great problem for this organization is the formulating of a system of scoring that will take cognizance of these traits of manhood or the development of traditions which will make it impossible for a college man to take advantage of an opponent, save in those qualities which the sport is supposed to require. The bane of basket ball to-day is the attempt to evade the laws of the game and even the rulings of the officials. There is no more reason why we should take an illegal advantage of an opponent in basket ball than that we should put our hand in his pocket and take his wealth. Few college men would take money or valuables from another, yet they are taught by the practices of our sports that it is not dishonorable to take an illegal advantage of another, if there is little prospect of being caught. To-day, a player hardly dares do the manly thing if it will mean a loss of points, lest he incur the ridicule of the bleachers and the sneers of his college mates. The man who does what he knows to be right, when he thereby fails to score points, too often incurs the wrath of the coach and the scorn of his team mates.

If athletics are to occupy the place that they might in the development of the college man of the future, they must take cognizance of the manly traits as well as of the development of physical skill and ability. This organization, composed mainly of faculty members whose interest is in the making of men rather than in the making of athletes, is the body to inaugurate such a movement. It should set the standard by which a sport is judged, and then, by education and, as far as possible, by legislation make the forward step in the development of intercollegiate contests.

As a member of the Basket Ball Rules Committee, I wish to say that that committee has done everything in its power to make the rules the very best possible. I believe that they are adequate to meet the situation, but their power is limited. While they may make rules of the very best, they have no power to enforce them, and each college is a power unto itself, and may make such provisions that the good of the rules is annulled. It is entirely within the province of this organization to take the next step in the development of an observance of the rules and the cultivation of true sportsmanship. If this body, composed of representatives of the great colleges of this country, and of representatives of the great athletic conferences of our colleges, should go on record as in favor of a rigid enforcement of the rules, clean sport, courteous treatment by players and spectators, and a fraternal spirit between college men, it would introduce a forward step in intercollegiate contests. The field would be broadened, and a true conception of a college athlete would ensue when we would realize that a college contestant is primarily a gentleman, secondarily a college man, and incidentally a basket ball player.

THE PROFESSIONAL VERSUS THE EDUCATIONAL IN COLLEGE ATHLETICS*

C. W. Savage
Oberlin College

The subject which I am to present to-day is not a small one. My treatment in the time allotted, therefore, must of necessity be fragmentary rather than full, suggestive rather than exhaustive. For this reason, lest my viewpoint be obscured and I be misunderstood, I wish to state at the outset that I am an ardent believer in intercollegiate sport in all its various branches; that I have been a 'varsity athlete myself, have coached 'varsity athletic teams, and am still closely connected with intercollegiate athletics. I trust, therefore, that my observations will not be considered as the maunderings of a "musty old high-brow," but rather as the conclusions of an ardent lover of, and believer in, athletic sports.

During the past ten years it has been increasingly borne in upon me that there are two great aspects of our athletic problem—two great tendencies, which I roughly characterize as the professional and the educational. In the early years of college athletics in America, only their recreational, hygienic and social aspects were recognized. In a surprisingly short time, owing to the innate love of sport and the growing intensity of athletic rivalry on the one hand, and to the conservatism and shortsightedness of educators on the other, we find strong student athletic associations flourishing and the entire control of college athletics vested in these associations. These organizations rapidly acquired great power. Young and inexperienced student managers abused this power and made embarrassing mistakes. The resultant bickerings and recriminations became so tiresome that it was

C. W. Savage, "The Professional Versus The Educational in College Athletics," *American Physical Education Review*, vol. XX, no. 4, April 1915, pp. 187-194.

*Read at the Ninth Annual Convention of the National Collegiate Athletic Association, Chicago, Ill., December 19, 1914.

rightly conceived that continuity and experience in management would reduce if not eliminate much misunderstanding and friction. This more efficient management shaped itself into what is now commonly called the graduate managership.

With a business man at the helm, the storms and perils of intercollegiate strife were largely dissipated, and the ship of sport for a time sailed smoother seas. College faculties breathed more easily, believing that the threatening clouds of athletic trouble had been dispelled.

But sports, well managed, grew in popularity both with the students and with the public. The graduate manager was a business man, and with an eye to business he saw that greater gate receipts meant better facilities, more equipment, and the means of attaining better results. Better results to the students, to the alumni, to the graduate manager, and even to the faculty meant more athletic victories. The business man's business grew. The training table, the training quarters, the return of star graduates to help coach, the high-salaried professional coach, magnificent athletic fields and imposing stadia were all made possible by good business methods and by the skill of the graduate managers in exploiting the loyalty of alumni. But the athletic association was not an educational body. The graduate manager was not an educator. He was closer to the alumni than to the faculty. His great enterprise assumed such proportions, and its exactions on the time and thought of the students became so heavy, that scholastic pursuits were considerably interrupted.

Here, with characteristic conservatism, college authorities came forward with a harmless prescription for faculty control—an advisory athletic committee, composed of some members of the faculty with sporting proclivities, a proportion of real sports from the alumni, and a representation of undergraduates. This committee advised the graduate manager and even did more, but the graduate manager still, for the most part, had his own way. The athletic associations have grown into corporations, and now hold property worth millions. Intercollegiate sport has gradually become commercialized and professionalized. The good name of the student athlete has often been smirched by proselyting and subsidizing, and our controversy of amateurism versus professionalism has grown ever more insistent. How can we expect professionalized sport to turn out amateur sportsmen? I believe that college and university presidents and thinking people in general, who have the courage to face the situation squarely, feel with President Wilson that there is real danger of the side show becoming more important than the main tent.

During the last few years slight indications of attempts at readjustment have appeared. The place of play is coming to be recognized. The educational world is in travail, and there is hope that a new athletic era is to be born, an era with an athletic policy that shall be the legitimate offspring of an educational system; a child, sane, sensible, sturdy and strong, who will, by the might of his clean ancestry and undoubted parentage, beat down his bullying braggart of a bastard brother until he shall come to recognize his rightful place in the educational family circle.

But possibly the sturdy younger son has already been conceived. In almost any college faculty you will now find a few men of vision who are beginning to preach the doctrine that play has a real and distinctive place in education, and even in higher education. What that place should be, I would like to discuss here, but it is outside the province of this paper. But what of the place of play in education at the present time?

For the sake of analogy, imagine the student body taking a great interest in the work of the Department of Expression and Public Speaking. A number of students form a dramatic association, secure a competent coach, and elect a manager. By patient training, a skilled debating team is developed, several prize orators are produced and a splendid cast of characters is trained to portray a Shakespearean play. Granted that contests for the orators and debaters and a theatrical engagement for the actors could be secured each week without the interruption of college work, will any educator here present advise that it would be good educational policy to schedule regular seasons of seven to ten weeks each year for these young people to travel about the country and appear before public audiences, while at the same time the great mass of the students should receive practically no instruction or training in any form of public expression?

This analogy cannot be pressed too far, yet it is apt enough to afford food for thought.

The facts of the case are that there is little or no justification of the present status of intercollegiate sport as a legitimate interest in an educational system. Some of you will say that it needs no educational justification, but with that position I must disagree. Thanks to the influence of this great association, and to the zealous and indefatigable efforts of the friends of good sport working through local conferences, the conditions surrounding intercollegiate sport have improved tremendously in late years, as far as public performances and external conditions are concerned. But we have not yet gone to the root of the matter. We are industriously pruning and trimming the athletic tree, plucking a leaf here and a diseased blossom there; but we hesitate to lay the axe to the root. With the great educational and moral principles underlying sport and with the question of amateurism I fear we are making little progress.

Now our difficulties in both these respects are largely due to one and the same cause. Under existing conditions promising young athletes in high schools and academies are rounded up by alumni scouts or other agencies, they receive inducements of one sort and another, in many cases legitimate and in many other cases such as to prostitute all moral integrity. But whether right or wrong, the athlete is zealously sought after, and that because he is an athlete. If possible he is placed under obligations before reaching college, he is even steered to the proper fitting school of the particular college. He thus enters college with the wrong idea of the relative importance of sport and study. Once in college he lives in an athletic atmosphere that is commercialized and professionalized. He joins the freshman squad and his training is begun. Neither time nor expense is spared to fit him "to deliver." He is promoted to the 'varsity squad. With professional coaches paid enormous salaries for a season's work, with the high-salaried trainer and his retinue, with a famous old grad a thousand miles away summoned by telegraph, expenses paid, to show him how to lengthen his punt a couple of yards, with scouts, who have watched every game of opposing teams throughout the season, returning for the week prior to meeting this or that opponent and coaching how to meet the particular opponent's play, with trips involving three or four days' absence from classes, with a week spent at the seashore or mountains away from the classroom—with all of these things and countless others, what idea of sport is the student to get? Is it sport or is it business, a pastime or a profession? Is it more important than studies or not? That our student athletes carry themselves as well as they do under these circumstances is a tremendous tribute to the stuff of which they are made. That they are able to do anything with their studies is almost inconceivable, yet here again they acquit themselves surprisingly well. But my contention is that the whole program is fundamentally wrong. The whole scheme is professionalized. Efficiency is developed down to the minutest detail. No captain of industry or corporation board of directors could map out a plan of campaign and carry it out with greater efficiency. The coaches and the managers in our great colleges leave no stone unturned that victories may result. Money is poured out like water. The student players are mere pawns, a band of picked men trained and groomed for the day of the contest. That the boys like this sort of thing and that athletic honors are coveted is neither here nor there.

I maintain that it is because of this system that to-day, in spite of multitudinous rules of eligibility, in spite of gentlemen's agreements, in spite of quasi-faculty control, we still have insistent calls for rule revisions, we still have men actually hired to play football on college teams, we still have men competing four and five years, we still have boys lying about their amateur standing, we still have charges made against the morality of intercollegiate sport.

All these things and countless others exist because of the system that has gradually been developed. There is nothing in the history of education to parallel this development. It is best likened to the war policies of Great Britain and Germany, now grappling in a struggle to the death. For a score of years each nation has been trying to surpass the other in preparedness for war. Similarly, since the beginning of intercollegiate football each institution has attempted to get ahead of its rivals in preparedness for the game. Gentlemen, the time for disarmament has come. To my mind our athletic troubles will never grow less, our discussions over the definition of an amateur never cease, until there is a radical readjustment of our athletic system, at least as far as intercollegiate football is concerned. Understand that I am making no charge against football as a game. I believe that our American game of football is the greatest game that the human intellect has ever devised. And let it be clearly understood that I am in no way censuring the special coach, be he graduate or professional. Neither do I blame the athletic associations or their managers. All alike are creatures of the system, and, like Topsy, the system has "just growed." The blame for the situation in the last analysis must rest upon the college authorities. Because of their lack of insight and of foresight we are where we are.

That our great universities will soon change their methods is doubtful. But eventually reformation, if not revolution, must come. At the present time, the trend is almost entirely in the other direction. Coaches who can "deliver the goods" are getting higher and higher salaries. Unsuccessful coaches must go. One bad season is enough. Or the coaching system is at fault and a new one must be tried. You know the ins and outs of the entire situation. But let me ask you a question. Do the presidents or the faculties or the trustees or the regents have anything to say in these matters? Very little. You may say that the educational authorities should have nothing to do with these matters. I maintain that they should have everything to do with them. As long as the students are in an educational institution, educators should direct and control all the educational influences to which they are subjected, and that, too, in such a way that the greatest good to the greatest number may result.

All games and sports in the last analysis have their genesis in the fundamental instinct of play, an instinct almost as powerful and as impelling as the instinct of self-preservation. The biological significance of this all-powerful play impulse is only beginning to be understood. That we as educators should not be content to dillydally with innocuous attempts at repression and control, but rather rouse ourselves to direct and utilize this tremendous force as a real means to education, is my plea.

Although I have already made a sad inroad upon your patience, I cannot close without a word along constructive lines. I have no panacea, no cure-all, to propose. But certain tendencies at least deserve commendation and certain policies can be suggested.

Certainly a readjustment all along the line is necessary, particularly in high schools and academies. Secondary schools are too prone to ape the colleges, but here and there they are showing signs of independence and originality. A high school on the Pacific slope maintains an interscholastic schedule but never sends out the same team to represent it. In the East the splendid Andover plan is certainly greatly to be commended.

In intercollegiate athletics, undoubtedly either schedules should be greatly cut down or different teams should be sent into the different games. In the one or two big games which every college always has on its schedule, surely the best team should represent its institution. But on such great days as these there should be no attempt on the part of the faculty to maintain college appointments. The day should be a holiday for both institutions. The one, both students and faculty, should be the guests of the other. Hospitality both before and after the game should be extended and received. I lay especial emphasis on the aftermath, for I think it would accrue greatly to the education of the victors were they to have an opportunity to learn how to comport themselves considerately and as gentlemen after a victory. The round of such a day of pleasure might fittingly end in a great athletic rally, with both teams present and the student bodies intermingling as friends. It would probably eliminate many of our troubles if gate receipts could be done away with and attendance be by student ticket and by invitation only. There is not the slightest reason why a sane athletic system should not be supported by endowment or by a student athletic fee, and athletics be run on a carefully prepared budget. The sport itself would then be running on a strictly amateur basis, and most of our evils would die a natural death.

The professional coaches would undoubtedly give place to men of faculty standing on the staff of the department of physical education. The practice now quite common in the Middle West of hiring the football coach for the entire year is a step in the right direction, but in too many instances the presence of the coach serves only to increase the stress on football. He is constantly "sizing up" and working with his material for the next season; he has them practice boxing and wrestling through the winter, gives a number of talks on the fine points of the game, and in the spring calls them out for unseasonable and senseless "spring practice." "In the spring the young man's fancy lightly turns to thoughts"–of football? Well, hardly!

Another suggestion would be to schedule intercollegiate meets between departments or classes. If intercollegiate games are good for twenty-five players out of five thousand students, why not for a hundred, or five hundred? Doubtless many other and better suggestions could be made, but enough has been said to serve my purpose.

In my judgment, it is the privilege and duty of every delegate in this convention to go back to his institution and say: "Let us do away with this ineffective scheme of faculty control of athletics, and let us hasten the day of faculty direction and utilization. Let us recognize the value of athletic sports in education and make a real place for them." In other words, the time has come for educational institutions, to incorporate the entire athletic life of the institution, intercollegiate as well as intramural, into their educational program. No longer should we be content with intensive athletics alone, even were they to be conducted in a manner above reproach. Our attention and effort should also be turned to extensive athletics as well, if we are to justify them in the life of students. Even should we claim that play and games afford nothing more than social and hygienic effects (and this I, for one, cannot admit), our athletic methods of to-day are preposterous, even scandalous, and almost entirely indefensible as a legitimate interest in the efficient working program of an educational institution.

"Ranting radicalism," I seem to hear many of you say. Others say, "Even if true, impossible and impracticable." Well, we educators always have been conservative. I will admit that I am taking a long look ahead, but I am emboldened to point the way to-day for two great reasons.

In the first place, we are met to-day in a great city of the Middle West and I am addressing a body composed largely of progressive western men. You men represent institutions with a future. Unhampered by a load of tradition, set yourselves seriously to this problem, and blaze a new trail. Remember, not everything that has been, or is, is right.

Secondly, this is a material age. Thanks to the wonders of invention and the miracles of modern science, no age and no nation has ever enjoyed the material advantages which we are enjoying to-day; and because of the stoppage of the ordinary channels of trade due to the European conflict, we see in the immediate future new opportunities for our commercial aggrandizement such as the world has never before afforded. But herein lies a tremendous national peril. Easy wealth and industrial prosperity do not make nations great. Our best civilization is already open to the charge of softness. Will not greater prosperity completely enervate and demoralize us?

The nations of Europe are to-day engaging in a titanic struggle which is transforming men from the easy-going "flanneled fools" of Kipling to prodigies of courage and physical endurance. A moral regeneration is sweeping all Europe. War has this virtue at least. But our nation is the prophet of peace. How are we, at the rising tide of a material prosperity never before dreamed of, to be able to keep our virility? War makes heroes, easy wealth makes mollycoddles and worse. Our manhood must possess virility, force, physical courage and endurance if this nation is to endure on the earth. And where so naturally and so well are these qualities engendered as on the athletic field? Therefore, I challenge you, not only for the sake of our national greatness but for the sake of our very existence, to help hasten the day when the participation in athletic sports shall be general, and when every college man shall leave his *alma mater* physically and morally, as well as intellectually, fit.

THE FUNCTION OF NEURO-MUSCULAR COORDINATION IN THE EVOLUTION OF THE INDIVIDUAL

December 15, 1917

Mr. E. T. Hartman,
3 Joy Street,
Boston, Massachusetts.

My dear Mr. Hartman:

In your letter of November 28th you ask me to state briefly the function of neuro-muscular coordination in the evolution of the individual. You rightly suggest that it is equivalent to the biological theory of human development. I think biologists and psychologists are reasonably well agreed on the significance of motor training in evolution and development of the neuro-muscular system relative to the evolution of the human mind. It is assumed that the great differentiation and high state of mental development of the accessory neuro-muscular system is particularly associated with the development of the higher human faculties, considered from a racial evolutionary standpoint. On that basis, probably, it is considered equally important in the evolution of the individual human. Without motor experience the child would have no basis for ideas or thoughts and no mechanism for their expression. Our general ideas of the world about us are in the last analysis based on, or at any rate partly associated with, kinesthetic sense perceptions and motor experience. Such, for example, are our ideas of space and distance, density of objects, speed of moving bodies,

William Skarstrom, "The Function of Neuro-Muscular Coordination in the Evolution of the Individual," an unpublished correspondence from Dr. William Skarstrom to M. E. T. Hartman, December 15, 1917. Edith Hemenway Eustis Library, Wellesley College.

etc. We estimate these things in terms of the amount of muscular effort it would take us to travel a given space, that would be exerted in squeezing a given object, or that it would take us to follow with the eyes or intercept by means of locomotion a moving object. While our basic ideas are no doubt closely associated with motor experience involving the fundamental neuro-muscular system, the further development of our ideas is largely dependent upon motor experiences involving the accessory, namely, the finer muscles of the forearm and hand, tongue, lips and pharynx (muscular movements involved in speech). So much for the general relation of motor experience and training (the latter would be an obvious corollary) to mind development.

In Physical Education in the ordinary sense we are concerned chiefly with the fundamental neuro-muscular system. The training of the accessory belongs in other fields. Properly I suppose it really does belong in the field of Physical Education. But it would be a difficult thing to organize, supervise and manage everything under the head of Physical Education, for it would include manual and industrial training, art work, and all work of that kind. That makes a practical division of labor necessary and I think the general concensus of opinion is that Physical Education concerns itself with the fundamental system only.

There are those who believe that after the age of ten or twelve there is no further need of training the fundamental system; that at this time the fundamental system has practically reached a point in which there is no further development worth mentioning; that, in other words, the nascent period for the development of that system is about over at that time. The general theory is, further, that play activities constitute the proper material for the development of the fundamental muscular system; that nature has attended to it by implanting the play instinct into the child and that, if given opportunity, the child, through the promptings of this instinct, will do the things which will insure sufficient development of the fundamental neuro-muscular system; also that, if there is any further development after the age of pubescence in this respect, play activities constitute the main agency. As to this last, I am one of those who believe that the advocates of play activities, while all right in the main, fail to recognize certain factors. One of these is the fact that most of us are not products of the law of the survival of the fittest; that, in a measure, we start more or less handicapped; are able to survive through scientific interference with the law of survival and are, therefore, not in a condition to depend entirely on what might be called natural means of reaching our full development. Furthermore, though we hope some day there will be abundant opportunity for varied play activities—sufficient in quantity and variety to insure complete all-round development of the fundamental system—the fact of the matter is that at present such conditions exist only in the dreams of the idealists with here and there occasional exceptions. I have no fault to find with the ideal, but I believe in facing conditions as they are and not basing my point of view and procedure on conditions as they ought to be.

Finally, in our time and generation there is a premium on the kind of motor control which might, tentatively at least, be called "subjective," that is to say, control of the body with reference only to its own parts, and to space, without reference to achieving any result outside of the body. Such control, of course, results to a certain extent from abundant and varied activity of any kind done in a hit-or-miss way; but without limited opportunities for sufficient quantity or variety of play activities, I doubt if the average individual develops as fully in the matter of "subjective" motor control as he ought to. When placed under favorable conditions and environment—refined home life, family pride, demanding not only good taste in dress and grooming, in speech and manners, but including also graceful and dignified carriage and motor habits in general—the child gets a fair amount of this kind of training, but the great masses of our youth do not. Hence it seems to me that Physical Education ought to attempt, at least, to meet the need for this training.

The means consist of gymnastics and dancing. These are in a true sense subjective activities. They aim to give the individual "subjective" motor control to enable him to solve given motor problems with more or less conscious direction of his movements. This, I believe, accustoms him to move about with assurance and absence of what is generally understood as self-consciousness, in the same way as a person trained in the language is able to speak good English in an unconscious way. The premium on such subjective motor control should be fairly evident to any one of an unbiased mind and reasonable opportunities for observation and experience of life. It is a business asset, it is a social asset (social in the narrow sense). In these days such subjective motor control would mean a great deal in the way of military efficiency. It is the possession of that which makes the difference between a loose organization and a disciplined army. Need I say any more along this line to have you understand what I mean? As I see it, this training by means of gymnastics and dancing, making for subjective motor control, is nothing but a further education of the fundamental neuro-muscular system, an education beyond the point where such education ceases for most people, namely, the point that has been reached at the end of childhood. In the case of most people, so far from progressing any further after this point, there is apt to be retrogression. How many adults (including the guardians of the peace) can cope with the healthy, lively, squirming young imp of twelve or thirteen in the matter of "subjective" motor control? Again who has not on social occasions noticed the awkward movements and the mental state of embarrassment and self-consciousness of young men who may be wonders on the football field or even in a baseball game, or who may be skilled in the use of their hands. When not having any particular object to accomplish by their movements, they are at a loss to know what to do with their motor machinery. This is also illustrated by the well known difficulty of the callow youth who cannot think what to do with his hands—and feet; who, indeed, seems to himself to be "all hands and feet." Gymnastics and dancing of the right kind aim to train the individual to be at ease with himself in a motor way, give him a consciousness of power to be able to do what he wants with his fundamental motor machinery. In short, these agencies aim to do in a specific direction what Physical Education in general aims to do, namely, increase the individual's intelligence on the motor side, that is to say, develop his motor personality.

In your last paragraph you asked something which I interpret to mean in substance: "What bearing has training of the fundamental neuro-muscular system on the nervous health and stability of the individual?" According to Tyler, Hall, Hetherington, and others, it has tremendous significance in this respect. Indeed, Tyler goes as far as to say that without thorough-going training and development of the fundamental neuro-muscular system, nervous instability later in life is to be rather expected than otherwise. To put it differently, he says that children of high strung, rather delicate parents need this fundamental neuro-muscular training particularly, in order to keep from breaking down nervously on the least provocation. The general idea of such training is that it makes the fundamental centers robust, rugged, able to stand a great deal of rough usage, that these constitute the foundation for the superstructure of the accessory centers, that the latter will be able to stand the strain better if the fundamental centers are all that they ought to be. In treatises on the increasing number of "occupation neuroses" it is generally held that a good foundation in the way of fundamental training and development would perhaps have saved the breaking down of the accessory centers, and in the treatment of them exercises of the large muscles of the trunk, shoulder and hip region are almost considered as specific. Someone of the above named writers has expressed it something like this: "The training of the fundamental centers through large muscle activities creates a fund or reservoir of nervous energy or stability on which the individual can draw in the stress of later life." This is probably figuratively speaking. I think your own experience of marked benefit from work involving both the fundamental and accessory systems is partly the result of beneficial exercise, done under favorable mental conditions, and partly the extreme interest in the work and achievement which it represents. The mental satisfaction undoubtedly had a great deal to do with it, but the principal effect was probably one of the physiological effects of general exercise, which was purely objective, in that respect resembling play activities. In a case of that kind undoubtedly that is the best form of exercise. Indeed, aside from the period of childhood and adolescence when gymnastics ought to be used intensively, I think play activities are the proper agency both of Physical Education and of the hygienic recreation that should be the logical sequel of a rational Physical Education.

Sincerely yours,

Wm Skarstrom

THE VALUE OF FOOTBALL

Professor Raymond G. Gettell
of Amherst College

A phenomenon of frequent recurrence in widely separated times and places has been the intense general interest in games or contests manifested by those peoples who held the leading place in the civilization of their day. The Olympic games in Greece, the gladiatorial contests in Rome, and the tournaments of the Middle Ages alike were characterized by the enthusiastic zeal of those actively engaged, by the presence of crowds of frenzied spectators, and by the interest and attention centered upon them by the public at large. All these athletic carnivals were subjected to severe criticism in their age, yet they increased in popularity in spite of opposition, and declined only with the decadence of the peoples interested or with changes in culture that made them no longer possible. In the modern world, Teutonic peoples hold the reins of power, and among them great football, baseball, and cricket contests inspire widespread interest and enthusiasm. One explanation of this phenomenon, using football as an example of the modern type, is here attempted.

As might be expected, football has been subjected to unusually severe criticism. The danger to life and limb, the accompanying evils of gambling, professionalism, or unsportsmanlike methods, the enormous expenditures, the comparatively small number who actually take part in proportion to the numerous spectators, the false standards created in the minds of growing school boys, the over-emphasis on athletics in general in colleges and universities—these are some of the direct accusations that the sport has been compelled to face. In addition, the complexity of its rules, making it difficult for the ordinary

Raymond G. Gettell, "The Value of Football," *American Physical Education Review,* vol. XXII, no. 3, March 1917, pp. 139-142.

spectator to understand much of what is taking place or to appreciate the finer points of the play, together with an almost annual tinkering with these rules, keeping the game constantly in an unsettled and experimental condition, would seem sufficient to ruin any except the most firmly grounded institution.

In spite of these criticisms and these defects, however, football has become during the autumn season the preëminent sport, especially in American schools and colleges. The football "star" is a college hero; ambition to "make the team" is a chief desire in the mind of many a student, and pride over football victories is a powerful stimulant to loyal college spirit. Nor does public interest in the game show sign of decline. Each Saturday during the season, thousands assemble to witness the contests, additional thousands, even in the remotest parts of the country, crowd around bulletin boards, which give detailed descriptions of the plays or announce the scores, and still other thousands turn first to the sporting columns of the Sunday morning newspapers. A game that inspires such widespread devotion must rest upon certain vital underlying principles of human nature.

A certain amount of its popularity, especially from the spectator's standpoint, may undoubtedly be explained by that fondness for excitement and for spectacular display which, especially in America, seems a logical corollary to the intense and nervous pace of our living. But a closer analysis of the fundamental nature of the game and of the physical, mental, and moral requisites of its players, shows that it reproduces, in unusual fashion, many of the essential features in human development.

Two opposed, yet closely interrelated, factors have characterized the process of human and social evolution. These factors, which are found even in the animal world, are (1) conflict and (2) coöperation. Conflict among individuals, the primitive and brutal struggle for existence, is modified by the formation of coöperating groups, within which competition is replaced by mutual aid, the conflict continuing among these larger units. Within the group are found organization, discipline, and obedience to authority and law. Even among the groups, rules to regulate inter-group contests arise and are enforced with more or less success. This process is most marked in the evolution of the tribe and state, in the rise of government and law, and in the formation of the coöperating and competing industrial groups, which, in the modern world, ordinarily substitute the rivalry of business for the earlier and cruder combats of physical force.

Conflict and competition, then, remain, even in modern civilization, but on an increasingly mental rather than on a physical basis. Besides, the struggle is a contest between organizations, not between anarchic individuals. Within these organizations, discipline and authority are found, and altruistic coöperation largely replaces selfish competition. Moreover, the whole process, both of coöperation within the group and of contest without, takes place under an orderly *régime* of law. Football epitomizes this entire process.

The love of physical combat, of the matching of man against man to determine bodily supremacy, is a masculine trait, especially strong in primitive and vigorous peoples, and in the young men of even the highest civilizations. The natural and unrestrained play of boys usually takes some form of pretended or real bodily contest. Wrestling, racing, fighting, and most boys' games show this tendency.

The elements involved in any struggle for physical supremacy are mainly (1) strength, (2) speed, (3) skill, and (4) cunning. All of these are directly applied in football. Strength, depending upon size, weight, and muscular force, is a requisite in interfering or in blocking opponents, and in opening holes or plunging through the line. Speed of foot is needed in the quick dashes around the end or down the field under kicks, and is combined in football with the natural animal instinct to chase, to seize, and to throw. Skill is demanded in the technique of the game, the execution of the various forms of the kick or in the forward pass, the handling of the body and of the ball. Cunning is demanded in the strategy and generalship of the game, in the constant need of striking the opponent at his weakest points, of concealing the nature and purpose of the attack, in quickly diagnosing the plans of the opponent and in taking advantage of his mistakes.

This physical combat, which exists in more varied phases in football than in any other sport, creates certain virtues. Aside from the bodily development that results from exercise and training, the game develops courage, endurance, resourcefulness, and self-reliance. There are, however, accompanying evils. Individual conflict creates selfishness and lack of self-control. These must be remedied by another phase of the game.

Football is not a contest between individuals. It is a contest between groups or "teams." The union of eleven men under their "captain" typifies the characteristic human factor of organization. In no other game is the individual, as individual, of so little moment, and the unit, or team, so closely integrated. The success of almost every manœuver depends upon a detailed division of labor, a distinct part being assigned to each member within the machine; and the success of a team in competition with others depends mainly upon the perfection of its organized "teamwork." Football, then, demands coöperation, the subordination of the individual interest to the welfare of the larger unit. It reproduces on a small scale that process of organized social effort by which man first attained supremacy over the world of nature, and by which the more highly organized and more closely coöperating peoples have conquered and surpassed their less advanced rivals.

Of even more importance, both in the evolution of mankind and in the development of a football team, is the discipline resulting from the necessary obedience to authority and rules, which coöperation demands. Coöperation implies a plan whose details must be worked out under order and regulation. The organized coöperation of primitive men created the chief and the sacred customs of the tribe. In a higher social order these become government and law. So in football, emphasis is laid on discipline and obedience. Strict self-control and physical fitness are secured by a rigorous system of training. Implicit obedience to the plans and directions of coaches and captain is demanded. Each play is preceded by a "signal," which assigns to each man his part, and the whole machine is put into motion by another signal, which secures concerted action. Thus within the team everything is orderly because of obedience to authority. The worst possible offense is to disregard a signal, in other words, to follow one's own inclination at the expense of the team as a whole.

But not only within the team is law enforced. Contests between teams are carried on under an elaborate code of rules, enforced by a corps of officials who impose severe penalties in case of disregard or violation of these rules. Indeed, the parallel between football and the larger world of politics is strikingly close. Each college is a sovereign state, represented on the battle field by its organized army, or football team. This army is levied, equipped, trained, and drilled. Rules of eligibility determine its make-up. Secrecy surrounds its plans and manœuvers; and woe to the traitor or the spy through whom the enemy secures much-desired information. All the excitement of a campaign precedes the contest, and a spirit of intense patriotism, with the accompanying irrational hatred of its opponents, permeates the entire collegiate body, and finds expression in the concerted cheering contests carried on between the rival groups of spectators. Moreover, the rules under which the game is played are a sort of international law. They are created by a convention of ambassadors from certain of the sovereign commonwealths, sitting as a sort of Hague Conference. They are sanctioned by intercollegiate public opinion and enforced by neutral arbiters, selected, after the fashion of the Hague Court, by a neutral board or commission, from an eligible list of ex-players.

Accordingly, football, while retaining the virtues of physical combat, remedies its worst evils by emphasizing organization, coöperation, and obedience. These necessitate self-sacrifice, subordination, mutual aid, and fair play. They discipline the individual, teach self-control, and inculcate principles of honor and loyalty. Especially do they build up an ideal. Just as the knight strove for his fair lady, or the warrior for love of native land, so the football hero performs mighty deeds for the fair fame of his college. In an age often accused of decadent materialism, it is an indication of national health and vigor that enthusiastic youths should sacrifice ease and luxury, should give and take hard bruises, under a *régime* of discipline and law, and in an honorable spirit of gentlemanly rivalry, for the sake of a vague ideal called college spirit.

If the above analysis of the essential nature of football be accurate the explanation of its popularity is obvious. More than any other sport it retains the vital elements of physical combat and necessitates an exhibition of all its essential factors—strength, speed, skill, and cunning. In addition to this primitive lust for battle, it satisfies the higher and distinctly civilized interest in organization, coöperation, and the skilled interrelation of individual effort directed to a common purpose. It typifies the highest human achievement in its unusual emphasis on discipline and obedience, on the subordination of the individual to authority and law. Finally, in its purpose and in its spirit, it represents that highest craving of the human soul, the striving for an ideal.

A UNIVERSAL SYSTEM OF PHYSICAL EDUCATION

Conference called by U.S. Commissioner of Education

A most significant meeting was held at Atlantic City on February 28, last, when, at the call of P. P. Claxton, United States Commissioner of Education, representatives of nineteen national organizations met to consider how in view of the proven lack of physical fitness on the part of our conscripted young men an adequate, successful system of physical education may become universal. There were present at the Conference the leaders of physical education—Doctors Sargent, McKenzie, Wood, Storey, Crampton, the President of the American Physical Education Association, and representatives of the following organizations: College Directors Society, Bureau of Child Hygiene, Town and County Nursing Service, Committee of Physical Education of Secondary School Principals, Child Helping Department of the Russell Sage Foundation, Life Extension Institute, Southern Sociological Congress, Social Hygiene Society, American Posture League, War Department Training Camp Activities, American Medical Association, and the American Federation of Labor.

Commissioner of Education Claxton was authorized to appoint a committee of nine to carry out the Recommendation presented by Thomas D. Wood, M. D.

I. That a comprehensive, thoroughgoing program of health education and physical education is absolutely needed for all boys and girls of elementary and secondary school age, both rural and urban, in every state in the Union.

II. That legislation, similar in purpose and scope to the provisions and requirements in the laws recently enacted in New York State, and

"A Universal System of Physical Education," from "News Notes," *American Physical Education Review*, vol. XXIII, no. 3, March 1918, pp. 179-180.

New Jersey, is desirable in every state, to provide authorization and support for state-wide programs in the health and physical education field.

III. That the United States Bureau of Education should be empowered by law, and provided with sufficient appropriations, to exert adequate influence and supervision in relation to a nation-wide program of instruction in health and physical education.

IV. That it seems most desirable that Congress should give recognition to this vital and neglected phase of education, with a bill and appropriation similar in purpose and scope to the Smith-Hughes law; to give sanction, leadership and support to a national program of health and physical education; and to encourage, standardize and, in part, finance the practical program of constructive work that should be undertaken in every state.

V. That federal recognition, supervision and support are urgently needed, as the effective means, under the constitution, to secure that universal training of boys and girls in health and physical fitness which are equally essential to efficiency of all citizens both in peace and in war.

The members of the Association should coöperate with the secretary of the conference, Dr. W. Small of the Bureau of Education, Washington, D. C.

A CONSTRUCTIVE PROGRAM OF ATHLETICS FOR SCHOOL GIRLS
Policy, Method and Activities*

Elizabeth Burchenal, A.B.†

Assistant State Inspector, New York State Military Training Commission; Chairman Committee on Girls' Athletics of American Physical Education Association; formerly Executive Secretary, Girls' Branch Public Schools Athletic League of New York, and Editor of its official Handbook of Girls' Athletics.

It is thoroughly recognized that the problems involved in girls' athletics are quite different and more difficult than those in boys' athletics, since the athletics of boys and men have been established by them through a long history of evolution, while girls have nothing which has been evolved by them in a corresponding way, the subject for them being a comparatively new one which of necessity has been largely experimental.

If athletics are to become a successful part of the health education of girls, they must have some definite policy and purpose back of them, and definite forms of athletic activities must be established which (1) have fundamental interest and appeal for girls; (2) are desirable from the standpoint of health and recreation; (3) are practicable for the average girl from the standpoint of physical strength; and (4) are mechanically practicable in view of the build of the average girl—for as the girl matures the conformation of her body alters, and her figure becomes different from that of a boy, her weight being greater in proportion to the strength of her muscles, and distributed differently. It is this that places her at a disadvantage in certain of the boys' athletic events (such as high and broad jumping, pole vaulting, high hurdles, weight throwing, long dashes, etc.) and makes these events more or less impracticable and inconsistent for general use in competitive sports for girls.

Elizabeth Burchenal, "A Constructive Program of Athletics for School Girls: Policy, Method and Activities," *American Physical Education Review,* vol. XXIV, no. 5, May 1919, pp. 272-279.

*Prepared for the New York State Military Training Commission.

†On leave of absence doing Americanization work in "Community Service."

During the past fifteen years consistent experiments in athletics for schoolgirls have been carried on on a large scale by responsible organizations and women with training and experience in athletics who are most vitally interested in the subject, as a result of which certain general policies have crystallized and certain methods and forms of activities have been gradually established. The following suggestions are founded on some of the most extensive and successful results as yet accomplished* and represent the general trend of girls' athletics to-day:

1. *Policies.*

(a) Athletics for girls should be developed only on the bases of play, wholesome pleasure, health, and character building—"Sport for sport's sake."

(b) Athletics should be for *all* the girls (Extensive Athletics). Any form of athletics is a failure which does not include, and is not suitable for and interesting to, *at least* 80 per cent of all girls.

(c) Eliminate all the disadvantages and mistakes of boys' athletics (such as development of individual stars and "crack" teams—intensive athletics), creation of interest by large public meets with paid admission, intense excitement, applause, newspaper notoriety, individual prizes, exploitation of the few best performers and teams, professionalism, etc.

(d) Athletics carried on *within* the school (intramural, interclass athletics) and no interschool competition.

(e) Athletic events and games in which *teams* (not individual girls) compete.

(f) Athletics chosen and practiced with *regard to their suitability for girls* and not *merely in imitation of boys' athletics.*

(g) Girls' athletics directed by competent *women* instructors and leaders.

2. *Guidance.*

A Girls' Athletic League or Committee, formed in a free school district or a village or city school system, has been found very helpful in bringing about a uniform adoption of the above policies and in encouraging and guiding the development of athletics for girls in the schools.

(a) Such a committee might consist of the supervisor of physical training (preferably a woman), several representative women of the school community (approved by the superintendent) who have a special interest in girls' problems, and an equal number of women from the teaching force (who have special interest and ability in girls' athletics) appointed by the superintendent.

(b) This committee could recommend policies, methods, activities, and athletic rules for uniform use in the schools, and could encourage the development of athletics in the schools according to the above policies by—

*Girls' Branch of the P. S. A. L. of New York.

(1) Providing trophies and badges for certain events, such as interclass athletic meets, all-round athletics, interclass championship games, swimming tests, etc.
(2) Providing free instruction for grade teachers who volunteer their services after school, when the Board of Education is unable to do this.
(3) Assisting to organize Girls' Athletic Clubs.
(4) Securing enlarged facilities for girls' athletic work indoors and out, by cooperation with public departments or private individuals controlling desirable grounds, buildings, swimming pools, skating ponds, etc.
(5) Protecting girls' athletics from public exploitation.

3. *Organization.*

All the girls of the school (from third to eighth grades in elementary school, and from first to fourth year high school) who have been found by the medical inspector to be physically fit, may be organized into a "Girls' General Athletic Organization, or Athletic League," and subdivided according to class or grade, or by arbitrary division into "clubs." Each of these groups or clubs should in turn consist of two or more teams. Each club meets regularly during the school year for active practice, receives instruction in the various athletic activities suggested below, and carries on competition between teams within the club for pleasure and interest, and occasionally combines with other clubs of the school in an "athletic meet." Individual members of clubs may also work to qualify in all-round athletics. (See descriptions of Athletic Meets and All-Round Athletics given below.)

4. *Dress.*

It is vitally important to the success of girls' athletics that clothing should be worn which allows full freedom of movement and removes the handicaps ordinarily imposed on a girl by her dress. The following is suggested as desirable:

(a) Light weight one-piece knitted union suit.

(b) Stocking supporters attached to belt or yoke worn around the hips *well below* the *waist.*

(c) Dark bloomers, washable loose blouse or Norfolk worn outside, serviceable stockings. Sweater.

(d) Rubber-soled gymnasium shoes or "sneakers."

The addition of a skirt to this costume provides a universally becoming, appropriate, economical and healthful school dress for general use.

5. *Eligibility.*

The following eligibility requirements for elementary and high school girls and athletic clubs have been found satisfactory:

A. Elementary Schools.

(1) *Eligibility of Girls.*

(a) Athletic membership is open only to girls from the third to the eighth school year, inclusive.

(b) Eligibility for membership in clubs is left to the discretion of the principal with the one proviso that a physician's statement be secured in cases of doubtful physical fitness;

But

(c) Any girl to be eligible to compete in an athletic meet of the school or qualify in all-round athletics must meet all of the following requirements:

1. The girl must have been in the school at least one month.
2. She must be a member of a club that has fulfilled the requirements for amount of work done.
3. She must have taken part in active practice of at least 20 sessions of her club.
4. She must have a standing in school work of a majority of B's (or better) in Effort, Deportment, Proficiency and Posture, from the beginning of the year to the time of the contest or completion of her record.
5. Girls taking part in unsanctioned events render themselves liable to suspension.

(2) *Eligibility of Clubs.*

In order that the members may be eligible to take part in athletic meets or qualify in all-round athletics, a club must—

(a) Organize and begin practice not later than November 1.
(b) Hold at least 24 practice meetings during the school year.
(c) Keep an accurate official record of the season's practice.
(d) Practice only sanctioned events.

(Events at which admission is charged or the general public attends are not sanctioned and no girl taking part in such events will be eligible for qualification in all-round athletics or participation in athletic meets of the school.)

B. High Schools.

(1) *Eligibility of Girls.*

(a) Athletic membership is open to all high school girls.

(b) Any girl to be eligible for membership in an athletic club, or to take part in any athletic events, or to win any pins or trophies, must have a physician's certificate of physical fitness, and the personal approval of the instructor in charge.

(c) Every girl must be approved by the principal as being in good standing both in deportment and scholarship, including work in physical training.

(d) No girl who takes part in athletic competitions outside of school shall be eligible to take part in athletics of the school.

(e) No girl who has represented any outside organization or taken part in any interschool competition, shall be eligible to compete in any event until twenty school weeks have elapsed from the time of such competition.

(f) *Girls taking part in any unsanctioned events render themselves liable to suspension.*

Events at which admission is charged or the general public attends are not sanctioned, and, therefore, no girls who take part in such events will be eligible to take part in school athletics.

(2) *Eligibility of Clubs.*

Same as Eligibility of Elementary School Clubs.

6. *Athletic Activities for Girls.*

(Note.—Full descriptions of the following may be found in "Girls' Athletics," the official Handbook of the Girls' Branch of the Public Schools Athletic League of New York City. Published by American Sports Publishing Company, 45 Rose Street, New York City.)

(a) *Team Games.*

1. Indoor Baseball—Elementary and High School.
2. Basket Ball—Elementary and High School.
3. End Ball—Elementary and High School.
4. Punch Ball—Elementary and High School.
5. Captain Ball—Elementary and High School.
6. Newcomb—Elementary and High School.
7. Pin Ball—High School.
8. Volley Ball—High School.
9. Field Hockey—High School.

(b) *Track and Field Athletics.*

1. All Up Relay—Elementary School.
2. Pass Ball Relay—Elementary School.
3. Shuttle Relay—Elementary and High School.
4. Potato Relay—Elementary and High School.
5. Hurdle Relay—Elementary and High School.
6. Basket Ball Throw (for distance)—Elementary and High School.
7. Baseball Throw (for distance)—High School.
8. Simple Relay (circular track)—High School.

(c) *Miscellaneous Athletic Activities.*

1. Walking—Elementary and High School.
2. Swimming—Elementary and High School.
3. Skating: Elementary and High School.
   Ice Skating.
   Roller Skating (out of doors).
4. Bicycling—Elementary and High School.
5. Coasting—Elementary School.
6. Hand Tennis—Elementary and High School.
7. Horseback Riding—High School.
8. Rowing and Paddling—High School.
9. Golf and Lawn Tennis—High School.
10. Heavy Gymnastics—High School.
11. Folk Dancing—Elementary and High School.

(No. 11 refers only to the folk dances which have the strongest game element, are sturdy and vigorous, and develop agility, endurance, and teamwork by the group.)

7. *All-Round Athletics (Elementary and High Schools).*

(a) *Eligibility.*

To qualify in all-round athletics, a girl must be eligible (see "Eligibility of Girls" above): she must have actively participated in at least 24 athletic meetings of a club which is eligible (see "Eligibility of Clubs" above), and which has held at least one-third of its practice meetings out of doors (and more if possible); she must complete a *required record* in all-round athletics specified below, and in addition she must have passed in *at least three* of the *personal proficiency tests* listed below.

(b) *Required Record.*

It is required that a girl shall, during the school year, have devoted an *equal amount of time* to the practice of each of the three different groups of *Athletic Activities for Girls* (listed above) as indicated:

Group 1. Team Games—any or all.
Group 2. Track and Field Events—four or more.
Group 3. Miscellaneous Athletic Activities—any or all.

(c) *Personal Proficiency Tests.*

(In addition to the above record each individual girl must have qualified in at least three of the following tests.)

1. *Walking.*
   a. One 3-mile Walk, 3-A to 5-A, inclusive, Elementary School.
   b. One 5-mile Walk, 5-B to 8-B, inclusive, Elementary School.
   c. One 10-mile Walk, High School.

2. *Throwing for Distance.*
   a. 30-ft. Basket Ball Throw, 3-A to 5-A, Elementary School.
   b. 40-ft. Basket Ball Throw, 5-B to 8-B, Elementary School.
   c. 50-ft. Basket Ball Throw, High School.
   d. 60-ft. Baseball Throw, High School.

3. *Swimming.*
   (In water shallow enough to stand in.)
   a. Push off and float face down in water
      and
      Push off and swim at least 5 good strokes, 3-A to 8-E, Elementary School, and High School.

4. *Bicycling.*
   a. One 3-mile Ride, 3-A to 5-A, Elementary School.
   b. One 5-mile ride, 5-B to 8-B, Elementary School.
   c. One 10-mile Ride, High School.

5. *Throwing Ball in Basket.*
   a. Two out of five 8-ft. distance from goal, 3-A to 5-A, Elementary School.
   b. Three out of five 10-ft. distance from goal, 5-B to 8-B, Elementary School.
   c. Four out of five 15-ft. distance from goal, High School.

6. *Skating—Ice.*
   a. Forward 20 strokes and quick stop, 3-A to 5-A, Elementary School.
   b. Outer edge forward 6 strokes, Inner edge forward 6 strokes, } 5-B to 8-B, Elementary School.
   c. Outer edge forward 20 strokes, Inner edge forward 20 strokes, } High School.

7. *Rope Skipping.*
   a. Single Rope—Enter front, skip, and leave by rear of rope, Enter rear, skip 10, leave by front. } 3-A to 5-A, Elementary School.
   b. Double Rope—Enter front, skip 10, and leave by rear, Enter rear, skip 10, leave by front, Twenty skips forward, turn about and return without stopping. } 5-B to 8-B, Elementary School.

8. *Batting Ball (as in Baseball).*
   a. Three hits out of five, 3-A to 5-A, Elementary School.
   b. Placing ball right field, center field, left field, (3 trials for each field), } 5-B to 8-B, Elementary School.

Sample of Club All-Round Athletic Record.

Meet-ings	Date	Time Devoted	Indoors or Outdoors	Team Games	Track and Field	Miscellaneous
1	Nov. 1	1½ Hrs.	Outdoors	Baseball		
2	Nov. 8	2 Hrs.	Outdoors		All Up Relay Shuttle Relay Potato Relay Ball Throwing	
3	Nov. 15	1 Hr.	Indoors			Walking to Pool and Swimming
4	Nov. 22	1½ Hrs.	Indoors	End Ball Punch Ball		
5	Dec. 5	2 Hrs.	Outdoors			Skating

(And so on for at least twenty-four meetings.)

Sample of
Certified List of Successful All-Round Athletic Candidates.

I hereby certify that the following girls have met all the eligibility requirements both for girls and clubs, have fulfilled the *required record* for all-round athletics, and have passed the necessary *proficiency tests* as indicated.

Signed ...., Principal.

Name	*Personal Proficiency Test Passed*
1. Mary Hutton	Swimming, skating and throwing.
2. Katherine Jones	Walking, swimming and bicycling.
3. Mary Brown	Throwing, swimming and bathing.

(And so on.)

8. *Athletic Meet.*

(a) To take part in an athletic meet, both the clubs and their individual members must be eligible. (See "Eligibility" above.)

(b) Meets should be held on the school premises wherever possible.

(c) The meets should be between clubs or classes of one school. No interschool competition should be allowed.

(d) Competitive events should be *between groups,* and there should be no competition *between individuals.*

(e) *Preliminary Contests.* When these are held during the year their total scores may be added and the club with the highest total may receive 5 points (on the score of the final contest) for first place for the year's games; the club with second highest score, 3 points; and third highest, 1 point. In this way the year's practice may be taken account of on the score of the final contest as if this were another event on the program. At least three preliminary contests are desirable.

(f) *Selection of Events.* Should be selected from the track and field athletics listed under paragraph 6. There should be at least five competitive events, and *every club* competing in the meet should take part in *each of these events.* One of these five events may be folk dancing, in which case each group's dancing is judged on the basis of memory (possible 10 points) and game spirit (possible 10 points), and as in the case of all the other events, 5, 3, and 1 points are awarded for 1st, 2d, and 3d places respectively. (See Sample Score Card, p. 350.)

(g) The success of the meet depends upon the interest and enthusiasm of the girls themselves. It should be managed without any atmosphere of regular school discipline. The girls should be where they can observe each event from start to finish, see what fouls are made, etc. They should be allowed freedom to talk, comment on the events, cheer, sing, etc.

(h) The floor, or grounds, should be plainly marked for all the events before the meet, start and finish lines for the relay races, distance lines and throwing circles for ball throwing, etc.

(i) *Good Sportsmanship:* All games should be conducted strictly in accordance with the rules agreed upon. Players should be instructed prior to a meet on the points of good sportsmanship, which should include especially how to lose with good spirit; never to question the decision of an

Sample Score Card

Girls' Athletic Meet. Elementary School .... Date ....

Events	Points Scored Class	Class	Class	Class	
Hurdle Relay					Points are scored in all *events* as follows: 1st Place–5 Points 2d Place–3 Points 3d Place–1 Point To decide 1st, 2d and 3d places in folk dancing, judge each dance on the following basis: Memory–possible 10 Points Game Spirit–possible 10 Points
Ball Throw					
Shuttle Relay					
Potato Relay					
Folk Dancing					
Preliminary Contests					
Total Score					

Name of Winning Class ....

Signed ...., Chief Judge.

The clubs and individual girls taking part in this meet have met all the eligibility requirements.

Signed ...., Principal.

---

official; to cheer for a defeated opponent; and to play a game for the game's sake rather than to win at all costs.

High School Interclass (or Interclub) Championship Games:

(a) *Competing Teams:* High School Championships shall be decided within the school by a series of games whereby each team of the school shall play each of the other teams entered in the school championships. The team winning the greatest number of games is the winner of the school championship.

(b) *Sanctioned Games:* Only team games sanctioned for High Schools shall be used for Championship Series.

(c) *Supervision:* All games shall be under the direction of an instructor (preferably physical training instructor) appointed by the Principal.

(d) *Schedule:* The instructor in charge of the games shall arrange the schedule.

(e) *Preliminary Tournament:* If more than four teams are entered, preliminary games should be played to pick the four strongest teams to play the final Championship Series of six games.

(f) *Place:* The games shall be played in the school building or grounds except in case there be no suitable space. In this case another space may be secured, only on the consent and approval of the Principal.

(g) *Eligibility:* All girls taking part must be eligible. (See "Eligibility" above.)

(h) *Officials:* The six final games in a championship series must be under the direction of a Chief Official. It is the duty of the Chief Official to decide all questions relating to the actual conduct of the game whose final settlement is not otherwise covered in the rules. The decision of this official shall be final and without appeal.

(i) *Marking Grounds:* The floor or ground should be plainly and accurately marked before the hour of the game.

(j) *Good Sportsmanship:* Players should be familiar with the rules of good sportsmanship and athletic courtesy, which include how to lose with good grace; never to question the decision of an official; to applaud a defeated opponent; and to play the game for sport's sake rather than to win at all costs.

(k) *Score:* The official score of the series shall be kept by the Chief Official.

9. *Trophies and Badges.*

An added interest and pleasant incentive are often created by the presentation to a school of a perpetual trophy for girls' athletics, to be awarded each year to the class or club of the school winning the final meet, or having the greatest number of girls qualifying in all-round athletics. The name of the winning club is inscribed each year on the trophy as a permanent record.

In many cases it has been found successful to award small, inexpensive individual badges, or other insignia, to each member of the winning club in a meet, or each individual qualifying in all-round athletics.

The awarding of such trophies or badges to the winning club is done at the close of the meet, when the victorious club is announced.

Tests of Success

1. Are your girls' athletics carried on solely on the basis of healthful play and recreation?

2. Are at least 80 per cent of all the girls interested and taking regular active part in athletic practice?

3. Do they enjoy athletics for their own sake? Do they practice when no instructor is present, and do the older, more adept girls act as leaders for the younger beginners?

4. Have all adopted suitable dress for athletics?

5. Are their athletics providing them with an opportunity to develop into happy, wholesome, active young *human beings* and allowing them to forget, for the time being, that they are girls?

"A girl should be a tomboy during the tomboy age, and the more of a tomboy she is, the better. If a girl does not become a good sport before she is fourteen she never will, but will be condemned to premature young ladyhood. She ought, indeed, to be caught somewhere about the age of eight, or ten at the latest. Of course, we must beware of adhesions to a passing phase. It is not a permanent tomboy we are trying to produce, but the *enduring values* that are to be acquired during that period. . . . To learn during these precious years to be a good team mate and a good comrade is for any girl an education experience that will bear fruit through her whole life, and in more than one relation." (From Lee in "Play in Education.")

THE PHYSICAL TEST OF A MAN

One of the strongest of the natural forces with which man is constantly contending is gravity, or the tendency of his body to be attracted and held to the surface of the earth. The infant first crawls, then creeps on its hands and knees, and finally by the aid of crib or chair or mother's assistance, gets onto his feet. The raising of the head, the straightening of the spine, grasping with the hands and feet, and striking out and kicking with the arms and legs are only preliminary movements necessary to prepare for the standing position. All the twisting, rolling, wriggling, squirming, crawling, creeping, and occasional stiffening and straightening of the trunk and limbs an infant can be induced to do, the better it will be for his future development.

A child must first get a footing in the world and be able to move in the erect position before the adult may properly function as a human being. In other words, the child must pass in a few months from the animal stage of its existence where all its organic inheritances for thousands of years had fitted its body to resist the force of gravity in a horizontal plane, to a vertical position where gravity acts in a perpendicular plane. Is it any wonder that over 75 per cent. of our youth of both sexes have a bad posture, and that so few ever attain the ability to meet this comparatively new strain—the ability to sit and stand erect?

If there is any doubt as to the seriousness of failing to measure up to this test of young manhood, ask your physician as to the fundamental causes of the following list of physical imperfections: spinal curvature, knock knees, bow legs, flat feet, drooping head, round shoulders, weak backs, varicose veins, hernia, sagging of the abdominal

D. A. Sargent, "The Physical Test of a Man," *School and Society,* vol. XIII, no. 318, January 29, 1921, pp. 128-135.

organs, misplacement of the pelvic organs, and many other physical weaknesses and defects which afflict mankind.

These prevailing weaknesses are mainly due to the failure of the body to make provision to resist this constant force of gravity to pull us down from our top-lofty, vertical position to a horizontal plane. We pay our respect to this natural force by availing ourselves of every opportunity to lean, sit and recline at our work throughout the day, and we finally yield to it completely by assuming a horizontal position for sleep at night.

Many of these bodily weaknesses and imperfections to which I have referred have arisen largely from civilized man's neglect to care for the form and strength of his bodily mechanism as an African Zulu or Sandwich Islander would do. Instead of priding himself upon his ability to sit straight without support for his spine and legs, as shown by many of the savage tribesmen, civilized man luxuriates in upholstered chairs and lounges moulded to his physical defects,—and then wonders why he has a weak back and can not stand in a vertical position.

Yet the ability to stand erect, thereby relieving the arms and hands from supporting the body, and conserving their strength to be directed into self-chosen activities constitutes man's supreme inheritance.

How is this ability attained? By gradually strengthening and developing the muscles all up and down the front and back of the trunk and legs. These muscles hold the body balanced in perfect equilibrium over the two feet, which, in length and breadth taken together, average about one sixth the perpendicular height. When the body is thus accurately balanced on the bones of the legs and spine, gravity is acting parallel with these bones, and consequently the strain is taken largely from the muscles and thrown onto the bones and ligaments.

If one relaxes from this vertical position, and stands with the body flexed or bent forward at the knees, back and neck, the strain is then brought upon the muscles and after a little while the effort of standing becomes intolerable. But strain or pain means loss of power and energy. This is the reason why a perfect poise in standing or sitting is the most economical position that can be maintained.

Although the ability of a man to stand on his feet and maintain perfect poise is of vital importance, it is not the only requisite. He has other things to do. During the growing period of youth, while one is acquiring his stature, gravity should be used so as to stimulate the growth force, not to retard it, as is often done by keeping children too long on their feet either in working or playing. It is better to continually fall and try to rise again than to remain standing too long.

A young man having acquired full stature, and learned to stand and sit correctly in defiance of the laws of gravity, must generate still more force and let gravity act in harmony with his physiological necessities and his mental and physical desires. In other words, he must add to his weight as well as his height before he can cut any figure in the world, bear his own burdens, fight his own battles and render service to others. This means that he must extend his growth force and developmental energies into body breadths, depths and thicknesses as determined by given measurements, as well as into lengths or vertical directions. The only way of adding effective weight is through the development of the muscles which constitute nearly 50 per cent. of all the tissues of the normal man, and determine to a large extent the size and function of the other organs. By this use of the term muscle, I do not refer to the large superficial voluntary muscles only, but to the muscles of digestion, circulation, respiration, glandular organs, special senses, etc. The only way that any muscle tissue may be developed is through the activities; and our responsibility for the proper training, nutrition, and consequent development of this part of our anatomy is great indeed.

The primary object of all the efforts of physical education through athletic games, sports, plays, and general gymnastics, is to add to the power and efficiency of mind and body through the agency of the muscular system. This efficiency is determined largely, I shall hope to show, through the intimate relation of body height and weight. These two factors are always taken into consideration in publishing the names of players on the great football teams, boat crews, and in other athletic organizations. Why? Simply because in a vague way, there is thought to be a correlation between the height and weight and a man's physical efficiency. Up to the normal limit, a man's strength is supposed to increase with his height and weight. Men are matched in boxing, wrestling, and tug-of-war contests according to their weights, such as light weights, 135 lbs.; middle weights, 160 lbs.; heavy weights, 175 lbs.; etc. In boxing and wrestling, at least, this weight classification is further refined by having a bantam-weight class of 115, a feather-weight class of 125 and a heavy-weight class for all men over 175 lbs.

No team, crew or individual contestants would be considered well-matched if they had to give or accept much difference in weight from their opponents. So we find in studying the characteristics of different types of athletes and gymnasts that variations in stature or total height, sitting height, height of knee, and relative length of trunk and limbs, tend to favor different classes of athletic performers. As a rule, the oarsman is favored by having a long body, and relatively short legs, the middle distance runner, jumper, and hurdler by having long legs and a relatively short body; the gymnasts by having short arms; and the heavy lifter by having short thighs. And so through the whole range of athletic specialists, each gains some mechanical advantage from the development that is peculiar to him.

Woman's incapacity for certain kinds of physical activities as compared with man's, arises largely from the fact that she is on the average 25 lbs. lighter and five inches shorter than he is. The whole Japanese race averages only 5 ft. 4 in. in stature, due largely to their relatively short legs, that have undoubtedly been made so by their long-continued racial habit of sitting on their heels with their legs sharply bent under them. These facts and many more have come to us through our studies in anthropometry and the classification of physical measurements.

Age, sex, and race are rightly considered the dominant factors in evaluating any body measurements, and the height, weight and chest girth are admittedly the most important of these measurements. Moreover, there is a probable standard of height, weight, and chest girth for every age, each sex and all the different races. These facts are known in a general way by those whose business it is to make physical examinations, such as surgeons in the army and navy, life insurance examiners, and physicians who examine school and college students, candidates for civil service, and employees in all the different trades and industries where physical conditions are now being taken into consideration.

So, in theory at least, it may be well said in support of the relationship of bodily measurements and vital functions "that the greater advance we may make in inquiries of this nature, the more perfectly is the law of proportion that governs the typical man demonstrated; rendering it equally apparent how undue or imperfect development of any one organ or function throws the remaining organisms out of gear, and constitutes a greater or less tendency to disease."

In popular estimation it takes so many inches and so many pounds and a certain size chest girth to make a man, and this estimation is borne out largely by experience. Hence, the universal interest in the physical measurements of the human body. However, those of us who are engaged in making physical measurements of men by the thousand soon learn the limitations of the information which comes to us from this source alone. While it is true that the strength and functional capacity of a part generally increases with the size of that part, other things being equal, the number of cases where other things are not equal is so numerous that the generalization should be greatly modified.

The measurements alone do not tell us anything of the texture and quality of the parts covered, *i.e.*, how much is fat or bone, and how much muscle, nor do the measurements alone give us any information of the innervation of the parts upon which power and efficiency so frequently depend. Even if we accept the physical measurements of a man as an indication of his potential power, as so many of us almost intuitively do, we are soon taught by experience that there is in many men an unknown equation which makes for power and efficiency which has never been determined and which can only be measured by an actual test.

The important question is, what is this unknown equation and how can it be simply and practically tested and numerically expressed? With a good many others, I have been wrestling with this problem for years by the way of strength tests, endurance tests, speed tests, etc., but have never come across any one that satisfied me or quite met the demands of the situation. It is said that every pioneer or inventor or discoverer, if he lives long enough, goes through three stages in his career. The first one is where his propositions are unfounded and absurd; the second stage is where if proven true, they are not original; and the third stage is where they are so self-evident that any fool ought to have thought of them. I have now arrived at the third stage in my career, and want to share what seems to me the simplest and most effective of all tests of physical ability with the other fools who have been looking for one. I have dwelt at some length upon gravity as a constant force to be overcome and its relation to the height and weight and other measurements of the body. The new test that I offer consists of using the constant factors of height and weight which one always has with him, in a little different way than is commonly thought of. It is so simple and yet so effective for testing the strongest man or weakest woman or child that one feels almost like apologizing to the general public for mentioning it.

The New Test

The individual to be tested stands under a cardboard disk, or paper box cover, heavy and stiff enough to hold its form, about twelve inches in diameter, held or suspended from ten to twenty or more inches above his head. He is then requested to bend forward, flexing the trunk, knees and ankles, and then by a powerful jump upward, straightening the legs and spine, to try to touch the cardboard disk with the top of the head. Swinging the bent arms forward and upward at the time the legs, back and neck are extended, will be found to add to the height of the jump. When the disk has been placed at the highest point above the head that can be just touched in jumping, this height is measured. The difference between this height and that of the total stature is of course the height actually jumped.

Now, if this height is multiplied into the total weight of the body at the time of making the jump, it will give one some idea of the amount of work done in foot pounds as usually calculated. But it will be observed, no credit is given for lifting the full weight of the body from the deep knee or squatting position to the perpendicular standing position, which difference represents about half the height. The total work depends upon how heavy and how tall the individual is. Thus, if a man weighs 150 lbs. and is 70 in. tall, one half of that height would be 35 in., which, multiplied into the full weight and divided by 12 (to reduce inches to feet) would equal 437 foot pounds, thus:

$$\text{Formula } A = \frac{\text{Weight} \times \text{Half the Height}}{12} = 437 \text{ F. P.}$$

In estimating work done outside of the body, this amount of energy expended is not always taken into consideration as power expended. In the new test, however, an individual must not only do a certain amount of work in physical effort in rising from the crouching attitude to the perpendicular postion, but he must generate force enough to project his body 10, 20, or 30 inches into the air, above the height attained in the standing position. If this person weighing 150 lbs. should jump 20 in. above his height, this weight multiplied by 20 and divided by 12 would equal 250 F. P. thus:

$$\text{Formula } B = \frac{\text{Weight} \times \text{Height jumped}}{12} = 250 \text{ F. P.}$$

This amount of work done would be acceptable according to the usual methods of estimating man power. Both the *A* and *B* formulæ are frequently used for tests of the physical basis of efficiency. The height jumped will depend a good deal upon the length of the legs and trunk that make up the total stature, the tall man being favored—therefore an exact ratio of the height jumped to the stature would seem to make the test more equitable. Thus, if the man weighing 150 lbs. was 70 in. tall and jumped 20 in. above his head, the ratio of 20 to 70 would account for this advantage in height. This ratio may be obtained by the following formula:

$$\text{Formula } C = \frac{\text{Height jumped} \times 100}{\text{Total height}} = .285$$

Although the formulæ *A*, *B*, and *C* are interesting in enabling one to account for his efficiency or deficiency in the test, these formulæ may be dispensed with in favor of one including the three important factors which we are considering. If then in the new test we multiply the total weight by the height jumped and divide this product by the total height of the person in inches the result will give a fair index of the effort made in the smallest number of figures. This is always an advantage in making a test and handling the data for statistical purposes.

Thus if the individual tested weighed 150 lbs. and jumped 20 in. above his head and was 70 in. tall, the formula for his efficiency index would be as follows:

$$\text{Index} = \frac{\text{Weight} \times \text{Jump}}{\text{Height or stature}} = \frac{150 \times 20}{70} = 42.8$$

As an example of the way this formula works out in the practise, I have selected the first ten pupils graded according to this test from the Sargent School of some four hundred pupils. It must be borne in mind that none of the girls had any preliminary practise for this particular test, other than that which comes to them in their regular school work. With the freshmen at least it was largely a question of natural ability. (See Table I.)

TABLE I

First Ten out of Four Hundred Tested at the Sargent School of Physical Education, Cambridge, Mass.

	Class	Age	Jump, Inches	Height, Inches	Ratio Jump to Height	Weight, Lbs.	F. P. of Work	Index
1. L. V. M.	Jun.	20	20.0	67.5	.300	152	253	45.0
2. M. N. G.	Sen.	20	20.0	61	.328	132	220	43.2
3. M. E. W.	Sen.	20	20.5	65.5	.312	132	226	41.3
4. M. J. O.	Jun.	20	18.8	60.2	.312	132	217	41.0
5. H. W.	Sen.	22	15.3	64.2	.238	176	224	40.5
6. M. E. F.	Fresh.	19	16.9	60.6	.260	145	204	40.5
7. J. I. J.	Fresh.	23	14.0	68	.206	196	240	40.3
8. E. M. B.	Sen.	23	20.5	61.5	.333	117.5	200	39.1
9. H. A. B.	Fresh.	23	16.0	68	.236	163	217	38.2
10. B. S.	Fresh.	18	17.5	64.5	.271	146	213	38.0
Average		20.5	17.9	64	.279	148	221	40.95

No. 1 is a vigorous athletic girl, being 67.5 inches in height and 152 lbs. in weight. She jumps 20 inches above her head which is .300 of her height, does 253 foot pounds of work (as shown by multiplying her weight by her height jumped and dividing that product by 12) and has an energy index of 45.0.

No. 2 has an energy index of 43.2. Although she is shorter and lighter than some of her mates and does less foot pounds of work than four others in the group, she lifts her weight higher in proportion to her height, and therefore gets a high score. She is an earnest student and a good all-round athlete, but not a star.

No. 3 is the star athlete of her class, excelling especially in running and jumping. In this test she jumps 20.5 in. above her height, but she is 4.5 in. taller than No. 2 and does not lift her weight as high in proportion to her height.

No. 4 although of the same weight as Nos. 2 and 3, and jumping the same proportion of her height as the girl above her, does not jump as high and therefore gets a little lower index.

No. 5 jumps nearly five inches less than those who have preceded her, but she is a strong husky girl weighing 176 lbs. and to raise this weight a less height requires a high index.

No. 6 has the same index as No. 5, although she is 3.6 in. shorter and weighs 31 lbs. less. She makes up for this difference in weight and height by jumping an inch and a half higher, and jumping a greater per cent. of her height.

No. 7 is the heaviest girl in the school, weighing 196 lbs., and is 68 in. in height. As might be expected she jumps the least of any in the group, and the least percentage of her own height. But she projects 196 lbs. fourteen inches above her head and thereby does 240 F. P. of work—which makes her the second strongest one on the list.

No. 8, although she lacks the mechanical advantage in height that a girl of 67 in. or 68 inches would possess, and has the least advantage in weight of any in the group, still manages to project her 117.5 lbs. 20.5 in. above her head, which is the highest ratio of her own height of any in the group (.333). This girl is quite strong for her height and weight and very energetic—she also has the distinction of being the highest ranking scholar in her class.

The records of Nos. 9 and 10 are self-explanatory. They are girls of fine natural physiques, good athletes, superior to the average in height and weight, and will show a much higher index after a little more training.

I have commented upon the variations in physique as shown by the height and weight in these seven individuals, because these variations illustrate the compensating nature of the test. With a variation of 7.4 in. in height and 78.5 lbs. in weight, there is little difference in their physical ability as shown by the test, as all were able to make the first ten in the school. What one lacks in height and length of limb, she makes up in strength, speed and energy; what another lacks in weight she makes up in height and energy; what still another one lacks in energy and speed she makes up in superior height, strength and weight; while still another who lacks both in height and weight has to make up for this deficiency by greater determination, will power, nerve force, or some other unknown quality, that makes for physical efficiency. If any one of the factors chosen for the formula had been adopted as a standard, it would have brought a little different type of girl to the front. This is shown by the following table:

TABLE II

Relative Standing of First Ten According to Other Factors as, Jump, Height, Weight, etc.

Index	Jump	Height	Ratio of Jump to Height	Weight	Foot Pounds
1. L. V. M.	1. M. E. W.	1. J. I. J.	1. E. M. B.	1. J. I. J.	1. L. V. M.
2. M. M. G.	2. E. M. B.	2. H. A. B.	2. M. M. G.	2. H. W.	2. J. I. J.
3. M. E. W.	3. L. V. M.	3. L. V. M.	3. M. E. W.	3. H. A. B.	3. M. E. W.
4. M. J. O.	4. M. M. G.	4. M. E. W.	4. M. J. O.	4. L. V. M.	4. H. W.
5. H. W.	5. M. J. O.	5. B. S.	5. L. V. M.	5. B. S.	5. M. M. G.
6. M. E. F.	6. B. S.	6. H. W.	6. B. S.	6. M. E. F.	6. M. J. O.
7. J. I. J.	7. M. E. F.	7. E. M. B.	7. M. E. F.	7. M. M. G.	7. H. A. B.
8. E. M. B.	8. H. A. B.	8. M. M. G.	8. H. W.	8. M. E. W.	8. B. S.
9. H. A. B.	9. H. W.	9. M. E. F.	9. H. A. B.	9. M. J. O.	9. M. E. F.
10. B. S.	10. J. I. J.	10. M. J. O.	10. J. I. J.	10. E. M. B.	10. E. M. B.

It will be observed by referring to Table II. that, if the height of the jump had been the only factor considered M. E. W. and E. M. B. would have come to the front as 1 and 2; or if height and weight had been the prime factors, J. I. J., who was 10 in the jump, would have been put in the first place. If the height jumped in proportion to her own height had been accepted as the final test, E. M. B. would have reached first place, though she ranked 10 in weight and strength. Then again, if foot pounds of work done as usually calculated, had been adopted as the standard, J. I. J. would have come up from 10th place in height really jumped and ratio of height jumped to second place. The foot-pound formula is perhaps the best test for real strength and gives the taller and heavier girls a decided advantage.

It must be admitted, however, that the three girls who come the nearest to the front in all the factors that make up the test are those that stand 1, 2, and 3, according to the index adopted. What this index as thus obtained really indicates is a question that may well engage our attention.

First, no one would deny that the ability to project one's weight 20 or 30 inches into the air, against the force of gravity requires *strength* on the part of the muscles engaged in the effort. No one would deny that the effort would have to be made with a certain degree of velocity or *speed* in order to create impetus enough to carry the body twenty inches above its own level in the standing position. Further no one would deny that back of the requisite strength of muscle fibers and rapidity with which they are made to contract there must be *energy,* "pep," "vim," vitality, or whatever it may be termed which drives our internal machinery. Overlapping all of course is the skill or dexterity with which the jump is executed.

I think, therefore, that the test as a whole may be considered as a momentary try-out of one's strength, speed, energy and dexterity combined, which, in my opinion, furnishes a fair physical test of a man, and solves in a simple way his unknown equation as determined potentially by his height and weight. It will be observed that the parts tested, namely, the muscles of the feet, calves, thighs, buttocks, back, neck, anterior deltoid, chest and biceps, are the muscles most used in all forms of athletics, sports, track and field games, setting up exercises, posture drills, etc., and are of fundamental importance in all the active industries. For this reason, I think it should precede any other all-round physical test in basic value.

In presenting this paper for discussion, I have intentionally narrowed myself down to a consideration of the factors involved in making the test, omitting the experience that has led up to it, and the application that may be made of it, and the method of conducting it.

To those who wish to try the experiment, I would suggest that the jump be made in gymnasium slippers or at least in shoes with low heels, and as the factors, weight, height and height jumped are to be multiplied and divided in the calculation, that all the measurements be made with the greatest accuracy.

If the test is of any value, then the standardization of it, and the collection of different data concerning it will of course be of the greatest importance, and follow naturally for the benefit of those who want to make use of it.

D. A. SARGENT.

Cambridge, Mass.

PRESENT DAY PROBLEMS IN PHYSICAL EDUCATION*

C. L. Lowman, M.D.
Los Angeles, Cal.

As an interested observer and one closely associated with physical educational activities for seventeen years, I wish to call the attention of educators to some of the needs not filled by the present methods of teaching physical training. As an orthopaedic surgeon, I have had occasion during the past thirteen years to become intimately acquainted and associated with many physical directors from many schools, and consequently feel justified in commenting on their activities with the hope that these observations may lead to some constructive changes in university methods in this department.

The possibilities for physical directors were never brighter than they are today. There never have been so many avenues of activity opening up for them. This, however, is a day of specializing, and in order to specialize in any one of a dozen branches in physical education it is perfectly obvious that preliminary education looking forward to these special branches must be given. At present there is not sufficient continuity of activity between the school life and the future position, except in the limited fields of recreational games and athletics, floor gymnastics, folk dancing and play ground work. There is, however, a gap between the school course and all specialized lines which are now open, and others which of necessity must open in the future to the student of physical training.

C. L. Lowman, "Present Day Problems in Physical Education, *Mind and Body,* vol. 28, no. 301, September-October 1921, pp. 705-712.

*While we agree heartily with the author so far as the trend of his article is concerned we must say that the better normal schools and colleges of physical education are doing much more along the lines indicated than Dr. Lowman gives them credit for. With our schools, as with others, it is all a matter of the amount of time at the disposal of the school. Good beginnings have been made. Based upon these it will easily be possible, if one or two additional years are added, to train the specialists spoken of.—*Editor.*

Chief among these specialized lines are the various branches using physiotherapeutic procedures.

(1) Orthopaedic corrective work, both as an assistant to orthopaedic surgeons and in physiotherapy departments of orthopaedic institutions.

(2) Speech disorder correction is a special field only just opening which furnishes another new and promising opportunity for the student who has had proper preliminary training which should include applied psychology, dramatic art, with special emphasis on the study of psychomotor activities. This work is so closely allied to special training of the motor apparatus that the properly qualified student of physical training is the logical one to develop it, although he must know and emphasize the psychological aspects as much or more than the physical phases of the work.

(3) Reconstruction and rehabilitation of the human wreckage from industrial accidents and such injuries as are left from the carnage of the great war, also offer a new channel of activity for especially prepared students.

(4) Physical welfare departments in connection with large industrial plants is another field which is still untilled. Social welfare is becoming an established part of such organizations, and certainly the establishment of physical training departments should not be far behind. Play grounds, recreation parks, and gymnasia are already in operation on some plan, but no special effort that I know of is being made in schools of physical education to give directors the special work which should underlie this type of activity. Workmen and women who have some natural and beneficial outlet and relaxation from mental and physical tensions will certainly be less prone to seek unnatural and detrimental forms of relief.

(5) Young Men's Christian Associations, Young Women's Christian Associations, Chautauquas, many religious bodies, Knights of Columbus, Jewish Welfare Departments, Red Cross, Boy Scouts, Camp Fire Girls, and many other phases of physical welfare work are needing workers whose training should make them of special value to these bodies. The value of pageantry with its various elements of dramatic and terpsichorean arts is being more and more seen and appreciated, both for its educational value in schools and for its usefulness in stimulating and welding community interests. The dramatization of the nation's life and history, and the portrayal of primitive life and activities serve a valuable purpose in keeping alive the impulses and instincts leading to motor expressions; these need to be preserved as much as the historical facts.

(6) Specialized physical training in institutions of the mentally handicapped and defective, opens up another avenue of action in the field of psychiatry and neurology, interest in which is slowly awakening. The remarkable results obtained by the orthopaedic surgeon in correction and re-education has shown what can be done, and the cooperation developing with the neurologists is most encouraging. The next few years will see positions opening for specially trained physical directors in public and private institutions and sanitaria, and the outlook for both men and women along many lines was never brighter.

(7) The position of physical director and advisor in grade schools is another post, and to my way of thinking by all odds the most important. Every grammar school should have its gymnasium and director, but more particularly the latter, who should have specialized training for this position, and aside from the training she should possess a definite aptitude and fitness for this work. In addition to the regular physical educational subjects she should have paid especial attention to the problems of school and physical hygiene, growth, nutrition and child psychology—especially in relating the motor activities to sensory development. She must understand the sequence of development biologically, both mental and physical. In the school she should be the representative of school physicians and school health service. She should be the school detective whose duty it is to spot out and watch for the earliest signs of potential postural, motor and nervous faults. She should be able to size up a child as to type, attitudes, gait, appearance, and other physical changes, and know something of what these facts indicate. Her most valuable function would be to act as advisor on health and development to both parents and teachers. She could visit a child's home and find out about the environment there. Certainly a small amount of physical training in school is not going to accomplish much in correcting a child's bad posture if at home he sleeps on a faulty bed, sits in bad chairs, wears faulty clothing, or has improper food.

It has been my experience, that the average mother is anxious to cooperate in every way, to do anything in reason which would improve the health and future growth of her children. While the grade teachers have had some training in observing many of these factors of child hygiene, it should be realized that the plastic, grammar school period is the most important time, physically in the child's life. Certainly, this period is vital enough to need a special director or supervisor of health constantly "on the job" to carry out and elaborate the excellent work of school physicians and nurses who cannot, in the nature of things, do more than advise, and who are not trained along physical educational lines. The field for especially trained assistants to the orthopaedic surgeons is growing larger every year and the younger men in this branch will soon be needing assistants, so that the demand on orthopaedic training centers is almost constant.

(8) Hospital gymnasia. I am also going to prophesy that at no distant date, medical men and hospital directors will come to realize that every hospital should have its gymnasium and when possible its recreational field, for these two reasons: (a) Nurses: To keep the working personnel up to its proper efficiency. Nurses in training should be required to take thirty minutes a day of active gymnasium work similar to the "setting up" exercises in the army. They should all have physical examinations in which as much or more attention should be paid to their actual physical motor fitness as to other more general factors of vital capacity. More nurses are incapacitated from flat feet, bad backs, and other static faults than from bad lungs or leaky hearts. (b) Patients: Surgeons and physicians will come to recognize that their patients are not well when their incisions are healed, and they have recovered enough to leave the hospital. If the hospital had a physiotherapy department the physician could prescribe bed gymnastics, massage, and other corrective procedures which could be carried out by the director or assistant in the hospital physical department. Consequently, his patients could be sent out earlier and noticeably better, with more strength and a closer approach to normal health.

In the Orthopaedic Hospital-School gymnasium, we have found that the younger graduates in physical education coming to us, have very little conception of what is required of a technical assistant in orthopaedic surgery. It takes at least a year to add sufficient training to make even a good beginning in the development of these technicians. As the problems of crippled children have only begun to be appreciated thruout the country, and new institutions are arising to solve this problem, it can be readily seen that more and more men and women trained in orthopaedic technic will be needed. The big problem then, as I see it, is the modification of teaching methods to allow students to specialize more carefully and thus be fitted to step out of the university into a special branch, in which they will be as well equipped as they are now for taking up at once the usual lines of school athletics and gymnasium work. The refinement in technical detail, the enlargement of scope and importance of the larger field of activity is not at present presented by the medical departments, or by any other department of education. It is essential that this department be raised to the dignity of a school of physical education in the same sense that the medical, dental, or law departments are schools.

Plans should be made looking to the grouping of subjects basic to work in this more technical physical educational course, and credits given which would make possible the attainment of a degree. This diploma would consequently mean very much more than it does at present. This department should rank as high as any other educational branch, for the health and development of our children both physically and mentally is as much in the hands of the physical directors as in those of any other instructors.

It seems feasible to presume that a course similar to the premedical course could be arranged in which very nearly the same subject matter as that already covered in other departments could be brought together in such a way that regular requirements could be satisfied, while at the same time the basis for the advanced work is laid. For instance, certain elements in dramatic art are important for a student in physical education because expression in all forms, speech, gesture, or look, are all psycho-motor activities and correct understanding of them is essential in several branches of physical education and corrective work. A student could be credited then by the English department for work in dramatic art or literary courses whose subject matter is connected with some phase of physical education. Regular work in biology and elemental physiology and anatomy, chemistry and physics, especially the latter should all have a place in this preliminary course. This work should be put into the two years just preceding the course in physical education. This course should include three or four years of fundamental work with another year of practical clinical work to be done either at the institution or at an affiliated one whose work is accredited by the University. As early as possible a student should be assisted by the head of the department to decide just which phase of the ultimate work she is best suited to undertake, and those branches in the preliminary course which bear on such work should be majored so as to pave the way definitely for the last year of selected clinical or laboratory work.

I am well aware of the fact that some persons in high positions educationally, do not agree that it should be a function of the physical department of a university to attempt the teaching of specialized corrective work. However, unless the university and recognized schools of physical education change the character and type of their teaching so as to graduate competent and accredited students who have the weight of a university degree back of their training we shall find the large field of which I have spoken, filled with untrained and unqualified persons, many of whom are little more than incompetent charlatans. Already the land is filled with institutions of mechanotherapy and physical culture, nature cures, massage parlors, Swedish institutes, and medical gymnasia. These are frequently conducted by some one who has acquired a smattering of physiotherapy during a sojourn in some sanatarium as a masseuse or masseur, or as an orderly at springs or hospitals where mechanotherapeutic procedures are used.

Some may hold that medical institutions should take over teaching of this kind. Granted; but medical students are not the ones who will practice in this field; consequently, the task falls to the lot of the physical education students. If these students are properly trained they will tend to discourage the illicit and improper activities of those unqualified persons who at present prey upon an innocent public.

The following is a brief sketch schematically outlining the idea which I wish to suggest, merely as something to bring out and help to crystallize into action the more elaborate ideas of those more familiar with educational methods than myself.

1. Anatomy Applied.
2. Physiology Applied.
3. Psychology Applied.
4. Hygiene.
5. Dramatic Art Elemental.
6. Kinesiology.
7. Gymnastics Theory and Practice.
8. Drills—Dances.
9. Rhythmic Studies.
10. Other elements basic to regular physical education.

1st 2 years. University preliminary to physical education and other required work.

2. 2 years in physical education school, 6 months clinical.

Another year for selective clinical for bachelor physical education.

Physical Education 4 years.

Bachelor Physical Education 5 years.

1. Kindergarten physical education.
2. Playground.
3. Grammar Grades corrective advisory.
4. Regular Gymnastic indoor floor.
5. Regular Gymnastic indoor dances, drills and games.
6. Regular Outdoor athletics, Recreational.
7. Regular Outdoor folk dancing and pageantry.
8. Camp Fire Girls.
9. Boy Scouts.
10. Y. M. C. A. and Y. W. C. A.

11. Army and Navy physical director.
12. Orthopaedic corrective work.
13. Defective and Psychopaths corrective, educative and recreative.
14. Speech Defects.
15. Hospital Physical Director Physiotherapy Department patients and nurses.
16. Industrial reconstruction.

The first two years at the university could cover the required and prephysical preliminary work and fundamental physical educational subjects. The second two years the regular more advanced work, with the final six months of selected clinical work for the physical education degree, and another year of selected special training for bachelor's degree.

The subjects which should be given as outlined in the scheme need a little explanation, for at present there is not enough, or at least not quite the right kind of work given by other departments to the physical education student. For instance, the head of the physical department should be allowed to outline the quantity and character of the work given his students by these other departments, and not have to accept whatever may be given in accordance with the ideas of the other department heads.

Anatomy, should be applied anatomy—not as elaborate as that given to medical students, but it should be a working, living anatomy, not a matter of dry bones and dissections. Especial attention to the action of the bone levers and joint function should be given, and a correct idea of skeletal alignment, and the relation of muscle and ligaments in maintaining it. The effect of alignment on the organs should be presented in such a way that the physical education student actually visualizes visceral relations when the pupil is working in various gymnastic positions. The average student cannot think mechanically in three planes—anteroposterior, lateral, and rotatory—all at once, and this is absolutely essential to the handling of abnormal cases like spinal curvatures, foot and leg conditions, etc. A most essential primary subject in anatomy should be sufficient anthropology to enable the student to correlate quickly the various type differences in order to know later how to classify their pupils and outline procedures along lines best suited to the various types. At present, long and short, fat and thin, in given grades are given the same work. Certain types such as the long, lithe type are naturally more prone to postural deviations of back and feet, and allowance should be made for this fact. More exact information about the glandular and sympathetic nervous systems should be given than at present, and is very essential to the proper understanding of later physiological studies which deal with these factors. The blood and nerve supply to the glands and viscerae is as important as to the muscles, and the time is coming when the student specializing along these lines will need to know more than the action, blood and nerve supply of the muscles only.

Physiology.—A branch which should be presented in a very practical, applied manner, laying more stress on newer aspects which underlie a proper application of the best methods used in psycho-motor training. The neuro-muscular relations; the sympathetic and visceral neural connections should be studied, and enough brain physiology to make the student more capable of understanding our problems in reeducation, both physically and mentally, of the retarded and handicapped, should be given. Basic muscle physiology and more about glandular functionings and its relation to muscle tone should also have a place in this course. The thyroid gland being the energizing organ of the body and being especially related to the maintenance of muscle tone and essential fact in corrective work. The importance of glands of internal secretion in connection with growth and nutrition as well as physical and mental activity should be reasonably understood. A very important factor is an understanding of the balancing function, so elaborate in its working. The internal ear mechanism, the relation of eye balance to posture, the relation of shoulder and head muscles to visual effort used in balancing, studies in vertigo, and other abnormalities of balance, all are very essential and even basic to proper understanding of so vital a neuro-muscular function.

The department of psychology should present such subjects as the psychology of muscle training, the psychology of recovery, child psychology and methods of handling various types of children, and should insure a proper understanding of what sensory development means. We find few students who appreciate what motor activities are controlled by the sensorium, and the workings of various sensory centers is just as important as the motor centers.

For those students who wish to take up speech defects, orthopaedic corrective work, and work with feeble minded and defective children, more specially applied work along this very important branch will be needed. It is more particularly psycho-physiology that is needed, so that the average student will be well grounded for either the general or special branches of physical training.

Applied hygiene is a well recognized need, but is not usually given in such a way that the importance of its truths sink home to the average student. The personal hygiene of the child and of his environment, both at school and home, should be gone into. The relation of chairs, beds, school desks, clothing, etc., to posture and efficiency should be studied. The recognition of physical factors indicating potential functional faults; mouth breathing, faults in speech, early signs of tics, muscle spasms, signs of deafness and eye disturbances, and a long line of other things should be dwelt upon. There are enough facts of this kind to make fifteen lectures alone on applied hygiene without going into the sex question, sanitation, or housing, and the broader aspects of general interest.

An elemental or working acquaintance with a certain amount of dramatic art dealing with expression and the fundamentals which underlie gesture, speech, etc., should also be given. All expression is a motor activity and an acquaintance with the normal biological development of it is important.

Studies in rhythm, drill, dancing, etc., constitute a subject in themselves, as do games and athletic activities, both indoor and outdoor.

Kinesiology, the theory and practice of gymnastics, and the other basic subjects to the regular physical training course should all be arranged as needed.

I wish to bring out chiefly that the first five mentioned should be given more accurately and interestingly as being the subjects most needed to fit the students for a wider, and more scientific field of endeavor in this line. These are the branches in which the students are weakest, and this necessitates the taking of more post-graduate work before the newer lines of activity can be entered.

The large field of corrective physical education has scarcely been touched, and yet records are ample to show that the majority (from seventy-five to eighty-five per cent) of all our school children have some physical defect. Why then shall we continue in the old way, giving most attention to the minority when the major need is so great?

REPORTS OF THE NATIONAL AMATEUR ATHLETIC FEDERATION OF AMERICA

Report of the Committee on Organization of the Conference on Athletics and Physical Education for Women and Girls, April 6 and 7, 1923, at Washington, D.C.

Called by Mrs. Herbert Hoover at the suggestion of the National Amateur Athletic Federation of America.

Whereas, we believe that we are in the early stages of a great advancement in athletics for girls and women which is destined to be of incalculable value for the vigor, health, and character-training of girls and women as citizens and future mothers, or of great possibilities for harm; and we believe that the program of athletics for the welfare, health, and education of women depends upon the women experts on girls' and women's athletics organizing themselves as a deliberating and administrative body to deal with the special problems of athletics for girls and women; *whereas* we believe that there must be an organization concerned with the national problem in athletics common to both boys and girls and men and women:

Therefore, be it resolved,

First, that there shall be a special organization of women to stand as a deliberating, investigating, legislating, promoting, advising, and finally controlling body on the special problems of athletics for girls and women; and

National Amateur Federation of America, Reports of the Conference, April 6-7, 1923, Washington, D. C., *American Physical Education Review,* vol. XXVIII, no. 6, June 1923, pp. 284, 286, 288, 289.

Second, that the N. A. A. F. shall be considered the inclusive body concerned with the national problems and all problems of deliberation, investigation, legislation, promotion, and control in athletics which are common to both sexes.

Be it further resolved that the chairman of this conference shall, with the authority of the Board of Governors of the N. A. A. F. and the written suggestions of each member of this conference appoint a commission of not less than seven women which shall stand under the authority of the N. A. A. F. as the deliberating, investigating, legislating, promoting, advising, and finally controlling body on women's athletics for the next year, or until such time as the Commission can perform two special functions, as follows:

First, to work out with the officials of the N. A. A. F. the detailed organization of the N. A. A. F. in dealing with the national or common problems in athletics as they apply to both boys and girls and men and women; and

Second, the detailed organization of the special women's organization as a part of the N. A. A. F.

Be it further resolved,

First, thai the Commission shall strive to formulate a special organization on girls' and women's athletics which shall give the opportunity to bring together in the Federation representatives of all social groups of girls and women, and all agencies concerned with the athletic activities of girls and women.

Second, that the Commission in conference with the officials of the N. A. A. F. shall formulate a relationship according to the following terms:

a. The creation of a joint executive board composed of men and women, the women members to be selected by women.

b. That the special athletic and physical problems of girls and women shall be the function of the special organization of women.

c. That there shall be appointed a special executive secretary, who is a woman, qualified and authorized to promote and direct the women's program.

BLANCHE M. TRILLING, *Chairman*,
J. ANNA NORRIS,
HELEN MCKINSTRY,
HELEN FROST,
J. DANA CALKINS,

Committee on Organization.

Resolutions Adopted by the Conference on Athletics and Physical Recreation Held Under the Auspices of the National Amateur Athletic Federation at Washington, D.C., April 6-7, 1923

1. *Resolved:* That it be noted that the term "athletics" as used in this conference has often included the problems connected with all types of non-competitive as well as competitive physical activities for girls and women.

2. *Whereas,* the period of childhood and youth is the period of growth in all bodily structures, and

Whereas, a satisfactory growth during this period depends upon a large amount of vigorous physical exercise, and

Whereas, the strength, endurance, efficiency, and vitality of maturity will depend in very large degree upon the amount of vigorous physical exercise in childhood and youth, and

Whereas, normal, wholesome, happy, mental and emotional maturity depends in large part upon joyous, natural, safeguarded big muscle activity in childhood and in youth,

Be it therefore resolved, that vigorous, active, happy, big muscle activity be liberally provided and maintained and carefully guided for every girl and boy, and

That all governments, village, county, state, and national, establish and support adequate opportunities for a universal physical education that will assist in the preparation of our boys and girls for the duties, opportunities, and joys of citizenship and of life as a whole;

3. *Resolved,* that there be greater concentration and study on the problems and program of physical activities for the prepubescent as well as for the adolescent girl.

4. *Resolved,* in order to develop those qualities which shall fit girls and women to perform their functions as citizens

(a) That their athletics be conducted with that end definitely in view and be protected from exploitation for the enjoyment of the spectator or for the athletic reputation or commercial advantage of any school or other organization.

(b) That schools and other organizations shall stress enjoyment of the sport and development of sportsmanship and minimize the emphasis which is at present laid upon individual accomplishment and the winning of championships.

5. *Resolved,* that for any given group we approve and recommend such selection and administration of athletic activities as makes participation possible for all, and strongly condemn the sacrifice of this

object for intensive training (even though physiologically sound) of the few.

6. *Resolved,* that (a) competent women be put in immediate charge of women and girls in their athletic activities even where the administrative supervision may be under the direction of men;

(b) We look toward the establishment of a future policy that shall place the administration as well as teaching and coaching of girls and women in the hands of carefully trained and properly qualified women.

7. *Whereas,* a rugged national vitality and a high level of public health are the most important resources of a people,

Be it therefore resolved, that the teacher-training schools, the colleges, the professional schools, and the universities of the United States make curricular and administrative provisions that will emphasize:

1. Knowledge of the basic facts of cause and effect in hygiene that will lead to the formation of discriminating judgments in matters of health;
2. Habits of periodical examination and a demand for scientific health service, and
3. Habits of vigorous developmental recreation.

To this end we recommend,

a. That adequate instruction in physical and health education be included in the professional preparation of all elementary and secondary school teachers;

b. That suitable instruction in physical and health education be included in the training of volunteer leaders in organized recreation programs;

c. Definite formulation of the highest modern standards of professional education for teachers and supervisors of physical education and recreation, and the provision of adequate opportunity for the securing of such education.

8. *Resolved,* that in order to maintain and build health, thorough and repeated medical examinations are necessary.

9. *Resolved,* since we recognize that certain anatomical and physiological conditions may occasion temporary unfitness for vigorous athletics, therefore effective safeguards should be maintained.

10. *Whereas,* we believe that the motivation of competitors in athletic activities should be that of play for play's sake, and

Whereas, we believe that the awarding of valuable prizes is detrimental to this objective,

Be it resolved, that all awards granted for athletic achievement be restricted to those things which are symbolical and which have the least possible intrinsic value.

11. *Resolved,* that suitable costumes for universal use be adopted for the various athletics activities.

12. *Whereas,* we believe that the type of publicity which may be given to athletics for women and girls may have a vital influence both upon the individual competitors and upon the future development of the activity,

Be it resolved, that all publicity be of such a character as to stress the sport and not the individual or group competitors.

13. *Whereas,* certain international competitions for women and girls have already been held, and

Whereas, we believe that the participation of American women and girls in these competitions was inopportune,

Be it resolved, that it is the sense of this conference that in the future such competitions, if any, be organized and controlled by the national organization set up as a result of this conference.

14. *Resolved,* that committees be appointed for study and report on the following problems:

a. Tests for motor and organic efficiency;

b. The formulation of a program of physical activities adapted to various groups of the population;

c. The relation of athletics to the health of pre-pubescent and post-adolescent girls;

d. Scientific investigations as to anatomical, physiological and emotional limitations and possibilities of girls and women in athletics, and a careful keeping of records in order that results may be determined.

15. *Resolved,* that the sincere and hearty thanks of the members of this conference on athletics and physical recreation be extended,

a. To the National Amateur Athletic Federation for its suggestion that this conference be called; and

b. To Mrs. Herbert Hoover for her vision and devotion in organizing this conference and in making possible the vitally significant achievement of coordination of the various agencies for women's athletics.

16. *Resolved,* that the National Amateur Athletic Foundation be requested to publish these resolutions and to distribute them

a. To all members of this conference.

b. To all present members of the National Amateur Athletic Federation.

c. To the Associated Press.

d. To the American Physical Education Association, with the request that they be copied and distributed to all members of the Springfield convention.

J. ANNA NORRIS, *Chairman*,
ELIZABETH KEMPER ADAMS,
HELEN M. BUNTING,
HELEN MCKINSTRY,
EDITH HALE SWIFT,
Committee on Resolutions.

Report of the Committee on Recommendations Regarding Inter- and Intra-Institutional Activities

As adopted by the Committee on Women's Athletics of the American Physical Education Association, Springfield, Mass., April 14, 1923.

Your committee calls attention to the following excerpts from the resolutions adopted by the Washington Conference and approved by this committee, which have particular bearing upon the subjects of intra- and inter-institutional competitions, upon which there has been so much discussion.

Resolution 4.

a. That girls' and women's athletics be protected from exploitation for the enjoyment of the spectator or for the athletic reputation or commercial advantage of any school or other organization.

b. That schools and other organizations shall stress enjoyment of the sport and development of sportsmanship and minimize the emphasis which is at present laid upon individual accomplishment and the winning of championships.

Resolution 5.

a. That for any given group we approve and recommend such selection and administration of athletic activities as makes participation possible for all, and strongly condemn the sacrifice of this object for intensive training (even though physiologically sound) of the few.

Resolution 6.

a. That competent women be put in immediate charge of women and girls in their athletic activities even where the administrative supervision may be under the direction of men.

b. We look forward to the establishment of a future policy that shall place the administration as well as teaching and coaching of girls and women in the hands of carefully trained and properly qualified women.

Resolution 10.

Whereas, we believe that the motivation of competitors in athletic activities should be that of play for play's sake, and

Whereas, we believe that the awarding of valuable prizes is detrimental to this objective,

Be it resolved, that all awards granted for athletic achievement be restricted to those things which are symbolical and which have the least possible intrinsic value.

Resolution 11.

That suitable costumes for universal use be adopted for the various athletic activities.

Resolution 12.

Whereas, we believe that the type of publicity which may be given to athletics for women and girls may have a vital influence both upon the individual competitors and upon the future development of the activity,

Be it resolved, that all publicity be of such character as to stress the sport and not the individual or group competitors.

Your committee recommends that the Committee on Women's Athletics

1. Make themselves familiar with the complete set of resolutions.
2. Take active steps to see that they are applied to girls' athletics.
3. Use every opportunity to bring them to public attention.

Whereas, we endorse these resolutions, and

Whereas, we believe them to express the fundamental policies upon which any competition in athletics for girls and women should be based,

Be it therefore resolved, that no consideration of inter-institutional athletics is warranted unless,

a. The school or institution has provided opportunity for *every girl* to have a full season's program of all around athletic activities of the type approved by this committee.

b. That *every girl* in the school or institution (not merely the proposed contestants) actively participates in a full season of such activities and takes part in a series of games within the school or institution.

c. These activities are conducted under the immediate leadership of properly trained women instructors, who have the *educational value* of the game in mind rather than *winning.*

Resolved, that in cases where

1. The above conditions obtain and proper responsible authorities (preferably women) deem it desirable *educationally and socially* to hold inter-institutional competitions the following requirements are observed:

   a. Medical examination for all participants.

   b. No gate money.

   c. Admission only by invitation of the various schools or institutions taking part in order that participants may not be exploited.

   d. No publicity other than that which stresses only the sport and not the individual or group competitors.

   e. Only properly trained women instructors and officials in charge.

Note: The committee feels that it is questionable whether inter-institutional athletics are ever warranted for children under high school age, except where such competition is conducted by the chart system or communications by mail, telegraph, etc.

Your committee was unable in the short time available to prepare further recommendations for presentation at this meeting or for the proper elaboration of these here presented, but among other matters which they desire to emphasize and for which they wish further time are the following:

1. The undesirability of traveling away from the home town or community to take part in competitions, especially in the case of girls below adult age.
2. The necessity of limiting the number of games.
3. Desirability of working out some type of meet which
   a. Is an incident of the general program of athletics for all.
   b. Is a logical culmination of a season's program.
   c. Is not confined to one type of activity.
4. The desirability of working out a program of activities in which the competing unit is a group and not an individual.

Finally, the committee does not wish it to be inferred from these recommendations that it is advocating or attempting to promote a policy of inter-institutional games.

Respectfully submitted,

Elizabeth Burchenal, *Chairman,*
2790 Broadway, New York City.
Margaret Burns,
Margaret McKee,
Leslie Sawtelle.

PSYCHOLOGY AND ITS RELATION TO ATHLETIC COMPETITION

Coleman R. Griffith

Professor of Psychology
University of Illinois
Read by Coach Robert Zuppke

Although a great many men have hitherto used the words "psychology" and "athletics" in the same sentence, no one has, until the present, undertaken a thorough survey of all that might be done in this field. The time has not yet come, therefore, when papers about "psychology and athletics" can treat of special problems or of new groups of facts as do papers on well-established topics and sciences. Until psychologists, athletic directors, and coaches can come to an understanding of the general extent of the field, a paper such as is being read to you to-day must be written much as a map is drawn. Boundaries are to be laid out, parts of the country labeled, and the main features of the map described in a proper way. For this reason, we shall tell first of the reason why the words "psychology and athletics" go together at all and then we shall go on to lay out the general plan of this new field of inquiry and give illustrations of the problems that belong to it.

When an athlete goes out on the field for a contest he does not leave his mind tucked away in a locker with his shoes, his watch and his hat. Such a statement seems almost too obvious to make before this group; but, as we all know, there are some coaches and athletic directors who act as though they had to do only with human bodies. They speak of *physical* training and they coach their men to play as if weight and speed of muscle were the only factors involved in athletic competition. It takes but a moment, however, to realize that the best athletes use almost every faculty of their minds when they go into a contest. The men who are most alert mentally are the men who make the best teams. Witness the fact that we are always looking for "brainy" quar-

Coleman R. Griffith, "Psychology and Its Relation to Athletic Competition," *American Physical Education Review,* vol. XXX, no. 4, April 1925, pp. 193-199.

terbacks, "heady" open field runners, "thinking" pitchers and catchers, clever basemen and baserunners, and "shifty" boxers. In other words, when we go to athletic competition with an eye open to psychological matters we cannot help but come away with the belief that all athletic competition is purposeful, clever, intelligent, emotional, and skillful, and not merely mechanical. The athlete who goes into a contest is a mind-body organism and not merely a physiological machine. First, last, and always he is an intelligent person; and his success as well as the success of his coach rests upon how well the springs of intelligence have been touched and brought into play. Psychological facts appear also in another place. If athletic competition is going to stand against its enemies and if it is going to make strides in realizing the best hopes of its friends we must have an ever growing regard for athletic ideals. Honor, sportsmanship, courage, fair play and other fine things must be the daily accompaniments of competition if our stadia and our other monuments to athletic prowess are to mean anything in our national life. Now ideals do not belong to charging, fighting, human machines. Brute strength is almost always blind to sportsmanship. Ten pounds of flesh on a man's arms are not a sure sign of mental spirit. We come, then, to this fundamental proposition, viz., that the more mind is made use of in athletic competition, the greater will be the skill of our athletes, the finer will be the contest, the higher will be the ideals of sportsmanship displayed, the longer will our games persist in our national life, and the more truly will they lead to those rich personal and social products which we ought to expect of them.

Because of these facts, the psychologist may hope to break into the realm of athletic competition, just as he has already broken into the realms of industry, commerce, medicine, education, and art. He does not approach the athletic field, however, with any bag of tricks or with his hands and voice full of strange formulæ. A great many people have the idea that the psychologist is a sort of magician who is ready, for a price, to sell his services to one individual or to one group of men. Nothing can be further from the truth. Psychological facts are universal facts. They belong to whoever will read while he runs. There is another strange opinion about the psychologist. It is supposed that he is merely waiting until he can jump into an athletic field, tell the old-time successful coach that he is all wrong and begin, then, to expound his own magical and fanciful theories as to proper methods of coaching, the way to conquer overconfidence, the best forms of strategy, and so on. This, of course, is also far from the truth, although certain things have appeared in the application of psychology to business and industry to lead to such an opinion. During the last few years and at the present time, there have been and are many men, short in psychological training and long in the use of the English language, who are doing psychology damage by advertising that they are ready to answer any and every question that comes up in any and every field. No sane psychologist is deceived by these self-styled apostles of a new day. Coaches and athletes have a right to be wary of such stuff.

The real task of the psychologist on the athletic field can be illustrated in three ways. His first task is to make plain to young and inexperienced coaches those psychological laws and principles that are implied in the successes of our best coaches. There are a few men who stand out as physical directors and as coaches because they have been fortunate enough to hit upon those principles and laws, some physiological and some psychological, that make for success in coaching. Many times these men are not able to express to themselves or to others the secret of their success. As we say, they seem to have an intuitive or instinctive knowledge of how to teach plays to their men, how to prevent overconfidence, how to develop morale and spiritedness, how to get along with their fellow human beings. One task of the psychologist, then, is to interpret great coaches to inexperienced coaches; to write out in detail the well-tried laws and principles which great coaches may unconciously follow as they develop their own teams. The net outcome of this task of the psychologist will be to raise the whole level of coaching and of competition and to provide a way for the training of men in directions which are not now open to them. In the second place, the psychologist can adapt to athletics some of the facts which he has discovered in his laboratory and which, up to this time, have not been made use of on the field of competition. There are a great many facts about perception, attention, memory, reaction time, emotion, personality, crowd psychology, overconfidence, fear, and the like, which may not be known even to the best of coaches. By going slowly and by undertaking to apply these facts with care and with full sympathy for the nature of athletic competition, the psychologist ought to be able to make a few worthy contributions to this new field of interest. In the third place, the psychologist can bring his experimental laboratory to the aid of the coach and help him to answer in a scientific manner new problems and discover new facts. Experience is, of course, a good school; but everyone now knows that a sane use of laboratories and of scientific methods will take us in a day to results not gotten in years in other ways.

In order to illustrate still more exactly just what the psychologist is about, we shall run over in a little more detail some of the specific things that have already been done in the field. Consider for a moment the use which the average athlete must make of his eyes. In ordinary life we suppose that we get along solely by taking account of the objects which we see in the line of direct vision; but any of you who drive automobiles know that you run in and out of traffic, that you live up to the courtesies of the road, by making use of the whole field of vision. You see out of one corner of your eye that the man on your right has parked too far from the curb and out of the other corner of your eye you note that the man on your left is driving too close. As one approaches a side street, one depends upon the things seen in indirect vision for the safety of an attempted crossing. It takes time to move the head and the eyes from one side to another. These same facts are true of the athlete. The forward passer receives the ball, runs a yard or two as a feint, and then, with scarcely a look over the broken field, selects a person and a place and throws the ball. There is no time to turn the head here and there. The best forward passers seem to keep track of moving objects in the broken field out of the corner of their eyes. The linesman in a football field does about the same. He must keep his eyes on the ball and at the same time solve the intentions of his opponent. He must make use of the whole field of vision. The man who dribbles down the basket ball floor keeps his eye upon the ball; but he is, nevertheless, aware of the position of his teammates and opponents; or he may keep his eye on the men about him but in the meantime know the position of the ball which he is dribbling. The infielder on a baseball team keeps his eye on the ball but he always knows where to throw it to catch the runner as soon as the ball is fielded. A boxer may keep the center of vision on his opponent's chest and trust to the rest of the field of vision to warn him of coming blows. Now there are some rather important facts that have come out of a study of the outer portions of the retina and it is in a knowledge of these facts and in methods of practicing vision out of the corner of one's eye that successful dribblers, successful forward passers, and clever broken-field runners get their skill. If we practice muscles in the art of throwing a ball, why not practice retinas and perceptual abilities in the art of sizing up the field of vision without having to take the time to look, now here, now there, now over yonder? Also, in the experimental study of our ways of perceiving distance, and rates of movement, and in the study of the illusions to which our eyes are subject, we get further facts that may be of use on any athletic field, especially in the development of fast open field runners, and dribblers, boxers, and others.

One of the sources of information which most coaches do not often use lies in the field of somatic perception or the perception of bodily state. This whole problem can be illustrated nicely by an account of some experiments in animal psychology. As one of their regular laboratory tasks, white rats are forced to run through a maze or a labyrinth in order to get their food. The first time the rat is put into a maze, it may wander through all of the blind alleys and make every possible mistake; it is only after a long series of explorations that it finds its way to the center and thus to food. As the trials are repeated, however, the rat learns to go through the maze without any errors. Now the question arises, does the rat see its way through the maze or smell its way or does it make use of some other kind of experience? The matter can be tested in this fashion: Suppose that during the first trials the rat learns to run the maze when the maze is tilted at an angle of 20 degrees to the right. Part of the pathways will then be uphill and part downhill. Now, suppose that, after the maze has been learned, it is tilted to the left by 20 degrees. The pathways that formerly ran uphill will now go down and those that ran downward will now stretch upward. If the rat has learned the maze in terms of visual experiences, this changing of the level of the maze ought to make no difference in the performance. As a matter of fact, however, the rat has to re-learn the maze. This simple experiment shows that the learning is done in terms of the muscular experiences involved in running along paths of given distances and in turning at certain places. In other words, the rat learns the maze by what is commonly called the sixth sense or the muscular sense. It turns out, upon investigation, that athletes also make use of this sixth or muscular sense. The free-thrower in a basket ball game knows from his muscles when his throw is accurate, even before the ball has left his hands. So, too, the pitcher knows while the ball is still in his hand whether or not the throw he is just making will cut the plate as he desires. We have, after close study of this matter, found out that the muscular sense or muscular perception can be used far more often than it is. Many times the use of the muscular sense instead of the visual sense enables us to acquire degrees of skill that would not be approached by using the visual sense alone. Some football coaches have recognized this fact in asking their linesmen to spend the winter months on the wrestling team and in tumbling so that they will learn more about the feel of their own bodies. The writer has conducted several experiments on this problem and he has been able to show that basket ball players who formerly, could scarcely hit even the bank-board, learned in a short time to make such good use of their muscular experiences that they came to be fairly good shots. Golfers who have had trouble hitting the ball under the old instruction that one should keep his eye on the ball, have learned while blindfolded, to pay attention to the muscular feel of driving and so have greatly improved their game. All forms of athletic skill depend upon muscular experiences and the psychologist believes that the average athlete will find as much value in these experiences as professional gymnasts find in them on the vaudeville platform. In them lies a part of the secret of quickly acquiring skill in the finest forms of muscular coördination.

It is in the field of attention that most coaches are more nearly at home. In every play which he teaches, and in all of the forms of field strategy which are supposed to make up the inside story of football, the coach depends upon the fact that he can make men attend toward some objects and to some parts of the field and attend away from other objects and other parts of the field. The coach is very much like a sleight of hand performer who invites you to regard the object he holds in his right hand while he draws the rabbit out of your pocket with his left. In other words, much of modern football rests upon the question as to how attention can be commanded. It is, of course, an ordinary principle in psychology that sudden, new, strange, moving, repeated objects get themselves attended to most readily. The fact that in the ordinary shift play eight or ten men are in movement at once makes the shift play a difficult thing to handle because the moving bodies of men invite attention to themselves and away from the ball. We also attend readily to those things that we have learned to attend to and a large part of football strategy rests in the skill which a coach has in out-guessing another coach by making quick shifts or creating tricky plays which fall outside of the ordinary habits of attention of opponents. Take also the well-established fact that one cannot attend to more than five or six objects at once. This fact is known as the span of attention. When a player is forced to go beyond the ordinary span of attention, muscular incoordination is almost sure to result. A pitcher can attend to the ball he is about to throw, to the set of his arm, to the position of the batter, to the signals from the catcher, and perhaps to one runner on base, but when three men get on, he is taken beyond the ordinary span of attention. He is then apt, as we say, to "blow up." We think a six-ring circus is good not because the individual acts are good but often because we spend three hours at the limit of our abilities to attend. Almost all shift plays depend for their success upon the fact that the men in the line cannot be expected to attend clearly to more than five or six of their opponents. If every man is used in every play and if the shifts are short and snappy, much that takes place when the ball is snapped will lie beyond the range of attention. It is this fact more than the momentum of the shifting men that gives an offensive team the advantage in charging. The psychologist has made a great many detailed studies in the field of attention and he is prepared to say with a high degree of accuracy what kinds of plays, what shifts, and what other circumstances will take advantage of the facts of attention and he is also prepared to say how the span of attention may be increased, how to decrease the effects of razzing, how to command the attention of one's opponents, how to attend steadily at one part of the field for several moments, how to learn to pay attention to little things—signs and clews that betray the intentions of one's opponents—and so on. In other words, the psychologist is ready to handle with accuracy the many advantages and disadvantages which lie in what we might call single-mindedness versus multi-mindedness.

It is in the fields of habit, memory, and learning that the psychologist can, perhaps, be of most value. The coach has a task of instruction which is not paralleled anywhere else in the university. Within a few weeks he must teach a squad of twenty or thirty men all the details of an extremely complicated game and at the same time he must produce an amount of skill which the spectator, who looks on, thinks almost incredible. If the average university student were asked to get a corresponding amount of skill in mathematics or in language in the same time that is at the disposal of the coach, he would go on a permanent strike at so astounding an imposition. When the coach undertakes his very difficult task of instruction, he faces the fact that human nervous systems will not be hurried. It takes time to acquire habits and memories. One of the most fundamental laws of all learning runs something like this: the greater the distribution of practice periods, the more economical will be the expenditure of time, and the greater the reward in skill. That is, if a coach has ten hours to spend on the learning of any one play, it is far better, other things being equal, to spend a half-hour a day for twenty days, than to spend an hour a day for ten days, two hours a day for five days, or five hours a day for two days. It often happens, however, that his schedule or that injuries to men on his team force him to pile up repetitions into two or three days. Over night he must build a new team. In doing this he faces an almost impossible situation. The nervous systems of his men refuse to work as fast as necessary. Yet the game must be played on the coming week-end. It is at such a time that the coach must go to some of the other facts that have been discovered about learning and habit and so seek to get out of his difficulty as best he can.

In short, the coach has a definite amount of time to spend and in exchange for time he wants to purchase the highest degree of skill time can buy. The highest degree of skill comes out of a knowledge of the proper length of practice periods, the proper distribution of practice periods, the advantages of learning by wholes rather than of learning by parts, the methods of presenting new material, the laws that govern increases in the amount that can be learned in a given time, the effect of attention on rate of learning, the effects of relearning and overlearning, the effects of later habits on earlier habits, the relation of individual differences to learning, the ratio between the rate of learning and the rate of forgetting, and the advantages and disadvantages of cramming, the effect of incentives to practice, such as knowledge of the end sought, knowledge of scores and of records, knowledge of errors, and knowledge of when material learned is to be used.

In addition to these fields in which there is so much actual experimental fact, there are several fields in which the psychologist is prepared to act in an advisory way. We do not have, for example, very many experiments upon the problem of thinking but since thinking is a psychological matter, the psychologist ought to be able to pass some judgments in this field that would be more reliable than the judgments of the men in the barber shop. The most obvious thing which we can say is that thinking—real constructive mental effort—does not belong upon the athletic field. The time to do one's thinking is before the season starts and before the game is under way. During the heat and the emotion of the game, athletes are victims of the habits and skills which their coaches have taught them. They must have learned so well that they have become highly trained automatons even under partial concussion and certainly under extreme emotion. And there are dozens of other problems that have to do with feeling and emotion. We are just beginning to learn about some of the relations that obtain between the major emotions and certain glandular secretions. It seems to be fairly clear that a coach may, by putting his men into a high state of emotion, cause adrenalin to be thrown into the blood stream and thereby increase the amount of work that can be done and decrease the rate of which fatigue products will be developed. That is, there is a real physiological sense in which football players, basket ball players, and track men get their second wind. They can and do tap new reserves of energy. All of these facts, together with facts about the relation between moods and bodily states, ought to be common knowledge to coaches, if not to athletes. Sometimes, instead of exciting emotions, the coach must control emotions.

This is especially true of the emotion of fear and studies in the psychology of war have shown us how to control fear and turn it to account on the field of athletic battle.

Sometimes contests are settled by physical strength and at other times by differences in skill; but there are many times when victory turns on the matter of personality. Personality is a name for the persistent and insistent habits of a man. These habits may be habits of speech, habits of thinking, habits of feeling, habits of facial expression, or what not. Men use their personality or their individualized systems of habits to impress themselves upon other people. Strong coaches impress themselves upon their men; strong men impress themselves upon opponents. It follows that the psychologist who knows something about habits can suggest ways of developing personality, ways of adjusting personalities to each other so that captains may get along with their men, the men get along with each other and with their coach, so that a whole team will acquire a personality of its own. Closely related to personality is the fact of will power. The psychologist cannot, of course, believe in any mysterious, strange, hidden force called will; but he does believe in certain facts about habit which we all think of when we use the words "will power." In this sense of the word, there is a way to cultivate will power, a way to build up a spirit of determination or the will to win, a way to get rid of the yellow streak, on the one hand, and of overconfidence, on the other. Studies of this kind bring us pretty close to the topic of morale or mental spirit. Morale is the measure of the quality of men. It has to do with the mental temper of a man and of a team. In morale lies the answer to such questions as: how long can a linesman continue to look the opposing linesman in the face? how long can a pitcher preserve his fine muscular coördination when there are three men on base? how long can a quarterback stand in a position to receive a punt when he sees out of the corner of his eye two or three opponents rushing down upon him? how long can the server keep on cutting the corners when the set score is 5-2 against him? how long can any athlete carry on with whole-souled vigor when his breath begins to fall short, his ribs to hurt, his knees to weaken, and when the bleachers begin to fall silent? Here again the war has helped us for we have learned to know what morale is, how to control it, how to acquire it, and how to destroy it.

Other problems in which a psychologist might be interested do not so directly touch a coach at work on the field but they belong, nevertheless, to athletic competition at large. Everyone is agreed that athletics must justify themselves as being better for college students than a good old-fashioned wood pile. Competition does justify itself because the football field is a place where morale, spirit, courage, honor, sportsmanship, fair play, team work, and the like, are directly taught. We do not learn these things in our courses in mathematics, English, or history; we cannot learn them over a wood pile, or while digging ditches. It seems that hard and honest competition is the one great school for all those virtues which are sometimes called martial virtues. It is clear, of course, that we cannot go to war every time we find our bodies becoming soft and our minds losing their spirit. The athletic field is the only place where the best things of war can be taught. Ideals and traditions are, of course, psychological and the psychologist's place here is probably that of an interpreter. It may be his privilege to put the ideals of athletic competition into a psychological background and so make them convincing or reasonable to persons who think more closely of the money that is used in great stadia or of the hurts that come out of hard competition than they do of the fine moral and spiritual values that are tested and tempered in the heat of the contest.

If we had time we might mention in detail other problems of the same sort as, for example, the personal and social rewards of athletic competition, the relation between play, work, and fatigue, the psychology of crowds, and of cheer leading. We shall touch briefly on only one problem of this group; namely, the problem of selecting the best men for given places upon a team and the problem of selecting for any given game the men who are in the best physical and mental shape for that game. There ought to be some way of preventing a coach spending many hours upon a man who at the end shows he did not have the mental stuff in him; on the other hand, there ought to be some way of finding the man who will blossom out quickly under a little cultivating. As you all know, psychological tests of a great many kinds are being successfully used in industry, commerce, education, medicine, and law. These tests come out of a description, on the one hand, of the psychological capacities that any given task will require for its successful execution, and, on the other hand, out of the psychological capacities which any individual may possess when he appears at the "hiring-on" window. The problem is, of course, to fit individuals to tasks so that economy of time and effort will be gained. A certain number of these tests are of a general nature and they can be used in almost any kind of work. Athletic competition, however, demands tests of a specialized sort and we have every reason to believe that sometime it will be possible after an hour's work to select from a group of a hundred men those that are best adapted to play any given part in a game. Of the standardized tests there are some that already enable us to tell within a few moments as to whether a man is being overtrained or not. There are times during the football season when motor incoördination and mental fatigue result from a coach having pushed the nervous systems of his men too fast. It is easy to discover these moments and to prescribe for the team rest or change of practice. Of the specialized tests, we ought to have a means of selecting a pitcher from the pitching staff, a forward from a group of forwards, a gymnast from a group of gymnasts, or a golfer from a group of golfers.

It is now clear, from what has been said, that the psychologist is not proposing any revolutionary changes in the world of athletics. His interest is partly a scientific interest in the mind of the athlete, partly a practical interest in turning to account such facts as he knows, and partly a matter of ordinary human interest. Psychologists, like all men, desire to see games played at their best. All that we ask is that we be forgiven for our vague and technical vocabulary, and that we be given a chance to work out slowly and carefully the principles that are used in competition that is not of muscles only but of alert minds as well.

PHENOMENAL GROWTH OF INSTRUCTION IN SWIMMING AND WATERMANSHIP

By Elbridge Colby
Captain of Infantry
United States Army

Undoubtedly one of the most striking adventures in American pedagogy during the first quarter of the twentieth century has been the phenomenal growth of instruction in swimming and watermanship. Whether this has been due to the increasingly artificial modes of our modern urban life, and the consequent necessity of developing means of exercising, or to the phenomenal emulation-producing performances of Charles M. Daniels, Norman Foss, and John Weissmuller, or to the current tendency in academic circles to teach new tricks—it is not possible to say. Let it suffice to remark that swimming has increased to a tremendous degree. Pools are built in high schools. Playgrounds contain swimming facilities. Many colleges include ability at swimming as a prerequisite for a degree. Country clubs are not considered complete without tanks. At the colleges, aquatic teams take tank with basketball and hockey teams. In military posts, it has become increasingly emphasized that mobility across water is an essential to a moving body of fighting men, a fact ably proven by the experiences of the Fifth and Eighty-ninth Divisions at the Meuse River in 1918. At the summer training camps for civilians instruction in swimming is given as a matter of course. In a single city of average size, a single swimming installation accommodated an average of 2,755 persons a day for the four months of the hot season.

Swimming Now a Nation-Wide Sport

Let the details pass. The days when swimming was used only for heroic exploits, like those of Beowulf, or for amorous adventures, like

Elbridge Colby, "Phenomenal Growth of Instruction in Swimming and Watermanship," *Mind and Body,* vol. 32, no. 342, September 1925, pp. 673-677.

those of Leander, are gone. Swimming has become a nation-wide sport, and consequently two very important problems have arisen: The problem of developing a suitable technique for teaching swimming and the problem of training leaders and instructors in water safety.

Leading in the campaign for water safety and in the instruction of the general public in this is the American Red Cross, that semi-governmental agency which ministers to the dangers and ills of suffering humanity. Scrutinizing the tremendous casualty lists resulting from drowning, the officials of the Red Cross deemed it a proper function of their institution to apply their peace-time energies to this work. So for something more than a decade experts have gone forth who have given instruction and followed by stringent tests. In local Red Cross chapters special agents have been appointed who have promoted community action. A list of qualified life savers was created, and later supplementary examiners were authorized to give instruction and to give tests in the name of the national organization. By a decentralization of actual organization and a dissemination of correct principles and methods of water rescue, the Red Cross was able to multiply its instruction. With due deference to the signal successes attained by the United States Volunteer Life Saving Corps, notably those units in and about New York City and Providence, R. I., and to the notable work done in the name of the World Life-Saving Alliance, it is still possible to say that the American Red Cross has been the most powerful single force for the promotion of water safety.

Delegation of Authority Responsible for Success

A very large part of the recent success of the Red Cross has been due to its increasing willingness to delegate its instructional and qualifying authority to persons seriously interested in water-safety work and honestly responsible for the progress of instruction in local communities. By such delegation of authority to "examiners" the few traveling field representatives have been able to devote the major part of their time to general surveys of the field, the checking up technique and to spreading knowledge of new methods.

A very significant contribution toward the accomplishment of the Red Cross work has been the system of "institutes" held annually in mid-June under the auspices of the life-saving corps. At various boys' or girls' summer camps, the Red Cross has held preseason camps of its own, devoted to intensive 7 or 10 day instruction in water safety. To these camps come, as volunteer members of the "faculty," certain specially invited experts who give freely of their time; and young men and young women also come who are destined to become water-front directors at boys' camps, or counsellors at girls' camps, or instructors in physical training, or volunteer swimming teachers or life guards at scout camps. The type of students is of high grade; the majority of them are college people. In late June they put in seven strenuous days, jumping from one bathing suit to another, it seems, to fit themselves for aquatic responsibilities in the July and August camps of the regular recreational type. So favorably is this work of the Red Cross looked upon by the associated summer camps that the officials are able to secure camp sites for their pre-season courses by voluntary, gratuitous donations. So popular is this work that the "institute" camps are increasing in number from year to year. And as they increase, knowledge of watermanship and the habits of water safety are disseminated more and more widely.

Red Cross Camps Numerously Attended

To these camps, under a special invitation, and in view of the very special relationship existing between the Red Cross and the Army, come officers and enlisted men of the Regular Army; to learn the approved technique and insure proper precautions at the swimming pools and places maintained by the Army at its posts, camps, and stations. To these camps come also young and old, the spry and the sedate, the active instructors and the advisory executives—all ready to be indoctrinated and to secure the best advice on their work.

Other institutions which have taken up the work of making water sports safer are the Turnvereins of the larger cities of the United States. Many of them have installed swimming pools for the use of their own members and their turning school instructors are required to give instruction in swimming to the hundreds of pupils who make use of the gymnasium facilities. The Normal College of the Turner organization maintains a summer camp school at Elkhart Lake, Wisconsin, where prospective gymnasium teachers are taught the various methods of swimming in order that they may be fitted to train the pupils they will instruct in the Turnvereins.

It is not just to say that no systematic instruction in swimming is given in this country. In Chicago, New York, Boston, and Springfield are institutions of pedagogical learning that produce swimming instructors. Yet it is perfectly just to say that instruction in swimming is more heterogeneous and less uniformly organized than any other kind of instruction. Indeed, the varieties of method in teaching people to swim are multitudinous. "Use no artificial aids" demands one authority. "Use this or that one" answers a rival. "Teach the breast stroke first" says Mr. Sullivan of Princeton. "Do not teach the breast stroke at all" says the famous Mr. Lou Handley, of New York. "Teach the dog-paddle first" announces another authority. "Learning swimming is individualistic" declares Mr. Barnes from the West. And so—on—and on. All are agreed that the old system—hurl him overboard and let him sink or swim—is now improper; but that is the only agreement; and it may be pointed out that if that method were adopted there would be no need of swimming instructors, so the instructors naturally look upon it with disfavor.

It is proper to say, therefore, that swimming instruction is as yet in a heterogenous state; and the reasons for it are several. In the first place, we have been experimenting with the type of pedagogy only 25 years or so. Then we are teaching one of the most difficult things in the world, teaching what Thorndike would call "form" and "execution" in a process that can never become secondary; it must always be the result of conscious effort, and can never slip into the remoteness of automatic responses like typing by "touch system" on a standard keyboard. In teaching swimming the instructor is confronted more vitally with the problem of teaching confidence and with elemental instincts attempting to vitiate his work.

Must Overcome Natural Reactions

Man is not naturally amphibian. If forced into the water against his will, he revolts by nature. The problem is a problem in vitiating basic reactions—how to avoid the rigidity of fear and acquire the relaxation of easy grace. Many a man has produced his own pet scheme and the texts on swimming will show many pets. For the various uses of swimming there are many strokes. But for the beginner there is but one problem, the problem of counteracting an automatic almost reflex action of the muscles and of slowing the action to a cadence of rhythm and grace. In the Army the breast stroke is preferred because it is the stroke most easily swum with full field equipment, and in competitive circles the "crawl" is the one most generally swum, because it is the most efficient for a man with a silk racing suit. In the Red Cross, they emphasize the side stroke and the "reverse scissor" kick. There you have it.

I feel that swimming instruction has progressed and that American waterfront recreation is becoming increasingly popular and increasingly safe. But I can not feel the systematic study has yet produced any conclusive body of doctrine on the topic, soundly based on psychological laws and proved by widely gathered experimentations. The professional schools of pedagogy have experts working on the topics—or if they have not they ought to have. A scrutiny of the psychology of teaching swimming would not be nearly so academic as a scrutiny of teaching spelling or arithmetic, nor probably so universally used. Yet I somehow feel that such a scrutiny would be eminently more interesting because more concerned with innate prejudices, mental aversions, and general human traits, rather than with mere brain manipulation. I feel that the study has but just begun.

School Life.

THE LARGER ASPECTS OF THE DANCE AS AN EDUCATIONAL ACTIVITY

Margaret Newell H'Doubler

To discuss the subject of this chapter, the "Larger Aspects of the Dance as an Educational Activity" is really to sum up all that has been said before in the course of this discussion in what may be considered a formulation of the fundamental purposes of this type of dancing. Such a formulation is of value to the instructor and her class because it presents briefly the purposes which should inform all our work and the values which should reward our efforts if they have been made in the spirit of these purposes. They are at once the justification and the incentive of our work.

Such a formulation if it is to be intelligible must of necessity be more categorical than is wholly desirable. For any statement of the ends of an art should be an organic synthesis rather than an analysis. Yet the very exigencies of its statement demand a dividing and a marshalling that however systematic they may be, must of necessity let slip through their interstices the finer breath and spirit of the undertaking. It is with an ever-present consciousness of this inevitable difficulty that this final formulation of the larger values of the dance is undertaken.

The first thing to be noted is that all artistic values to be educationally significant must extend beyond the practice.

First of all, as cannot be said too often, the dance affords a source of pleasure to every normal individual. It is only recently that education has come to recognize the importance of recreation in the development of the individual, the necessity of providing everybody with some wholesome means of relaxation and recreation. Anything that affords a fresh source of pleasure is a genuine addition to life. Every

From *The Dance and Its Place in Education* by Margaret Newell H'Doubler, 1925. Reprinted by permission of Harcourt Brace Jovanovich, Inc., chapter IX, pp. 221-229.

normal human being enjoys the exhilaration of rhythmical movement, whether he is working in a group or by himself, and the sense of power that comes from the exercise of all his faculties in harmonious self-expression. And the pleasure is the more significant from the point of view of education in that the true lover of the dance can create its beauty for himself alone in a small room with a Victrola as well as on a stage with all the resources of a dance-drama.

This pleasure is also recreative in the best sense of the word. Too often recreation has been classed with amusement by people who have little respect for the great value of wholesome and refreshing amusement. But recreation is something larger than amusement. At its best it is a genuine re-creation, a relaxation of nervous tension, a freshening of interest and energy, a restoration of depleted powers. That is what the dance may mean. As one student has put it, "I can go into my dancing class tired physically and perhaps mentally, and actually feel rested and relieved. I don't know how to explain it in more æsthetic form, but I have a cleaned-out feeling." In other words relaxation is no mere flopping or collapsing of the body. It is not an end in itself, but a means to a larger end, the winning of that poise which prevents useless expenditure of energy. In experiencing relaxation the aim should be to learn to use just those muscles which are essential to a particular effort or movement. In so doing we relieve that stiffening of parts which constitutes such a serious and unnecessary drain upon our energy. Relaxation when properly used is a conservation of energy, because it promotes the rhythmical flow of energy through a body which is not inhibited.

Then, too, the dance contributes to the pleasure of life in that it helps the individual to express himself. Again, it is only recently that the necessity of self-expression to the healthy mental life of the individual has been realized. The average person tends to be constrained and awkward, and in certain parts of America, largely because of the Puritan tradition, exceedingly reserved. Often his feelings are so effectually repressed that they become thin and barren, and atrophied for want of exercise. Or often, finding no expression that refines or transmutes them, they remain powerful but crude. Again, the average person is both awkward and embarrassed in the presence of any call to totality of physical expression. There are few to-day who have that fine coördination of body, mind and feeling which permits them to move and act with any grace or surety. The average person finds his body, if not an expensive liability, at least an instrument over which he has limited control and with which he can express still less. Every teacher faces the problem therefore in both its forms, the fear of emotion and of emotional expression, and the imprisonment of the personality in a stiff, unresponsive body.

Unfortunate as such a condition is in itself, it would not be so disastrous if men could live without some emotional life. But they cannot. The emotional life of the normal human being must at once find some outlet of expression and some answering satisfaction from his fellows. But too often it is pent up within a hard and unresponsive exterior that repels rather than encourages the much desired fellowship of feeling. Here is where the dance, freeing the body from needless inhibitions, and breaking down some of the unessential reserves, frees the real man for a wider and more satisfying life.

In a more specific sense, the dance affords a medium of expression for those people whom Holmes has described in one of his poems as the singers who die with their songs unsung. There are many of these people who have beautiful things to say, but who can find no words for them. It is hoped that the dance may afford some of them a medium of expression that will give them the joy of embodying in a beautiful form some of the beauty within.

There is still another way in which the ability of the dance to afford the individual opportunity for self-expression serves his larger interests. Only in the present day are psychologists coming to understand those deeper emotional tensions that arise when powerful emotions must be left stopped within the mind with no opportunity for expression. Such an emotional tension often works havoc, where the same emotion understood and recognized with its energies transferred into some other channel becomes a source of personal power. Now it would be absurd to think that simply dancing a less powerful emotion could relieve one of these dominating tensions, but any form of free and joyous self-expression relieves tension, and opens the channels for more free and unimpeded expression of other emotions. Moreover, everyone has had some experience of those wider transmutations of feeling that artistic expression may work. Overwhelming grief has been known to find its greatest solace in comic creation. And the exquisite heightening of consciousness that sometimes results from pain may find its greatest relief in entering sympathetically into the delicate and the whimsical. Any medium of self-expression that gives the individual the chance to enter through the gate of his own experience into a more universal experience to make out of his little personal experience a thing of beauty and of universal significance should serve widely and permanently the health of the emotional life.

At the same time, the dance should help to make the self which the student is trying to express a finer self. That is, the real aim of this type of dancing is the development of personality. Of course, the dance cannot put into the student what is not already within the scope of his natural powers and interests, but it can help to develop the powers he has in the direction of greater fineness and effectiveness. The physical effectiveness to which the dance contributes is a resource for the development of a higher type of personality, for almost as many mental as physical elements go into its making. But of more importance from this point of view is the power of the dance to help the student to cultivate his sympathies, to refine his taste, and to strengthen his preference for the finer things in art and life. These, especially the last, are notable services, for half the battle of conduct is the preference of the higher to the lower.

Moreover, in the dance, the student learns that the narrower, meaner, more selfish and lazy self is not good material out of which to make art. He soon finds that the finer the self which he expresses, the more beautiful will be his creation. In the same way, he finds that the mere idiosyncratic expression of his own peculiarities does not make so interesting a dance for other people to watch as a more universal expression of his theme in which the elements find a wider validity than his nature affords.

That is one of the greatest services of any form of art—its power of carrying the individual beyond himself into a greater world of imaginative experience and understanding. There are few better ways of experiencing an emotion than by working it out in bodily movements. Such a problem makes the student more observant of the people around him, of the rich play of feeling that goes on constantly under the superficial surface of everyday life. And in this imaginative experience, he has a chance to become more understanding, more tolerant, more sympathetically respectful of the inner life of other people since sympathy is the natural fruit of greater understanding.

He may also secure from his dancing valuable experience of the working out of emotion in the lives of men, a knowledge that later may serve him well. Of course, no imaginative preconception of an emotional experience can ever do the reality justice in its fullness and its insistence, but it can make the student more sensitive to the impress of experience, and more intelligent in his reception of it.

Finally, the dance not only satisfies and enriches the student's sense of beauty in one form but in the understanding it gives him of the fundamental elements in all experience of beauty, rhythm, variety within limit, proportion, balance or symmetry, and unity and harmony of the whole, it carries him beyond the limits of one art into the wider realm of all art and makes him a citizen of its world of beauty and meaning. This is one of its greatest services for its ministers to one of man's oldest and most persistent needs. The history of art is the story of man's love for the beautiful, his search for those harmonies of form and meaning which would satisfy his craving for ideal perfection. When one realizes the struggles which the race has made, the numbers of times that it has fallen back into chaos, one acknowledges the gigantic power of this instinct which has led men out of the jungle and kept them resolutely on the upward path. Man's love of beauty is much like the thing of beauty itself; one can analyze and explain its parts, but there is always left over that intangible essence which men call spirit.

But even more important for this wider orientation than the knowledge of beauty is the attitude toward beauty which the dance helps to cultivate. For, here as elsewhere, the accessibility to experience depends largely upon the attitude with which it is approached. It is almost as hard to define the æsthetic attitude as to define beauty. Probably the most effective way of getting at its secret is to see how it works. The most significant characteristic of the æsthetic attitude is a detached, impersonal relation to the object observed. It is a "psychic distance" whereby the observer is enabled to appreciate the object as an object, judging it solely by its own appropriate standards. The æsthetic attitude enables him to love its beauty for the sake of beauty alone, with no thought of "possession, fame or success." It is only when the love of pure color, form, or movement is stronger, either as a result of natural capacity or of training, than the instinct to possess or the desire to win, that the æsthetic attitude is possible, that beauty can be "its own excuse for being." Obviously then, the æsthetic attitude demands a very considerable evolution and civilization of the personal instincts.

It is apparent from this definition, that the æsthetic attitude goes beyond art in the narrower sense. Indeed, there are few experiences toward which one could not maintain an æsthetic attitude, for there are few experiences in life which do not possess elements of beauty. We are so apt to make the mistake of thinking that only the fine arts contain these elements that we need to make the effort to remember that they may be present in anything from "the building of a house to the planning of an attack in football." He who has the æsthetic attitude recognizes this fact and appreciates these elements wherever he finds them, applauding the better artist in every field, even at the cost of his own material interest. Such a point of view will keep him from making the mistake of thinking that a work of art is great simply because it is expensive or is advertised as a model of the latest school, or is an expression of his favorite subject. The æsthetic attitude, then, is not determined by the object with which one is dealing, but rather determines one's relation to the object. It is a purely impersonal appreciation in the abstract of the difficulty of the problem, and the effectiveness and beauty with which it has been solved.

This valuing of things for their own intrinsic merit is the foundation of all the higher levels of human life. It frees the individual from the fetters of place and circumstance, and gives to him the essential possession of all that he can appreciate. And on the other hand, it may free him from himself, from self-seeking, from jealousy, from prejudice, and releases his energies for coöperation with all his like-minded fellows in the creation and appreciation of beauty.

This attitude toward art and life is the greatest contribution of the dance to modern education.

THE MEANS TO THE END

Celia Duel Mosher, M.D.

Associate Professor of Personal Hygiene
and Medical Adviser of Women
Stanford University, California

From the vantage point of three decades spent in observation and study of the surrounding conditions that govern the activities of women, the following conclusions may be of interest, since they are made with the long view which comes only with the passing of the years. All that will be said applies only to physical training and athletics as they concern the average girl and not at all as they concern the training of teachers.

The problems facing the teacher of hygiene and physical training of thirty years ago and those which face the teacher of these subjects to-day, differ greatly; in fact, if the signs of the times be read aright, the problems of to-morrow will differ almost as much. The teacher must always be keenly alert to avoid crystallization, which would mean failure to adapt her methods. She must not think in terms of yesterday in dealing with the girl of to-day, who is the woman of to-morrow. The successful teacher will be the one who recognizes that this most important training is a preparation for the still greater opportunities and duties which lie ahead of our splendid modern women.

From the prevailing type of girl in that earlier period, wasp-waisted and delicate, who fainted in an emergency, lost from five to seven days of her active life each month, and who exceptionally went to college, it seems a long journey to the superbly vigorous college woman of to-day, who calmly meets almost any situation with resourcefulness, seldom loses a day's work, and enters college as a matter of course.

When we consider the woman of thirty years ago and the conditions which produced her, we can understand how the idea of her traditional weakness and incapacity hamper us even now in our work,

Celia Duel Mosher, "The Means to the End," *American Physical Education Review*, vol. XXX, no. 10, December 1925, pp. 535-540.

interfering with the full development of the modern woman herself; and how she is unconsciously influenced by what we were taught, popularly and scientifically. Let us consider some concrete illustrations.

The entering students at Stanford may justly be regarded as a fair sample of the average college woman of the United States,[1] since their birthplaces are found in every state of the union with the exception of two—Delaware and North Carolina. Of the 4,170 Stanford women whose records I recently analyzed, only 1,567 were native born Californians. These records show that the women of thirty years ago were about an inch and two-tenths shorter in height, weighed three or four pounds less and were on the average a little older at the time they entered college than the women of to-day. The ideal of "Female Delicacy of the Sixties," so cleverly portrayed by Miss Reed in the October, 1915, *Century,* to a great extent still prevailed. The curved front corset was almost universal; only here and there a very advanced woman wore a corset-waist. It was so exceptional for a woman to go without a corset that, unless she was financially able to have her coats and clothes made to order, she had the greatest difficulty in being dressed like other girls. To be individually dressed in those days meant something even more serious than it does to-day in the United States. The little girl of that generation, who heard constantly: "You must not do this. You must not do that. It is not lady-like," had this bogy overshadowing her childhood, curbing her normal impulse toward physical activity; she was provided with a doll and expected to sit quietly playing house; and if her muscles demanded activity, her restless spirit to voice her feelings by shouting, if she played ball with her brothers or the neighbor boys, she was designated a "Tomboy."[2] It took a girl of more than ordinary vitality and with unusual parents to withstand this pressure. By the time the average girl entered college, her waist reduced to the then fashionable dimensions by those organs of destruction—the corsets of the day—she had reached puberty and was painfully familiar with the disability of being a woman, lucky if she did not spend at least from three to five days out of school and feel miserable for a week in addition. Required work in gymnastics was the exception. Athletics as we know modern sport did not exist. What impulse had this fragile creature toward physical activity?

The physiologists of that day taught us that women breathed costally and men abdominally. This was supposed to be wise nature's provision against the time of gestation when the gravid uterus would interfere with the descent of the diaphragm.[3] It was therefore most natural that so weak a creature should need the support of her corset to hold her upright. It was a real problem in those days to prevent the wearing of the corset in the gymnasium and on the athletic field. Fashion not only provided her with a corset, but decreed that she should wear voluminous skirts measuring from nine to fifteen feet in circumference; these were further weighted with crinoline and heavy canvas to make them hang properly. Her clothes weighed, on the average, something like from seven to twelve pounds, for under these voluminous skirts were worn seven or eight starched petticoats tied about her poor distorted waist. Sometimes these monstrous clothes were varied by the introduction of the long bustle or the voluminous sleeves, with cloth enough in a single sleeve to make a child's dress. The long, heavy skirts swept street and floors, adding to the unhygienic conditions surrounding the woman. The facts of life were not suitable for this sensitive girl to hear, and she fainted at the most guarded reference to the hygiene or physiology of her own body and its special functions.

There were, to be sure, unusual girls here and there who through some chance of unconventionally minded parents or other good fortune had developed normally, who belonged to that exceptional group of about nineteen in a hundred that did not suffer at their menstrual periods;[4] the waists of these girls were shockingly large and unconstricted; they flew in the face of convention and defiantly suffered the stigma of being different, in wearing no corset, few petticoats, somewhat narrower skirts, and those supported.

In 1894 it was demonstrated that the costal breathing of women was due to constricting clothing; that diaphragmatic breathing might persist to the eighth and even the beginning of the ninth month of pregnancy.[3] In 1911-1913 it was proved that menstruation was not a sickness;[6] that in the vast majority of cases the unduly long periods could be shortened and pain done away with by using the diaphragm and abdominal muscles, by correcting constipation, and by the removal of constricting clothing. In 1917 the difference in the muscular strength was shown to be determined by use and development of the muscles, there being between the strength of men and women no difference which is due to sex as such. In 1921 with more rational dress and much more universal physical activity in general, with the more perfect functioning which follows these changes, we find women increasing in height and weight, while with no special effort to correct the menstrual conditions, in 1916-1917, there were sixty-eight out of each hundred entering women who had no menstrual pain, instead of nineteen in a hundred as was the case in those years of wasp waist, heavy wide skirts, and little or no physical activity.[4]

Accompanying these changes in thought, came changes in activity and fashion. The bicycle arrived and women learned to ride. Bloomers and shorter skirts were necessary for the long trips which women began to make. The small beginnings of basket ball were made. In April, 1896, the Stanford Women's Athletic Association sent a team up to San Francisco to meet the women of the University of California, in perhaps the first intercollegiate game of basket ball played by women. The audience was limited to women. The daily papers, east and west, heralded this first intercollegiate game, and printed pictures of wasp-waisted bloomer-clad figures in amusing plays and attitudes—evolved from the minds of the artists who in absence of any photographs drew on their imaginations for the players as well as the plays. Then the weeklies followed, and even St. Nicholas appeared with an article on the innovation. That girls should play intercollegiate basket ball was a seven days' wonder.

The fashion makers in alarm at all of these many changes in ideas and activities of women tried to reintroduce the hoop skirt, but the automobile, which had come to stay, prevented their adoption, while with lighter, looser clothing women were gradually learning the joy of physical activity. Next the world war called on women to do unprecedented work. To meet the need these splendidly active women, trained in gymnasia and developed on the athletic field, cast aside convention and the remnants of the traditional view of their weakness and did what there was to do, finding themselves no more injured than the men of corresponding weight and size.[5] To save cloth, skirts became shorter and narrower, a fashion which taught more women the comfort of being unhampered by long heavy skirts, the delight of feeling more alive. The corset[7] was more and more relegated to the dump heap, and left to the middle aged and overfat. Why should these splendid young women with perfectly developed bodies—with trunks firm and muscular—put themselves into a surgical appliance?

The bogy of the tomboy has been laid. Go along the streets now in any small town and you will see the school girls out playing ball with brothers and neighbor boys—the promise of a new day, when not only the college woman, but all women will have their chance.

Delicacy is no longer the fashion. If the young woman has not rosy cheeks and red lips, she applies rouge to her cheeks and uses her lip stick. What does it mean? Ask one of them—"I'm pale and I don't look healthy."

So, since health is the fashion, if she is not rosy, she resorts to the camouflage of the color of health, a remnant of the old ideas when the woman was always what she was expected to be.

With the ideal of health firmly fixed in the mind of the girl other problems have come. The delicate girl of the earlier periods had to be urged and tempted into the gymnasium; her splendid successor needs sometimes not urging, but holding back. Usually physically fit, she is not only ready for any physical activity, but is impatient if she loses a single day of work or play and, intoxicated with the sheer joy of living, filled with the sense of freedom and energy, she overdoes, burns the candle at both ends, and, cutting short her sleep, lengthens out her day to undesirable lengths in the effort to crowd all of life into the four years of college. When she comes to class tired and pale, do we notice her as she goes on the floor? Do we see the individual girls, or are we so intent on the perfection of our class achievement or on the winning of the game that the individual is lost in the mass—the emphasis on the means rather than on the end?

Perhaps it was because in the early days, lacking better models, we took over the methods and aims of the men's physical training, modified perhaps, and adapted in some degree to the traditional weakness of women, that we have emphasized so much the athletic ideal. Valuable as is this form of physical work, is it not possible that we may be overstressing athletics at the expense of other equally important forms of physical training? Is there not a chance that we may be including in the discard the very things which would be most valuable? There are simple exercises which can be easily carried over into the everyday life of the girl, encouraging her to continue the habits of exercise when gymnasia and athletic fields are not available. These are the exercises whose practical value we should point out to the girl and which we need rather to emphasize than to discard.

When the class exercise is perfectly carried through, when the team brings home a victory, the results of training are obvious. But who notices the real and vital thing we have done for the individual girl whose personal welfare we have influenced by changing her position from forward to the back field, even at the cost of victory? The girl herself, who naturally prefers the more strenuous position, does not like the change, but she will appreciate it later. The team may be crippled, but turning out winning teams to the glory of the college is not our only aim. Noticing that one of our most efficient students is pale and is pushing herself more than she should, we suggest that she drop out for the remainder of the hour: our class performance is less complete, less perfect, and the visitors in the gallery miss a star performance. But we have done for the individual girl what was best and made possible her more rapid recuperation.

If this girl had broken down, or that girl had been hurt by playing on the team, we cannot say that the individual matters little or that the responsibility should be placed on the girl herself. She ought to have been going to bed earlier; she should not have taken part in the play or danced in the opera; she should have "queened" less;—very true, but the fact remains that her lack of judgment in arranging her life should have been supplemented by our sacrifice of a brilliant effect in our work to her individual well-being.

In this transition period, when we have so many girls who have always exercised and who have had some form of athletics since childhood, we are in danger of thinking of all modern women in terms of physical fitness and arranging our programs too often for ideal conditions. But the weak girl is still with us, and we must find means to gain her cooperation. Hampered as she often is by a holding over of mid-Victorian tradition—often instilled by a mid-Victorian mother—she fails to realize her capacity for health; she needs vision, incentive, belief in physical vigor as attainable for her.

The unpopularity of the corrective class may be because the women have the feeling that if they go into it they are in some way labelled "unfit." If so many of the girls are unwilling to do the work to make themselves perfect, to correct their deficiencies, may it not be because we are too machine-like in our methods, too little human in our dealing with the girl?

One of the serious problems of the teachers of hygiene in the early days was how to induce those delicate undeveloped women to eat enough; to substitute proper nourishing food for the usual lunch of a chocolate éclair and a cup of tea. The vigorous modern girl physically fit, is hungry, and eats not only a hearty lunch, but in season and out is as hard to satisfy as a growing boy. She comes to-day to have us tell her how to keep her weight within reasonable bounds. This again calls for an individual and personal solution.

No present-day problem is of more vital importance to the welfare and efficiency of the women of to-morrow than the question of shoes. And no teacher of hygiene or physical training is doing her full duty toward the future of women who is not meeting this crying need. The Y. W. C. A. has made it possible for us to aid this reform. Most of the manufacturers of shoes have been induced to put out a line of shoes which are hygienically satisfactory. By writing to the Y. W. C. A., 600 Lexington Avenue, New York, anyone may obtain the list of manufacturers and their addresses. The next step is to write to these factories and find what shoe shops in our neighborhood carry these approved shoes. Then start a campaign of education among the girls and supplement teaching with a list of the places in the vicinity where sane shoes may be obtained at a reasonable price. Several results will be accomplished:

(1) The girl will be able to apply practically what she has learned and will get sensible shoes while our teaching is fresh in mind.

(2) The manufacturers will be encouraged in putting out sensible footwear at a price as low as the passing style of undesirable shoes.

(3) The local dealers will be forced to carry sensible shoes.

(4) The women of the next generation will not be disqualified by distorted feet for any demand which the future may make.

This personal, individual side of our work is the side that should be emphasized. The true measure of our success or failure should be the product we turn out and its adaptation to everyday life. The spectacular game is naturally attractive, and the desire to shine is only human. Physical training and athletics, however, are not an end in themselves, but a means to an end. And that end is to train the girl to habits of exercise and to fit her for more perfectly filling her great function in life—motherhood.

In the early days of physical activity for women, dire were the predictions of what was going to happen to the mothers of the next generation. Recently in London one of these school mistresses who prefers the Victorian type of girl has revived these ancient superstitions. Re-inforced by a single woman doctor with a book based on an untenable scientific theory, and backed by excellent newspaper propaganda, the echo of her entertaining statements has come across the Atlantic. In spite of their absurdity it may be worth while to spend a moment in meeting these astonishing and scientifically amusing assertions. The statement that these splendidly developed modern women injure the male germ plasm is a cause of laughter to the student of genetics. The contention that the athletic girl, well developed and perfectly functioning, will bear only girl children, or, if she has sons, that they will be inferior, is contrary to fact. Figures cannot yet be given, but a few instances may be cited.

One of the best all-round athletes among our women—a little girl who was captain of her basket ball team, held the tennis championship again and again, rode her horse like an Indian, played every kind of game, tramped, and more nearly approximated the development of the average boy athlete—is the mother of four stalwart sons. In this later period of life she is strong and well and an important factor in the civic life of her home city.

Another tennis champion sent a picture of her splendid little son and ascribes the vigor and fine development of her little boy to the physical training she had had in college. She ends her letter by saying, "I consider physical training the best possible preparation for motherhood."

It seems evident, then, that our main task in the physical training of women is to set our girls free from the hampering effects of lingering tradition, to create ideals of health, to form habits of exercise which shall carry over into those years beyond the college games, and to develop in all perfection the physical possibilities of women, as workers, wives, mothers.

Bibliography.

1. "Concerning the Size of Women" (Preliminary Note), Reprint from the *California State Journal of Medicine,* Feb. 1921.
   "The Height of College Women" (Second Note), *Medical Woman's Journal,* Nov. 1921.
2. "The Strength of Women," *Proceedings of the First International Conference of Women Physicians,* Vol. I, N. Y., Woman's Press, 1919.
3. *The Frequency of Gall Stones in the United States,* Johns Hopkins Hospital Bulletin, Vol. XII, no. 125, Aug. 1901.
4. "Some of the Causal Factors in the Increased Height of College Women," *Journal of the American Medical Association,* Aug. 18, 1923, Vol. 81, pp. 535-538.
5. *Woman's Physical Freedom,* N. Y. Woman's Press, 1924.
6. "Functional Periodicity in Women and Some of the Modifying Factors" (Second Note), *California State Journal Medical Association,* Jan. and Feb. 1911; American Physical Education Review, Nov. 1911.
7. *Proceedings of the First International Conference of Women Physicians,* Vol. I, pp. 12 and 154, N. Y., Woman's Press, 1919.

THE MEASUREMENT OF ACHIEVEMENT IN PHYSICAL EDUCATION*

David K. Brace, Ph.D.
Professor of Physical Education
School of Education
University of Texas
Austin, Texas

Physical education is now included in all modern courses of study. The amount of time devoted to this subject has been, on the whole, steadily on the increase. Our teachers are now better trained than ever before, both as to general and as to professional preparation.

The subject matter and methods of physical education have improved and developed in step with education in general. The modern program, at its best, is vastly improved over the old formal program, at its best. Opportunities for the development of the pupil are no longer confined to his physical side, but now provide situations which favor mental and social development as well.

The aims, or general objectives, of a modern natural program, at first glance, do not appear to differ greatly from those of the formal programs common a few years ago and still found in some parts of the country. There is, however, a real difference, which is due to the fact that the modern program provides activities through which the expressed objectives may be reached, while the older programs made no such provision.

An illustration may be seen in the case of a specific aim, namely, the development of initiative. This has long been an aim of instruction in physical education and yet there is practically no possibility of developing initiative through calisthenics or other exercises given on command from the teacher. The development of the initiative of the pupil may be expected only where he is given opportunity to exercise choice in the things he does and in how he does them. The mere statement of objectives does not at all mean that they will be attained.

David K. Brace, "The Measurement of Achievement in Physical Education," *American Physical Education Review,* vol. XXXII, no. 8, October 1927, pp. 563-568.

*Read before the Physical Education Section of the Texas State Teachers Association at El Paso, Texas, November, 1926.

It becomes necessary, therefore, to try to determine the degree to which objectives are satisfied by the activities taught in the physical education program. Those advocating a program watch the results of their teaching and hold some belief as to the extent to which the objectives set up are being attained. But the judgment of one teacher on this point may differ widely from the judgment of another and equally capable teacher. It is easily apparent that the best judgment will be that which makes the best use of information or data in its support.

Achievement in physical education, as in any other subject, is the attainment of objectives. Evaluation of the type of activities taught, of the method of teaching them, and of the success of the teacher demands a determination of the extent to which specific objectives have been achieved. In other words, the measurement of achievement is essential to efficient instruction in physical education.

Accepting the establishment of this premise it will be the remaining purpose of this paper to show that the measurement of achievement in physical education demands:

(1) Establishment of specific objectives to be achieved.
(2) Measurement of the achievement of these objectives.

We can know whether or not and to what extent students are achieving only in so far as we know what they are to try to achieve. We can tell when a pupil has learned to recite the multiplication table because the multiplication table is a definite and specific objective. So, in other phases of education there are specific bits of information and specific skills and attitudes to be learned. Achievement is expressed in terms of the mastery of these specific objectives.

The measurement of achievement in education demands, first of all, definite and specific educational objectives. Unless we can state in specific terms just what are our objectives in physical education, we shall certainly be unable to measure pupil achievement wisely. We will be unable to tell whether or not our teaching methods are accomplishing that which we have expected them to accomplish.

It is necessary to understand and to be able to state clearly and in specific terms just what it is that we are aiming at, *i.e.*, just what are the objectives of instruction. The more general and the more vague our statement, the more difficult and uncertain will be our knowledge of attainment. The more concrete and specific the statement of our objectives the easier and more certain will be our knowledge of their attainment.

Heretofore programs of physical education have rather generally failed to state objectives in specific and detailed form. We have stated them in such terms as bodily strength, health, sportsmanship, neuromuscular coördination, athletic skill, etc. But we have failed to state just what coördination should be developed and at just what age, and to just what degree of proficiency this development should occur.

Good posture may be taken as an illustration. We believe physical education should help pupils to develop good posture. However, few courses of study explain specifically what constitutes good posture in standing. Still fewer programs state what constitutes good posture in sitting, in lying, and in performance of physical activities, such as play and athletics. Few courses of study state what achievement in posture should be expected of first grade pupils, of fourth grade pupils, of sixth grade pupils, of junior high school pupils, and of college pupils. Perhaps all pupils should be held to a single standard, but the chances are that the development of good posture occurs through gradual stages, or at least differs with different ages.

We are at once confronted by the fact that our difficulty in stating objectives in specific terms is due to the fact that we do not have the necessary exact information to allow us to make valid assertions. We do not know just what weight the average sixth grade boy should be able to lift, just how fast he should be able to run forty yards, just how far he should be able to jump from a run, just how accurately he should be able to throw, or just how much sportsmanship he should display in a specific game.

On some of these points we do have sufficient data to enable us to state, tentatively, specific objectives. On other points we have practically no objective evidence. It is necessary that our efforts in gathering such data be continued and increased.

Until there is sufficient evidence we may be compelled to state our objectives in more general terms. We should, however, see them as clearly as possible and state them as specifically as possible. We should always be revising them and making them more definite. The following list of objectives relating to certain elementary skills are more detailed than will be found in most courses of study and yet have retained a certain indefiniteness necessitated by absence of accurate data.

Running.

1. Run forward, backward, sideward.
2. Run carrying an object, as a ball.
3. Run at a jog 220 yards, 4th grade; 440 yards, 6th grade; 660 yards, 8th grade.
4. Run at full speed 60 yards, 8th grade.
5. Run in a circle.

6. Run, stop, and turn and run back.
7. Run in a zigzag fashion.
8. Run holding a comrade's hand.

Jumping.

1. Leap and land on both feet.
2. Leap (from one foot and land on the other), holding the balance.
3. Jump (from both feet) and land on both feet, holding balance.
4. Jump, landing on either foot.
5. Leap over an object knee high.
6. Jump down from a height knee high.
7. Run and leap.
8. Run and jump.
9. Run and jump over an object knee high.
10. Run and jump a distance equal to own height.
11. Several consecutive runs and leaps.
12. Hop, step, and jump.
13. Three continuous jumps forward.
14. Vault an object (fence, buck, etc.,) waist high.

Throwing and Catching.

1. Toss a large ball with two hands.
2. Throw an indoor baseball or other small ball a fair distance.
3. Play catch with a comrade.
4. Catch and throw while on the run.
5. Catch a bouncing football.
6. Catch a large ball, as basketball or football.

Batting and Striking.

1. Bat a ball, with fair form and success.
2. Bat a ball with the hand.
3. Strike a small ball on the bounce, as in handball.
4. Bat a tennis ball with a racket.
5. Use the arms to protect against a blow.

Swimming.

1. Ability to hold the breath under water for at least ten seconds.
2. Stand and walk in water shoulder deep.
3. Ability to float on the face a few seconds.
4. Ability to stand from a face submerged floating position.
5. Float on the back with the assistance of the hands.

6. Regain standing position from floating on the back.
7. Ability to come to the surface from a position under water.
8. Pick up an object from the bottom in water waist deep.
9. Swim with elementary back stroke.
10. Swim on the face a distance of twenty feet.
11. Assist a playmate from water, waist deep.
12. Coil and throw a life line.
13. Perform artificial respiration.

Dancing and Rhythm.

1. Execute simple steps and rhythm with music, as run, skip, hop, slide, etc.
2. Keep time while marching.
3. Perform simple folk dances and gymnastic dances.
4. Proper form in social dancing (including executing dance technique).

Where shall these objectives come from, how shall we get them? In the final analysis they must come from the pupils themselves. Adults must not sit down and decide what children should be able to achieve. They must get their knowledge from the actual achievement of pupils and measured in accurate units of some sort.

We must know the abilities and capacities of average pupils of the kind of group with which we are dealing in order to set standards of achievement. It is apparent that the accurate measurement of pupil achievement in terms of abilities and capacities is essential to the formulation of specific objectives.

I have tried to show: (1) That pupil achievement should be expressed in terms of specific things, or objectives, to be accomplished; (2) That a definite knowledge of achievement demands a definite and concrete statement of specific objectives; (3) That the definite determination of objectives should come from an accurate measurement of pupil performance and not from subjective opinion.

Under such a treatment, a course of study for sixth grade girls, for example, would state in more or less definite terms, objectives relating to health and physical fitness, to posture and bodily mechanics, to physical skills to be acquired, to information to be gained, and to habits and attitudes to be formed. Such objectives would be stated in terms as definite and as detailed as available data would permit.

The second part of the problem of measuring achievement in physical education relates to the tests and methods to be used.

Such measurement has the prerequisites of other educational testing, among which may be mentioned the following.[1]

(1) Tests and methods used must be valid, *i.e.*, really measure what they are supposed to measure.

(2) Tests must have reliability and objectivity allowing them to be given by the same or different examiners, to the same pupils at the same or different times, with equal results.

(3) Tests must be accurate. They must be objectively measured by appropriate units which are absolutely equal at all points on the scale. These units should be expressed in figures where possible.

(4) Tests should have satisfactory norms determined in relation to age, grade, sex, and nationality.

(5) The directions and procedure should be standardized and be as simple and clear as possible.

Lack of time prevents mention of a large number of additional characteristics which good tests should display.

Remembering that it is the function of achievement tests to measure pupil attainment, let us consider some illustrations. Suppose, for example, a high school class of boys is being instructed in basket ball. One of the skills to be mastered is that of "shooting fouls." This activity is well standardized. The equipment used and the regulations controlling it are exact and uniform. Achievement is measured in terms of successful throws out of the total number of trials. It is a valid test because it is identical with the skill being measured. This particular test might also be called a practice test and is an unique illustration. It is not, however, the best test of general skill in "shooting baskets."

If we wish to measure skill in handling a basket ball rapidly, *i.e.*, catching and passing it, some other test must be used. The speed pass[2] is such a test. This consists of standing eight feet from a brick or other solid wall and bouncing a tightly inflated basket ball against the wall and catching it on the rebound. The push pass or chest pass must be used and the ball is passed and caught ten times in succession as rapidly as possible. The score is the time, taken with a stop-watch, from the instant that the first pass strikes the wall to the instant that the tenth pass strikes the wall.

It will be seen that this test meets the criteria of a good test. It is measured in objective units. The directions and equipment are simple and uniform. It is non-coachable, since students are not given practice in taking the test, but get their practice through play and other teaching methods.[3]

Track and field events constitute another illustration of achievement tests. Probably most of us have used these, as tests of our ability to teach running, jumping, and throwing.

We have available achievement tests in more or less experimental form for all of the major sports such as football, basket ball, baseball, track and field, soccer, field hockey, tennis, and swimming.[4]

Few of these tests are out of the experimental stage, many of them are not accurately constructed, and few provide scales or norms to allow the best use of scores. All of them, however, will be found instructive and useful by the teacher who wishes to begin the accurate measurement of the achievement of pupils.

The decathlon tests, of Hetherington, used in California, posture tests, apparatus tests, and most of the so-called physical efficiency tests[5] are examples of achievement tests. They measure the learning of pupils in physical education activities.

The achievement tests mentioned so far have mainly had to do with athletic game skills taught in the junior and senior high schools and in colleges. It is, however, equally necessary that the elementary school teacher measure pupil achievement in the activities of physical education.

If objectives are expressed in specific and concrete terms achievement in them may be measured simply on the basis of success and failure. The following list of objectives relating to ability in hanging and climbing will serve as an illustration.

(1) Ability to hang by either hand a few seconds.
(2) Hang by both hands.
(3) Hang and bring both knees up to the chest.
(4) Hang and swing.
(5) Ability to climb a rope.
(6) Ability to come down a rope or pole a distance of twenty feet.
(7) Ability to climb up and descend a ladder.
(8) Climb and descend a rope ladder.
(9) Travel forward and backward while hanging on an overhead bar or horizontal ladder.
(10) Hang from a bar, high horizontal ladder, or rope and climb up onto the bar, etc.
(11) Jump and catch a bar above the reach of the upstretched hands.
(12) Mount to riding position on bar, fence, etc., waist high.

It will be noticed that the above list of objectives are specific in one sense and are yet general in that exact distances, speed, and form are not set down. Until we know just what pupils of different ages or sex may be expected to accomplish, it may be necessary to state objectives in this way.

It is important to note that such objectives are much more definite than would be the case if they were all lumped under the one heading of "hanging and climbing."

An elementary school teacher could easily examine her pupils, as to their ability to perform or to fail in each of the activities listed. She would also be able to set up degrees of difficulty and so secure finer grading of achievement. If proper criteria of test construction were followed, she would be able to develop and standardize achievement tests which would measure the varying degrees of pupil proficiency in meeting the objectives of her program.

We all know that achievement is not confined to physical skills. Successful teaching in physical education should result in achievement in the fields of attitudes and appreciations, and knowledge. The following objectives relating to attitudes and appreciations may be cited.

Attitudes and Appreciations.

1. Obey the rules when not watched.
2. Willingness to take turns.
3. Readiness to help playmates.
4. Subjecting personal desires to the good of the group or team.
5. Obeying the captain or leader.
6. Willingness to be selected as a leader on the basis of merit only.
7. The habit of not taking adversity as a personal affront.
8. Willingness to cheer a good performance even if made by an opponent.
9. Ability to lose without complaint or making alibis.
10. Ability to win with modesty.
11. Perseverance in the face of adversity.
12. Honesty in play.
13. Good sportsmanship.
14. Self-evaluation on a rational basis.
15. Optimism and cheerfulness.
16. Calmness and control.
17. Appreciation of good performance when "choosing-up."

Some objectives relating to information are as follows.

Information.

1. The elements of good sportsmanship.
2. Rules of simple group games.
3. Rules of playground ball or baseball.
4. Rules of handball.

5. The characteristics of a good captain.
6. The duties of a teammate.
7. The proper execution of fundamental motor techniques.
8. How to swim, run, skate, throw, bat, kick, climb, etc.
9. What constitutes a good performance.
10. How to go about learning new skills.
11. How to protect the body when falling.
12. How to help playmates.
13. Simple first-aid treatments.
14. How to care for the health when engaged in active play.
15. How to relax, rest and conserve energy during activity.
16. The essential elements of good form in motor activities.
17. How to evaluate success.
18. What steps to take to improve matters if one's efforts, or one's team's efforts seem poor.
19. How to play safely.
20. How to regard fear and what to really fear.
21. How to keep from getting excited.

Enough has doubtless been said to show the great possibilities in more accurate and scientific measurement of pupil achievement in physical education. Any teacher of ordinary ability, training and enthusiasm can make a beginning in the objective measurement of achievement. All that is necessary is that he or she get into definite and specific form a statement of the objectives of the program of instruction and then keep accurate records in numerical units, if possible, of what achievement each pupil makes in the specific objectives selected.

If pupils are given an opportunity to have considerable voice in selecting objectives and are used in measuring and recording achievement, the work of the teacher will be greatly lessened. Pupils will be much more interested in their work when they can understand and see the results they accomplish in activities they, themselves, have helped select.

The teacher using such methods will be able to diagnose difficulties and to grade and promote pupils on a logical and scientific basis. Such methods are followed in teaching other school subjects, they should be used in teaching physical education.

Perhaps a word should be said as to the difference between achievement tests and motor ability tests. The latter are intended to measure the amount of native motor ability that a pupil possesses and can bring to bear in making achievement. True motor ability tests will not be used to measure specific instruction or learning. Achievement tests are only intended to measure learning. Of course, achievement tests covering a wide variety of activities in which all pupils have had equal learning opportunity will give an indication of motor ability. There are, however, motor ability tests which can produce the same information about any sized class in a single lesson period and should be used for this purpose.[6] A discussion of these tests is not within the scope of this paper.

In conclusion, two steps have been presented as being necessary to the measurement of achievement in physical education. The first was the establishment of specific objectives to be achieved. The second was the accurate measurement of the achievement of these objectives by use of tests accurately constructed and measured in comparable units.

References

1. McCall, Wm. A., "How to Experiment in Education," pp. 82-83.
2. "Testing Basket Ball Technique," D. K. Brace, American Physical Education Review, April, 1924.
3. This and other basket ball achievement tests are described and scaled in the American Physical Education Review, April, 1924 and in *Measuring Motor Ability,* D. K. Brace, A. S. Barnes and Co., 1927.
4. 1. *Football:* "Reprint on Motor Ability Tests," American Physical Education Review, March, 1926.
   2. *Basket Ball:* previously referred to.
   3. *Baseball:* Wardlaw, C. D., *Fundamentals of Baseball,* Scribners, 1925; and Brace, D. K., *Measuring Motor Ability,* A. S. Barnes and Co., 1927.
   4. *Soccer:* Brace, D. K., *Measuring Motor Ability,* A. S. Barnes and Co.
   5. *Field Hockey:* Frost and Cubberly, *Field Hockey and Soccer for Women;* also *Report on Motor Ability Tests.*
   6. *Tennis:* Reilley, *Rational Athletics, Report on Motor Ability Tests,* and Anderson, *Tennis for Women,* A. S. Barnes and Co.
   7. *Track and Field:* Spalding Handbook.
   8. *Swimming: Swimming in all its Branches,* Sheffield, L., and N.
5. Proceedings of Athletic Research Society, 1920-1921.
6. Brace, D. K., *Measuring Motor Ability, and Scale of Motor Ability Tests,* A. S. Barnes and Co., New York City, 1927.

THE CONTRIBUTION OF PHYSICAL EDUCATION TO THE EDUCATION OF THE COLLEGE STUDENT*

By Jesse Feiring Williams, M.D.
Professor of Physical Education
Teachers College

We are gathered here to-day to dedicate the Women's Building. At best it can be only an awkward gesture that we make. Words never substitute for deeds, and the faithful work of those who have builded here outstrips in power and direction any words of ours to express its worth. Why try to match with symbols of pride, zeal, or enthusiasm the vision of those who conceived this building; the patience, courage, and high purpose of those who directed its construction; or even the skill, strength, and pride in work well done of those who labored to fashion the raw materials of nature into this edifice of man?

But in a larger view there is ample reason for the efforts we make. Words alone avail to express the purpose that may call the women of the college to dedicate themselves to the causes and achievements which beckon as they come up to the university. Here is no idle dream; this is no vain hope. Within this building, personifying its purposes, plans, and outcomes, is enshrined a lovely womanhood. What could be more fitting than the dedication of the women of this college to the realization of their best, the fulfillment of their possibilities, the accomplishment of their goals? Only in this way can a mere building come to have meaning.

When a biologist places upon the stage of his microscope the thin sections that show the development of the cell, he has upon that bit of glass one of the wonders of the world. There is the picture of vast changes in minute detail. The biologist looks and wonders. He sees

Jesse Feiring Williams, "The Contribution of Physical Education to the Education of the College Student," *Teachers College Record*, November 1927, pp. 109-121.

*An Address at the dedication of the Women's Building of the Oregon State Agricultural College, Corvallis, Oregon, on May 7, 1927.

the shift of tissues from one part to another, and follows in successive sections the outcomes of great pioneering projects in protoplasm.

When a university receives upon the stage of college life a student enlisted in the enterprise of education—another name for development—it takes unto itself a great adventuring in human life. There are to be vast changes, but they are not subject to microscopic analysis. The university prepares carefully for this experiment. It arranges curricula, assembles staffs, and erects buildings. As the years pass, and generations of students and faculties come and go, these devices of the institution are touched by what is known as the Spirit of the College. Does not the Spirit that broods over a college say, as it watches the parade of possibilities upon the stage of university education, "Here is a bit of life! What can be done to help that life realize its potentialities?" As the Spirit of this college comes to find a home in the Women's Building, will it not croon softly to itself of the future for Oregon womanhood?

There are remarkable differences as well as similarities between the laboratory of the biologist and the workshop of college life. The worker with the microscope observes changes, but he is powerless to alter them. Embryonal cells march in majesty across his stage to form the structures and to shape the functions which ultimately he must describe. But in the laboratory of university education these early biological outlines have been laid. The marvel in the college student is not the organization of tissues, nor the interdependence of organs, but the nascent possibilities to be changed into realities in human lives, the development of new powers, sound guides, and worthy standards. "There," says the biologist, pointing to his slide, "is the *record* of a great transformation." "Here," says the university, as it welcomes the student, "is the *promise* of great transformations."

My theme, to-day, deals with the contribution of physical education to such transformations, with the gift it promises to the education of the college student. This is no simple theme, although some would not appreciate that the contribution of physical education is anything worth talking about. Guided by popular beliefs, its contribution could be stated in terms of certain physical exercises, considerable vocal gymnastics at games, and a curious mixture of terpsichorean stunts and heliotherapy. To some persons physical education is a fad, a newfangled idea, a frill upon the educational garment that in many ways seems to lack the wearing quality, the fastness of color, and the utility that characterized the product of the little red schoolhouse two generations ago.

To justify the erection of this building that we dedicate to-day, to warrant your coming here, to excuse my trip across the continent for this occasion, physical education must be more than an exercise, more than raucous sounds, more than futile, even though aesthetic, movements.

The first physical educator was the parent who taught his child to throw, to jump, and to climb, and, in company with others, instructed him in the standards of the group to which he belonged. Savage initiations, as a part of the introduction to responsible manhood and womanhood and to social standards, have always been taught by the elders to the young. Along these lines of effort flow the source and purpose of physical education: to train the intelligence, to develop the organic systems, to master certain fundamental skills inherent in the individual's nature under the force of the social requirements; and to shape the young to understand, interpret, and uphold the standards of conduct approved by the group.

Little is known of physical education in these earliest days of savagery. There are no chronicles to tell us the complete story. Scattered bits of information are revealed by the explorations of geologists and anthropologists; the life activities of primitive peoples to-day help to portray the picture of this early education, but it is all partial, limited, and only in outline.

The plain truth of the matter is that little is known of educational beginnings previous to the time when the Greeks made their contribution to the world. We go back to the Greeks to explain many things, and particularly to understand the relationship between physical education on the skill side and physical education on the side of the social education of the citizen. We do not stop there, however. The remarkable conception of Greek thinkers who related gymnastics and music for the development of the individual; the altogether different notion in Rome that viewed physical education as an agency for military purposes; and then later, the withering hand of asceticism laid upon the physical body of man,—all represent variations of the same effort that surged through primitive man, driving him to train the young to meet social needs. When the philosophy of the day was harmony and beauty, when civil power through military conquest was the *summum bonum,* when the goal of man's effort was to reach God by denial of life, and when the vagaries of St. Augustine's early days pointed out the handicaps to spiritual excellence, physical education was turned or twisted this way or that to serve the needs of the group concerned. Even Vittorino da Feltra at Mantua, in the year before America was discovered, incorporated in his school, "La Casa

Giocosa," the ideas of the group of noblemen that influenced his thoughts and acts.

The contribution of physical education in any situation, at any time, or in any place is to be measured in terms of the ideas that control it. This has always been so. The conspicuous, nationalistic developments of physical education illustrate the force of political, economic, and social influences shaping its contribution. Germany at the mercy of Napoleon, lack of unity among the German peoples, and the force of feudalism in their social institutions are the conditioning factors that controlled physical education in Germany during the nineteenth century. Physical education, an aspect of education engaged in the procedure of handling human beings, must use methods that conform to prevailing ideas. Thus, one understands the drill room flavor of Swedish gymnastics, and sees in the military character of Swedish physical education the loss of Finland and the Alan Islands to Russia, the abdication of Gustavus IV, and the blockade of Swedish ports by British battleships.

In simple agricultural communities free from the constant threat of war and the ambitions of kings and princes, the life activities of the people themselves furnish a kind of motor training. There is no need of mass drill; occupations serve in a limited way the developmental needs of the people. What such simple living lacks in enthusiasms, in joyousness, in personal and social culture, it makes up in part by the rigor and hardiness of life. But with the coming together of peoples into cities, the organization of state and national life, the migration and rapid communication of citizens, a set of influences and associated ideas begins to shape physical education in relation to the needs of the time and place.

For the first one hundred and twenty-five years of our nation's existence, the people were engaged in a frontier type of life. Establishing independence, reclaiming a wilderness, building the physical body of the nation were the chief ends. Conquering a continent called for resourcefulness, initiative, leadership, and independence in the citizens. In these years, life in the United States was free from the fungus of feudalism. We have been opposed to military developments; even the fervor of 1918 was unable to establish universal military service.

Nevertheless, European nations, with their ideas of nobility, of discipline for the masses, of privilege, have been too frequently our examples. The influence of a pseudo-nobility and war captains, posing as men who knew how to rule, had to compete with the ideas of the common people and their notions of democracy. It was the ideas of John Quincy Adams versus those of Andrew Jackson.

The third decade of the nineteenth century saw sporadic efforts at physical education in the work of Partridge, with his military academies, the German refugees, Beck, Follen, and Lieber, the manual labor movement, and the calisthenics of Catherine Beecher. But the nation was primarily engaged in agriculture and its allied affairs. The energy of the population was poured out in wresting from nature a livelihood. It was a grim business, and no time was left for leisure and little for education. The ideas of personal development and self-expression had little opportunity for realization.

With the industrial revolution came remarkable changes. New peoples coming into the cities found the church and the private and charity schools unable to meet the educational needs. "In 1833," says Cubberley, "it was estimated that one-eighth of the total population of New York City was composed of public paupers and criminals, while the city had one saloon for every eighty men, women, and children in the total population." The strict moral code of the rural districts, living remnants of Puritanism, broke down in the cities, and the political ideals of those "fit to rule" fought in the open against the claims of the common man.

After the Civil War, the industrial revolution opened new and varied economic opportunities which were eagerly grasped, with the result that in the latter half of nineteenth century the distribution of the population in rural and urban communities was altered profoundly, and the factory, instead of the home, became the center of vocational life for many people.

The factory system and urban life changed the social groups in many ways, so that from time to time people questioned concerning the need of proper physical development. Consequently, at the sessions of the famous Physical Training Conference held in Boston, in 1889, the outstanding view regarding physical education was that its purpose was corrective rather than developmental. Moreover, the Conference was not a meeting of specialists in physical education alone; it was also attended by educators, and these school people set up a number of conditions that reflected the ideas they had concerning the function of education. In effect, the school men proposed that any physical training that was to be taken into the school must require very little time, must be inexpensive, must not demand specially trained teachers, must conduct its activities in the classroom, and must not require equipment.

In brief, this represents the beginning of physical education in the schools of the United States. No study was made of the kind of activities boys and girls need for developmental purposes, nor of the uses to which physical activities can be put in the setting up and acquirement of standards of conduct. The schoolroom stoop and physical exercises loomed large as the problems. A ready cure was offered for a very complex disturbance, with the results which usually characterize the use of such unscientific methods. An antiseptic request will always produce a sterilized program.

This type of physical training (for it was nothing more than a training procedure) never caught the imagination of boys and girls. The child was asked to go through an innumerable number of stupid "posturings" and his whole being was calling for a kind of activity based on the neuron connections already set up and organized in his nervous system. Consequently, from time to time, youth took into its own hands the business of physical education. In colleges and high schools, teams were organized for the playing of games, meets were held with other teams, and soon the institutions represented found themselves involved in disputes, financial arrangements, and real embarrassments. Not yet appreciating the place of physical education in the education of young people, school men set up faculty advisors, or managers, to control an activity with which they had little sympathy and no understanding.

Thus, quite characteristically, examples of two types of physical education in the school may be found. One is composed of artificial exercises that arose in response to a group of ideas wholly foreign to the traits, characteristics, and needs of American boys and girls, and that are justified by those who propose them on the grounds of correction of defects, acquirement of health, or promotion of military discipline. That such exercises, given *en masse*, do not correct the defects which require accurate diagnosis and specific, individual treatment, that they are not conducive to health interpreted in the light of present-day available knowledge, and that the discipline they promote is that of the barracks, is not yet sufficiently understood by educators.

The other type is represented by the extreme development of competitive athletics that arose as a natural activity of youth, stimulated by the commercial and advertising values of games, and without the educational leadership which such an activity should attract. The early days of sport in America bear the marks of the gambler, pugilist, and "plug-ugly." Some of its present-day manifestations reveal these early scars. Games have been continued, however, not so much because educators desired them as educative activities, but because those in control were helpless to prevent them, or because the leaders saw in them an advertising asset. It has rarely occurred to educators to use physical education for worthwhile educational goals. If one wished to teach children the value of international good-will, one would not select as a teacher a believer in war. If one desired to teach science in the schools, one would not place the children under the guidance of an anti-vivisectionist or an anti-vaccinationist. In the teaching of school games, however, the teacher (coach) is selected frequently, not because of his educational qualifications but because of his reputed ability to turn out a winning team. That he may be a cussing, raving, roaring type of bully makes little difference, because, too frequently, the goals are commercial rather than educational.

In the light of the experience of other nations, and the forces of our own national life, physical education to-day in the American college is being subjected to careful analysis. Educators are asking questions concerning aims, objectives, procedures, and results of its program. Quite clearly the contribution of physical education to the development of the college student is conditioned by the answers to such questions. Those who are interested enough to inquire will find several distinctive qualities in the mood that characterizes those who deal with the problem.

In the first place, science is being invoked as never before. There is a passion to get at the facts, to know the truth. Traditional procedures are being overturned not for the purpose of indulging in mere iconoclastic revelry, but to examine their bases, and to evaluate their claim to support. Health practices based on superstitions are questioned, and their counterpart among primitive peoples helps truth seekers to understand the almost universal appeal of the magical and mysterious. As a result this mood is unwilling to tolerate the superstitious, whenever science has something to report. Students of history remember that throughout the centuries fetish power has always been cheap. Nothing is easier than thinking against the facts! Moreover, magic has always been economical down to a certain point. St. Simeon Stylites on his pillar, seeking,

> "The meed of saints, the white robe and the palm,"

could deny the physical, could escape the facts, could seek his kind of excellence. Such was fetish power and magic. It cost nothing; passers-by could be healed by merely touching the garments of such saints. In such an atmosphere no university could afford to construct a costly building devoted largely to the physical activities of students, when an occult force, at no expense, could be followed as a pathway to excellence. Consequently, in the great universities of the Middle Ages no provision was ever made for the physical education of the students. Abelard, at Paris, gathered about him great numbers of students, but education, whether in theology, law, medicine, or philosophy, served occult and magical masters.

How far we are removed to-day from the fettered existence of the cathedral schools of France and Italy! Man's place in nature, dignified, worthy, acceptable, stands free from the tyranny of superstition and magic that challenged Luther, Montaigne, Locke, Bacon, and Spencer. And yet this scientific spirit must still contest with vestiges of scholasticism. Scotus Erigena rules no university to-day, but his spirit lurks in the academic mind that frowns on play, deprecates recreation, and leads to a narrowness in university education that sacrifices the physical for so-called mental gains.

In the second place, physical education is emphasizing to-day as never before the unity of mind and body. This view sees life as a totality. Correct in their appraisement that the cult of muscle is ludicrous, those who worship at the altar of mental development too frequently neglect the implications that should follow from thorough exploration of the facts of the social inheritance. "Socrates with a headache" is always preferable to a brainless Hercules, but the modern mood in physical education seeks to evaluate the physical in terms of mental and spiritual worth. It is the plain truth of the matter that no individual, no community, no nation can depend upon any one aspect of life for the whole of living. Deification of the physical, mental, or spiritual alone leads to disaster.

In A.D. 410, the barbarians sacked Rome. Alaric fell upon a slave-ridden nation and rent it asunder. Agricultural Western Europe went to pieces. The people were disturbed because Christianity, conceived by them as a magical force, had not been an effective barrier against the barbarian. In the failure of the Cross to protect the citizens from the horrors of Alaric's wrath, the church turned to Bishop Augustine of Hippo. He answered by defending the Civitas Dei which had taken the place of Civitas Romae. Physical education in its modern mood seeks no single justification for its service to man. Draft boards may reveal unparalleled physical deterioration in our young men, but no modern physical educator, sensitive to the mood of the profession, will hurry from Hippo to Rome to proclaim the superiority of Civitas Corporis over Civitas Animae. Neither the body nor the mind alone supplies an answer to the vexing problems of modern life. Science has taught too well! Physical education views man as a unity. Not yet knowing the possibilities of the physical, it follows Aristotle in declaring also that we shall never know until the physical finds its true function as instrument for the spirit. Materialism consists not in frank recognition of the physical, but in assigning it to a spurious supremacy. "There can be no materialism in utmost emphasis upon physical education," writes MacCunn, "so long as 'Body for the sake of soul' is, as it was with Plato, the presiding principle of educational action."

This recasting of the scene for physical education is no superficial move but a tendency of deeper growth. It holds that we need to aim higher than health, than victorious teams, than strong muscles, than profuse perspiration. It sees physical education primarily as a way of living, and seeks to conduct its activities so as to set a standard that will surpass the average and the commonplace. There is in such a view something of the loftier virtues of courage, endurance, and strength, the natural attributes of play, imagination, joyousness, and pride, and through it all, the spirit of splendid living,—honest, worthy, competent.

In the third place, nothing seems clearer than the inevitable character of the forces shaping the place of physical education in American life. While past generations may have thought of it as a rehabilitating procedure devised to serve restorative and therapeutic purposes, the steady march of social forces shifts the emphasis. The swing of the population to the cities, the increasing tendency to industrialize society, the social and political ideals of the citizens, demand full recognition in all plans for education. American life is extremely complex, and yet the main currents are well marked and clearly defined. To a people with social and political beliefs which express a faith in and desire for freedom, liberty, and individual development, there has come an unprecedented material prosperity. Out of this tremendous economic development has resulted an unheard of amount of leisure for great numbers of the people.

The increase of leisure time does not itself guarantee richness and fullness of life. People may have a great deal of free time and not know what to do with it. The tremendous financial success of commercial recreation indicates, however, leisure time opportunities and some of the interests of the people.

It must be clear that the only recreation that rebuilds is an active kind. Such active recreation may range all the way from the minor arts to the major ones; but if there be a saving grace in any of them, it will come through the opportunity for the individual to lose himself in the world of the activity that he pursues. This may be in the dance, in painting, in camping, in writing, in a hundred activities that are carried on, not for any economic returns, but for the mere love of the thing.

The craftsmen of two generations ago in this country, as in some few places in the world to-day, got joy out of the work they did. To-day, too frequently, the industrial worker in shop and factory works only for the monetary return, and as soon as he is free from the demands of the schedule he is eager to get away, and then for him, if possible, comes the chance to do something that provides satisfaction. He works to earn money with the hope that in some way he can buy happiness. He has never had a philosophy to help him understand that happiness cannot be bought, for like beauty it comes from within and cannot be acquired from without. Thus the happiness that the industrial worker finds is likely to be the kind catered to by professional and commercialized forms of recreation, and these, too frequently, have been associated with characteristic and lewdsome forms of vice. Stevenson is reported to have said, "One may travel the whole world in search for beauty and never find it unless he has it with him in his heart."

But to speak of joy of work when the whole process is the repetitive task of placing nuts on bolts, or throwing levers, or stacking trays, or watching for a thread to break in the rapid and phantasmagoric evolutions of a textile machine, is to call for that species of unbelief that greeted Dr. Eliot's address on the rights, duties, and privileges of the manual laborer. Cabot's analysis of the main features of this problem indicates clearly that the work of the industrial laborer is lacking in those qualities so essential for self-expression and self-realization.

In this service to leisure time education, physical education in the college must contribute skills, attitudes, and appreciations that will seek constantly throughout life for wholesome expression. In short, this contribution must continue into life after college days are left behind. This view requires adjustment of many traditional practices, but it denies that it is utopian. Education, during college years, for the proper use of leisure time may constitute the fence that will save many who now fall over the cliff of social or biological disaster. Dramatic rescues always thrill. Rushing to the base of the cliff with an ambulance to pick up those who have toppled over, because of improper living, degenerative diseases, social maladjustments may be dramatic; it is hardly educational.

The imperative necessity of viewing physical education in relation to fundamental human problems forces itself upon us continually. Hence, it should be kept clear that physical education is a form of education. It is a way of life. Its activities are engaged in because of the satisfactions to him who participates. To him who enters the lists of its activities there will come as by-products health, skills, good postures, strength, endurance,—the many results so frequently sought as direct ends. Physical education then makes its contribution primarily as an attitude, a way of living, a point of view; only incidentally is it a technic, a performance, a particular skill. Given the former, the latter incidentals are acquired readily; without the former the latter are rarely secured or fall early into disuse.

One last word! There will always remain in any condition of society the need of physical vigor and fine personal character. The day of democracy and the international spirit goes back to tribal practices in these things. Our civilization must ever rely upon these bulwarks.

If perchance those hardy pioneers who trekked across the prairies and mountains to found this great state should look down upon this scene to-day, what would they ask that physical education contribute to our women? They would wish them to be physically strong, surely. Paraphrasing an old French philosopher, they would remark, "It is not a soul, it is not a body that we are training up, but it is a woman." From out the dim past would come another voice speaking. "The weaker the body the more it commands; the stronger the more it obeys." Oh, glorious girlhood, may these tumultuous years find you growing strong!

They would ask, also, I am sure, that you have courage and self-reliance; that you be able to say, with confidence,

"I am the master of my fate,
I am the captain of my soul."

Barrie tells of the circumstances under which Henley wrote those lines. "I was a patient," writes Henley, "in the old infirmary of Edinburgh. I had heard vaguely of Lister, and went there as a forlorn hope on the chance of saving my foot. The great surgeon received me as he did and does everybody, with the greatest kindness, and for twenty months I lay in one or other ward of the old place under his care. It was a desperate business, but he saved my foot, and here I am." Yes, there he was, singing during the "desperate business,"

"I am the master of my fate,
I am the captain of my soul."

It seems clear to me that these voices from the past would ask our women not only to be physically strong, not only to be brave, but also to be good sportsmen. To follow through, to finish the task, to play the game—not only on the athletic field, but everywhere in college and in life—these shall be their aims. No doubt remains of the right of those pioneers to speak to us to-day. The strength and physical hardihood of our forefathers, their courage and self-reliance, and their faithfulness to high causes and noble ends remain our common heritage.

The biologist looks at the sections of the cell upon his stage and wonders. The university looks at the young folks coming to its doors and builds. In this enterprise, physical education seeks to serve.

ATHLETICS FOR GIRLS

By Jay B. Nash

Associate Professor of Physical Education

New York University

The mere mention of "athletics for girls" is sure to stimulate a heated argument in almost any assembly today. It is a modern No Man's Land. Vigorous vocal action can always be assured by the announcement of such a topic. Proponents and opponents in all walks of life will be found to be fairly evenly divided. The argument is never settled because of the fact that few people use the same vocabulary. They may use the same words but with different meanings.

"Competitive athletics" is the phrase that is many times used. It, in itself, is a misnomer, because all athletics are competitive. It is simply another way of saying competitive competition. When one person talks about athletics, he visualizes the emotionalized interschool contests of the modern high school or college. When another person speaks about athletics he may have reference to the great mass of athletic games which go on in connection with the physical education programme in the school, without spectators and conducted in a perfectly natural way.

In this ever present argument some people visualize girls' athletics in their worst possible form. They see State championship matches in basketball, where girls are called upon to travel long distances and play in exhausting elimination tournaments. They see track meets for girls who have been coached by men. They see great stadiums with throngs of spectators in a highly emotional state. They see games played under boys' rules, coached, managed, and officiated by men. They see an utter disregard for the girls' physiological conditions. They see the girl athlete in the Sunday supplement. They see as an object city, State, National, and possibly International championships for girls.

Jay B. Nash, "Athletics for Girls." Reprinted from *The North American Review*, January 1928, pp. 99-104, by permission of the University of Northern Iowa.

On the other hand, those who see good in girls' athletic activities see a participation which involves all the girls of an institution in activities adapted to the organic needs of the girl. They see the girl properly costumed. They see the teams coached, officiated and managed by well trained, mature women leaders. They see the group of girls building up an organic capacity and acquiring standards of behavior of a very high order.

So it is that the mere phrase "competitive athletics", or "athletics for girls", has in reality no definition. One might as well ask, "How long is a string?" as to ask, "Are athletics for girls bad?" It all depends upon conditions. What are these conditions?

The conditions relative to girls' athletics are precisely the same as the conditions relative to boys' athletics. Boys' athletics which involve activities not adapted to the needs of the boy and conducted under highly emotional situations, with selfish leaders who care more for the click of the camera, the scratch of the reporter's pen and the gate receipts than they do for the boy, are bad. Much of the athletics in junior and senior high schools and colleges fall under this category. It is obvious, then, that if girls' athletics merely ape boys' athletics, they are likely to be bad for the very reason that many of the boys' activities are bad. The earmarks of bad athletics, whether they involve boys or girls, will always centre around *intensive coaching of a few, neglect of the many, spectators, gate receipts, State and National championships.* Such activities are not educational. They exist to give publicity to the coach, the principal of the school, the president of the university, the alumni, some local newspaper, the town boosters' club, and the players.

An interesting situation presents itself; namely, that those who today are most vigorous in their condemnation of athletics, both for boys and for girls, are the ones who are at fault for the muddle in which we find the present athletic situation. This group of people, who have only themselves to blame, are high school principals, Boards of Education, college presidents, and Boards of Directors of colleges and universities. This is the group of people who, over a series of years, refused to recognize the educational content of athletics. They are the group of people who forced student associations to organize, raise their own money, build their own stadiums, hire their own coaches, and, incidentally, spend their own gate receipts. This is the group of people who refused to finance a programme of athletics as one of the important phases of education.

That situation is largely a thing of the past. The school men of the country are vigorously taking hold of the athletic situation both for boys and for girls and a solution is in sight. Education today is upon an activity basis. All learning is through some form of activity, mental or physical. In physical activities all of the value lies in participation: none in the onlooking. No longer can we make excuses that the spectators acquire "loyalty to the school", or "get relaxation", or "are out in the fresh air." These are platitudes. The value is in the *doing of the activities*. Therefore, plans must be so laid that every child in the school is given an opportunity to take part in *activities adapted to his capacities*. It is through activities that individuals are educated. Looming large in these activities, especially in connection with physical education, are what we call playground activities, "athletics", or "athletic games". Physical activities adapted to the needs of the girl, conducted under proper leadership, lay the basis for development. Development which is laid in this way is fourfold.

One is the development of organic power. This is probably best illustrated in what we call endurance or vitality. It means simply the power to expend great energy and to withstand fatigue. This organic power is today tremendously needed. It is a matter of common knowledge that many of the men in present day positions of great responsibility were raised on the farm. In the big-muscle activities on the farm their organic power or endurance was obtained. More and more there is a strain upon the nervous system. There is the hurry and worry of business life. If men are to stand under this strain, there must be built up through big-muscle activities—playground activities during childhood and youth—great organic capacity.

A second is menti-motor development. This means that the latent powers in the neuro-muscular mechanism called strength and skill are developed; and that millions of nerve cells are brought into functional activities under the control of the will. This power is greatly needed today in connection with the varied and highly mechanical life that we live. Quick responses learned on the athletic field or in simple games may save a life in the crowded traffic, or prevent accidents in connection with our modern factory system.

A third is the development of the impulses. In the games of childhood and youth the most powerful impulse tendencies of human nature are exercised. Character traits are developed. In the stress of the game the temptation is particularly strong to be unsportsmanlike and violate the rules for the sake of winning. Probably the most effective instance where the child distinguishes right from wrong is when other children point their fingers at him and say, "You didn't play fair." Playground activities offer a tremendous range of opportunities for guidance and the development of the impulses in an approved direction.

Finally, there is the development of judgment. In no phase of education is it necessary to think situations and to will coördinations so rapidly as in playground activities. Judgment is necessary. Action must be instantaneous. A slight error in judgment is fatal to the individual and to his team. The entire being of the player is set upon making a good showing for his team mates. He thinks because thinking is imperative in play to do his best.

Based upon these fourfold objectives are the intermediate and the remote objectives, or what we term standards of behavior; namely, health and character. Over all these objectives and ways of acting is the adult adjustment to the recreational life, namely the right use of leisure.

Several factors are necessary to insure this development. These may be enumerated as follows:

1.—A recognition of athletics as a phase of physical education. Athletic games are in reality the heart of the physical education programme of the adolescent, and are definitely concerned with the "want" of both the boy and the girl.

2.—A recognition of physical education as a phase of general education. This makes necessary a recognition of the educational values of physical education, not just for the physical, but through the physical. It is one of the approaches to education and today must be recognized as one of the most vital approaches.

3.—A scientific classification of children. All children must be classified in accordance with sex, age, capacity and individual differences. Skilled leadership is necessary. Physical examination must be given. The individual capacity of each child for activity must be determined in order that activities adapted to the individual's need may be prescribed. As soon as this classification of children is properly made, the next step is the adaptation of activities to these needs.

4.—Adaptation of activities to needs. As soon as individual needs have been determined the programme of activity can be planned. Here is where the programme of activities for girls will differ very decidedly from that of activities for boys. Girls who have spent a relatively inactive early childhood, which up to the present time has been less vigorous than the boys, can not suddenly plunge into vigorous activities. On the other hand, physiological differences begin to appear at adolescence. The dangers which are involved in throwing a girl suddenly into the highly charged emotional situation of an athletic game, where she is a representative of the school and there are many spectators, is well pointed out by the experience of Dr. St. Clair Lindsley, who has had a wide experience in her capacity as advisor for girls in connection with the Los Angeles public schools: "The entire endocrine balance is being established and the adolescent girl who is subjected to highly emotional situations is but sowing the seed for a nervous breakdown later on by putting undue stress on these glands of internal secretion, which are trying to adjust themselves to the physiological changes taking place at that time, and are really having all they can do. Moreover, many of our chronic backaches in later life are the results of the 'sacroiliac spreads' which occur through the abuse of the body when not sufficiently developed to withstand the sudden and difficult training involved in athletics."

5.–A proper leadership. This involves thoroughly trained physical directors–men to have charge of boys' activities and women of girls' activities. Without this leadership, good results can not be expected either in connection with physical development or in connection with standards of behavior which are involved in character education and health education.

Athletics for girls? Certainly! It is one of the basic phases of education. How much? Just as much as the organic examination indicates will give benefit to the individual. When? Throughout life. Where? Anywhere, where results as indicated above can be a product.

As a matter of practical administration this means trained women physical directors, capable of classifying children and adapting activities to their needs. It means an intraschool programme which involves every girl in the institution. It involves the elimination of gate receipts, because gate receipts merely start a vicious cycle. It involves the elimination of the pyramiding games which involve city championships, State championships, National championships, and International championships. It practically means the elimination of the spectator, who, after all, represents the "deep-dyed villain of this drama." Athletics can not be run both as a financial proposition and as an educational proposition, and this is true not only for girls' athletics but also for boys' athletics, whether conducted in high schools, colleges, or universities. If the school does not finance athletics as part of an educational procedure, it can not control athletics. We can squirm and dodge, but we have to go back to what actually happens in practice. If it is finance, it is a desperate try for a winning team, and educational results take second place.

Girls' athletics can be conducted as a phase of education–must be conducted as a phase of education. It is a phase of education upon which we must depend to build organic capacity, the development of the impulses involved in good citizenship and good sportsmanship, upon which we must build our programme of standards involved in character training and health.

STORIES OF PLAY DAY—AN OLD INSTITUTION WITH MODERN VARIATIONS

From colleges East and West come reports of Play Days held last year. The idea of Play Day is old but the various ways in which it has been carried out are anything but that. From the University of Denver at Denver, Colorado, there comes this extremely interesting letter:

"Of the past year, the most outstanding day of interest and importance to all of us was the annual Play Day, at which the Rocky Mountain Colleges were our guests. We entertained eleven representatives and a coach from each of five colleges. We are particularly proud of our wonderful new stadium, consequently we entertained our guests there. The stadium, of Greek architecture, made an ideal setting for our sports and games.

"As we decided to be entirely true to form, and when in Greece do as the Grecians do, we divided all of the girls into two large groups, the Athenians and the Spartans. Each girl was given a red or yellow band with a border of Grecian design as her mark of distinction. A program, 'Order of Events in the Arena,' was given to each guest. The events included: a chariot race, discus throw, javelin throw, baseball throw, basketball throw, running high jump, hurdles, indoor baseball, volley ball (three games), and archery."

A very small but a very interesting portion of the letter from Mount Holyoke College, at South Hadley, Mass., is devoted to Play Day. "At the end of October comes Field Day and the annual A. A. banquet. It has become customary upon such days for each class to bring out some special costume or toy usually in their class color. These take various forms such as yellow smocks, blue tams, red mittens. Great care is taken to keep them secret."

"Stories of Play Day—An Old Institution With Modern Variations, *Newsletter of the Athletic Conference of American College Women,* April 1, 1928, pp. 10-11.

Cornell College W. A. A. at Mt. Vernon, Iowa, held one of the first Play Days to be given in the Middle West. Here is their description of it: "The local W. A. A. invited the Coe College W. A. A. to participate in a dual Play Day. Three sports were featured: hockey, swimming, and tennis. Teams were divided so that each team was composed of girls from both schools. The names chosen were Cor-Hawks and Cor-ells. The Play Day was brought to a close by a luncheon at which ribbons were given the Cor-Hawks, who were the winners."

Leland Stanford Junior University writes: "And lastly, and probably most important, are plans we are making for the Mills College, University of California, and Stanford Play Day to be held in March. This year we are to be hostesses of the Triangular Conference and we are hoping to make it a bigger and better Play Day than ever before. However, we have decided to call it a Sports Day and that is what we are going to make it. There will be competition in basketball, tennis, archery, and swimming in the morning. Also the University of California will give an exhibition of fencing."

This year the W. A. A. of Iowa State College at Ames, Iowa, is eagerly looking forward to Iowa's first Play Day with Drake University and Grinnell College as its guests."

Gustavus Adolphus College at St. Peter, Minn., says of its Play Day. "Women's Day has become an annual event observed under the auspices of the W.A.A., starting at 6:30 in the morning with a breakfast in the 'Valley of the Moon,' and continuing with a track and tennis meet in the afternoon and a banquet in the evening. This is followed by an initiation of new members."

The description of Play Day at the University of Pittsburgh is so fascinating that it is impossible to omit one word of it. "As each girl reached the stadium she registered at the Headquarters Booth. The general plan was to equally divide the members from each school into four groups, i.e., Blue, Gold, Red, and Green, the leaders of which had been chosen beforehand. At this booth the girl registering received a name card, the color depicting the group to which she belonged, a 'pinny' of the same color, worn to identify the player easily, and a milk ticket which entitled her to one serving of milk and crackers any time in the afternoon. At an assembly at headquarters the program was explained to the contestants.

"The activities of the afternoon are classified into Major Sports and Novelties. Each individual participated in one major sport in her group. For the team winning any major sport an award of two points was given. The purpose of the Novelties was to give the girls an opportunity to be active or inactive as they desired, to give a place for individual accomplishments, and to add 'pep.' The method used was the challenging system; that is, any girl could challenge any member of another team, not participating in a major sport, to individual competition. The program of events suggested novelties, such as: basketball throw, volley ball serve, tennis serve, marbles, quoits, jacks. No one could refuse a challenge and an effort to meet that challenge had to be made. An award of one point was given to the team of which the winner was a member. All results had to be reported at the Headquarters Booth in order to count. At any time during the afternoon when the Master of Ceremonies so desired, a whistle or bugle was blown. This was a signal for the groups to line up to listen to score announcements, change in program, or whatever might occur to the Master of Ceremonies. The group lining up in the shortest time was awarded one point.

"Activities began at 2:30 promptly and continued until 4:30, at which time the concluding point event was held in the form of a Shuttle Relay, all girls participating, all groups competing. From 5 o'clock until 6:15 everyone was free to do as she wished. The swimming pool containing 100 colored balloons was open and a miniature water carnival was soon in progress.

"In direct contrast to the strenuous, informal activities of the afternoon a formal banquet was held as the concluding event. Everything—food, songs, speeches, program, tables arranged in a huge circle—was made to conform to the main idea of the day, 'all-round.'"

The girls of Miami University, Oxford College and Western College met Saturday afternoon, November 5, on the Western College athletic field for a Play Day. "The object of the Play Day was to establish better acquaintanceship between the girls of the colleges through play," writes Western College for Women at Oxford, Ohio, in describing the event. "In the contests no idea of competition and rivalry existed between the colleges. All teams were composed of equal numbers from each college, about 150 girls taking part. The events of the afternoon included hockey, soccer, volley ball, a golf-driving exhibition, and archery."

The University of Vermont writes in a similar strain, "Play Day with Middlebury is at present one of the rosy dreams which the co-eds of Vermont are harboring. The plans are to have the girls of the two colleges get together and enjoy a general good time playing games. There will be Vermont and Midd girls on each team and the object will be 'Play for Play's Sake' without rewards or any desire for competition. This is distinctly a new feature for us and we hope to make it a flaming success."

And here is the report of a Winter Carnival, also from the University of Vermont. "Winter Carnival is a day given over to winter sports and general jollification. All sorts of ski, snow-shoe and handicap races are run. Everyone is there, laughing, stumbling, falling into the snow, or being pelted with snow, but having a dandy time all the same.

"The lawn at Redstone, our most beautiful dormitory, is a perfect bevy of girls, either tussling with suitcases, umbrellas and long full skirts in the obstacle races, or swiftly gliding in the ski races or maneuvering snow-shoes along the track as quickly as they can. It is loads of fun even to watch such a performance."

A CRISIS IN GIRLS' ATHLETICS

By Ethel Perrin

Chairman of the Executive Committee of the Women's Division of the National Amateur Athletic Federation, for ten years head of the Department of Physical Education of the Detroit public schools.

The problem of training our millions of schoolgirls in the principles of good sportsmanship is upon us. The Olympics of 1928 are past history. The Olympics of 1932 are history in the making. In part that history will be made out of the lives of girls now in our junior and senior high schools. They are the individuals who must first be selected and then trained for the women's events of the 1932 Olympics which are to be held in San Francisco.

A consideration of some of the purposes of the Women's Division of the National Amateur Athletic Federation shows at once that the Division cannot sponsor the training of teams for the 1932 Olympics. It works to promote the best type of athletics for girls. It can only oppose strongly a program that it considers harmful for the girls who may be chosen to train for teams, that requires an enormous expenditure of money and effort in order to produce a huge spectacle of exploitation and that necessarily diverts attention and interest from the sound purpose of athletics for girls—the increased opportunity for physical and mental health and for joy for all.

Already the organizers of the American Olympic teams are at work. They have a selective program. In other words, they have a program which they will present to the school officials throughout the land. It will clear out the "dead wood" in the shortest possible time and leave the green timber of our adolescent girls to be bent and fashioned by a program of intensive athletics.

Do we want this selective program accepted by the schools? Do we want the adolescent girls of the junior and senior high schools

Ethel Perrin, "A Crisis in Girls' Athletics," *Sportsmanship*, vol. I, no. 3, December 1928, pp. 10-12.

trained to enter the 1932 Olympics? Our answer to these questions will be profoundly serious in its effect. If we answer "yes," we shall have turned girls' athletics back many years. If we answer a courageous "no" we shall have set it many years ahead. It is the concern of us all to decide what part we want athletics to play in the lives of our adolescent girls.

When American women first took part in Olympics, there was no national women's organization to sponsor the women's teams. Therefore, the American Amateur Athletic Union undertook to do so with the help of women advisors whom they appointed.

Girls are not suited for the same athletic programs as boys. The biological difference between them cannot be ignored unless we are willing to sacrifice our school girls on the altar of an Olympic spectacle. Under prolonged and intense physical strain a girl goes to pieces nervously. She is "through" mentally before she is completely depleted physically. With boys, doctors' experienced in this problem of athletics maintain, the reverse is true. A boy may be physically so weak that he has not strength to "smash a cream puff," but he still has the "will" to play. The fact that a girl's nervous resistance cannot hold out under intensive physical strain is nature's warning. A little more strain and she will be in danger both physically and nervously.

Women directors of physical education and of recreation know this as they know the other physical handicaps under which girls play. All athletics for girls are more safely conducted by women than by men. If, however, we send our girls out to train for Olympic teams, we will be sending them to work under men trainers. I have been asked why this is, why men rather than women, train the girls for Olympics. The answer is that the women will not do it. They know that the necessary training for those events is always dangerous and at best subversive. Therefore, they will not undertake to give that kind of training.

Furthermore, women leaders and all those interested in athletics and recreation for girls are working for a very different purpose. They are working to give *all* girls a life foundation of recreational athletics. They are building bodies and characters and supplying the means of recreation which the girls may carry with them into adulthood. Slowly, but strongly, girls' athletics, under their leadership, have been developing into a broad program that includes all sports, that emphasizes the spirit of sport, that is adapted to the physical and mental equipment of girls, that is free from exploitation and overstrain, and that constitutes recreation for all.

The coming glory of the American Olypiad throws, not light, but a cloud of darkness over a program that is as wide as the nation.

It is black with menace to progress in athletics for girls. You will hear many arguments, many clever phrases in defense of the combing of junior and senior high schools for possible material. You will hear sportsmanship spoken of. Perhaps you will ask yourselves "sportsmanship for whom?" For a few hundred or for millions? You will hear that interest in athletics for women will be increased. In whom will it be increased? In those who are willing to exploit the girls? Yes, certainly. In the girls selected for special training? Yes. In the "dead wood" whom the selective program has cast aside? Hardly. I think for the millions who will be classified as "dead wood" athletics will more probably be a sore subject. I think those millions of school girls will not feel any particular enthusiasm for sport. I think their ardor for athletics as a great source of recreation and happiness will be cooled.

Further when you hear that interest in athletics for women will be increased you may care to ask what kind of interest. Will it be interest that has the welfare and happiness of the girls at heart? Or will it have the success of the Olympiad at heart? How much will it be concerned with the individual girls? How much will it consider what the ultimate effect on them will be? Very little. And for the rest, the great mass, it will not care at all. It will already have disposed of them—"dead wood." But they are not "dead wood." They are normal, adolescent American school girls, who have a right to the opportunity for athletics and many of them will be told that the training of Olympic teams takes nothing away from the girls who are not on the teams, that their program goes on just the same. Perhaps it does, but they know and you know that it is comparatively speaking an inferior program. They are, so to speak, getting an athletic diet of left-overs. Another falacious argument which I, at least, have heard, maintains: "Girls want it. God bless them—they shall have it." We might as well approve of giving matches to a child or of giving ice cream to one child while all the others watch him eat it.

What, then, are we going to do in the next four years to further the right kind of athletics for girls? We can not evade the question today. It has been growing more and more insistent for years. Now with the preparations on foot for the 1932 Olympics it must be answered. Here is an answer which the Women's Division of the National Amateur Athletic Federation will give "Competitive Athletics for Girls—More Rather Than Less—but of the Right Kind."

In April, 1923, women leaders and experts were called to a conference at Washington on athletics and physical recreation for girls and women. Out of this conference developed the Women's Division of the National Amateur Athletic Federation.

"To inaugurate and foster a national movement for sane and constructive athletics and physical recreation for the girls and women of America;

"To make it possible for all groups interested in such activities to come together in a central and unified body for better understanding and more effective service;

"To formulate standards and establish them nationally for the sound conduct and development of girls' athletics;

"To assist groups to put these standards into concrete effect in their work.

"To make possible for girls and women a wider participation in suitable athletic activities;

"To serve as the national research body and clearing house for all problems of athletics and physical recreation for girls and women."

THE CASE FOR COMPETITION

By Dr. Clarence C. Little

In a previous issue Miss Ethel Perrin, in an article entitled "A Crisis in Girls' Athletics," stated that "girls are not suited for the same athletic programs as boys" due to biological differences. Hereunder is presented another view on the subject of girls' athletics by Dr. Clarence C. Little, which, by permission, is reprinted here in part from The Pentathlon, journal of the Middle-West Society of Physical Education.

All that a mere man can do, I believe, is to discuss a problem of this kind in a preliminary way, for I do not think that any one man will influence very markedly our attitude toward women's physical training, or indeed the rest of the curriculum.

First of all, I do not see that there is any inherent difference physically between men and women which makes it desirable to expect of women anything less in the way of physical achievement, in proportion to their strength, than what we expect of men. In other words, if a man has a certain unit of strength that we may call 100 and a woman has a unit of strength that we may call 80, and we expect a man to develop his body so that he can use 100 units of his strength when he wants to—that is to say, use his full ability—then I see no reason why women should not face their problem along those same lines and expect to develop themselves physically so that they can use all the units of strength which they can possibly possess. They should look towards their program of physical training exactly on the same basis as men look towards theirs.

It is very clear that our civilization has developed an attitude toward women which has taught them first that they are not expected to make any great physical effort if they are to be successful. A successful woman in our civilization is very apt to be looked upon as a woman who can afford to be lazy. I think this view has arisen because, when we were less civilized, the way of women was a very rocky path. They had an enormous amount of drudgery, and therefore it became a sign of a happy situation and of advancement when they

Clarence C. Little, "The Case for Competition," *Sportsmanship,* vol. I, no. 5, February 1929, pp. 5-7.

could avoid physical effort and simply be lazy and live "on the man" or on invested earnings—something that meant that they would not have to work for their own support.

Then, too, there is a second attitude which I think was prevalent, certainly in the Victorian period, and which has lasted over in some degree, and that is that the woman most likely to get a husband is the "clinging vine" type, physically indolent, more or less versatile in the form of demonstrating such attractions as she may have in a quiescent way, a way that does not depend upon any physical vigor or alertness in order to impress the man. In other words, I mean the old game of man-hunting by dependency of the woman, the woman needing protection and thus appealing to the man's sense of vanity.

That being the case, it has been a very remarkable thing that American girls and American women have turned as they have toward an increasing program of physical development and proficiency. Yet there is a real reason for it. The truth of the matter is that while the indolent, clinging vine, dependent type may catch a husband, it takes the other type to hold him after he is caught. There is more truth than fiction in that, because woman, naturally not as strong as man, maturing more rapidly and aging more rapidly—in spite of all efforts to disguise the latter fact—is in need of real physical vigor, to be a real partner to the one who happens to be her mate or husband, and the man of her particular choice. It is, therefore, I think, a matter of actual natural selection value that women are building up their physique to compete with men on a more or less equal basis.

When we come to decide how they are to do this, different theories at once arise. As in every other field, you get a normal curve of variation. The conservative people say that women should not get into sport clothes, and should not play rough games, that a game like field hockey provokes conduct that is unladylike and therefore should not be played. On the other extreme of the curve are the people who say that a woman should do everything that she possibly can that is rough and rugged. She is likely some day to be a mother of boys. She is likely some day, whether she is a mother or not, to be a teacher of boys. She is certain, whether she is a mother or a teacher, to have a very distinct voice in public health measures and the care of other people's boys. At all events, she needs to understand rough, rugged, happy-go-lucky activity first hand so that she may be more intelligent in facing the problems which come to her for a decision. In between the extremes there are all sorts of intermediate conditions: people who feel that it is quite all right for women to play certain restricted games, but that they should not take part in competitive games; people who feel that it is all right for them to have competitive games, but that they should not be by organized groups—there should be more in the way of individual competition; people who feel that it is perfectly satisfactory for them to have competition by organized groups, but that it must always be within their own institution; and, finally, people who feel that it is entirely proper for them to have organized group competition outside of their own institution, provided it is carefully controlled and does not become national in its scope with intersectional matches or international competitions. Then there are also people who feel that the extramural type of competition is perfectly reasonable, no matter what the limits are. To these it is just as natural to have an Olympic team of women track athletes as to have an Olympic team of women swimmers.

I should like to analyze very briefly some of the objections which I have heard made to intercollegiate or interscholastic athletics for women. We can remove a lot of possible objections by saying that some women feel that their intercollegiate athletics must necessarily be exactly like men's intercollegiate athletics. They do not see that it is quite possible to develop a different type of interscholastic or intercollegiate contact, and they say that because men's athletics are full of weaknesses, full of commercialism, and various other undesirable qualities, that women's intercollegiate athletics must of necessity have those same unpleasant attributes. I think that point of view is entirely unproven, if, for example, one means that there will have to be professional athletics by women. I doubt very much whether that will be the case. In the first place, women will not be able to compete in the same games that men can with equal proficiency. As a general thing, a women's baseball team, a women's football team, a women's crew, if you have such organizations, could not beat men's teams in those sports. Ninety-nine times out of a hundred or nine hundred and ninety-nine times out of a thousand the men would win. Therefore, men will not go to see contests between women if they can go to see men's contests in the same sports, and there will be men's contests in various sports professionally, I imagine, as long as we have our present type of civilization.

I say then that women need not worry about drawing hundreds of thousands of spectators. It hardly seems that women are infantile enough to place that over-emphasis on their intercollegiate contests which men have frequently placed on theirs. And yet, what are women doing now about intercollegiate athletics for men? It seems to me that they show toward men's intercollegiate athletics all the weaknesses and all the stupidities that they could possibly show toward their own.

In other words, we have gotten at present all the undesirable participation of the woman student body in the intercollegiate athletic situation for men without any of the physical or moral benefits that might be derived from that situation. Surely the girls follow the football team. Surely they go and yell their heads off over the basketball teams and make fools of themselves over the men athletes. At least, it looks to some of us men as though they do make fools of themselves about these outstanding young gentlemen who are able to run eighty yards for a touchdown or who are high scorers on the basketball team. There will always be, as you know, young women wasting their time and wasting their energy in following the men's athletic teams. What would happen? What would be the tendency? Would it be toward more normality or less normality if women had their own intercollegiate or interscholastic teams?

It is quite true that a number would follow the women's teams, but I submit that it is quite as healthy a relationship, and quite as likely to lead to educational and intellectual proficiency, if they are interested in the athletic prowess of their own sex as if they are interested in the athletic prowess of the opposite sex. I submit also that there will be no more time wasted nor will a less desirable situation arise by their following women's field hockey teams or basketball teams than there will be in their going off in automobiles or in overnight sleepers to attend football games of the Big Ten, as they do now. On the other hand, if there was a girl who was vigorous and healthy and an outstanding star in an athletic team, and popular as well, I have an idea that a number of the other girls would want to be like her. Her example would be wholesome.

Now, as I see it, this question comes: Would such a procedure allow a gradual enough development of intercollegiate or interscholastic athletics to insure the probability at least that undesirable overemphasis will not be attached to it? I believe that it will. I believe that women are inherently more balanced, more sensible, and more conservative than men. I believe that they are less likely to fall into the mistake that men have made.

The objection has been raised that a woman would be made coarse and unattractive by intercollegiate competition; that she would get to be "hard-boiled," so to speak, and impersonal about it all, and her truly feminine charm would vanish. I think that the experience of those who have dealt at all with girls is that quite as much undesirable toughness, both of conversation and behavior, may occur as the result of an education in some of the so-called very elite boarding schools and institutions of that type, as well as on athletic trips. In fact, the reactions, physiologically, psychologically, and sociologically, of a group who are physically fit, preparing to play a game with other girls of their own age and training, will be more normal, more sane, and more healthy than would those of a group of girls who might be going to the same place to attend an inter-sorority function, or a "Junior Prom," or bridge tournament, or something of that kind. I believe that there is really much evidence to show that the more active persons are physically, the more normal they are apt to be in their sense of proportion toward these various temptations and "time wasters" that appear on every hand.

I have felt all along that women have been tremendously handicapped in their contact with people whom they do not know well. Men are apt to be very jolly, perhaps even "gladhand" artists. We have Rotary clubs, Kiwanis clubs, Lions clubs, Exchange clubs, where everybody calls the other fellow by his first name, and where they go through at least the semblance of friendship once a week. Women as yet do not do that sort of thing as naturally as men.

PHYSICAL EDUCATION IN PRESCHOOL YEARS*

Arnold Gesell, M.D.
Director of the Yale
Psycho-Clinic
New Haven, Conn.

The Commissioner of Education in Connecticut has just sketched for you an impressive picture of the work of the public school system in the field of physical education.† It is significant of the trend of the times that he did not leave the preschool child out of the picture.

Within the past ten years the preschool child, to say nothing of his parents, has been rediscovered. He has of course, existed as long as the race has existed, but his significance in the scheme of things has recently risen into bold and arresting prominence. He is the focus of attention from many quarters. He has a new status in educational planning, in public health, and even in science. Although the number of preschool children in the community is almost as great as that of the elementary school population, we are scarcely aware of the great size of this preschool army, because the army is a very scattered one and it never assembles to make a show of its numerical strength. These preschool children are now in cradles and perambulators. Or they are making brave excursions on their runabout kiddie cars in the nursery, in the back yard, or on the front sidewalk. Only one in nine of eligible age attends a kindergarten. A small but interesting fraction are attending nursery schools under private, public, or semipublic auspices. It is too early to suggest that the public school system should at once make room for the preschool population, but it must be granted that the developmental welfare of the preschool child is already coming under increasing social control.

Arnold Gesell, "Physical Education in the Preschool Years," *American Physical Education Review,* vol. XXXIV, no. 9, November 1929, pp. 528-529.

*Abstract of a paper given before the Physical Education Convention at New Haven, April 19, 1929.

†See October Review, pp. 449-456.

This is all very natural when we look at the situation in its full perspective. It takes many years of growth to acquire and organize the human physique. In a biological sense one may think of this growing period as terminating in the early twenties. The preschool years are the first six years which precede the eruption of the school entrance molar. At every stage of this cycle of growth, physical education is of importance. One would not wish to set the claims of any one period against another; but the preschool years cannot be left out of the reckoning, even in physical education. They are of fundamental significance for the simple but sufficient reason that they come first in a developmental sequence.

At no time in child life does the growth of the neuro-muscular system proceed at such a swift rate as during the preschool years. There is a stupendous amount of growth to be accomplished. The child begins life limp and "molluscous." He can scarcely lift his head or make a well-directed movement of arm or leg. But at four months he begins to rear his head and shoulders in an apparent zeal to sit up. If we assist him for a moment to attain the sitting posture, even at this early age he seems to get a kind of athletic thrill out of the experience. At six months he sits up with slight support; at nine months he sits without support; at 12 months he is assuming the standing posture; at 15 months he walks; at 18 months he toddles; at 24 months he runs; at three years he can poise himself on one foot. By six years he normally has a considerable motor capital in the way of hopping, skipping, jumping, dancing, dodging, throwing, and innumerable other motor coördinations which lie at the basis of games and sports and body control.

Fortunately he acquires much of this equipment through the process of natural growth. Even if his physical education is much neglected, he attains to certain levels of ability through sheer maturation and through casual experience. But his optimum growth, in the physical sense, will not be realized unless, even in these tender years, he enjoys ample opportunities for training, practice, exercise, and adventure.

Modern mothers are conscious of his needs and sometimes make ill-advised efforts in the field of infantile calisthenics. It is dangerous to use gymnastic procedures without the advice and supervision of a physician. A premium should be placed on natural forms of play activity. In passing, it may be noted that in the playground movement the preschool child has been somewhat overlooked. He needs more play provisions planned in his special behalf.

The motor hygiene requirements of the preschool child are coming into clearer focus through the observations now being made in laboratories and in nursery schools. It will of course be impossible to meet these needs by mere extension downward of the devices and procedures which are now in vogue with children of more advanced age. But the fundamental principles of physical education apply to tender ages. There can be little doubt that posture, skill, and grace are fostered by fortunate experiences in spontaneous play, in rhythmic games, and physical activities on staircase, sidewalk, hill, seesaw, slide, kiddie car, and jungle-gym. Through plays and games which give an opportunity for effort and failure, for success, for judicious risks and thrills, the child accumulates a store of experience which builds up morale. This morale has several aspects. It is not purely muscular. It means the capacity to endure and to "stand the gaff" of plays and games; it involves elements of sportsmanship. Positively, it also means pleasurable interest in physical activity and in outdoor life. In this broad sense, the concepts of physical education reach down into early life. The higher orders of mental and bodily control have a substratum.

The profounder and pervasive emotional attitudes which color and condition the physical organization of the individual are acquired, in considerable measure, in early childhood. Whether it be the complexities of baseball and of golf, or the robustness of rough-and-tumble play, the inner personal attitudes of the growing child are modified by what he experiences in the field of physical expression. He gets a subtle something by exposure to and preliminary participation in feats beyond his immature powers. Such early experience gives bent to his interests and may even impart a flare to some expertness realized in later life. The mechanics of his posture, the patterns of his postural control, are moulded by a host of influences, and it is because his physique enjoys this degree of plasticity, that the philosophy of physical education must include the preschool years of childhood.

Modern science is bringing mind and body into interpenetrated relationships. There is much to learn about these interrelations. The more fundamental methods of physical education of young children can be worked out only after patient research and by judicious, controlled educational experiment. But as the biological sciences bring body and mind more closely together, the more important appears the developmental significance of physical education in the preschool years.

METHODS OF RESEARCH IN PHYSICAL EDUCATION*

C. H. McCloy, Secretary
National Council, Y.M.C.A.

Events in the field of physical education seem to move in waves. We have had tidal waves of chest weights, of folk dancing, of posture instruction, of worrying over under weight, of badge testing, of Danish gymnastics, and of "natural" programs. At present the beginnings of a flood tide of emphasis upon research in physical education seem to be discernible. All of these new movements have swept in and many have subsided but all have left deposits of something useful on the beach. Most of those that were compounded largely of mistaken enthusiasms have entirely passed away.

The tide of interest in research offers promise of help. While much of this wave will prove to be effervescent enthusiasm and froth yet physical education on the whole should be lifted to a higher level than it was before and future research should carry it higher still.

It has been said that the methods for the determination of truth have passed through three major stages. The first was that of reference to authority, where questions were decided by the oracle of the profession. The second was that of speculation, where students were less fettered by tradition and at least did their own thinking. The third was that of hypothesis and experimentation. Fields of knowledge have not really attained to the right to the title of *science* until this third stage has been reached. The leaders in physical education in general have passed well beyond the first stage and into the second. They have for years utilized the experimental results of physiologists and psychologists; but it is but recently that they have begun in any

C. H. McCloy, "Methods of Research in Physical Education," *American Physical Education Review,* vol. XXXIV, no. 1, January 1929, pp. 10-16.

*Read at the Research Section National Convention A.P.E.A., Baltimore, Md., May 25, 1928.

large number to use the methods of research. If we can judge from the analogy of other sciences, the more extensive use of this tool should presage a new day in physical education.

The adoption of even a well-understood method into a new field is not infrequently accompanied by a period of adjustment while the old garment is being cut to fit the new usage, and it is at this period that systematic presentation of the methods used may be of real help to prospective users. Within the limits of the time available I shall endeavor to give a review of the methods used in the research field as they may be applied to physical education.

Research is simply an extraordinarily earnest and organized endeavor to ascertain the real facts about something. It involves constructive, creative thinking based upon experiments, documents, observations, or analysis of data, all of which are of as objective a nature as it is possible to secure. The different types of problems to be studied however necessitate many types of approach. There are definite techniques in research methodology in as real a sense as there are in art, in the writing of novels, or in the planning of ships. A knowledge of the fundamentals of these techniques may be of real help to one contemplating work in this field. I shall try to present the methods most frequently employed and to give some illustrations of work already done and a few problems which fall within the various fields.

I. Bibliographical Research

Bibliographical research involves finding all of the literature bearing upon a question. The results of this type of research are well illustrated by any complete bibliography. The most complete bibliography of physical education which has come to my attention recently is that by a Spaniard, Dr. Sanchez, which contains a rather complete outline of all of the literature in all of the scientific languages bearing upon the field of physical education. Some bibliographical research is necessary as a preliminary to almost any type of problem and is frequently one of the most troublesome and tedious parts of the study.

To succeed in bibliographical research involves a knowledge of sources and of library aides. Any competent librarian can show one how to find and use these tools but most librarians are apt to neglect to even mention the medical and physical educational reference guides which are not usually found in public libraries and frequently not in universities. Usually the best start can be made by securing the most recent treatise upon the subject and starting with the bibliography given there, working backward through the literature. If nothing of this sort is available and the worker has to proceed from other sources, the best procedure usually is to make a list of catch words which are apt to locate the material in the various indices and readers' guides rather than to laboriously hunt through individual books and journals. Further discussion of this type of research here would be superfluous.

II. Historical Research

Research in the field of science deals with observed facts: historical research deals with the past. Constructive historical research endeavors not only to determine what has really happened in the past but to interpret it and bring out facts bearing upon the present and the future.

Historical research is based upon the most reliable records of the past that are obtainable. The student must evaluate the genuineness and reliability of the sources. A list of questions which he must answer to his satisfaction will perhaps serve as well as any other simple method of showing something of the scope of this difficult type of research. Are the sources what they appear to be? Are they what they are thought to be? When, where, and by whom were they written? Is there a possibility that the documents were falsified or faked? Could they have been influenced by propaganda or by the bias of the writer? Are the sources direct or indirect—that is, did the writer see the occurrence or know the facts or is he retailing secondhand information? What sort of man was the writer, learned or ignorant? Did he write carefully and conservatively or carelessly and with wide-sweeping claims? Is there any reason for doubting his good faith or his accuracy? Are both sides of the question reported in the source material? It would be obvious that newspaper accounts written in war times or political speeches written for a campaign would be relatively untrustworthy sources of information. Scholarly treatises by authorities who were on the spot would be much more reliable. Original statements by actual observers would be better than reports of such statements made by others.

After the selection of source material has been made must come the establishment of the probable facts. The study of the historical problem will enable one to form a picture of what probably happened in the light of all of the source material. He will have to synthesize it, to image and group the facts, considering the environment, and by constructive reasoning build up an integrated picture of the whole, filling in the gaps the best way he can. He will also endeavor to apply the experience of the past to the present and to the future where it is possible to do so.

In the field of physical education *The History of Physical Education* by Leonard is a classic example of this type of research. A more recent and much less difficult example is seen in *Tests and Measurements in Physical Education* by Bovard and Cozens.

As illustrations of the service this kind of research might render I should like to suggest one or two problems that would lie in this field.

To adequately referee a game of basket ball calls for a profound knowledge of the rules. This knowledge must be a knowledge not simply of the letter but of the spirit. A very constructive historical research which would contribute to this understanding could be made by conducting a critical study of the minutes of every meeting of the basket ball rules committee and of the yearly basket ball guides as well as by checking this information and humanizing it by interviews with contemporaries, who, fortunately in many cases, are still living. By such a method one could study the situation created by new developments of technique, and the rule changes which were made in order to meet these developments. Thus one would work from situation to response, year by year from the beginning of basket ball to the present. This would be a relatively simple task because of the recentness of the problem and because of the fact that hundreds of men who know these changes intimately are still living.

A more difficult but immensely important problem would be that of tracing the relationships between physical education and the development of civilization from the earliest times. This would be a task to challenge the most ambitious, and one which would probably take from 10 to 20 years for its completion.

III. Descriptive Research

This general title is given to a type of research that embraces a number of methods of fact finding and it can perhaps be adequately treated under these several methods.

1. *Observation and Fact Recording.*

This method is simply that of observing and recording facts as they are available, classifying and sorting them, and reporting on the result. It is the method commonly used by insurance companies and is well illustrated by the study, *The Intelligence of Varsity Athletes* by Burtt and Nichols.[1] There are many useful problems to be studied by this method. A study of the norms and of the range and distribution of pulse rates and blood pressures for each age of both sexes and under the different conditions of position and exercise would be an example. A study of the relative success and failure of athletes and non-athletes in after life would be another.

2. *The Questionnaire.*

This much maligned instrument is a necessity in research and has extensive use. Its limitations are as important as its contributions. The most common defects associated with the use of the questionnaire in research are, first, that of asking leading questions which would prejudice the answers, and, second, that of publishing opinion—and in many cases ignorant opinion—as fact. To illustrate, the opinions of 500 Y. M. C. A. physical directors as to whether or not the tote-box system is advisable in business men's locker rooms would not necessarily be conclusive. There would probably be a large and emphatic majority upholding the negative. Experiment might show the exact contrary. The recent study by Lehmann and Witty published under the title of *The Psychology of Play Activities*[2] is a good illustration of a study based upon a questionnaire. The questionnaire lends itself well to studies involving a job analysis, interests of children, and studies of current practice in the field of administration. The methods of constructing a good questionnaire are presented in a number of standard texts.

3. *The Case Study.*

This is a method in which the individual is studied and analysed either by careful, systematic observation or by interview. This method has its own techniques, one of the most important being that of not influencing the answer. Questions must be presented clearly and without giving undue weight to one side of the problem and without the opinion of the questioner being made known. Hamilton in a recent study of a hundred married men and a hundred married women safeguarded the personal equation to the extent of presenting all questions in writing without comment. This method is used too little by physical educators. Such studies as that of what causes excessive membership turnover in a Y. M. C. A. department of physical education would be one illustration of the use of this method. A very much needed research is a case study of 1,000 women who have been exploited upon commercial basketball teams, checked by a concurrent study of 1,000 women of the same age, social status, educational background, etc., but who have not been exploited athletically. This method can also be wisely used in preliminary experimental and causal studies in which a study is first made of selected individuals for the purpose of determining the variables which are significant to the study.

IV. Experimental Research

In experimental research the important factor is that the experimenter endeavors to control and render as constant as possible all factors other than the one factor experimented upon. Tests before and after or concurrent with the experiment are made, usually upon two or more groups, though this type of research is occasionally done upon only one group alternating the use and disuse of the experimental factor. It is one of the most common methods used by physiologists. Examples in the field of physical education are seen in the recently published study of *Exercise and Basal Metabolism in Dogs* by Steinhaus[9] and in the study of the effects of a natural program as contrasted to a formal program which was published in 1922 in the *Teachers College Record.*[3]

This type of research is rich with possibiilty, and hundreds of possible problems could be suggested. It would for example be easy to experiment with the "part vs. the whole" methods of teaching folk dancing, track athletics, or swimming. Studies could be made upon the efficiency of different distributions of teaching time in the various activities such as basket ball or dancing. For example, how long does it really pay a team to practice batting each day? It would be relatively easy to experiment upon the question of how skilful it is necessary to be in the different athletic games before the activities become really educationally useful. What is the upper level of such skill beyond which no additional educational advantage accrues? How much does Danish gymnastics accomplish of what its enthusiastic admirers claim? There are hundreds of other problems that can be attacked by experimental research, the main element in which is adequate control of experimental conditions.

V. Causal or Correlative Research

This type of research in a certain sense is experimental research done backward. Data concerning all of the elements or variables probably involved are collected and analysed, usually utilizing some form of the correlation technique and, in some cases, causative factors are sought. An example is seen in the relationships of strength to athletics made by Rogers[4] and in the study of motor ability by Brace.[5]

An excellent study that should be better known to physical educators and which has been made by these techniques is that by Karl Pearson on the relationship of health to the psychological and physical characteristics in school children.[6]

This method is one that is full of pitfalls but is one that offers very great possibilities to those who can command it. The dangers lie in the ever present possibilities of the misuse of statistical methods and the misinterpretation of results—of the "taking a pint of fact and whipping it up into a barrel of statistics."

This method offers us hundreds of problems. With it one might study the methods of accurately predicting athletic skill and motor ability. By refinements of this method, anthropometric norms of a high degree of accuracy might be obtained. For example, Dr. Franzen* has recently been able to predict body weight to such a high degree of accuracy as to obtain a multiple correlation of .97. By such methods it might be possible to predict lung capacity, which at present is predictable only to within about an 8 per cent accuracy, with a very much higher degree of accuracy and reliability.

VI. Philosophical Research

In many cases it is impossible to obtain accurate and objective measurements in a specified field. In some such cases it may be possible to borrow adequate facts from some other closely related field and to formulate an adequate theory by analysis. In many cases, to meet a real need, it may be necessary to formulate a tentative theory that is based upon absolutely no adequate objective data. In such cases a profound knowledge of all the associated researches and the ability to philosophize constructively may give excellent results. This is what roughly is included in philosophical research. Examples are seen usually in any new advance in the field of the philosophy of physical education. Much that appeared in Hetherington's *School Programs in Physical Education*[7] is a case in point.

Illustrations of the use of this method can be seen in an attack upon such a problem as that of character education through physical education. In such a problem philosophical research might approach through the field of general or mental education, applying the laws of learning and the psychology of original nature and of individual differences from the field in which measurements can be made with a fair degree of accuracy to the character field in which accuracy of measurement

*Unpublished study of the American Child Health Association.

is not at present even remotely possible. A large amount of philosophical research should of course be a part of almost all other forms of research.

VII. Comparative Research

This is a relatively new term in the research family. Some authors do not grant that it is deserving of a distinctive name, for it frequently utilizes all other methods. The distinctive contribution of comparative research lies in the field of comparing things that do not lend themselves easily to experimentation. Illustrations will make this clearer than a long discussion.

In any field of physical education, it is vital that the individuals participating should so far as possible be contented and satisfied with everything concerned with both plant and program. If for example the locker room is too crowded, oppressively dark, and ill ventilated, the concomitant results might be serious indeed. It would be very wasteful of time and money to experiment upon such a problem. It would however be quite feasible to make comparative studies of entirely different plants. I believe that this type of research has a large usefulness in the field of physical education.

VIII. Research in Methods of Research

This picture of methods of research would not be complete without pointing out the necessity of constantly seeking for more efficient tools. The field of physical educational research abounds in problems for which as yet no adequate statistical techniques have been devised. The same is probably true of physiological techniques. It is therefore necessary that research studies will in addition to the solution of "practical" problems also endeavor to develop more adequate research techniques in order that other problems may be better solved. The methods presented above comprise all that are apt to be of use in the solution of problems in the field of physical education. Very many problems of course will necessitate the application of more than one of these methods.

In attacking a research problem, experience has made clear the fact that in general the best procedure is somewhat as follows:

1. First, select the general problem to be studied. This will probably be too broad and inclusive for practical use and will have to be narrowed down to a content consistent with the possibility of solution. A study of "Physical Education Activities for Business Men" for example would be too inclusive a problem; but "The Effect of Singles in Handball on a 20 x 40 Foot Four-walled Court, as Measured by

Changes in Blood Pressure and Pulse Rate" would be a more attackable problem, providing a standard for interpreting the changes in the vascular system were available.

2. Formulate the problem clearly so there will be no ambiguity as to what is to be attempted. The wording of the formulation need not of course be the title of the study.

3. Next do the necessary bibliographical research, accumulating the entire bibliography needed before beginning to read it. This should be done on cards with sufficient space for annotation.

4. Do the necessary reading on the bibliography. It is usually not at all necessary to read everything. Many individual studies are summarized in later studies. In this reading one should keep careful notes and give references that can later be easily followed up. This reading will usually give many suggestions as to the techniques to be followed and as to methods of attack as well as suggest subsidiary problems which are usually best filed away for future reference and study but not included in the present study.

5. Outline the study from beginning to end so far as may be possible. Write down the questions which it is hoped the study will enable one to answer and then organize the study carefully and in detail. A major problem may consist of a number of subsidiary problems all bearing upon the larger study. The study may involve some preliminary experimentation of a somewhat simple nature either for the development of techniques or for the ascertaining of the direction of the experiment. These five items involved in setting up the problem not infrequently take from half to two-thirds of the time given to the study.

6. Collect the data necessary for performing the experiment. In case the reading of the bibliography or some other source has led to suggestions concerning closely related problems, it may be quite possible with the same set-up to collect additional data which can be analysed later for the solution of more than one problem. In this way economies in time may be effected.

7. Analyse and interpret the results.

8. Draw the necessary conclusions and in so far as possible answer the questions asked in the preliminary organization of the study.

9. Write up the study. Even in this there is an accepted technique. Adequate helps in this technique are available for those who need them.[8]

In conclusion it should be emphasized again that research is not at all an abstruse or particularly difficult thing to do. It has its techniques and can no more be effectively done without some knowledge and mastery of these techniques than can football coaching, flying an aeroplane, or playing a saxophone. Most of the studies of dubious values in the field of physical education have been made by men who would know better than to attempt to make a coat, but who have begun a complicated research with no knowledge of the methods involved. It was with the hope that an outline presentation of this subject of the methods of research might open up the possibilities in this field that this paper has been prepared. In so far as we, as a profession, desert from the ranks of those who hang upon the words of the oracles and of those who depend solely upon reason, and in so far as we enlist in the ranks of those who in ever increasing measure depend upon ascertained fact, will the physical education of the future move forward.

Publications Cited or Referred To

1. *The Intelligence of Varsity Athletes.* H. E. Burtt and J. H. Nichols, American Physical Education Review. March, 1924.
2. *The Psychology of Play Activities.* H. C. Lehman and R. A. Witty, Barnes, 1927.
3. *A Comparative Study of Formal Gymnastics and Play for Fourth-grade Children.* J. F. Williams, R. V. Atkinson, and D. K. Brace, Teachers College Record, September, 1922.
4. *Tests and Measurement Programs in the Redirection of Physical Education.* F. R. Rogers, Bureau of Publication, Teachers College, Columbia University, 1927.
5. *Measuring Motor Ability.* D. K. Brace, Barnes, 1927.
6. *On the Relationship of Health to the Psychical and Physical Characteristics in School Children.* Karl Pearson, Cambridge University Press, 1923.
7. *School Program in Physical Education.* C. W. Hetherington, World Book Company, 1922.
8. *How to Write a Thesis.* W. G. Reeder, Public School Publishing Co., 1925.
9. *Studies in the Physiology of Exercise.* A. H. Steinhaus, American Journal of Physiology, January, 1928.

A Brief Bibliography of Methods of Research

1. *An Outline of Methods of Research with Suggestions for High School Principals and Teachers.* Bulletin No. 24, 1926, Department of Interior, Bureau of Education, Washington. Price 10 cents.
   This is a brief outline of a number of methods of research. It contains a good, short bibliography.
2. Watson, G. B., *Experimentation and Measurement in Religious Education,* Association Press, 1927. Price $3.
   A recent book giving an excellent presentation of some research methods. Much information is given for guidance in questionnaire construction. An elementary book.

3. Alexander, Carter, *Educational Research.* Bureau of Publication, Teachers College, Columbia University, 1927. Price 50 cents.
   This pamphlet gives most of the sources for bibliographical research in the educational field. It is well worth having. For the fields of physical education and medicine, the following additional sources should be known:
   (a) *Bibliografia general de la Educacioń Fisica,* Dr. Don Rufino Blanco y Sánchez, Libreria y casa Editorial Hernando, Calle del Arenal, num. 11, Madrid, 1926. 2 volumes. This gives an excellent modern bibliography covering all scientific languages.
   (b) "Selected Bibliography of Physical Education and Hygiene." G. B. Affleck. Appears three times a year in the AMERICAN PHYSICAL EDUCATION REVIEW. This bibliography covers most of the current American publications on Physical Education, but occasionally misses some of the important research publications. Not well classified for finding references easily.
   (c) *Quarterly Cumulative Index and Index Medicus.* This gives all medical publications in English. Can be found in any medical library.
4. McCall, W. A., *How to Measure in Education.* Macmillan, 1922. Price $3.35.
   Describes how to build tests.
5. McCall, W. A., *How to Experiment in Education.* Macmillan, 1923. Price $2.60.
   Gives the essentials of experimental and causal research.
6. Fling, F. M., *Outline of Historical Method.* Lincoln. Miller, 1899.
   Now out of print and must be consulted in a library. Gives a very thorough treatment of historical research.
7. Monroe, W. S., and Johnston, N. B., *Reporting Educational Research.* University of Illinois, Bulletin No. 25, 1925. Price 50 cents.
   Gives thorough instructions for reporting all types of research.
8. Statistics.
   (a) Thurston, L. L., *The Fundamentals of Statistics,* Macmillan, 1925. Price $2.
   Simple, elementary treatment, good to start with, but not complete.
   (b) Yule, G. U., *An Introduction to the Theory of Statistics.* Griffin & Co., 1924. Price $5.
   Thorough, but very mathematical, and is hard reading. Uses nothing more advanced than algebra, however.
   (c) Kelley, T. L., *Statistical Method.* Macmillan, 1923. Price $4.
   Very good, very complete, but very hard to understand unless well prepared in mathematics.
   (d) Holzinger, Karl J., *Statistical Methods for Students of Education.* Ginn and Co., 1928. Price $3.60.
   This is a new text which is unusually successful in giving a wide scope of methods without too much complicating the mathematics. One of the best books available.